D1582221

HARVARD ORIENTAL SERIES

Edited by MICHAEL WITZEL

VOLUME FIFTY-ONE

The Goindval Pothis:
The Earliest Extant Source of the Sikh Canon

THE GOINDVAL POTHIS

THE EARLIEST EXTANT SOURCE OF THE SIKH CANON

GURINDER SINGH MANN

PUBLISHED BY THE DEPARTMENT OF
SANSKRIT AND INDIAN STUDIES
HARVARD UNIVERSITY

DISTRIBUTED BY
HARVARD UNIVERSITY PRESS
CAMBRIDGE, MASSACHUSETTS
AND LONDON, ENGLAND
1996

Library of Congress Cataloging in Publication Data

The Goindval Pothis:
The earliest extant source of the Sikh canon
Gurinder Singh Mann

(Harvard Oriental Series; v. 51)
ISBN 0-674-35618-7

I. Mann, Gurinder Singh, 1949- II. Title
III. Series: Harvard Oriental Series; 51

CIP

For Rita, Mana, and Raj

Acknowledgments

Research in the field of manuscripts has its peculiar problems, and when these texts are part of the sacred inheritance of a family, any attempt at their rigorous examination is further complicated. How these problems were overcome and the present book completed is a story of collective endeavor, involving a number of friends and family members. It is a real pleasure to acknowledge their invaluable help.

I am indebted to the Bhalla families, the descendants of Guru Amardas, for allowing me to conduct a sustained examination of the pothis in their custody at Jalandhar and Pinjore. I am grateful for their gracious and warm reception every time I visited them in the past six years. It is a complex feeling to be a member of the select group of less than ten scholars who have had the opportunity to examine these manuscripts in the twentieth century and to have had the good fortune to have spent the maximum time with these rare manuscripts.

I am thankful to Dr. John Stratton Hawley for constant support and encouragement since I moved to Columbia University in 1987. He introduced me to the field of medieval Indian manuscripts and with great dedication guided my research and other activities related to the Sikh Studies program at Columbia. I am extremely grateful for the time he invested in helping me think through the issues that appear in this book and are at the center of my forthcoming work on the formation of Sikh canon. It has been a unique privilege to know and work with him.

A number of other scholars deserve my deep gratitude. Dr. Ruth Katz, formerly of the Florida State University, offered detailed comments on my doctoral dissertation, of which this project is an offshoot. Her critique helped my research attain further clarity. I am also indebted to her for her valuable help in putting the present book in its final form. Dr. Ainslie T. Embree, Dr. Mark Juergensmeyer, Dr. W. H. McLeod, and Dr. Michael Witzel, have been sources of support and encouragement during the past years and I appreciate all that they have done for me. Dr. Winand M. Callewaert graciously sent me the original film of the Banno Pothi, Kanpur, he made some years ago. I am thankful for this help.

I am thankful to two senior Sikh scholars, Professor Piara Singh Padam and Giani Gurdit Singh, for generously sharing with me their wealth of information regarding Sikh manuscripts. Their first-hand accounts of the debates relating to the early manuscripts in the mid-decades of the twentieth century were extremely useful to understand the broad issues and the positions taken by major scholars in the field.

My sister Jatinder and brother-in-law Manmohan Singh spent long hours working out arrangements to reach the Goindval Pothis and other important manuscripts. This project could not have been completed without their unstinting support. My uncle Iqbal Singh Dhillon introduced me to Guru Amarjit Singh Sodhi of Kartarpur, resulting in my extended access to the Kartarpur Pothi. My friend Kulwant K. Singh was always there to assist. I am thankful to them all.

On this side of the globe, Rita, my wife, played an important role in patiently listening to reports of my early research and my efforts to draw some hypothesis out of it. Mana and Raj, my daughter and son, have grown out of their childhood waiting for Dad to have more time to spend with them after he finishes his work. I dedicate this book to Rita and to them, for their love and forbearance during these difficult years.

I owe a particular debt of gratitude to Harjeet and Jagjit Singh Mangat for their keen interest in the publication of this work, and Balwinder and Rabinder Singh Bhamra for their steadfast support in the past years.

This book was originally prepared in Punjabi, but the problems relating to its publication in the Punjab and the suggestion of making the research available to wider range of scholars shaped its final form. Farina Mir of Columbia University translated Chapter 1; she created a draft of this in a little over three weeks, and I then worked on that, to give it its present form. I am indebted to her for this timely assistance. I am deeply grateful to Paul Arney also of Columbia for his help at various stages of development of this project.

I am indebted to Columbia Council for Research and Faculty Development for a Summer Grant in 1993, which provided me with time to prepare the first draft of this book. I am thankful to Harpreet Mahajan, executive director of information technology, SIPA, Columbia University, for her guidance in computer related problems; and Robin Dale, head of the preservation reformatting department at Butler Library, for her help in creating microfilms of important seventeenth-century Sikh manuscripts.

My work on the Goindval Pothis, manuscripts which must have received the physical touch of three Sikh Gurus, Guru Amardas, Guru Ramdas, and Guru Arjan, proved to be of great personal benefit. Each visit to these pothis resulted in profound solace and this spiritual revitalization kept the research going afterwards, even though from a great distance. I hope that this book will be useful for scholars interested in medieval Indian literature in particular the evolution of the text of the Adi Granth.

Columbia University
May 3, 1996   Gurinder Singh Mann

Note on Transliteration

No diacritical marks are used in the text, but the pronunciation of the Punjabi words is recorded in parentheses in the glossary. The Punjabi vowels /a/ /i/ /u/ /e/ /o/ /ai/ /au/ are fairly close to the sounds that appear in the English words *but, bit, book, bait, boat, bat,* and *bout*. A macron (‾) is used to indicate an increase in the length of /a/ /i/ and /u/, and these sounds correspond to vowel sounds in the English words *balm, beat, boot*.

The Punjabi stops /kh/ /ph/ correspond closely to the aspirated /k/ and /p/ as used in initial syllabic position in words such as *cat* and *pat*. The Punjabi stop /ch/ corresponds to affricate used in the English word *chair*. I have used /chh/ to mark the aspirated /ch/ in Punjabi. The Punjabi /th/ comes close to the dental fricative used in English words *thick* and *myth*. The Punjabi retroflexes /ṭ/ /ṭh/ /ḍ/ /ḍh/ /ṇ/, and the flap /ṛ/, for which there are no corresponding sounds in English, are marked with a subscript dot throughout the text.

Contents

1
Introduction to the Goindval Pothis

Among early Sikh religious documents there is a set of manuscripts known as either the "Goindval" Pothis or the "Mohan" Pothis. The two separate names emerge from the close association of these manuscripts with, respectively, town of Goindval in central Punjab, founded by the third Sikh Guru, Guru Amardas (1551-1574), in which they are said to have been prepared, and Baba Mohan, Guru Amardas' oldest son, in whose care they remained after the Guru's demise. Throughout the present book, the former name will be used.

At present, two of these pothis are in the custody of the Bhalla descendants of Guru Amardas. One of them is at 371 Lajpat Nagar, Jalandhar, and the other is at Sundar Kutia, Pinjore. If traditions available in Sikh literature and Bhalla family memories regarding the Goindval Pothis are historically accurate, then the two extant Goindval Pothis have a unique status within the context of early Sikh manuscripts.

According to firm tradition, the Goindval Pothis were used as primary sources for the preparation of the Kartarpur Pothi (1604), a manuscript prepared during the time of the fifth Guru, Guru Arjan (1581-1606), to the contents of which the compositions of Guru Tegh Bahadur (1664-1675) were added in the closing decades of the seventeenth century, to give the Sikhs their canonical text, the Adi Granth ("original book") or Guru Granth Sahib ("the honorable Guru in book form").[1] If this tradition reflects actual events, then the Goindval Pothis, compiled prior to the Kartarpur Pothi and the Adi Granth, can play a crucial role in our understanding of the evolution of the text of Sikh scripture, and are thus a rare and important item in the Sikh religious inheritance.

Along with their claim to priority among early Sikh manuscripts, the extant Goindval Pothis are notable insofar as they contain the earliest extant version of the hymns of medieval non-Sikh saints.[2] Among these hymns are several that to my knowledge are not present in any other available collection of the compositions of these holy men. In addition, the Goindval Pothis shed crucial light on historical issues, such as the existence in the Punjab of the hymns of the non-Sikh saints in the second half of the sixteenth century and the relationship of this literature to the Sikh sacred writings.[3]

This chapter begins with an analysis of the information about the Goindval Pothis that is to be found in Sikh sources. Next I draw upon my first-hand scrutiny of the two extant manuscripts and, coordinating this with previously unnoted historical facts, I attempt to address in detail the history of the Goindval Pothis, the time of their recording, their original number, their internal structure, their place in the transmission of the early Sikh sacred corpus, etc. The purpose of this investigation is to firmly establish the role of the Goindval Pothis in the history of the compilation of the Adi Granth. In a brief section at the end of this chapter, I have attempted to place before the reader the theoretical limits of this research. I hope that this statement will help to put the task of a textual scholar in correct perspective and clarify that this research does not pose any challenge to the Sikh belief that the contents of their scripture are revealed in nature.

1. 1. *The Goindval Pothis as understood by Sikh tradition*

In Sikh literature the Goindval Pothis, instead of being an independent subject of interest, surface in traditions regarding the compilation of the Adi Granth. Given the importance of the Adi Granth in the Sikh community, traditional scholars addressed the issue of its making, and in their reconstructions included basic information about the Goindval Pothis.

Sarupdas Bhalla's *Mahima Prakash* ("The Rise of Glory"), written in 1776, is the earliest Sikh text in which we find reference to the Goindval Pothis.[4] Three main points emerge from this account. First, the Goindval Pothis were prepared during Guru Amardas' lifetime and their actual inscribing was accomplished by his grandson, Sahansram. Second, after Guru Amardas passed away, these pothis remained in the custody of Baba Mohan in Goindval. Third, Guru Arjan himself went to Goindval, borrowed the pothis from Baba Mohan, his mother's elder brother, and utilized them as the primary sources for the Kartarpur Pothi.

The traditions regarding the Goindval Pothis in *Mahima Prakash* also appear in another late eighteenth century text, *Sikhan di Bhagatmala* ("Garland of Sikh Saints").[5] This text's author clearly claims that the Goindval Pothis were prepared during Guru Amardas' period and that they were later used as a source for the Kartarpur Pothi by Guru Arjan. Both *Mahima Prakash* and *Sikhan di Bhagatmala* provide a detailed account of how Guru Arjan himself went from Amritsar to Goindval to borrow these pothis, sat in the lane in front of Baba Mohan's house, and sang a *chhant* (hymn of four stanzas of six verses each) in *rag* Gauṛi ("Mohan, your high abodes and palaces are boundless," the Adi Granth, p. 248) to persuade Baba Mohan to lend him the pothis. Pleased with this singing, Baba Mohan did indeed give Guru Arjan the pothis. Whether the association of Guru Arjan's *chhant* with his trip to Goindval to get the pothis was part of Bhalla family lore, or an outgrowth of the technique we find so frequently in the literature that developed about Guru Nanak's life (Janam-sakhis) whereby stories are woven around his hymns, will be discussed later in this chapter.

Two famous Sikh texts of the mid-nineteenth century created by Nirmala scholars, *Sri Gur Bilas Patishahi 6* ("The Splendor of the Sixth Master") and *Sri Gur Pratap Suraj Granth* ("The Book of the Guru's Glory") build on the details regarding the Goindval Pothis in the eighteenth century sources.[6] The authors of both these texts accept that the Goindval Pothis were written during Guru Amardas' time and that after his death they stayed in the custody of Baba Mohan. These authors do not, however, seem to be satisfied with the earlier brief accounts of Guru Arjan's borrowing of the Goindval Pothis. On the one hand, they expand on the difficulties faced by Guru Arjan in collecting the pothis; on the other hand, they relish the prestige and glory showered on the pothis as they were brought to Amritsar.

In the final decades of the nineteenth century we see, along with the aforementioned *chhant*, a *chaupada* (hymn of four stanzas of four verses each) of Guru Arjan, also in *rag* Gauṛi ("We are the lucky ones," the Adi Granth, pp. 185-186), added to the narrative concerning the Goindval Pothis' role in the preparation of the Kartarpur Pothi. According to an account that appears for the first time in the authoritative commentary on the Adi Granth prepared under the patronage of the Sikh state of Faridkot and completed in 1883, Guru Arjan is said to have composed this particular *chaupada* on the occasion of the first ceremonial opening of the text of the Goindval Pothis at Amritsar.[7] According to the famous Sikh commentator Giani Badan Singh Sekhvan, the use of the word *khazana* ("treasure") in this hymn refers to the Goindval Pothis. The view presented here is in all likelihood based upon some oral tradition prevalent in the Sikh community, but it reveals an important point: that the Faridkot commentary, a result of the collective effort of a wide range of Sikh scholars, endorses the tradition about the use of the Goindval Pothis in the compilation of the Kartarpur Pothi.

A few years after the completion of the Faridkot commentary, the famous Sikh historian Giani Gian Singh presented quite a different understanding of the role of the Goindval Pothis in the compilation of the Adi Granth. According to Giani Gian Singh's *Tvarikh Guru Khalsa* ("The History of the Guru Khalsa"), first published in 1891, Guru Arjan collected the hymns of the Sikh Gurus with great effort and labor from a variety of sources, not primarily a single one. In his view, hymns of Guru Nanak (1469-1539) were secured both orally and in written form from distant Sikh congregations. Guru Arjan "wrote commands to all Sikhs around the country that whoever had the word of the Guru should come forth. . . . The few remaining writings were recorded in the two pothis in the care of Baba Mohan and these Guru Arjan himself went and borrowed."[8] The difficult task of collecting the hymns of Guru Nanak continued for many years, and at the end of this enterprise, Guru Arjan edited the text of Sikh scripture. Giani Gian Singh's view of how the Sikh scriptural text was compiled came to be accepted as true by most Sikhs, but it is important to remember that it was apparently a novel view at the time he put it forward. In this new statement about the compilation of the holy text during Guru Arjan's time, Giani Gian Singh greatly reduced the importance assigned to the Goindval Pothis in earlier accounts. He reduced it b'cos it contained Hindu stuff.

It is interesting to note that Giani Gian Singh was the first scholar who had an opportunity actually to examine the Goindval Pothis. According to a footnote introduced in the later edition of the *Tvarikh Guru Khalsa*, he saw the pothis in 1895.[9] At that time, the Goindval Pothis had been brought to Patiala at the invitation of the Sikh royal family. Given Giani Gian Singh's scholarly credentials, he could no doubt have read the text of the pothis with ease and would clearly have seen that the corpus of hymns available in them was much larger than he had earlier supposed. Giani Gian Singh, however, made no effort to revise his theories about the contents of the Goindval Pothis or their role in the compilation of Sikh scripture. He only introduced a note about his viewing of the pothis. Having seen the two Goindval Pothis in Patiala, he declared two to be their original number. Later writers accepted this as a statement of fact, but it is a fact we have reason to question.[10]

At this point we must step back and see these events against the background of other larger developments in Sikh history. It is to be stressed that we are attempting to understand Sikh traditions regarding the Goindval Pothis, not the history of the pothis themselves. In this endeavor we must keep in mind that the earliest of these traditions to appear in written form dates only in the late eighteenth century, 200-odd years after the accepted period of the compilation of the Goindval Pothis. During the long intervening period, the text of the Sikh scripture attained its canonical form, and at the time of his death, Guru Gobind Singh (1675-1708), the tenth and the last Guru, is traditionally believed to have replaced the office of the living Guru with the text, thus assigning it the status of Guru Granth Sahib, the manifest Guru in the community. The impact of these developments upon the oral traditions regarding the compilation of the sacred Sikh text, which had been passed down since the sixteenth century, was considerable. The very description of how the pothis were brought from Goindval to Amritsar, as presented by nineteenth century authors, offers one example of how the changed status of Sikh scripture, which was so substantially elevated at the beginning of the eighteenth century, may have affected the way stories about scripture were told. Nineteenth-century authors have us witness conch shells being blown in front of the caravan carrying the pothis to Amritsar, musicians singing hymns, the pothis being carried in a palanquin on the shoulders of Sikhs. They are constantly fanned with a fly whisk, and behind the palanquin Guru Arjan and the rest of the company walk barefoot. The ceremonial honor given to the Adi Granth during Sikh rule of the Punjab at the turn of the nineteenth century must have been a major factor in generating such descriptions.[11]

These would seem to be external developments in which nineteenth-century reality shaped Sikhs' understanding of events that happened two centuries earlier. But there were internal developments as well--a process of evolution that can be observed in accounts regarding the Goindval Pothis themselves. In the story found in *Mahima Prakash*, Guru Arjan first sends a Brahmin priest to get the Goindval Pothis; after he returns empty-handed, Guru Arjan himself goes to get them.[12] According to the description in *Sikhan di Bhagatmala*, Guru Arjan tells Bhai Gurdas (d. 1637), a Sikh savant traditionally thought to have been the scribe of the Kartarpur Pothi, to go to Goindval, but Bhai Gurdas thinks that Guru Arjan himself should go for

5

such an important task; accepting this suggestion, the Guru goes.[13] Later writers portray Guru Arjan's trip to Goindval in a very picturesque manner. According to *Sri Gur Bilas Patishahi 6* and *Sri Gur Pratap Suraj Granth*, first Bhai Gurdas and then Baba Buddha (d. 1631), two leading Sikhs of Guru Arjan's time, make unsuccessful trips to Goindval to get the pothis. Only after this, does Guru Arjan himself arrive in Goindval. He bathes in the sacred well (*bauli*), and having encountered the visible form of the founder of this well, Guru Amardas, who offers him his blessings, he goes and sings his *chhant* in *rag* Gauri in front of Baba Mohan's balcony. In the end, after earning Baba Mohan's good will, Guru Arjan succeeds in getting the pothis. With this mission accomplished, he visits his other maternal relations in Goindval and the descendants of Guru Angad (1539-1552) in nearby Khadur, before returning with the pothis to Amritsar.[14]

Thus we see a pattern of steady expansion and elaboration over the years. Understandably, the active role of the Guru involved--Guru Arjan-- tends to grow. Equally understandably, he is increasingly shown as being surrounded by a court full of attendants. It is a measure of the Sikh community's ever firmer devotion to the Guru that their actions prepare the way for his.

One also detects evidence that later writers experienced difficulty with some of the traditions passed down regarding the Goindval Pothis. For example, the authors of *Sri Gur Bilas Patishahi 6* and *Sri Gur Pratap Suraj Granth* feel the need to question Baba Mohan's possession of the Goindval Pothis. These authors think that the manuscripts of Sikh sacred writings should have been with Guru Amardas' successors, Guru Ramdas (1574-1581) and later Guru Arjan. Both texts present a solution to this dilemma of ownership in dramatic fashion. Guru Amardas is said to have left these pothis with Baba Mohan on purpose so that Baba Mohan could rectify the wrong of not having appeared at the succession ceremony of Guru Ramdas, his brother-in-law, when Guru Ramdas was chosen as his father's successor instead of himself. Baba Mohan responded to this gesture, thus redeeming himself. By giving the pothis to Guru Arjan, and thus helping in the compilation of sacred text, Baba Mohan sought forgiveness for his earlier mistake.[15] On this matter and other issues relating to the descendants of Guru Amardas which will be discussed in the present book, see the table below.

6

TABLE 1. GENEALOGY OF GURU AMARDAS' DESCENDANTS

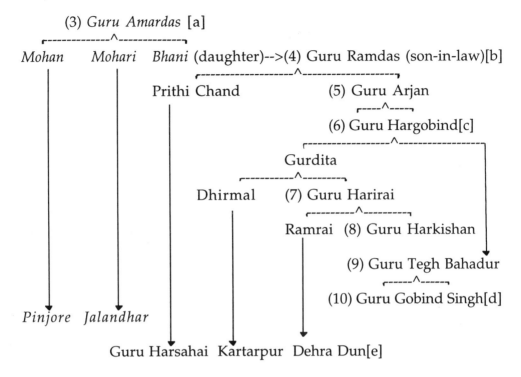

[a] Italics indicate Bhalla family; all others Sodhi family.
[b] Guru Ramdas had another son, who played no role in history.
[c] Guru Hargobind had three more sons, who played no role in history.
[d] Guru Gobind Singh had four sons, who predeceased him.
[e] The descendants of the sons of the Sikh Gurus who did not make it to Guruship live in Pinjore, Jalandhar, Guru Harsahai, Kartarpur, and Dehra Dun, and all have early pothis in their custody.

It is not difficult to understand the background of Giani Gian Singh's depreciation of the role of the Goindval Pothis in the compilation of the Kartarpur Pothi. Giani Gian Singh believed that Guru Nanak had, in his long travels, established many Sikh congregations (*sangats*) and that the Sikh faith had spread far and wide during Guru Nanak's lifetime.[16] On the one hand Giani Gian Singh's claim that Guru Arjan had collected the sacred hymns from these distant congregations authenticated these congregations' existence; on the other, it served to glorify the enterprise of compilation of the Sikh sacred text. Apparently Giani Gian Singh's commitment to these purposes was so strong that even when he had a chance to see the actual contents of the Goindval Pothis, he did not care to revise his general

7

argument about the compilation of Sikh scripture. His persistence caused a degree of confusion in Sikh thought.

Aside from Giani Gian Singh's *Tvarikh Guru Khalsa*, a strong belief that the Goindval Pothis are the primary source for the Kartarpur Pothi is constantly found in Sikh literature, and a respect for the importance of their role goes well beyond Bhalla family sources.[17] At the same time, however, one does not see any concerted attempt to understand the Goindval Pothis as a key landmark in the formation of the Sikh canon. The credit for the compilation of Sikh scripture has tended to be assigned to Guru Arjan and Guru Arjan alone. In these writings, however, there is no evidence of first-hand knowledge of the actual contents of the Goindval Pothis. Anything that has been said about them is based upon either orally transmitted memories or knowledge of hymns present in the Adi Granth.[18]

In the last quarter of the nineteenth century, the widespread introduction of Western education and the arrival of printing press in the Punjab, left a deep impact on Sikh way of thinking about the scriptural text.[19] Sikh scholars for the first time attempted to understand the history of the compilation of the Adi Granth in a systematic manner. Under the guidance of Teja Singh, educated at Gordon Christian College, Rawalpindi, and Sahib Singh, a graduate of Government College, Lahore, a new school of thought was born which dated the beginning of the task of the compilation of Sikh scripture to Guru Nanak's period. These two scholars built their case on the evidence available in the seventeenth century Janam-sakhi literature, in the compositions of Bhai Gurdas, and in the hymns of the Gurus themselves.[20]

In making a strong claim that the work of recording Sikh scripture began during Guru Nanak's period, twentieth century Sikh scholars refuted Giani Gian Singh's contention that Guru Arjan had been the first to gather scattered hymns.[21] With this new understanding of the compilation of Sikh scripture, it was natural to want to understand more about manuscripts compiled in the sixteenth century and their importance in the Sikh community. The preparation of the Kartarpur Pothi, the immediate basis of the Adi Granth, was the central focus of attention. But that meant that the Goindval Pothis were also important. Preeminent scholars like Bhai Kahn Singh Nabha, Bhai Vir Singh, Bhai Jodh Singh, Teja Singh, Piara Singh Padam, and Giani Gurdit Singh all endorsed the traditional view that the Goindval Pothis had been compiled during Guru Amardas' period, had stayed in Goindval in the custody of the Bhalla family, and had played a pivotal role in the preparation of the Kartarpur Pothi.[22]

Among twentieth-century scholars who attempted to understand the process by which Sikh scripture came to be compiled, research of two scholars is of particular importance. In *Sri Guru Granth Sahib dian Prachin Biṛan* ("Old Manuscripts of the Adi Granth"), published in 1944, Gurbaksh Singh (G. B. Singh), a pioneer in the study of Sikh manuscripts, attempted to understand the evolution of Sikh scripture on the basis of information found in manuscripts he had examined, particularly those dating from the seventeenth century.[23] G. B. Singh understood the importance of the Goindval Pothis among sixteenth century Sikh texts and attempted to draw a relationship between them and, on the one side, the Kartarpur Pothi created by Guru Arjan and, on the other side, a pothi prepared, according to a prominent Sikh tradition, during Guru Nanak's time. The latter manuscript, known in Sikh literature as the Guru Harsahai Pothi, was in the custody of the descendants of Guru Arjan's older brother, Prithi Chand (d. 1618), until 1970.[24] G. B. Singh was not successful in his persistent attempts to examine any of these three early pothis and, as a result, was unable to give a considered opinion about the transmission of the Sikh sacred corpus in the sixteenth century. But his dedication to the task before him qualifies him as the first scholar to try to understand in rigorous ways the traditional views about the role of texts like the Goindval Pothis in the context of other sixteenth-century compilations.

A second scholar whose work deserves to be noticed is Sahib Singh, who in the middle decades of the twentieth century, made a special contribution to understanding the first stages in the process through which Sikh scripture came to be compiled. According to him, Guru Nanak himself must have prepared a pothi of his own hymns, which he then gave to Guru Angad at the time of his succession. In similar fashion, later Gurus created pothis of their own hymns and along with that of Guru Nanak entrusted them to their successors.[25] According to Sahib Singh, Guru Arjan received the compositions of his predecessors when he became Guru, and added his hymns to the material in these sources, thereby preparing a new text, the Kartarpur Pothi.[26] This line of thinking affirms that the compositions of the Gurus were available in written form during the sixteenth century, much before the compilation of the Kartarpur Pothi. By postulating that the pothis

9

were an important part of the succession ceremony, it gives recognition to their important status within the Sikh community, long before 1708, when Guru Gobind Singh is traditionally believed to declare scripture to have an authority tantamount to the Gurus themselves.

Sahib Singh rejected the standard tradition to which he was heir, the one asserting that the Goindval Pothis were importantly used in the compilation of the Kartarpur Pothi during Guru Arjan's time. He did not have the opportunity to examine the Goindval Pothis, but in the place of the earlier tradition about their role, he put forward an argument for the existence of other pothis, which he thought would have been handed over to Guru Arjan when he ascended to leadership of the community. He pointed out the weaknesses to be encountered in connecting the story of the Goindval Pothis being brought to Amritsar with that of Guru Arjan's *chhant* in *rag* Gauṛi. According to him, the term "Mohan," which meant "beguiling," was to be understood more generally, as an epithet for God. Sahib Singh claimed that there was no historically factual basis for the story of Guru Arjan's trip to Goindval and his singing in front of Baba Mohan's house.[27] It was unnecessary for Guru Arjan to go to Goindval, he said, because he already possessed a collection of the hymns of the earlier Gurus.

This reconstruction of the early compilation of Sikh scripture has received much recognition in the Sikh community and in academic circles, but its fundamental shortcomings cannot be overlooked. If Sahib Singh's contention that every Guru had a pothi of sacred compositions prepared during his period of leadership is correct, then by the time of Guru Arjan's succession there should have been four successively prepared collections of these writings: those prepared by the first four Gurus and given to their successors. Sahib Singh did not think it necessary to examine issues regarding these sources, such as their condition, where they went after the sixteenth century, or why there is not even a single mention of them in Sikh literature.[28] The absence of any documentary evidence regarding these primary sources and the complete silence about them in Sikh literature are in direct contradiction of Sahib Singh's argument. Their absence shows his reconstruction of history to be elegant in its simplicity, but entirely devoid of any evidential basis.

This may not always remain the case. In the last few decades, important manuscripts have surfaced and it is likely that in the future, with the expansion of research, others will come to light. Of those manuscripts newly found, the Bahoval Pothi in the library of Bhai Vir Singh Sahitya Sadan, New Delhi; Manuscript 1245 at Guru Nanak Dev University, Amritsar; and Manuscript 1192 at the Panjab University, Chandigarh, are important. But no one has ventured to argue that any of them dates to the earliest period of Sikh history. They may shed light on Guru Arjan's period, but they can make no contribution to a discussion of the propagation of Sikh writings in the sixteenth century.[29] At this juncture in research, therefore, it is very difficult to accept any argument that forgoes the use of the Guru Harsahai and the Goindval Pothis in the making of the Kartarpur Pothi. These two are the only pothis, extant or otherwise, that tradition recognizes as belonging to the sixteenth century.

The problem Sahib Singh detected in the story of Guru Arjan's trip to Goindval is easy to solve. Sahib Singh's rejection of the authenticity of this story was an extension of his rejection of the historical value of the Janam-sakhi literature, a hagiographical genre dating from the early seventeenth century, and focusing on Guru Nanak, the founder of Sikh tradition. In Janam-sakhi literature, as we have already observed, it is a standard practice to create stories that would establish the historical setting for hymns of Guru Nanak, and in this context Sahib Singh's suspicions about the historical reality in any of these stories is perfectly justified. Sahib Singh felt that stories told about Guru Arjan could be similarly rejected, but he was not necessarily correct in this assertion. Our earliest Janam-sakhi collections come from the seventeenth century; Guru Nanak lived a century earlier. Hence there was plenty of room for story tellers to invent ties between Guru Nanak's hymns and the events of his life. Guru Arjan, by contrast was a near contemporary. Many of the events of his life--which do indeed correspond to themes in his hymns--might well have been accurately recorded. Hence there appears to be no reason for rejecting out of hand the connection between Guru Arjan's *chhant* in *rag* Gauṛi and the story of his journey to Goindval.[30]

Even if one leaves aside the possibility of a contemporary knowledge of actual background to the topics introduced in Guru Arjan's hymns and accepts Sahib Singh's idea that the *chhant* in *rag* Gauṛi was simply in praise of God, this does nothing to nullify the tradition of Guru Arjan having sung this hymn before Baba Mohan's house in Goindval.[31] After all, Baba Mohan was the Guru's maternal uncle and a revered figure in the early Sikh community. What difficulty would it pose to use his name in this *chhant* in praise of God? Yet even if this *chhant* by Guru Arjan had absolutely no relationship to Baba Mohan, and the story of Guru Arjan going to Goindval to borrow the pothis were not true, the presence of the pothis in Goindval and their use in the preparation of the Kartarpur Pothi is a separate issue.

In sum, the foundation of Sahib Singh's understanding of the compilation of the Sikh sacred text in the sixteenth century is weak. On the one hand, he provides no documentary proof on the basis of which it could be said that Guru Arjan possessed pothis of the complete hymns of the earlier Gurus, which were used as the source for the Kartarpur Pothi. On the other, if the traditional story of bringing the Goindval Pothis to Amritsar is not true, that in itself does not prove that the authenticity of these pothis is questionable, or that the strong tradition of their role in the preparation of the Kartarpur Pothi is historically inaccurate.

In Sikh traditions, the Guru Harsahai and the Goindval Pothis are said to have been prepared before the Kartarpur Pothi. Thus in traditional Sikh thought the first three crucial stages of the community's evolution, under the leadership of Guru Nanak, Guru Amardas, and Guru Arjan, are related to a parallel expansion of Sikh scripture: the Guru Harsahai Pothi, the Goindval Pothis, the Kartarpur Pothi. G. B. Singh embarked upon an inquiry about these primary pothis after accepting this traditional belief as historical reality, but because he was unsuccessful in reaching these pothis, he was unable to provide us with a clear picture of the early development of Sikh scripture. Sahib Singh, the other major contributor to this area of study, attempted to radically rewrite the tradition of early Sikh manuscripts. This revised understanding primarily resulted from Sahib Singh's inability to accept the validity of traditions regarding sixteenth century manuscripts. According to him, Guru Arjan should have received pothis of sacred hymns at the time of his succession. Instead of being in Guru Arjan's possession, however, the Guru Harsahai and Goindval Pothis were actually in the custody of those relatives who challenged his succession. Sahib Singh is not the first scholar to have been confronted with this discrepancy. Nineteenth century writers also felt a need to clarify the fact of the Goindval Pothis being in Baba Mohan's care and, as mentioned earlier, created a story in which this was part of the scheme to forgive Baba Mohan for having shown disrespect to his brother-in-law, Guru Ramdas.

Sikh scholars have shown great hesitancy in scrutinizing the role of the Gurus' relatives in tussles for authority within the community.[32] But we must learn to be more realistic. I believe that what later happened to the Kartarpur Pothi, when it fell into the hands of Dhirmal, the grandson of Guru Hargobind (1606-1644), allowing him to make a strong claim to Guruship at Kartarpur, in the seventeenth century; the same pattern seems to have evolved with the sixteenth century pothis as they were taken into custody by the sons of Gurus who were competing with what was to later emerge as the mainstream leadership.[33] As a result of his inability to resolve this complexity, Sahib Singh failed to give due recognition to the Guru Harsahai and Goindval Pothis and attempted to fill the vacuum with some other non-existing pothis. There is no historical or documentary basis for the argument that the first four Gurus prepared successive sources of their hymns and passed them on to their successors.[34]

With the advent of new ideas relating to textual studies in this century, a fundamental need to accurately understand the contents of the Goindval Pothis in order to evaluate their contribution to the compilation of the Adi Granth was felt for the first time. The custodians of these pothis were not helpful, yet work in this direction was started by Bawa Prem Singh, himself a distant cousin of the Bhalla family. In 1945 Bawa Prem Singh had an opportunity to examine the two extant Goindval Pothis, and the description he prepared during this inspection became the primary source of knowledge about them. Bawa Prem Singh's essay about the pothis was published only many years later in the literary journal *Alochna* ("Criticism"), in 1984, and in 1987, through the efforts of Gursharan Kaur Jaggi, a scholar of early Sikh and Punjabi literature, it appeared in the form of a booklet; but in the intervening years it had been widely disseminated to scholars.[35] In 1969, Bhai Jodh Singh, who had made an important contribution to the preparation of the authoritative version of the Adi Granth published by the Shiromani Gurdwara Prabandhak Committee, included a traced copy of a folio from the section on *rag* Ramkali in the pothi at Pinjore, in his book, *Sri Kartarpuri Biṛ de Darshan* ("An Examination of the Kartarpur Pothi"); the tracing, which made a sample of the writing of the Goindval Pothis available to the readers for the first time, had been obtained from Bawa Prem Singh.[36]

Meanwhile, a leading scholar of early Sikh manuscripts, Giani Gurdit Singh, had been making concerted effort to get to the pothis. In 1976 he

13

managed to photograph the pothi presently at Jalandhar, but unfortunately, photographs of the complete text of the pothi could not be taken. One copy of his incomplete but extremely important set of photographs is in the library of Punjabi University, Patiala, and the other is at Giani Gurdit Singh's residence in Chandigarh.[37] The photographs at the Punjabi University library helped Nirbhai Singh, a scholar of philosophy of religion there, conduct research on Namdev in the 1970s, but for some reason, Nirbhai Singh's interest did not expand to include a detailed study of the Goindval Pothis themselves.[38] In 1990 Giani Gurdit Singh published his findings about the Goindval Pothis in the last section of *Itihas Sri Guru Granth Sahib, Bhagat Baṇi Bhag* ("The History of the Adi Granth, the Section on the Saints"); recognizing the crucial importance of the research relating to early manuscripts outlined in this work, the Shiromani Gurdwara Prabandhak Committee, Amritsar, honored Giani Gurdit Singh in early 1991.[39]

Two senior scholars of early Sikh manuscripts at Guru Nanak Dev University, Amritsar, have been engaged in research related to the Goindval Pothis for many years. In his *Gatha Sri Adi Granth* ("The Story of the Adi Granth"), published in 1992, Piar Singh expanded the discussion on the contents of the Goindval Pothis and their role in the compilation of Sikh scripture.[40] According to information given by Pritam Singh, he has already edited the pothi at Jalandhar; this piece of important research is being published by Guru Nanak Dev University, Amritsar.[41]

In a recent article, W. H. McLeod, the leading scholar of Sikh history and religion in the Western world, has cogently discussed issues relating to the compilation of the Sikh scriptural text and the possible role of the Goindval Pothis in this process.[42]

In the following pages an attempt has been made to address the fundamental issues that have arisen in discussion regarding the Goindval Pothis. My precise aim is to examine thoroughly the traditional claim concerning the role of these pothis in the compilation of the Kartarpur Pothi/Adi Granth. The foundation of this investigation is information I have gathered through detailed examination of the two extant Goindval Pothis at Jalandhar and Pinjore over the last several years, and I make use of that information here to determine the pothis' position in the evolution of Sikh scripture.[43]

According to Bhalla family tradition, the two extant Goindval Pothis, from the time of their completion during the lifetime of Guru Amardas to the beginning of the twentieth century, remained in the custody of Guru Amardas' descendants, at Goindval. According to Sikh tradition, Guru Arjan temporarily brought these pothis to Amritsar at the turn of the seventeenth century and used them in the preparation of the Kartarpur Pothi. It seems natural that after this task was completed, the pothis were sent back; there is even a palanquin in a Goindval gurdwara ("Sikh temple") which, according to a popular local tradition, was used to transport the pothis to and from Amritsar.[44] Only after about three hundred years do we come across a reference of the Goindval Pothis leaving Goindval again--this time to be brought to Patiala for viewing by the Sikh royal family in 1895.[45]

During the Gurdwara Reform Movement (1920-1925), the thinking of the Bhalla family took a new twist. The Shiromani Gurdwara Prabandhak Committee, created under the laws of the Punjab government, challenged the traditional custodians of historic gurdwaras and rare Sikh relics. In order to prevent the pothis from falling under the control of this newly formed Sikh body, the Bhallas sent the pothis to family members living outside Goindval. At first, it was impossible to obtain knowledge of the new locations of the pothis, but later it was found that one had reached Bawa Dalip Chand Bhalla in Ahiapur, District Hoshiarpur, and the other, Bawa Bhagat Singh Bhalla, who was a resident of Hoti Mardan in the Peshawar area.[46]

A few years ago Bawa Dalip Chand's family left Ahiapur and settled in Jalandhar. The pothi they had received is presently in the custody there of his son, Vinod Bhalla. In Ahiapur, it was customary to display the pothi every *sangrand* (the first day of the month according to the local calendar), but in Jalandhar this practice was largely discontinued because of Vinod Bhalla's busy routine. In special circumstances, if the Bhalla family is exceptionally kind to some visitor, then the pothi is put up for display on the morning of the *sangrand* and one is permitted briefly to view the compositions entered in the text (see photograph, p. 191).[47]

The other pothi came to Ludhiana, Patiala, and then to Pinjore, as the Peshawar Bhallas relocated after the partition of the Punjab in 1947. Now it is in the custody of Bawa Bhagat Singh's son, Kanwarjit Singh Bhalla, and his family in Sundar Kutia, Pinjore. According to family tradition, the pothi is displayed on the morning of *puranmashi* (full moon night). At about ten o'clock a congregation begins to gather. After about an hour of singing hymns (*kirtan*), traditionally beginning with Guru Arjan's *chhant* in *rag* Gauṛi, the pothi is unveiled and the congregation is given permission to view it (see photograph, p. 208). Normally, the pothi is open at folio 94; according to Bhalla family memory, the writing there, *gulam mast taiḍa* Jeth Chand ("Jeth Chand your intoxicated slave"), is Guru Ramdas' signature. Jeth Chand was Guru Ramdas' name before he received the Guruship. At 12, the pothi is ceremonially put to rest and members of the congregation are treated to a meal (*langar*), with great hospitality, by the Bhalla family.

There appears to be little confusion in this history of the two Goindval Pothis. We have the testimony of Bhai Gurdas that after Guru Amardas passed away, his eldest son, Baba Mohan, established his own seat of authority at Goindval.[48] It is not surprising that Baba Mohan would have taken possession of the manuscripts of the sacred hymns of the Gurus that were in his home and not given them to Guru Ramdas, the nominated successor of his father, Guru Amardas. Goindval had been founded by Guru Amardas, and even today it is known as the central site of the Bhallas. There appears to be no doubt that the pothis remained in the care of the Bhalla family there. Nor is it difficult to understand the Bhalla family's sending the pothis away in fear of their going under the protection of the Shiromani Gurdwara Prabandhak Committee, at the beginning of the twentieth century.

1. 3. *The time of their recording*

The two extant Goindval Pothis at Jalandhar and Pinjore contain no colophons to reveal their precise dates, but on the basis of internal and external information, it is possible to establish decisively the time at which they were written. The shapes of both vowels and consonants used in the pothis are extremely old. There is a clear difference between the shapes of letters in the pothis and their forms in later Gurmukhi. Take, for example, the vowels. The appearance of the *hoṛa* (as in English "boat") is the inverse of what emerged later. On the right end of the *aunkaṛ* (as in "soot") and *dulainkaṛ* (as in "boot") there is a curl that disappears in later writings, and instead of their lines being straight, they droop downward; the lines of the

16

sihari (as in "bit") and the *bihari* (as in "beat") are not straight either. The symbol for the vowel *kanna* (as in "balm") is frequently left unrecorded, and when it does appear, it is in the form of a dot instead of its later shape of half a line. As for the consonants, some letters have not yet attained their Gurmukhi forms: ੲ (/i/), ਛ (/chh/), ਠ (/ṭh/), ਦ (/d/), ਯ (/j/), ਲ (/l/), and ਅ (/a/) and ਘ (/gh/), like Devanagri letters, have a line on the top. There are differences of usage as well. For example, one does not see the symbol of *kanauṛa* (the vowel sound as in English "route") used in the pothis, one certainly finds /r/ in conjunct form, but it appears relatively rarely; the *ṭippi* (marker of nasal sounds) has been used, but as yet with no uniformity.

TABLE 2. THE GURMUKHI CHARACTERS AS RECORDED IN
THE EXTANT GOINDVAL POTHIS

In the context of other Sikh manuscripts, the letters in the two extant Goindval Pothis confirm that they were prepared at an early stage of the evolution of Gurmukhi writings.[49] All scholars who have studied these pothis in the past decades agree that they were written in the second half of the sixteenth century, the time period beginning with Guru Amardas and coming up to Guru Arjan. As to the exact year of their recording, however, there are two different views.

According to one group of scholars, the pothis were prepared during Guru Amardas' lifetime. On the basis of one old manuscript, *Sakhian Guru Amardas Bhalle kian* ("Stories of Guru Amardas Bhalla"), Pritam Singh placed the period of the pothis' compilation at 1565-1574.[50] Bawa Prem Singh had specified the period of writing of the pothis to be between 1570 and 1572, on the basis of information available in another Bhalla family manuscript, *Sakhian Guru Bans kian* ("Stories of the Guru Families").[51] Three other eminent scholars of this century, Teja Singh, Piara Singh Padam, and Giani Gurdit Singh, supported the dates given by Bawa Prem Singh.[52] In accepting that these pothis had been prepared during Guru Amardas' lifetime, all these scholars fully endorsed Sikh traditional thought on this matter.

In a challenge to the supposition that the Goindval Pothis were prepared in the period 1570-1572, Kaliandas Udasi gave 1595 as their year of preparation.[53] By supporting this date in *Gatha Sri Adi Granth*, Piar Singh has brought this view to the attention of scholars and has necessitated a detailed investigation of this issue.[54] At this juncture one must remind the reader that in these two distinct opinions as to the date of the Goindval Pothis, the difference of twenty to twenty-five years is important. If 1595 were to be accepted as the correct date of preparation for the pothis, then it would be necessary to reject the whole tradition that places their compilation during the lifetime of Guru Amardas. Note that Piar Singh himself ignores the importance of this fact, however: on the one hand, he dates the preparation of the pothis in 1595; on the other, he argues that their compilation began during Guru Amardas' time.[55]

It is interesting that while Bawa Prem Singh and Pritam Singh used manuscripts, albeit obscure ones, as testimony for their argument that the Goindval Pothis had been written during Guru Amardas' period, Kaliandas Udasi's claim of 1595 as the date of writing was based only upon a brief statement recorded in the opening folio of the pothi at Jalandhar. Before one accepts the date found there, it is important to determine the manner in which this statement enters the pothi, and its real purpose (see photographs, pp. 192-193). The statement runs as follows:

> One God, the grace of the true Guru. Name, person who creates, without fear, without form, unborn, self-born. The pothi was written by Guru Amar Baba in Samat 1652 Magh *vadi* 1 (1595). This blessing was given by Guru Baba [Guru Nanak] to Guru Angad, who gave it to the third generation [Guru Amardas]. [The blessing was] that if someone would put his heart into the hymns of the Gurus, he would attain liberation, and would be comfortable both here and hereafter, and not be wanting in anything. He will attain liberation and will enter the presence of the Guru. [The Guru] is God, and there is no doubt or suspicion about it. This statement should be taken as the blessing. If someone leaves the Guru who comes from our family, and follows another, he will definitely go to hell. (folio 1*)
>
> O God! O Immortal persons, Baba Nanak, Angad, Amardas, the true kings, let my heart stay with the hymns of the Baba. There is no boon above this. O my God! Whomever you accept-that person will meet Baba Patishah [Guru Nanak]. (folio 9*)

The beginning of this statement, which presents itself as a blessing, is on folio 1* (* is the symbol I use to mark the left-hand side of the folio) and the last sentence is recorded on folio 9*. How might one explain the fact that this blessing starts on folio 1* and, instead of continuing on the blank right-hand side of folio 1, finishes on folio 9*? The first folio of the opening gathering of manuscripts is normally kept blank so that the document may be protected from the outer side until it is bound. Both sides of folio 1 are blank in the pothis at Pinjore and at Kartarpur and the pothi at Jalandhar must also have been this way originally. In my view, the blessing was inscribed later, in the folio left blank in the original writing. A scribe began to record the blessing on folio 1*, but when he found that he did not have sufficient room, he completed it on folio 9*. There is a clear reason for not having written on the blank right-hand side of folio 1. The pothi's text actually begins on folio 2, which is illustrated with cubic designs in blue and gold on the top half of the left-hand side of the folio, and a wavy design in between the lines of text (see photographs, pp. 194-195). Because of this decorative work, the back part of folio 2*, which is actually right-hand side of folio 1, has become slightly weakened. Any careful scribe would see that ink used here might come out on the other side and damage the pothi's opening decorations. That is why the scribe completed the remaining sentence on folio 9*, which happened to be the first blank folio left in the original writing of the pothi. All this suggests that the date 1595 refers to the time at which the blessing was inserted, not the date on which the pothi was originally completed.

We need, however, to address the fact that the text of the blessing is recorded in the hand of the primary scribe of both the extant pothis. An explanation for this may lie in the traditional claim that Sahansram, son of Baba Mohan, was the original scribe of the Goindval Pothis. If this is the case, and there are no grounds to suspect otherwise, it is reasonable to argue that he himself had later recorded the text of the blessing in the opening folios originally left blank in the pothi.

A study of the contents of this blessing points to the specific reason for its having been recorded. It is clear that this blessing has no relationship to the text of the pothi. Typically, at the beginning of a manuscript, an invocation to God (*manglacharan* or *bismillah*) is written, in which a scribe, before starting an important work, prays for its completion; but the text at issue here, instead of being a literary device, insists upon two strange claims.

The first is related to the beginning and transmission of the blessing. According to its author, this is Guru Nanak's blessing, which was given to Guru Angad and then reached the third Guru, Guru Amardas. The idea appears to be that inasmuch as Baba Mohan is Guru Amardas' son, he and his family are the rightful recipients of Guru Nanak's blessing. In other words, Guru Nanak's blessing did not go to the Sodhi family of Guru Ramdas and his successor Guru Arjan; as a result, the Sodhis' claim against the Bhallas for the Guruship is not authentic.

The other claim is that whoever is devoted to the hymns of the Gurus will be successful in this life and receive liberation at the time of death. Apparently the very reception of the pothis was to be taken as the sort of this worldly success the author had in mind, so the Bhallas family's superiority over that of the line of authority represented by Guru Arjan is clear. The point of these two claims is thus to establish the Bhalla family's spiritual status. The statement that the family (that is, the Bhallas) are the rightful heirs of Guru Nanak's authority and that anyone who disputes that and accepts someone else as Guru will go to hell, arises from this same background.

If we glance at Sikh history, we see that in 1595 the construction of the Darbar Sahib (the present day Golden Temple) in Amritsar, if not already complete, was nearing completion.[56] After this new sacred center at Amritsar came into existence, it was only natural that the eminence of Goindval in the expanding Sikh community would diminish. It is also likely that Guru Arjan would have started to think about compiling an updated Sikh scriptural text. An additional anxiety is likely to have arisen in the ranks of the Bhalla family, namely, that with the preparation by Guru Arjan of a new sacred text in direct competition with the Goindval Pothis, the Bhallas would again be left behind. The pothis, after all, were their principal treasure. Hence we can easily understand the recording of such a blessing in the context of Bhalla-Sodhi family competition.[57] My opinion is that 1595 is the date at which the blessing was inserted; that the blessing is, in itself, positive proof that the pothis were prepared at an earlier date; and that when this was entered in 1595, the pothis were in the possession of the Bhalla family at Goindval.

In support of the argument that the pothis were recorded in 1595, Piar Singh has presented additional internal evidence. According to him, in the pothi at Jalandhar, "two hymns attributed to Guru Ramdas and one to Guru Arjan carry the preparation date of the pothi to Guru Arjan's time."[58] There are difficulties in accepting Piar Singh's contention. First, in this context it should only be a question of two of these hymns: the third not being available in the Adi Granth, one can make no argument about it.

As for the rest, we must first of all understand the peculiarities of the two hymns in question. One, beginning with the verse "O Lord I get comfort by having your sight," is recorded on folio 137 of the pothi, in a pen and penmanship identical with those of the hymns on the previous folios (see photographs, pp. 200-201). In later manuscripts this hymn, appearing in the Kartarpur Pothi, folio 503, and in the Adi Granth, page 670, is attributed to Guru Ramdas; but the Goindval Pothi at Jalandhar records it as the last in the series of *chaupadas* by Guru Nanak. The other hymn, of two stanzas, begins with the verse "Human beings indulge in expensive fragrances"; it is recorded without authorship, and in handwriting not that of the primary

21

scribe, on folios 137-138 of the pothi at Jalandhar (see photographs, pp. 201-202). This hymn is recorded in the Kartarpur Pothi, folio 507, and in the Adi Granth, pages 678-679, attributed to Guru Arjan. Interestingly, in the Kartarpur Pothi and the Adi Granth, the hymn begins with what constitutes the second stanza in the Goindval Pothis: "O my loved one! The best search is that of the Lord."

Just as with the subject of the date recorded with the blessing, there are weaknesses in the argument for a late dating of the Goindval Pothis based on the evidence of these two hymns. My opinion about the tangled situation of the first hymn is different from that of Piar Singh. I would favor a possibility he did not consider: that this hymn, recorded under the name of Guru Ramdas in the Adi Granth, could actually have been by Guru Nanak, as the pothi at Jalandhar claims. Under some circumstance or other, the attribution could have been changed later. This would not be the only example of such variation of attribution of the compositions of the Gurus.[59]

In the Kartarpur Pothi, the hymn does not appear in the subsection of *chaupadas*, its normal place, but instead is recorded later, at the end of a sequence of six hymns of two stanzas (*dopadas*); it is also recorded in a different pen and in writing different from that of the material that precedes it.[60] This manner of the hymn's recording in the Kartarpur pothi and the issue of its attribution certainly require further investigation, but as it stands one cannot make a firm argument about the date of the Goindval Pothis on the basis of its presence in the pothi at Jalandhar.[61]

The second hymn is recorded in the pothi at Jalandhar on a folio originally left blank, between the end of the *chaupadas* (folio 137) and the beginning of the *chhants* (folio 139); it is not included in the overall count of hymns present in the *rag* section. It is appropriate to ask when and why this hymn by Guru Arjan was recorded here, but in my view, it is so clear that this hymn was added to the manuscript after it was initially completed that it makes little sense to use it as worthwhile evidence for dating the Goindval Pothis to the lifetime of Guru Arjan. This particular hymn may have been added then, but the pothi as a whole clearly antedates it.

Rather than the two hymns just discussed, we should turn our attention to the fourteen compositions recorded in the Goindval Pothis under the name of Gulam Sadasevak (whose identity will be addressed in a moment). These compositions can prove to be very important as evidence about the pothis' date. They are clearly part of the original writings of both the extant pothis, sometimes appearing under the full title "Gulam Sadasevak," and in other cases simply under "Gulam." This group of writings is recorded in the two Goindval Pothis between the hymns of the Gurus and those of the non-Sikh saints. Each composition of this group ends with a verse including the signature of "Nanak." Strikingly, the entire group has been crossed out of both extant pothis, but all these compositions can be read in their entirety (see photograph, p. 203). Their complete text is available in Chapter 3 of the present book.

TABLE 3. COMPOSITIONS ATTRIBUTED TO GULAM SADASEVAK
IN THE EXTANT GOINDVAL POTHIS

Pothi at Jalandhar

Rag Suhi	three (folios 54-55)
Rag Prabhati	two (folios 102-103)
Rag Dhanasri	one (folio 150-151)
Rag Basant	two (folios 211-212)
Rag Bhairo	three (folios 255-256)
Rag Maru	one (folio 284)

Pothi at Pinjore

Rag Sorathi	two (folio 160)

According to Giani Gurdit Singh's research, which was endorsed by the Shiromani Gurdwara Prabandhak Committee in 1991, the title Gulam Sadasevak was used for Guru Ramdas prior to his receiving the Guruship; in other words, these fourteen compositions were written by Guru Ramdas prior to 1574.[62] Piar Singh does not agree with this contention. According to him, "these were fake writings, which during Guru Amardas' time had begun to be composed under the signature of Nanak. In order to cause dissension between young Jeth Chand [Guru Ramdas' name before he received the Guruship], and Guru Amardas, their enemies introduced these writings under the name of Gulam Sadasevak. . . . Afterwards, when the truth was revealed, they were crossed out."[63] Piar Singh's analysis does not work. He has felt no need to address such basic issues as the actual identification of Gulam Sadasevak, why an attempt was made to create dissension between Guru Amardas and his successor, when these compositions were entered into the pothis, when it was revealed that they were fake, and who struck them out. As usual, the conspiracy theory leads no where.

Giani Gurdit Singh's view is far more convincing. As we have noted earlier, "*gulam mast taiḍa* Jeth Chand" is written on folio 94 of the pothi at Pinjore, and according to Bhalla family tradition, this is understood to be Guru Ramdas' holy signature. If this belief is based on historical reality, then the pairing of "Jeth Chand" with "Gulam" points to the likelihood that Guru Ramdas used the latter word as a name at the same time he was using Jeth Chand. Moreover, it is likely that when Guru Amardas decided to make Jeth Chand his heir, he gave him permission to use the authoritative signature of Nanak. In the Adi Granth, we have other examples of hymns composed by Gurus prior to taking up the Guruship.[64]

It is likely that Jeth Chand referred to himself as "Gulam Sadasevak" as a sign of humility: *gulam* translates as "slave" and *sadasevak* means "eternal servant." Such humility would also explain why, even if it was known that he was to be the next in line for the Guruship, he would have recorded his compositions somewhat separately from those of the earlier Gurus, and after them. When, later, Baba Mohan, at Goindval, found himself in competition with Jeth Chand, now become Guru Ramdas, it is not surprising that he would have crossed out of the writings of Jeth Chand/Gulam Sadasevak from the pothis in his possession.

Thus several indications--Bhalla family tradition, the placement of Gulam Sadasevak's compositions in the text of the Goindval Pothis, and the most likely scenario as to why they were struck out of the text--support the argument that Guru Ramdas, before actually becoming Guru, was the author of the compositions attributed to Gulam Sadasevak.[65] One can imagine the objection that if this were so, these writings should also be found in the Kartarpur Pothi prepared on the basis of the Goindval Pothis, by Guru Arjan, Guru Ramdas' son. To this we would suggest that the collection of the hymns of Guru Ramdas as it appears in the Kartarpur Pothi/Adi Granth was probably put together by Guru Ramdas himself, who may well have decided to omit the writings of his youth.[66] Once this omission had been made and writings attributed to Gulam Sadasevak in the Goindval Pothis were absent from his own family source of Guru Ramdas' hymns, Guru Arjan would have refrained from including them in the Kartarpur Pothi.

In support of our conclusion that the Goindval Pothis were prepared during the time Guru Amardas, we may call upon two additional pieces of evidence. First, there is the absence of the hymns of Guru Amardas' successors in the pothis, and second, as we shall see later in this chapter, the text is organized in a form that evidently suggests it was completed earlier than the Kartarpur Pothi. The corpus of Guru Amardas' hymns in the pothis is almost identical with his hymns as found in the Kartarpur Pothi (see Table 7). It can thus be stated decisively that all of Guru Amardas' hymns had been composed by the time the Goindval Pothis were prepared and that after this task was complete he did not create any new hymns that needed to be included.[67] From this, one can conclude that the task of compiling these pothis was accomplished during the final years of Guru Amardas' life and that Bawa Prem Singh's view as to their 1570-1572 dating appears to be correct.

1. 4. *Their original number*

There is no doubt that in Sikh literature the hymns collected at Goindval were understood to have been placed in more than one pothi, but there is no clear agreement as to just how many pothis there were.

The first reference to the number of these pothis comes in Giani Gian Singh's *Tvarikh Guru Khalsa*. He says there were two pothis and this would seem to tally with the fact that there are indeed two extant Goindval Pothis.[68] The difficulty, however, is that the description of the contents of one of the pothis discussed in *Tvarikh Guru Khalsa* does not accord with what we find in either of the extant pothis. In the Goindval Pothis he examined at Patiala, Giani Gian Singh saw hymns in *rags* Ramkali, Sorathi, Malar, and Sarang in one pothi, and hymns in *rags* Asa, Gauri, Sri, Vadhans, and Kanra in the other. In the second pothi the *rag* section on Kanra would have included only the hymns of Namdev, since the early Gurus did not compose hymns in this *rag*. The first pothi in this description is identical with that presently to be found at Pinjore; but the second is not the same as the pothi at Jalandhar. Instead of the *rag* groupings outlined by Giani Gian Singh, the pothi at Jalandhar contains hymns in *rags* Suhi, Prabhati, Dhanasri, Basant, Bhairo, Maru, and Tilang. There is no overlap, so it would seem clear that until the beginning of the twentieth century there were at least three Goindval Pothis, two which were taken to Patiala, and one which is now at Jalandhar.

According to Piara Singh Padam and Giani Gurdit Singh, two scholars who have extensively studied the early Sikh manuscripts, there were initially four Goindval Pothis, but neither has made an attempt to present any detailed supporting evidence.[69] According to information related to me by Man Singh Nirankari, another respected Sikh thinker, there were actually four pothis at Goindval in the early decades of the twentieth century: he saw them all during a visit there with his grandfather, a Nirankari Guru, Sahib Gurdit Singh (1907-1947), in 1924-25.[70] To my knowledge, Man Singh Nirankari is the only person to have made the crucial claim that there were four Goindval Pothis and he has actually seen them all. On the basis of internal and external evidence, a strong argument can be made to confirm that the Goindval Pothis were originally four in number.

The Kartarpur Pothi/Adi Granth contains hymns by Guru Nanak and Guru Amardas in nineteen *rags*, the hymns in each being grouped as a section of the manuscript. Of these nineteen *rags*, only eleven are represented in the two extant Goindval Pothis. The third Goindval Pothi, the one examined by Giani Gian Singh, contained hymns in four additional *rags*. If we accept as likely, on the basis of information earlier advanced, that the Kartarpur Pothi/Adi Granth essentially contains, in the appropriate *rag* sections, only such hymns of these two Gurus as were already present in the extant Goindval Pothis, then it would also seem likely that hymns in those of the nineteen *rags* that were not represented in the first three Goindval Pothis would have comprised the fourth pothi.[71] These are hymns of the two Gurus' in *rags* Gujri, Tukhari, Majh, and Bilaval, and a set of seven long compositions comprising couplets and stanzas (*vars*) that appear in *rags* Asa, Gujri, Majh, Malar, Maru, Ramkali, and Suhi, in the Kartarpur Pothi/Adi Granth.

The combination of *rags* in each of the Goindval Pothis whose contents we know appears to reflect an interest in the equal pairing of male and female *rags*, that is, *rags* and *raginis*. A hypothesized fourth Goindval Pothi would have fit nicely into such a scheme: the four *rags* it would have contained are half male and half female. This finding is especially compelling in light of the fact that one finds no such clear distinction between *rags* and *raginis* in the Kartarpur Pothi/Adi Granth.[72] The Kartarpur Pothi/Adi Granth seems to preserve thus a silent record of just what we would expect to find in its Goindval predecessor.

TABLE 4. THE LIST OF *RAG* SECTIONS IN THE GOINDVAL POTHIS

	raginis	*rags*
Jalandhar	Suhi, Prabhati, Dhanasri	Basant, Bhairo, Maru
Pinjore	Ramkali, Sorathi	Malar, Sarang
Pothi at Patiala	Asa, Gauri	Sri, Vadhans[73]
Fourth pothi	Gujri, Tukhari	Majh, Bilaval

One and the only remaining *rag* in which Guru Nanak composed hymns would seem to challenge this neat arrangement: *rag* Tilang, which does not fit into this pairing of the *rags* and *raginis*.[74] It is a small collection of hymns originally written on the last folios of the pothi at Jalandhar, and seems not to have been a part of the large design of the Goindval Pothis. My feeling is that because of its affinity with *rag* Suhi, hymns in this *rag* were appended in this pothi at Jalandhar.

The relationship between the *rags* and a particular time of day also seems to be basic to the arrangement of *rag* sections in the Goindval Pothis. According to the belief systems prevalent in the sixteenth century regarding the *rag*-time relationship, the following broad scheme emerges: Gujri, Tukhari, and Bilaval *rags* pertain to the early hours of the morning; Suhi, Prabhati, Dhanasri, Basant, and Bhairo are of the morning; Asa, Gauri, and Sri belong to the evening; and Ramkali, Malar, and Sarang are *rags* that can be sung at any time of the day.[75] The *rags* in the Goindval Pothis are apparently arranged according to exactly such a scheme.

The historical context of Sikh scripture also contributes to a determination of the proper number of the Goindval Pothis. We have already discussed the fact that the compilation of the scriptural text had begun from Guru Nanak's time. There would have been, I believe, two key aspects to this compilation and we shall see presently how they bear on the question of number. First, it is natural that Guru Nanak would have been eager to compile the divine message revealed in his own hymns. As he says, "The bard sings the message of God," Adi Granth, p. 148.[76] Second, a Sikh pothi of revealed hymns, recorded in a new script, Gurmukhi, would have been a great advantage in the context of religious and political thought about *ahl-i-kitab* ("the people of the book") in the sixteenth century Islamic (Mughal) rule. The existence of such a "book" during Guru Nanak's time would have functioned as a symbol of the distinct character of the growing Sikh community at Kartarpur.[77]

In the light of this, the continuing expansion of the Sikh scriptural text during Guru Amardas' time fits in well with other developments at this crucial phase in the early Sikh history. At that time, the growing community was actively attempting to establish a separate existence for itself--separate from the various communities that surrounded it. Sikhs issued to both Hindus and Muslims an open invitation to come into the shelter of the Guru if they wanted liberation. The words of Guru Amardas to the Brahmins were clear: "Your faith in God can only work if you listen to the advice of the Guru," Adi Granth, pp. 849-850. Living under Islamic rule, his invitation to Sufis to join the Sikh fold and submit to the leadership of the Guru was strikingly bold: "O Shaikh! Leave violence and with the fear of God control the inner madness. Many have attained liberation by fear of the Guru," Adi Granth. p. 551. He further stated: "O Shaikh! Bring your mind to focus on the One. Discard your futile pursuits and realize the word of the Guru. If you follow the Guru, you will gain respect in the divine court," Adi Granth, p. 646.

Sikhs clearly understood their community as unique and distinct from those of Hindus and Muslims, the early Gurus--certainly Guru Nanak and Guru Amardas--created the scriptural text as an indicator of this independent identity. In the case of Guru Amardas, his effort to structure the sacred Sikh text as four pothis can be explained in terms of the significance of this number for both Hindus and Muslims. On the Hindu side, one had the conception that the Veda forms itself into four collections (*samhitas*): Rig, Sama, Yajur, and Atharva, and according to early Sikh thought, Judaism, Christianity, and Islam as a group also possessed four divine texts: Toret (the Torah), Jumbur (the Psalms), Injil (the New Testament), and Qur'an. We find this conception clearly articulated in early Sikh literature.[78] Evidently the existence of four pothis belonging to the Nanak-panth ("the community of Nanak")--the Goindval Pothis--would have seemed a fitting symbol of the Sikh claim to be a distinct religious tradition, parallel to the Hindu tradition on the one side, and the Islamic on the other.

If one looks from a number of angles, then, four as the number of the Goindval Pothis appears to be correct. But only two are extant: where are the two missing pothis? One, plainly, is the Goindval Pothi seen by Giani Gian

Singh in Patiala in the 1890s. We have seen how neatly his description of it accords what we would expect to find. That leaves one remaining, and for that we must call to mind one of the memories of the Bhalla family residing at Pinjore. According to them, one Goindval Pothi was given away as part of the dowry of a Bhalla girl married into a family in Phagwara. Unfortunately, they retain no information about when this marriage took place or where this family is now.[79] Hence it is quite possible that the two missing pothis still exist, but at unknown locations. Before it is accepted that two of the Goindval Pothis are lost, it is necessary that a community-wide attempt be made to find them.

1. 5. *Their Internal structure*

By now we can say with confidence that Sikh traditions about the Goindval Pothis contain important historical truths that cannot be discarded as having been simply invented by later writers. As we have demonstrated, it seems quite clear that these pothis were prepared during Guru Amardas' time, and that they remained in Goindval until the beginning of the twentieth century. Moreover the information contained in the two extant pothis gives very important clues as to the structure of early manuscripts of Sikh scripture and the evolution of their organization, as well as the actual hymns that they contained. Further information that help us build a refined understanding of the way in which the pothis were structured can be gleaned from a close study of the appearance of the manuscripts themselves. I will now, therefore, turn to a rather minute description of the extant Goindval Pothis. The bearing of this on the question of their structure will become clear.

In both the extant pothis, the same light brown paper, which is becoming worn out in certain places, has been used. Each folio is carefully framed, but the custodians have no memory of when this repair was done. The folios are thirteen inches long and ten-and-a-half inches wide, and on the seam between each folio and its frame, a border of five lines is drawn. The text of both pothis begins with folio 2 and on the upper left-hand corner of these folios, geometric designs have been drawn in blue and gold. In the portions of the folios left empty between lines of text, decorations in a wavy style have been drawn (see photographs, pp. 194, and 204). The pothi at

Jalandhar has 300 folios and the pothi at Pinjore, 224. In both the pothis, there are two separate numberings of the folios: one is given in the middle of the top side of the right-hand folio and the other, in the top right corner. In literature on the pothis, the number in the top corner has been used: therefore, I have also used that number here. Although the number is written on the right-hand side of the folio, it is intended to include the left-hand side as well. As I have said, I follow the convention of giving the number listed on the right side of the folio, but to indicate the left side of any given folio I have added asterisk ("*") along with the number.

At the time of binding of both pothis, some problems of numbering resulted from the dislocation of folios from their original place, and we must now attempt to understand what these were.[80]

In my view, the present appearance of the extant pothis can be explained as follows. The original sheet of paper would have been folded four times to create a gathering of eight folios. Then before the actual writing began, each of these folded gatherings was given a number, which was written on the lower right-hand corner of the last folio (see photographs, pp. 193, and 200). At the time of binding, the spines of the gatherings were sewn first; then the gatherings were collected and sewn together. The pothi at Jalandhar now contains thirty-seven gatherings and the pothi at Pinjore, twenty-eight. Both pothis, exhibit certain structural peculiarities, but these can be explained by close study and need not detain us here.[81]

As for the physiognomy of the pothis, it exhibits a close affinity with Islamic manuscripts. This is so in several respects. First, the extant pothis display a beautifully drawn border on all four sides of each page. Second, there is actual style of the drawings on the opening folios (folio 2) in both the pothis, which is also continuos with what we see in sixteenth-century decorations of the Qur'an and other Islamic texts (see photographs, pp. 194, and 204). Third, there is the technique of collecting folios in gatherings, sewing them on the spine, and then placing them in exterior leather binding with a free edge flap.[82] Plainly the "pothis" created by Guru Nanak and Guru Amardas were intended to be of an entirely different order--perhaps not specifically "Islamic" in appearance, but certainly "scriptural." It is noteworthy that the characteristics we have mentioned more or less continued in the preparation of Sikh manuscripts until the 1860s, after which time the printing press completely took over the production of Sikh texts.

Both of the extant Goindval Pothis are primarily in a single handwriting. The writing is very clear, and alterations in words, duplications, mistakes in counting of hymns, and other such discrepancies rarely occur. Where a word or verse has been left out, the scribe has made a "+" symbol and entered the text in the bottom margin. If a word has been accidentally duplicated, it is crossed out or covered in ink with great care. If a mistake has been made in the writing of a verse, it is carefully pasted over with a yellow substance, the correct version being written on top of that.

In addition to that of the primary scribe, another handwriting appears in both pothis as part of the section of the pothis that contain hymns of the saints (see photograph, p. 196). Among other observable differences, the point of the pen used by this scribe must have been somewhat thicker than that preferred by the primary scribe. The second scribe's writing is invariably found in the last portion of various *rag* sections, where the hymns of the non-Sikh saints appear. To be, specific, these are folios 61-62 (*rag* Suhi); folios 159-164 (*rag* Dhanasri); folio 214 (*rag* Basant); folios 270-273 (*rag* Bhairo), in the pothi at Jalandhar; folios 101-106, 120-121 (*rag* Ramkali); folios 174-176 (*rag* Sorathi); folios 214-215 (*rag* Malar), in the pothi at Pinjore. Hymns recorded by the second scribe have two special features. First, these hymns seem to have been inscribed on folios left blank at the end of *rag* sections in the original writing of the pothis. Second, not all hymns written in this hand appear in the Kartarpur Pothi. There are fifteen such compositions in each of the extant Goindval Pothis, but only nine from the pothi at Jalandhar and five from the pothi at Pinjore are present in the Kartarpur Pothi. There has clearly been a selection made with regard to inclusion of these compositions in the Kartarpur Pothi, but why or on what basis is not entirely clear.

Additionally, in the pothi at Jalandhar, there are five hymns recorded in a third handwriting, a writing that makes unusually sparse use of vowels (see photograph, p. 197).[83] These hymns are in *rags* Vadhans, Malar, Bilaval, Asa, and Gujri, all of which fall outside the *rags* otherwise appearing in the pothi at Jalandhar. They have been written on folios left blank in the original writing (folios 38, 39, 165, 185, 186, 273, 299). The *rag* Malar hymn is present in the pothi at Pinjore (folio 213), and all are also found in the Kartarpur Pothi.

This analysis shows that the extant Goindval Pothis are primarily written in the hand of one scribe, whose work indicates excellent professional skills. To this original text of the extant pothis, thirty hymns of the non-Sikh

31

saints were added by another scribe. Since several of the hymns from this group do appear in the Kartarpur Pothi, one could surmise that this addition was made in the pothis soon after their compilation. The insertion of five hymns in a third hand and some odd additions in the titles, made at some point later in time, are not instrumental to our argument.

The Goindval Pothis have a very important bearing on the issue of blank folios in early Sikh manuscripts.

Table 5. RECORD OF BLANK FOLIOS IN THE EXTANT G. POTHIS

Pothi at Jalandhar

Suhi	1*-1, 9*, 10*, 12*-12, 38, 39*-39, 47*	10
Prabhati	81*, 82*-82, 85*-85, 87*, 89*, 90*, 104*-104	10
	[114-119]	11
Dhanasri	145, 148*, 151*-151, 162*, 163*	06
	[165-168]	07
Basant	179-180, 181*-181, 185*-186, 187, 201*-201,	12
	[213*-213, 215*-220, 221]	15
Bhairo	246, 247*-247	03
	[274*-276]	06
Maru	291, 292*	02
	[294-299*]	10
	total	92

Pothi at Pinjore

Ramkali	1*-1, 23*-23, 33, 34*-34, 54*-54, 73*-73, 81*, 87*	13
	[93*-100, 105, 106*, 107-110]	25
Sorathi	131*, 143*, 145*, 162*, 166*	05
	[176-182]	13
Malar	190	01
Sarang	212*, 223*	02
	total	59
	Grand total	151

Numbers in brackets indicate blanks at the end of the hymns of the Gurus or *rag* section as such. Here it is necessary to remind the reader that the text of the blessing discussed in 1. 3. of the present chapter is on folio 1* and 9*, and the hymns written in the handwriting of the third scribe appear now on folios 38, 39, 165, 185, 186, and 299.

The blank pages in both the pothis can be divided into two distinct types. First includes the pages that the scribe seems to have left blank because ink has seeped through or might seep through from the back of the page. For example, in the section on *rag* Sorathi, recorded in the pothi at Pinjore, there are five blank pages (131*, 143*, 145*, 162*, 166*). These are actually the back sides of folios 130, 142, 144, 161, 165, on which text is recorded. These blanks are thus connected primarily to the quality of paper.

The other large set of blanks appears either at the end of a *rag* section or between the hymns of the Gurus and those of the non-Sikh saints. From the table above it may be seen that there are forty-nine pages of this category in the pothi at Jalandhar and thirty-eight in the pothi at Pinjore. These blanks resulted from the scribe's effort to keep various *rag* sections, and subsections within *rags*, separate from one another. In the same manner, the scribe has sometimes left blank pages at the end of groups of *chaupadas*, *chhants*, or *ashtpadis*, within a given subsection of hymns of the Gurus.

Here, it is necessary to reiterate that blank folios are found at the end of *rag* sections, subsections of the hymns of the Gurus, and of groups of *chaupadas*, *chhants*, *ashtpadis*. This fact leaves no doubt that the scribe knew he had all the hymns available to him prior to writing the Goindval Pothis. Thus after Guru Nanak's *chhants*, for example, Guru Amardas' *chhants* begin directly; after Guru Nanak's *ashtpadis*, begin Guru Amardas' *ashtpadis*; and so forth. Hymns in all these groups are given a separate count.

The traditional explanation for the presence of blank folios in early Sikh manuscripts pertaining primarily to the need of incorporating Guru Nanak's hymns that may be found later is not supported by the data available in the extant Goindval Pothis.[84] The writing of the Goindval Pothis clearly runs *ad seriatim*, and there is no provision whatsoever left by the scribe to add a hymn of Guru Nanak in the text.

Another tenet of received wisdom about how early Sikh manuscripts were compiled is also challenged by the origin of the Goindval Pothis. This is the view popularized by Bhai Jodh Singh in his elaborate discussion of the Kartarpur Pothi: that the scribe set aside a given number of gatherings for each *rag* section at the outset, later recording the various hymns into them, as their texts became available to him.[85] The evidence from the extant Goindval Pothis bearing on this hypothesis of compilation of early texts is given in the following table.

TABLE 6. THE BEGINNING OF EACH *RAG* SECTION IN THE EXTANT GOINDVAL POTHIS

Pothi at Jalandhar

rag	first folio.	gathering no.	folios in gathering
Prabhati	folio 63*	gathering 8	folios 57-65*
Dhanasri	folio 120*	gathering 15	folios 113-121*
Basant	folio 169*	gathering 21	folio 163-171*
Bhairo	folio 228*	gathering 29	folio 227-235*
Maru	folio 277*	gathering 35	folio 275-283*

Pothi at Pinjore

Sorathi	folio 122*	gathering 16	folio 119-127*
Malar	folio 183*	gathering 23	folio 175-183*
Sarang	folio 216*	gathering 27	folio 209-217*

From this table it is clear that instead of each *rag* section beginning on the first folio of a new gathering, it begins in the current gathering after a few blank folios. There is no evidence in the pothis that would suggest that particular gatherings were assigned in advance to particular *rags* and then hymns recorded in them. It seems perfectly clear that the text of the Goindval Pothis was written serially. It is therefore untenable to argue that at the time of the Kartarpur Pothi's preparation separate gatherings were kept for each *rag* section, even when the complete corpus of the text to be copied in it was available to the scribe.

In both of the extant Goindval Pothis, one finds a special notation that presents further evidence that the writing was accomplished *ad seriatim*. In both pothis, after recording nine or ten folios' worth of text, the scribe has drawn three or four lines at the end of a hymn and has entered a number below them, a number that becomes consecutively larger (see photographs, pp. 198-199).[86]

According to Bawa Prem Singh, this notation should indicate the end of a section recording the hymns of one Guru.[87] This notion was quite correctly rejected by Piar Singh, but he too was unsuccessful in unlocking the meaning of this unusual system of notation.[88] Here, I think is the answer: the sign denotes the work accomplished by the scribe in a single sitting. It seems likely that this was how scribes kept records of their work in those days; Interestingly, there are regular shifts, and somewhat exceptional ones. The sign is absent, for example, in the texts of Guru Nanak's *Dakhni Aunkar* (folios 35*-53) and *Siddh Gosht* (folios 55*-74), and Guru Amardas' *Anand* (folio 80*-92), all of which are found in the pothi at Pinjore. The scribe completed these long compositions in one sitting each. If the sign does denote a sitting of a scribe, then the pothi at Jalandhar was written in thirty sittings and the pothi at Pinjore in twenty.

On the basis of important information found in the extant Goindval Pothis, our understanding as to the manner in which early Sikh manuscripts were prepared needs revision in several respects. In the case of the Goindval Pothis, the primary scribe began writing on folio 2* and, leaving some folios blank in the process, wrote consistently until the end. Such an endeavor could only have been possible if the scribe already had at hand all of the text he wanted to copy. This leads us once again--and from a different point of departure--to the important conclusion that we can no longer accept the Sikh traditional belief that the work of collecting the Sikh sacred hymns and its organization first occurred during the time of Guru Arjan. It was a much more gradual process, in which all the early Gurus played a role, and very likely it extends back to Guru Nanak.

1. 6. Their place in the transmission of the early sacred corpus

Yet if this study challenges certain long-held notions, it confirms others. These, as we have seen, are the various traditions that relate to the Goindval Pothis themselves. In one particular regard, however, there is more to be said--about the strong traditional claim that the Goindval Pothis are the primary source for the Kartarpur Pothi. This will enable us to determine insofar as possible, the precise place of the Goindval Pothis in the early expansion of Sikh scripture. This we may do by keeping in mind two principle aspects: the actual corpus of sacred hymns and their arrangement in a particular order.

We may begin by calling to mind, in another form, what we had already learned about the contents of the two extant Goindval Pothis. Hymns in seven *rags* are available in the pothi at Jalandhar: Suhi [folios 2*-62], Prabhati [folios 63*-113], Dhanasri [folios 120*-163], Basant [folios 169*-227], Bhairo [folios 228*-273], Maru [folios 277*-292], and Tilang [folios 182*-184, and 300*]. The pothi at Pinjore includes hymns in four other *rags*: Ramkali

35

[folios 2*-121], Soraṭhi [folios 122*-175], Malar [folios 183*-215], and Sarang [folios 216*-224]. To approach the issue of the evolving corpus of hymns in the early manuscripts, it will be useful to take this information and compare it with what we meet in the Kartarpur Pothi.

Let us first consider the hymns of the Gurus. In the table that follows, column 1 gives the name of the *rag* section; column 2 indicates the number of hymns in a given *rag* in the extant Goindval Pothis; column 3 shows the number of hymns recorded in the corresponding section in the Kartarpur Pothi; column 4 gives the differences in terms of hymns added (+) and absent (-) in the Kartarpur Pothi from the corpus present in the Goindval Pothis. *Rag* Maru also appears in the Goindval Pothis and the Kartarpur Pothi, but it presents special complications.[89] I have therefore excluded it from Table 7, below.

TABLE 7. A COMPARISON OF NUMBER OF HYMNS OF THE GURUS' IN THE EXTANT G. POTHIS AND THE KARTARPUR POTHI

rag	G. Pothis	K. Pothi	differences	
Suhi	31	32	2+	1-
Prabhati	34	33	1+	2-
Dhanasri	25	24	0	1-
Basant	38	38	0	0
Bhairo	32	32	0	0
Tilang	05	06	2+	1-
Ramkali	29	29	0	0
Soraṭhi	31	31	0	0
Malar	29	30	1+	0
Sarang	07	08	1+	0
Total hymns	261	263	7+	5-

As will be seen from the table above, there is only a minimal difference between the number of hymns of the Gurus included in the extant Goindval Pothis and those that appear in the Kartarpur Pothi. The difference between these texts is further reduced when one takes into consideration two of Guru Nanak's hymns that appear in *rag* Prabhati in the Goindval Pothis, ("Yoga is not in the patched quilt, the staff, or the ashes," and "What scale, what weights, and who I should call to test?"), but are recorded in *rag* Suhi in the

36

Kartarpur Pothi, folio 542, Adi Granth, pp. 730-731. The actual difference thus is limited to three hymns that appear in the Goindval Pothis but not in the Kartarpur Pothi, and five hymns that are present in the Kartarpur Pothi but are not available in the extant Goindval Pothis. The possible explanations for the dropping of three hymns from the Kartarpur Pothi are offered in Chapter 2, and their complete text is presented in Chapter 3.[90] The five added hymns, by contrast, are well known to Sikhs and are listed in Table 8, below.

TABLE 8. HYMNS OF THE GURUS IN THE KARTARPUR POTHI
THAT ARE NOT PRESENT IN THE EXTANT GOINDVAL POTHIS
1. "O beloved! This body is Maya immersed in greed," Mahala 1,
rag Tilang, Kartarpur Pothi, folio 534/Adi Granth, p. 721
2. "O my little one! What are you proud of?" Mahala 1,
rag Tilang, Kartarpur Pothi, folio 534/Adi Granth, p. 722
3. "O my mind! The praise of the name of the Lord," Mahala 3,
rag Sarang, Kartarpur Pothi, folio 876/Adi Granth, p. 1233
4. "That rare one on whom grace falls he knows," Mahala 3,
rag Malar, Kartarpur Pothi, folio 887/Adi Granth, p. 1258
5. "O my mind, praise the Guru," Mahala 3,
rag Prabhati, Kartarpur Pothi, folio 924/Adi Granth, p. 1334

If the Goindval Pothis were the basis for the Kartarpur Pothi, as tradition asserts, how is one to explain this discrepancy of five additions? As it turns out this is not entirely difficult, but we must proceed on a case-by-case basis. Let us begin with absence from the Goindval Pothis of the two hymns of Guru Nanak (Mahala 1) in *rag* Tilang. This is a mystery easily solved, relating as it more than likely does, to the construction of the pothi now to be found at Jalandhar.

The group of hymns assigned to *rag* Tilang appears in the final folios of this pothi. At some point in time, however, three folios from the final gathering of this section (and of the pothi as a whole) were somehow transferred into the section on *rag* Basant; meanwhile, one folio of the section on *rag* Basant became attached to the original section on *rag* Tilang. This switch may be clearly observed through the inclusion of a few hymns in *rag* Tilang in the section on *rag* Basant (folios 182*-184) and vice versa (folio 300). It is likely that the two hymns in *rag* Tilang that appear in the Kartarpur

Pothi but not in the Goindval Pothis were originally recorded in the final gathering of the pothi now at Jalandhar. The folios that contained them would seem to have been lost at the same time that other folios were rebound in the wrong way. Today, only two folios that apparently belonged to the original final gathering are attached to the end of the pothi. Three additional folios are those rebound into the section on *rag* Basant. This leaves three missing folios out of the usual eight that make up a gathering, and these are the folios that would have contained the missing hymns in *rag* Tilang. This excludes, of course, the one now transplanted at the end containing the opening section of hymn in *rag* Basant. Evidently the mistaken rebinding of the manuscript took place after the creation of the Kartarpur Pothi, since hymns, missing in the pothi presently at Jalandhar survive there.[91]

A different explanation can be offered for the presence of three additional hymns in the Kartarpur Pothi from our set of five in Table 8. As noted above, two hymns of Guru Nanak recorded in the Goindval Pothis in *rag* Prabhati are shifted in the Kartarpur Pothi to *rag* Suhi. We find other examples of such changes among the hymns of the non-Sikh saints as well.[92] Inasmuch as *rag* changes did occur, it may be suggested that these three hymns found in the Kartarpur Pothi may have been recorded originally in the Goindval Pothis in a different *rag* section, not extant.

As we have already discussed, the compilation of the Goindval Pothis took place during Guru Amardas' period. On the basis of a comparison of Guru Nanak's and Guru Amardas' hymns in the Goindval Pothis and the Kartarpur Pothi, one can safely say that almost all hymns of the Gurus available in the Kartarpur Pothi/Adi Granth are present in the corresponding *rag* sections in the Goindval Pothis. The Kartarpur Pothi thus included the text of the Goindval Pothis and the hymns created after their compilations by Guru Ramdas and Guru Arjan.

As with the hymns of the Gurus, the hymns of the non-Sikh saints that appear in the extant Goindval Pothis are closely reproduced in the Kartarpur Pothi. 148 such hymns appear in the two extant Goindval Pothis and of these, 129 are found in the Kartarpur Pothi. The nineteen omissions do not constitute a major difference. Only three of the omitted hymns are in the hand of the primary scribe of the Goindval Pothis. The other sixteen are in the hand of the second scribe. Why only these sixteen, out of the total of thirty, were omitted is still not clear to me at this stage of my research.

Besides the 129 hymns of non-Sikh saints in the Kartarpur Pothi that correspond to hymns in the extant Goindval Pothis, the Kartarpur Pothi includes thirty-four others. Where did these come from? One possibility is that these thirty-four hymns in the Kartarpur Pothi were assigned other *rags* in the Goindval Pothis--*rags* that appeared in the pothis no longer extant. These would then have been transferred to new *rag* sections when the Kartarpur Pothi was compiled. Another possibility is that at the time of the preparation of the Kartarpur Pothi, Guru Arjan, with the assistance of some independent source, expanded the size of the collection of the hymns of the saints beyond the number included in the Goindval Pothis. After all, we do have a very strong tradition in Sikh literature of Guru Arjan's having collected the hymns of the saints. Unfortunately, it is impossible at this stage to know which expansion is correct. We could only reach a decisive solution if we had at hand all of the Goindval Pothis. Even so, there remains the impressive fact that eighty-one per cent of the hymns of the saints present in the Kartarpur Pothi are available in their corresponding *rag* sections in the Goindval Pothis.

Thus a comparative study of the hymns of Guru Nanak, Guru Amardas, and non-Sikh saints that appear in the extant Goindval Pothis and the Kartarpur Pothi, a clear relationship can be seen between the two collections. The presence of the hymns of the saints in the Goindval Pothis illustrates that by Guru Amardas' time the writings of certain well-known saints who had no direct relationship to the expanding Sikh community, had become a part of Sikh sacred literature. It is possible that Guru Arjan expanded the corpus of saints' hymns already available in the Goindval Pothis, but we cannot accept, as has sometimes been argued, that he was responsible for including hymns of such saints in the canon.[93] He primarily added his own and Guru Ramdas' hymns to the sacred poetic corpus.

A comparison of the arrangement of hymns in the Goindval Pothis and in the Kartarpur Pothi clearly illustrates that the evolution of the organization of the Sikh sacred text during the sixteenth century was a gradual process. As we will see in Chapter 2, by the time the Goindval Pothis were written, the work of arranging the hymns was well advanced. A comparison with the Kartarpur Pothi therefore reveals on the one hand, a close relationship, but on the other, additional intricacies and progressive refinements in the organizational scheme. The basic principles of organization that ordered the text of the Goindval Pothis remained in force; they were merely expanded in the Kartarpur Pothi. We have already seen that there is a close correspondence in the hymns actually present in both documents: the numbers match very well. Now let us consider the order in which they are given. There too, the Goindval Pothis and the Kartarpur Pothi are generally parallel, and wherever there is a difference, an appropriate explanation can be found.

Let us first take as an example, Gurus' hymns assigned to *rag* Prabhati. These are found on folios 63*-101 of the pothi at Jalandhar and on folios 921-924 and 928-930 of the Kartarpur Pothi. The correspondence between Guru Nanak's and Guru Amardas' hymns in these two collections is as follows:

TABLE 9. A COMPARISON OF THE SEQUENCE OF GURUS' HYMNS IN *RAG* PRABHATI IN THE G. POTHIS AND THE K. POTHI

Goindval Pothis	Kartarpur Pothi
24 *chaupadas*	24 *chaupadas*
1-17 Mahala 1	1-17 Mahala 1
18-22 Mahala 3	18-22 Mahala 3
absent	23-24 Mahala 3
1-2 Mahala 1	absent
10 *ashṭpadis*	9 *ashṭpadis*
1-7 Mahala 1	1-7 Mahala 1
8 Mahala 3	absent
9--10 Mahala 3	9-10 Mahala 3

The table clearly illustrates the close relationship between these two texts. Regarding the differences between them in the sequence of hymns in this *rag*, they can be divided into two types. The first has to do with transference from one *rag* section to another. Guru Nanak's two *chaupadas* in *rag* Prabhati (technically Prabhati-Lalat) appear in *rag* Suhi in the Kartarpur Pothi (folio 542). The second type of difference has to do with transference vis-à-vis form. The *chaupada* of Guru Amardas (Mahala 3) entered as number 23 in the section on *rag* Prabhati in the Kartarpur Pothi is actually *ashṭpadi* number 8 in *rag* Prabhati in the Goindval Pothis. This hymn has only five stanzas. Therefore, at the time of the preparation of the Kartarpur Pothi, it seems to have been considered more appropriate to record it with the *chaupadas*

40

(usually four stanzas long) than the *ashṭpadis* (usually eight stanzas long) with which it had been placed formerly. Once the problem regarding this hymn has been solved, the *ashṭpadis* in this *rag* become completely synchronized. We have already referred to Guru Amardas' other *chaupada* in *rag* Prabhati, which is absent from the Goindval Pothis but recorded as number 24 in the Kartarpur Pothi. It is likely that this hymn was recorded in some *rag*, not extant, and was moved from there to its present position in the Kartarpur Pothi for reasons we cannot at present determine.

In the arrangement of the text in the Kartarpur Pothi, an additional music-related classification of *ghar* (literally "home"), the meaning of which is not clear to present-day scholars, has been introduced.[94] Along with this, in some *rag* sections other new principles have been added. For example, in the section on *rag* Sorathi, the number of verses per stanza has been made the guiding principle for arranging the hymns, as a result of which differences in ordering between the pothi at Pinjore and the Kartarpur Pothi are far greater than in sections where no such principle has been applied.

TABLE 10. A COMPARISON OF THE SEQUENCE OF GURUS'
HYMNS IN *RAG* SORAṬHI IN THE G. POTHIS AND THE K. POTHI.

Goindval Pothis		Kartarpur Pothi	
24 *chaupadas*		24 *chaupadas*	
1-12	Mahala 1	1-2, 5, 3, 6-8, 10, 12, 9, 11, 4	Mahala 1
13-24	Mahala 3	18-19, 21-24, 20, 13-17	Mahala 3
8 *ashṭpadis*		7 *ashṭpadis*	
1-4	Mahala 1	1-2, 4, 3	Mahala 1
5-8	Mahala 3	7, 5, 6	Mahala 3

The reason for every change in the ordering of hymns between the two pothis is readily clear.

The fourth hymn in the series of Guru Nanak's twelve *chaupadas* in the Goindval Pothis has been moved to the end of this group in *rag* Sorathi in the Kartarpur Pothi. This is apparently because this hymn, alone in this series, has been classified as belonging to *ghar* 3; all the others are in *ghar* 1. *Ghar* classification--whatever its meaning was--is also apparently responsible for many other rearrangement of hymns between the Goindval Pothis and the Kartarpur Pothi.

41

The other change in the series of Guru Nanak's *chaupadas* involves hymns numbers 9 and 11, which were also moved from their original place to a later position. Both these hymns are recorded under the title *ghar* 1, but they have apparently been moved to a later position in the sequence because they are five stanzas long, instead of four. This sort of change, affecting hymns whose form does not fit perfectly with their placement in the Goindval Pothis, occurs frequently. One example from the section on *rag* Prabhati has already been noted

At the basis of other sequential changes between the Goindval Pothis, and the Kartarpur Pothi, the new principle of arrangement according to number of verses per stanza is at work. The new placement is as follows:

Chaupadas of Guru Nanak:

1-2 (three verses); 5 (four verses); 3, 6-8, 10, 12 (two verses).

Chaupadas of Guru Amardas:

18-19, 21-24 (three verses); 20 (four verses); 13-17 (two verses).

Ashtpadis of Guru Nanak:

1 (four verses); 2, 4 (three verses); 3 (two verses).

Ashtpadis of Guru Amardas:

7 (three verses); 5-6 (two verses).

Other than this, the hymn entered as number 8 in the *ashtpadi* series in the Goindval Pothis is absent in the Kartarpur Pothi. This is actually a hymn of four stanzas, which was entered as number 13 in the *chaupada* section of the Goindval Pothis, but was somehow repeated in the section on *ashtpadis* as well. This hymn appears as number 13 in the *chaupada* section of the Kartarpur Pothi, but it seems that when the scribe of the Kartarpur Pothi found out the duplication, he made a correction by dropping it from the *ashtpadi* series. This is the only example of duplication that appears among hymns of the Gurus in the extant Goindval Pothis. In this instance the scribe of the Kartarpur Pothi made a correction, but problems of this sort are also found in there. In writing a work of such large size, their appearance is not at all unnatural.[95]

As we watch the way in which the corpus of Sikh scripture expanded from the Goindval Pothis to the Kartarpur Pothi, we see with some satisfaction that the traditional view regarding the relationship between these pothis appears completely correct. Put simply, the Goindval Pothis became the basis for the further elaboration in the Kartarpur Pothi. Besides, we have no other manuscript comparable to the Goindval Pothis that could be considered to have served as the source of the Kartarpur Pothi. If we understand the Guru Harsahai Pothi as having been compiled before the Goindval Pothis, and the Kartarpur Pothi afterwards, then three phases of the evolution of the Sikh sacred text in the sixteenth century come into clear focus. This story begins with the Guru Harsahai Pothi. Here, only Guru Nanak's hymns appear--for the simple reason, I believe, that only they were available. The classification of *rags* according to which these hymns were to be sung was given in the titles, but in recording this manuscript there appears to have been no effort to organize the hymns on the basis of *rag*.[96] In the Goindval Pothis, the size of the sacred corpus expands. Furthermore, it has been arranged according to *rag* sections, and the internal structure of these sections has become much more elaborate. We see the next stage of this evolutionary process in the Kartarpur Pothi. Here, along with the hymns recorded in the Goindval Pothis, we find new hymns by Guru Ramdas and Guru Arjan, including compositions in eleven *rags* that were not used by the earlier Gurus, and a still more complex system of organization. With the addition of the hymns of Guru Tegh Bahadur, in the 1670s, the text of the Kartarpur Pothi expanded to take the form of the Adi Granth.[97]

In addition to the information given above in support of the argument that the Goindval Pothis were the main source for the Kartarpur Pothi, important external evidence from Sikh history can also be presented. We have already referred to Bhai Gurdas' writings, according to which Baba Mohan was unwilling to accept Guru Ramdas as his father's successor and established his own separate seat of authority at Goindval.[98] Under the circumstances of this competition, it is not surprising that Baba Mohan did not give the Goindval Pothis, which were in his house, to Guru Ramdas. Starting with the Bhalla family, the presence of early manuscripts in the homes of families who were in direct competition with the mainstream community is a historical fact. In Goindval, Baba Mohan had the Goindval Pothis; during the seventeenth century, in the Darbar Sahib at Amritsar, Prithi Chand had the Guru Harsahai Pothi; in Kartarpur, Dhirmal had the Kartarpur Pothi; and in Dehra Dun, Ramrai had the sacred manuscript (1659) prepared during Guru Harirai's time (1644-1661). This array presents rather a remarkable picture, and it appears that these documents played an important role in claims for authority within the early Sikh community (see Table 1).[99]

43

The later history of the Bhalla family is fundamentally different from that of the other three families who made claims for spiritual authority, and I believe this difference may account for the use of the Goindval Pothis at the time of the preparation of the Kartarpur Pothi. After Guru Ramdas passed away, the Bhallas continued to struggle for leadership, now against Guru Arjan. The text of the blessing at the beginning of the pothi at Jalandhar, discussed earlier, is clear evidence of the ongoing tension. In the beginning of the seventeenth century, during the time of the Kartarpur Pothi's preparation, the family struggle between Bhallas and Sodhis appears to have ended with the lending of the Goindval Pothis by the Bhallas to Guru Arjan. Whether this burying of the hatchet was a result of Guru Arjan himself going to Goindval, as remembered by tradition, or whether it was made possible in some other way is not instrumental to our argument.

It is important to keep in mind that the seats of authority of Prithi Chand's family (Guru Haresh Singh Sodhi's family, in Guru Harsahai), the descendants of Dhirmal (Guru Amarjit Singh Sodhi's family, in Kartarpur), and the followers of Ramrai (Mahant Indresh Charandas' seat, in Dehra Dun) remain firmly established entities even today.[100] But in the Bhalla family, no such tradition of a Guruship ever became fixed. The impact of this fundamental difference is clearly found in Sikh documents related to the Khalsa *rahit* (code of conduct). Any association with the families of Prithi Chand, Dhirmal, and Ramrai, and their devotees, is proscribed, and the ban is still in effect in the Sikh community. Yet the Khalsa *rahit* contains absolutely no mention of any such proscription vis-à-vis the Bhallas.[101] On the contrary, a tradition recorded in an important eighteenth century source, Kesar Singh Chhibbar's *Bansavlinama Dasan Patishahian ka* ("Genealogy of the Ten Masters"), makes a strong claim for there having been a relationship of mutual love and admiration between Baba Mohan and Guru Arjan.[102]

It is fair to argue that by giving Guru Arjan the Goindval Pothis at the time of the Kartarpur Pothi's preparation, the Bhalla family not only gave the Guru essential assistance at this all-important stage of the compilation of the Sikh scriptural text, but also accepted his spiritual leadership. After this new turn in the Bhalla-Sodhi relationship, there would no longer have been any purpose in retaining a seat of authority at Goindval, and the Bhalla family's running struggle with Guru Arjan would have been permanently ended. The inclusion of Guru Arjan's *chhant* in *rag* Gauṛi in the Bhalla family's ceremonial worship, and their displaying to the congregation the holy signature held to be that of Guru Ramdas, have long symbolized Bhalla-Sodhi congeniality.

Thus we find no tension between three important sources for reconstructing the early history of the Sikh scriptural text. These are, namely, the internal evidence available in the Goindval Pothis and the Kartarpur Pothi, the history of the families that have been claimants to the Sikh Guruship, and the traditions about the prominent place of the Goindval Pothis in the evolution of Sikh scripture. The Goindval Pothis were not only prepared before the Kartarpur Pothi, they are also its primary source. On the basis of the hymns of the Gurus and the non-Sikh saints that were included in these pothis, and of information about the evolution of the arrangement of their contents, a clear picture of the development of the Sikh sacred text in the sixteenth century can be obtained. No other major religious tradition possesses manuscripts that make the evolution of its scriptural sources clear in a comparable way. Hence the Goindval Pothis and the Kartarpur Pothi are incalculably precious resources. A firm history of the evolution of the text of the Adi Granth constructed upon these documents can make a distinctive contribution to the comparative study of how scriptures are compiled, and canons formed.

1. 7. *Boundaries of this research*

To conclude this discussion of the role of the Goindval Pothis in the history of the compilation of the Adi Granth, it is well to ask how the materials found in these manuscripts become useful to the ongoing Sikh community, and what are the limits of such use. This issue arises in the context of the Sikhs' fundamental belief regarding the text of the Adi Granth, namely, that it is revealed truth. But this belief has several parts, and it is not without its historical context in an environment where other religions are also present.

With respect to their conception of God, Sikhs clearly belong in the company of adherents to monotheistic religions that emerged in the ancient Middle East. Similarly, Sikhs, like Jews and Muslims, give key recognition to the idea of a holy book. The followers of all three religions believe that the text recorded in their scripture is revealed, that the answers to all religious questions are in some way available in this text, and that this text is immutable, unchangeable.[103] By according the Adi Granth the status of the manifest Guru (Guru Granth Sahib), the Sikhs have in one sense taken their conception of the sacred book further than that of Jews and Muslims. As a result, the fundamental Sikh belief as to the status of their scripture has become increasingly firm through the years.

The authoritative edition of the text of the Adi Granth, as published by the Shiromani Gurdwara Prabandhak Committee, and Bhai Chatar Singh Jiwan Singh (a commercial publishing house in Amritsar), and dispersed worldwide, is known as the Damdama version. Manuscripts of the Damdama version can be found starting from the time of the tenth and the last Sikh Guru, Guru Gobind Singh.[104] Prepared at the end of the seventeenth century, this text obtained the status of Adi Granth/Guru Granth Sahib. The importance of manuscripts prior to those of the Damdama version--the Guru Harsahai Pothi, the Goindval Pothis, and the Kartarpur Pothi--is historical and not religious, inasmuch as all of these manuscripts represent incomplete versions of scripture. The examination of these early texts can prove helpful in understanding details pertaining to the process by which the Adi Granth, was compiled, but the presence of non-canonical writings there or the availability of textual variants need not affect the substance of faith. Debates on such matters are academic, not religious.

Research on the contents of the early manuscripts cannot be used to reopen the text of the Adi Granth. Such an endeavor, being contrary to Sikh religious faith, is beyond the reach of any individual.[105] The writings of Gulam Sadasevak as recorded in the Goindval Pothis, have no status in the Sikh community, even if their author can be shown later to have become Guru Ramdas. The writings of Kabir in *rag* Asa ("Look people, it is God's engagement," folio 374) and *rag* Sorathi ("Yogi, that one is my Guru," folio 497), Mirabai's writing in *rag* Maru ("Mother, my mind has been fascinated by his beautiful eyes," folio 810), and a few additional couplets (*shaloks*) included in the original writing of the Kartarpur Pothi but not present in the Adi Granth, are in the same situation. This has nothing to do with the authenticity or inauthenticity of these writings, which is an academic issue. It relates, rather, to the completeness of the canonical text of the Adi Granth. Compositions present in the early pothis which have for some reason not entered the Adi Granth cannot be added now, nor can they in any way be given the status of sacred writings. The canon is closed.

Just as no compositions recorded in the early manuscripts can be added to the text of the Adi Granth, similarly nothing can be taken out of it. From the time of Bhai Santokh Singh, in the mid-nineteenth century, to the recent times, many scholars have made the claim that the *Ragmala* is not a composition of the Gurus and a debate has been going on as to the validity of its presence in the Adi Granth.[106] Again the disposition of this debate is clear. The issue of *Ragmala*'s attribution may be argued for a long time to come, but no attempt to expunge it from the text of the Adi Granth has any chance of succeeding.

The text of the Adi Granth now bears a seal in the Sikh community that is three centuries old. But there is nothing in that fact that should discourage an attempt to understand the history of the making of the Adi Granth using the earlier manuscripts. Indeed, any attempt to argue that the Goindval Pothis are spurious because of the non-canonical writings contained in them, is liable in the long run to do more harm than good.[107] Instead of clarifying the history of the Adi Granth, this line of thinking is likely to create further confusion. As I have tried to show, the remarkable clarity with which we can trace the process by which the Adi Granth came to be is its own precious resonance, giving us rare access to the historical circumstances surrounding the definition of the Adi Granth. Seen in comparison to modern knowledge about the historical situations-- surrounding the canons of other religious traditions, this is a precious advantage--a bulwark against any future misunderstandings or distortions.

The issue of textual variants is a little different from that of non-canonical writings. On the basis of the information found in the early manuscripts, an investigation into the reasons for such variants can be made. And indeed, in the last few years, discussion on this issue has produced some new ideas. At one extreme we have Pashaura Singh, who associates the existence of textual variants in the early manuscripts with Guru Arjan's editorial policy at the time of preparation of the Kartarpur Pothi and sees in them an effort at making doctrinal and theological changes.[108] At the other, we have Piar Singh, who feels that the Sikh sacred text was compiled in quite a loose manner. He believes its contents were for some time recorded variously in Sikh congregations that were often quite distant from one another and from the center. It was a task of some magnitude, and inevitably discrepancies arose in the text.[109] My own view differs from the opinions of both these scholars.

In my view, Pashaura Singh's idea that Guru Arjan scrutinized or edited the hymns of the earlier Gurus is closely related to the conception that the text of Sikh scripture was collected and organized by him for the first time. But the fact that the corpus of Guru Nanak's and Guru Amardas' hymns is essentially identical in the Goindval Pothis and the Kartarpur Pothi, however, leaves no historical basis for this particular expression of the traditional view of Guru Arjan's importance in the process of canon formation. Nor is it possible to accept that Guru Arjan would have needed to make doctrinal changes in the hymns of his predecessors, in the process of preparing these hymns to be recorded into the Sikh sacred text. Moreover, the textual variants between the Goindval Pothis and the Kartarpur Pothi simply are not great enough to warrant the idea that Guru Arjan was in any serious way working as an editor.[110] To the text found in the Goindval Pothis, Guru Arjan added the compositions created by the Gurus who lived after these pothis had been prepared. He compiled the Kartarpur Pothi as an updating of the existing scripture. From all we can determine, Guru Arjan's reverence for scripture meant that hymns recorded in the Goindval Pothis were considered to be above any need for a detailed process of selection or thematic editing. What does seem to have happened in the process of preparing the Kartarpur Pothi, however, was an attempt to improve the early writing system, add a missing word or a verse, make appropriate changes in *rag* assignments, and revise the placement of hymns on the basis of their length. This argument may be clearly supported by the variants marked in Chapter 2 of the present book. Guru Arjan's purpose, apparently, was to display what he has received with the greatest possible clarity--but that is a far cry from any desire to alter the substance of what had come to him from the Gurus who preceded him.

The basis of Piar Singh's argument is not firm either. Consider this: in the second half of the sixteenth century, in the overall context of the evolution of the community at that stage, how many Sikh congregations could there have been in which collections of the hymns of the Gurus were being continuously prepared? Any idea that there number was legion could only be accepted if we had quite a number of independent early pothis, but besides the Guru Harsahai and Goindval Pothis, we do have not a single example of a sixteenth century document of this sort. I therefore feel strongly that the first compilation of the Sikh sacred text was accomplished during Guru Nanak's time and quite probably under his own direction, and that the pothi thus created during the first phase of the Sikh community's development, further evolved in the central Sikh congregation. The results are the Goindval Pothis and the Kartarpur Pothi. Only from the second half of the seventeenth century onward, quite a while after the preparation of the Kartarpur Pothi, do large number of copies of the Sikh scriptural text begin to be found.

To my mind, the textual variants found in the Goindval Pothis and the Kartarpur Pothi arise at a different level altogether. They are a simple consequence of the complexities of the writing process. On the basis of the information to be presented in Chapter 2 of the present book, it appears that during the preparation of the Kartarpur Pothi the text was being dictated orally from the Goindval Pothis. As the scribe wrote, he selected word forms in Punjabi according to his habit. Once he had done so, the sacred text was accepted by the overall Sikh community as having been securely recorded, though the respect assigned to the earlier manuscripts resulted in their continued preservation. Hence from the time of the Kartarpur Pothi the number of textual variants greatly decreases.

The investigation of textual variants in the early manuscripts is in no way meant to contest the belief that the text of the Adi Granth is revealed. It merely relates to changes made as a result of the human difficulties faced by scribes. The use of whiteout (hartal) to make corrections, and entries recorded in the margins of the Kartarpur Pothi: "this is correct" (shudh hai), "correct it" (shudh kichai), "this is repetition" (duhragat hai), all manifest the practical difficulties of inscribing the revealed word.[111]

In the controversy that has arisen from the researches of Piar Singh and Pashaura Singh, it has been claimed that their arguments are attacks upon fundamental beliefs relating to the Adi Granth, and a strong plea was made that textual studies of the Adi Granth should be banned.[112] Fortunately, the effects of this line of thinking have not spread far; and the activities of the Akal Takhat in 1994 were an affirmation of the Shiromani Gurdwara Prabandhak Committee's historical inclination toward openness and leniency on such academic matters.[113] At least in regard to the results of my own investigations of variants, the question of leniency would scarcely need arise. As I have said, such variants prove never to challenge the substance of scripture, but only details of its external form. In many religious traditions, a much more complex picture has emerged from textual scholarship, but not here.

As far as the issue of the *textus receptus* is concerned, I fully endorse the selection of the Kartarpur Pothi. Under the auspices of the Shiromani Gurdwara Prabandhak Committee, Teja Singh, Bhai Jodh Singh, and other scholars active in the middle decades of this century exerted great effort in order to prepare an authoritative edition of the Adi Granth in light of the text of the Kartarpur Pothi.[114] It has been suggested, however, by Sant Gurbachan Singh Khalsa that more work is in this direction leading to yet further refinements, still needs to be done.[115] Officials associated with the Shiromani Gurdwara Prabandhak Committee should look into the matter themselves and make a decision (*gurmata*). In any future attempt to reach a further level of accuracy of the text of the Adi Granth, the help of the extant Goindval Pothis can also be sought, if this be permitted. After all, there is no denying that the two extant Goindval Pothis contain hymns of Guru Nanak and Guru Amardas recorded prior to the preparation of the Kartarpur Pothi.

Belonging centrally to the remarkable process by which the sacred text of the Adi Granth came to be what it is, the Goindval Pothis and the Kartarpur Pothi are crucial sources of information regarding the history of Sikh scripture. With the help of these foundational manuscripts, we can draw a detailed picture of the expansion of the Sikh sacred corpus and its canonization. Thus the Goindval Pothis and the Kartarpur Pothi possess great historical importance. They do not challenge the central position of the Adi Granth in the belief system of the Sikh community. To the contrary, they reaffirm it.

The Contents of the Goindval Pothis

In this chapter the opening and concluding verses of all hymns found in the two extant Goindval Pothis are recorded. This is by far the most detailed presentation of the actual text of these two pothis that has yet been attempted. The information presented in this chapter is exclusively based on my own examination of the two pothis at Jalandhar and Pinjore; I hand copied these verses from the pothis themselves and then compared them several times with the original text, until I was fully satisfied with the accuracy of the transcription.

The detailed information pertaining to the contents of the Goindval Pothis presented in this chapter enables us to understand the precise extent and organizational structure of the sacred corpus in its pre-scriptural stage. By comparing this information with later collections such as the Kartarpur Pothi, we can understand the expansion of the contents of the Sikh scriptural text as well as the increasing complexity of its organizational structure.

As discussed in Chapter 1 (see Table 7), with the exception of hymns in *rag* Maru the other *rag* sections in the extant Goindval Pothis contain all the hymns of Guru Nanak and Guru Amardas found in the corresponding *rag* sections of the Kartarpur Pothi/Adi Granth. The situation regarding the hymns of the non-Sikh saints is by and large parallel: eighty-one per cent of their hymns recorded in the Kartarpur Pothi/Adi Granth are present in the corresponding *rag* sections in the extant pothis. This information confirms that the complete hymns of the early Gurus, and a large (if not complete) corpus of the hymns of the non-Sikh saints had been collected by the time of the preparation of the Goindval Pothis.

In addition, study of the organization of the contents of the extent Goindval Pothis shows that (1) the hymns in these pothis are organized according to their *rag* assignment; (2) each *rag* section opens with an early version of the *mulmantar* (invocation) that is slightly different from its canonical version in the Kartarpur Pothi/Adi Granth; (3) each *rag* section is divided between the hymns of the Sikh Gurus and those of non-Sikh saints; and (4) the subsections of the hymns of the Gurus are further divided into

51

groups based on the length of any given hymn, in terms of number of stanzas it contains (*chaupadas, chhants, ashtpadis,* and longer compositions). The hymns in each group were recorded in a chronological order. For example, the section of the *chaupadas* on each *rag* begins with the *chaupadas* of Guru Nanak, and goes on to record those of Guru Amardas.

The number of each hymn is recorded extremely carefully in the pothis. In the two-column numbering, the first records the number of *padas* in each hymn, and the second column indicates the number of each hymn within the subsection to which it belongs, and thus helps us understand the internal divisions of the various subsections within the overall section on each *rag.* See *rag* Suhi, note 22.

In addition to its *rag* classification, other instructions pertaining to the singing of a particular hymn are sometimes recorded in its title. For example, in folio 16 of the pothi at Jalandhar, the title of Guru Nanak's *chhant* in *rag* Suhi contains information as to the tune on which it ought to be sung (*chhant et dhuni gavana parthai hoi*). See *rag* Suhi, note 15.

In the internal structure of the *chaupadas* and *ashtpadis,* a verse normally appearing as number two in the hymn is assigned the status of *rahau* ("refrain") in the Goindval Pothis; at times more than one verse in a single *chaupada* is given this role. Likewise, the text of the *chhants* employs various sorts of fillers (*jiau,* Ram, etc.).

Thus, a good number of key principles of organization that were later used to codify the contents of the Sikh sacred text had already been established by the time of the compilation of the Goindval Pothis. These principles were further refined and expanded during the compilation of the Kartarpur Pothi, en route to the Adi Granth.

The sample verses of the Goindval Pothis provided in this chapter may be compared with the text of the Adi Granth to establish the relationship that exists between two texts recorded at different stages of the development of Sikh scripture. I have made a modest beginning in that direction and, at those places where I have found substantive differences between the texts recorded in the Goindval Pothis and the Adi Granth, have appended notes to point them out and to offer explanations, if possible, for the divergencies. Thirty-six hymns recorded in the extant Goindval Pothis that are not present in the Kartarpur Pothi/Adi Granth are marked with the symbol "#", and their complete text is provided in Chapter 3.

It needs to be emphasized that the study of variants presented here is of an extremely preliminary nature and makes no claim to being a comprehensive discussion of this issue, and that this brief discussion primarily involves the Goindval Pothis and the Adi Granth, which in traditional Sikh belief is supposed to have been an exact copy of the Kartarpur Pothi. For the text of the Adi Granth, I have used Teja Singh, ed., *Shabadarth Sri Guru Granth Sahib Ji*, published by the Shiromani Gurdwara Prabandhak Committee, Amritsar. When the need arose, I also referred to the Kartarpur Pothi and other early manuscripts.

In the following text, the number of the folio on which a particular hymn begins in the extant Goindval Pothis appears in a column on the left side of the page. As explained in Chapter 1, the folio number in both the extant pothis is recorded on the top right-hand corner. To indicate the left-hand side of the folio, I have used an asterisk.

In this statement of contents, I have tried my best to reproduce in standard Gurmukhi letters the text as it appears in the extant Goindval Pothis. In particular, if the spellings of certain words or the use of, say, a *tippi* (nasal marker), do not conform to their usage in later writings, this is not to be taken as a typographical error, but as the form in which the word actually appears in the pothis. The *kanna* (the symbol for a long /a/) is recorded rather inconsistently in the pothis. I have standardized its usage, but have appended the list of words in which it is sometimes arbitrarily dropped, see *rag* Suhi, note 1.

To make it easier for the reader, I have made three minor additions to the text of the extant Goindval Pothis reproduced here. First, in a running sequence of hymns by Guru Nanak, the scribe at times does not find it necessary to record the attribution. To help the reader, I have added the attribution at such places, in brackets. Second, in the titles of the hymns, the name of the *rag* may or may not be preceded by the word *rag*. For the sake of consistency and clarity, I have included the word *rag* in all cases. For example, titles of hymns in the opening section will always read "*rag* Suhi" and never merely "Suhi." Finally, at a few places, a word or phrase from a hymn, as found in the Adi Granth, has been omitted from the recording of the Goindval Pothis. In such cases I have added the missing verse in brackets, taking it from the text of the Adi Granth, and the detail of this addition is mentioned in the notes.

ਲਾਜਪਤ ਨਗਰ, ਜਲੰਧਰ, ਵਿਖੇ ਪਈ ਪੋਥੀ

ੴ ਸਤਿਗੁਰੂ ਪਰਸਾਦੁ ਸਚੁਨਾਮੁ ਕਰਤਾਰੁ ਨਿਰਭਉ

ਨਿਰੀਕਾਰੁ ਅਕਾਲ ਮੂਰਤਿ ਅਜੂਨੀ ਸਭਉ[1]

ਰਾਗੁ ਸੂਹੀ[2]

ਰਾਗੁ ਸੂਹਬੀ ਗੁਰੂ ਬਾਬੇ ਦੀ [ਮਹਲਾ ੧][3]

੨*   ਭਾਡਾ ਧੋਇ ਬੈਸ ਧੂਪੁ ਦੇਵਹੁ ਤਾ ਦੂਧੈ ਕਉ ਜਾਵਹੁ॥ . . .

     ਭਗਤ ਹੀਣੁ ਨਾਨਿਕੁ ਜਨੁ ਜਪੈ ਹਉ ਸਲਾਹੀ ਸਚਾ ਸੋਈ॥੪॥੧॥

੩*   ਅੰਤਰਿ ਵਸੈ ਨਾ ਬਾਹਰਿ ਜਾਇ॥

     ਅੰਬ੍ਰਿਤੁ ਛੋਡਿ ਕਾਹੇ ਵਿਖੁ ਖਾਇ॥ . . .

     ਹਮਿ ਨਾਹੀ ਚੰਗੇ ਬੁਰਾ ਨਾਹੀ ਕੋਇ॥

     ਪੰਟਵਤਿ ਨਾਨਿਕੁ ਤਾਰੇ ਸਾਚਾ ਸੋਈ॥੪॥੨॥[4]

੩   ਸਭਿ ਅਵਗਣ ਮੈ ਗੁਣੁ ਨਹੀ ਕੋਈ॥

     ਕਿਵ ਕਰਿ ਕੰਤ ਮਿਲਾਵੜਾ ਹੋਈ॥ . . .

     ਭਨਥ ਨਾਨਿਕੁ ਸਹੁ ਹੈ ਭੀ ਹੋਸੀ॥

     ਜੈ ਭਾਵੈ ਪਿਆਰਾ ਤੈ ਰਾਵੈਸੀ॥੪॥੩॥[5]

੪*   ਮਥੁ ਕੁਚਜੀ ਅਮਾਵਣਿ ਡੋਸੜੈ ਕਿਉ ਸਹੁ ਰਾਵਣਿ ਜਾਉ ਜੀਉ॥ . . .

     ਤੁਧੁ ਗੁਣ ਮੈ ਸਭਿ ਅਵਗਣਾ ਇਕ ਨਾਨਿਕ ਕੀ ਅਰਦਾਸਿ ਜੀਉ॥

     ਸਭ ਰਾਤੀ ਸੋਹਾਗਣੀ ਇਕ ਮੈ ਦੋਹਾਗਨਿ ਰਾਤਿ ਜੀਉ॥੧॥੪॥

੫*   ਜਾ ਤੂ ਤਾ ਮੈ ਸਭੁ ਕੋਇ ਤੂ ਸਚਾ ਮੇਰੀ ਰਾਸਿ ਜੀਉ॥ . . .

     ਗੁਰਸਬਦੀ ਸਹੁ ਪਾਇਆ ਸਚੁ ਨਾਨਿਕ ਕੀ ਅਰਦਾਸਿ ਜੀਉ॥੨॥੫॥[6]

੬   ਉਜਲ ਕਹਿਆ ਚਿਲਕਣਾ ਘੋਟਮ ਕਾਲੜੀ ਮਸੋ॥ . . .

     ਨਾਨਿਕ ਨਾਮੁ ਸਮਾਲਿ ਤੂ ਬੰਧਾ ਛੁਟਹਿ ਜਿਤੁ॥੬॥੬॥

੭*   ਜੋਗੀ ਹੋਵੈ ਜੋਗਵੈ ਭੋਗੀ ਹੋਵੈ ਖਾਇ॥ . . .

     ਨਾਨਿਕ ਇਹੁ ਤਨੁ ਕੰਮਿ ਨ ਆਵਈ ਜਿਤੁ ਤਨਿ ਨਾਹੀ ਸਚਾ ਨਾਉ॥੪॥੭॥[7]

੭   ਕਚਾ ਰੰਗੁ ਕਸੁੰਭ ਕਾ ਥੋਰੜਿਆ ਦਿਨ ਚਾਰਿ॥ . . .

     ਨਾਨਿਕ ਨਾਮੁ ਨ ਵੀਸਰੈ ਨਿਧਰਿਆ ਅਧਾਰੁ॥੮॥੮॥[8]

੬----੧੯[9]

ਰਾਗੁ ਸੂਹੀ ਮਹਲੁ ੩[10]

੬   ਜਪ ਤਪ ਕਾ ਬੰਧੁ ਬੇੜੁਲਾ ਜਿਤੁ ਲਘੈਹਿ ਵਹੇਲਾ॥ . . .

     ਨਾਨਿਕੁ ਕਹੈ ਸਹੇਲੀਓ ਸਹੁ ਖਰਾ ਪਿਆਰਾ॥

     ਹਮ ਸਾ ਕੇਰੀਆ ਦਾਸੀਆ ਸਚਾ ਖਸਮੁ ਹਮਾਰਾ॥੫॥੯॥

रागु सूही [महला १]

१० जिन कउ भाडै भाउ तिना सवारसी॥. . .
  नाउ नानक बकसीस जिसु नदरी करमु होइ॥४॥१०॥11

११* भाडा हछा सो जो तिसु भावसी॥. . .
  नानक आपि निहालु सभि कुल तारसी॥१॥११॥12

ੴ सतिगुर परसादु सचुनामु करतारु निरभउ
निरीकारु अकाल मूरति अजूनी सभउ॥

रागु सूही छंद बाबे दे [महला १]13

१३* भरि जोबनि मै मता पेईअड़ै घरि पाहुणी बलिराम जीउ॥. . .
  नानक वीछुड़ि ना दुखु पाए जे गुरमति अंकि समाए रामा॥४॥१॥१२॥14

१५* हम घरि साजन आए॥   साचे मेलि मिलाए॥. . .
  नानक अवगण सबदि जलाए गुण संगमि पिरु पाए रामा॥४॥२॥१३॥

१६ घरि आवहो साजना दरसनु देखह तेरा रामा॥. . .
  नानक गुरमुखि आपु पछाणै प्रभ जैसे अबिनासी रामा॥४॥३॥१४॥15

१८*----२

रागु सूही छंद महलु ३

१८* सुख सोहिलड़ा हरि धिआवहु रामा॥
  गुरमुखि हरि फलु पावहु रामा॥. . .
  नानक हरि आपे जोड़ि विछोड़े हरि बिनु को दूजा नाही॥
  साजन आइ वुठे घरि माही॥४॥४॥१५॥

१९ भगत जना की हरि जीउ रखै जुगि जुगि रखदा आइआ रामा॥. . .
  नानक आपे बकसि मिलाए जुगि जुगि सोभा पाइआ रामा॥४॥५॥१६॥

२१ सबदि सचै सचु सोहिला जिथे सचे का होइ वीचारे रामा॥. . .
  नानक जिस कै मसतकि लिखिआ तिसु परापति होई रामा॥४॥६॥१७॥

२३ जुग चारे धन जे भवै बिनु सतगुर सुहागु न होई रामा॥. . .
  नानक आपि मिलाई करतै नामु नवै निधि पाई रामा॥४॥७॥१८॥

२५ हरि हरे हरि गुण गावहु हरि गुरमुखि पाए रामा॥. . .
  नानक साचा सोहिला सची सचु बाणी सबदे ही सुख होई रामा॥४॥८॥१९॥

२७----३

२७ जे लोड़हि वरु बालड़ीए ता गुर की चरनी चितु लाए रामा॥16. . .
  नानक मेलि लई प्रभि आपनै गुर कै सबदि सवारे रामा॥४॥८॥२०॥

२९ सोहिलड़ा हरि राम नाम गुरसबदी वीचारे रामा॥. . .
  हरि हरि अनदु भइआ वडभागी नानक मनि हरि मीठ लगाए॥17
  गुर सेवनि सतिगुर दाता हरि हरि नामि समाए रामा॥४॥१०॥२१॥

55

राग सूही छंद दखणी [महला १]

३१*   # करि लालच मनु लोभाणा किउ करि छूटीऐ जी॥

        इहु साकतु करमि भुलाणा दरगह चुणि सुटीऐ जी॥ . . .

        सासि गिरासि कबहु न विसरै जा के जीअ पराणा॥

        नानक सतिगुरि टेक टिकाई गुरसबदी मनु माना॥४॥११॥२२॥[18]

राग सूही छंद [महला १]

३३*   जिनि कीआ तनु देखिआ जगो घंदड़ै लाइआ॥ . . .

        दानु देइ दाता जुगि विधाता नानका सचु सोई॥

        आपि करे किसै आखीऐ होरु करे न कोई॥४॥१२॥२३॥

३४   मेरा मनु राता गुण रवै मनि भावै सोई॥

        गुर की पवड़ी साच की सचा सुख होई॥ . . .

        हीनौ नीच करउ बेनंती सचु ना छोडा भाई।

        नानक जिनि करि देखिआ देवै मति साई॥४॥१३॥२४॥[19]

३८----੪

       ੧ੳ   सतिगुर परसादु सचुनामु करतारु निरभउ

        निरीकारु अकाल मूरति अजूनी सभउ गुरुपरसादि

राग सूही महलु ३ जिगुरु[20]

४०*   दुनीआ न सलाहि जो मरि जंमसी॥ . . .

        इस जुग महि विरले जाणीअहि नानक सचु लहनि॥१४॥१॥२५॥

राग सूही दखणी जिगुरु [महला १]

४४   मनहु न नामु विसारि अहिनिसि धिआईऐ॥ . . .

        गुण गावै नानक दासु सतगुर मति दे॥८॥२॥२६॥

४५----੫

राग सूही जिगुरु महलु ३

४५   हरि जी सूखमु अगमु है कितु बिधि मिलिआ जाइ॥ . . .

        जन नानक हरि अराधिआ गुरचरनी चितु लाइ॥८॥१॥२७॥

      ੧ੳ   सतिगुर परसादु

राग सूही महलु ३

४७   नामै ही ते सभ किछु होआ बिनु सतगुर नामु न जापै॥ . . .

        नानक तिसदा सभ किछु होवै जि विचहु आपु गवाए॥८॥१॥२८॥

५०*   काइआ कामनि अति सुआलिउ पिरु वसै जिसु नाले॥ . . .

        नानक सचि वडिआई पाए जिसनो हरि किरपा धारी॥८॥२॥२९॥

राग सूही दखणी [महला १]

५२*   मानस जनमु दुलंभु गुरमुखि पाइआ॥ . . .

ਮਨੁ ਤਨੁ ਹੋਇ ਚਲੰਭ ਜੇ ਸਤਗੁਰਿ ਭਾਇਆ॥

ਇਕ ਨਾਨਿਕ ਕੀ ਅਰਦਾਸਿ ਜੇ ਤੁਧੁ ਭਾਵਸੀ॥

ਮੈ ਦੀਜੈ ਨਾਮਿ ਨਿਵਾਸੁ ਹਰਿ ਗੁਨ ਗਾਵਸੀ॥੮॥੩॥੩੦॥

੫੩* ਜਿਉ ਆਰਣਿ ਲੋਹਾ ਤਾਇ ਭਨਿ ਘੜਾਈਐ[21] . . .

ਨਾਨਿਕ ਮੇਲਿ ਮਿਲਾਇ ਜੇ ਤੁਧੁ ਭਾਈਐ॥੮॥੪॥੩੧॥[22]

੫੪*----੬

ਰਾਗੁ ਸੂਹੀ ਗੁਲਾਮੁ ਸਦਾਸੇਵਕੁ[23]

੫੪* ਪਿਰ ਕੈ ਰੰਗਿ ਰਤੀ ਸੋਹਾਗਣਿ ਅਨਦਿਨੁ ਰਲੀਆ ਮਾਨੈ॥ . . .

[ਇਹ ਲਿਖਤ ਸ਼ੁਰੂ ਕਰਕੇ ਕੱਟੀ ਹੋਈ ਹੈ ਤੇ ੫੫* ਪਤ੍ਰੇ ਤੇ ਪੂਰੀ ਦਰਜ ਹੈ]

੫੪ ਮੈ ਅਵਗਣਿਆਰੀ ਕੋ ਗੁਣੁ ਨਾਹੀ॥

ਬਿਨੁ ਗੁਰ ਭੇਟੇ ਮਿਲਣੁ ਨ ਪਾਹੀ॥ . . .

ਭਨਥ ਨਾਨਕੁ ਪਰਭੁ ਅਲਖੁ ਅਬਿਨਾਸੀ॥

ਗੁਰਪਰਸਾਦੀ ਧਨ ਸੋਹੈ ਜਿਨਿਸੀ॥੬॥[24]

੫੫* ਪਿਰ ਕੈ ਰੰਗਿ ਰਤੀ ਸੋਹਾਗਣਿ ਅਨਦਿਨੁ ਰਲੀਆ ਮਾਨੈ॥ . . .

ਨਾਨਿਕ ਨਾਮੁ ਵਸੈ ਘਟ ਅੰਤਰਿ ਤਾ ਸਹਜੇ ਹਰਿ ਗੁਣ ਗਾਈ॥੪॥੨॥

੫੫ ਪਕੇ ਮੰਡਪ ਮਹਲ ਹਜਾਰਾ॥

ਖਿਨ ਮਾਹਿ ਜਾਤ ਨ ਲਾਗੈ ਬਾਰਾ॥ . . .

ਭਨਥ ਨਾਨਿਕ ਜਗੁ ਸਗਲ ਸੋਇਆ॥

ਗੁਰਪਰਸਾਦੀ ਜਨ ਮੁਕਤੁ ਹੋਆ॥੪॥

ੴ ਸਤਿਗੁਰੂ ਪਰਸਾਦੁ ਸਚੁਨਾਮੁ ਕਰਤਾਰੁ ਨਿਰਭਉ

ਨਿਰੀਕਾਰੁ ਅਕਾਲ ਮੂਰਤਿ ਅਜੂਨੀ ਸਭਉ

ਰਾਗੁ ਸੂਹੀ ਕਮੀਰੁ ਨਾਮਾ ਭਗਤ ਕੀ ਬਾਣੀ[25]

੫੬* # ਜੈਸੇ ਰੰਗੁ ਸੁਪਨੈ ਨਿਧਿ ਪਾਈ ਮਨ ਹੀ ਮਨਿ ਸਮਾਨਾ॥ . . .

ਕਹੁ ਕਬੀਰ ਸੋਈ ਜਨ ਉਬਰੇ ਇਕੁ ਰਾਮੁ ਜਿਨਾ ਮਨ ਮਾਹੀ॥੪॥੧॥[26]

੫੮* ਬੇੜਾ ਬੰਧਿ ਨ ਸਕਿਆ ਬੰਧਨ ਕੀ ਵੇਲਾ॥ . . .

ਕਹੇ ਫਰੀਦੁ ਸਹੇਲੀਹੋ ਸਹੁ ਅਲਹੁਸੀ॥

ਹੰਸੁ ਚਲਸੀ ਡੁਮਣਾ ਇਹੁ ਤਨੁ ਢੇਰੀ ਥੀਸੀ॥੩॥੨॥

੫੮ ਸਹ ਕੀ ਸਾਰ ਸੁਹਾਗਨਿ ਜਾਨੈ॥

ਅਬਮਾਨੁ ਛੋਡਿ ਸੁਖਿ ਰਲੀਆ ਮਾਨੈ॥ . . .

ਕਹੁ ਰਵਿਦਾਸੁ ਸਰਨਿ ਪ੍ਰਭ ਤੇਰੀ॥

ਜਉ ਜਾਨਹਿ ਤਿਉ ਕਰਿ ਗਤਿ ਮੇਰੀ॥੩॥੩॥

੫੮* ਊਚੇ ਮੰਦਰ ਸਾਲ ਰਸੋਈ॥

ਏਕ ਘੜੀ ਮਹਿ ਰਹਣੁ ਨ ਹੋਈ॥ . . .

ਕਹੁ ਰਵਿਦਾਸ ਸਭੋ ਜਗੁ ਲੁਟਿਆ॥

हमि ता एकु रामु करि छूटिआ॥४॥४॥

५८ जो दिन आए सो दिन जाही॥
करिऐ कूचु रहनु थिरु नाही. . .
कहु रविदास निदानि दिवानी॥
चेति रे बंदे दुनीआ फानी॥३॥५॥[27]

५९* तपि तपि लुही हाथ मरोड़े॥
बउरी होई ता सहु लोड़े. . .
तिसु ऊपरि है मारगु मेरा॥
सेख फरीद पंथु समालि सवेरा॥३॥५॥[28]

५९ अवतरि आइ कहा तुम कीना॥
राम का नामु न कबहू लीना. . .
कंठि गहनि तब करनि पुकारिआ॥
कहै कबीरु आगै ते न समारिआ॥३॥६॥

६०* थर थर कंपै बाला जीउ॥
न जाना किआ करसी पीउ. . .
कागु उड़ावत भुजा पिरानी॥
कहै कबीरु इह कथा सिरानी॥३॥७॥[29]

६०* अमलु सिरानो लेखा देना॥
आए कठन दूत जम लैना. . .
कहै कबीरु सेई जन भूले॥
खसमु विसारि माटी संगि रुले॥४॥८॥

६० तपि तपि लुहि लुहि हउ हाथ मरोरउ॥
बावलि होई सो सहु लोरउ. . .
उस ऊपरि जम मारग मेरा॥
सेख फरीद पंथु सवारि सवेरा॥४॥८॥

६१* # कुसलु कुसलु कर सभु जगु बिनसिआ पडिओ काल की फासी. . .
कहु कबीर फुनि हम तुम जाई है रहे रामु अबिनासी॥३॥१०॥[30]

६१ # मात कहै मेरे पूतरा घरि आनि किउ सरसी॥
जिनि एहु जगतु उपाइआ सो चिंता करसी. . .
काहू कै मनि कोऊ वसै काऊ किछु सुहाई॥
नामदे के मनि रामईआ छीपा हरि गुन गाई॥३॥११॥[31]

६२* # जिसु कारनि तनु मनु जालिआ॥
तिनि सरजनि कवलु न पालिआ॥
सेख सरफ न होहु उतावला॥
इकतु सटि न थीवहि चावला॥८॥१२॥[32]

58

ਰਾਗੁ ਪਰਭਾਤੀ[33]

ਰਾਗੁ ਪਰਭਾਤੀ ਬਾਬੇ ਦੀ [ਮਹਲਾ ੧]

੬੩*   ਨਾਇ ਤੇਰੈ ਤਰਣਾ ਨਾਇ ਪਤਿ ਪੂਜ॥
  ਨਾਇ ਤੇਰੈ ਗਹਣਾ ਮਤਿ ਮਕਸੂਦੁ॥. . .
  ਜਾ ਸਦੇ ਤਾ ਢਿਲਿ ਨ ਪਾਇ॥
  ਨਾਨਿਕ ਕੂੜੁ ਕੂੜੋ ਹੋਇ ਜਾਇ॥੪॥੧॥[34]

੬੪*   ਤੇਰਾ ਨਾਮੁ ਰਤਨੁ ਕਰਮੁ ਚਾਨਣੁ ਸੁਰਤਿ ਤਿਥੈ ਲੋਇ॥. . .
  ਨਾਨਕ ਮੂਰਖੁ ਏਕੁ ਤੂ ਅਵਰੁ ਭਲਾ ਸੈਸਾਰੁ॥
  ਜਿਤੁ ਤਨਿ ਨਾਮੁ ਨ ਊਪਜੈ ਸੇ ਤਨਿ ਹੋਹਿ ਖੁਆਰੁ॥੪॥੨॥

੬੪   ਜੈ ਕਾਰਣਿ ਬੇਦ ਬਰਹਮੈ ਉਚਰੇ ਸੰਕਰਿ ਛੋਡੀ ਲੇ ਮਾਇਆ॥. . .
  ਤੁਧੁ ਸਲਾਹਿਨਿ ਤਿਨਾ ਧਨੁ ਪਲੈ ਨਾਨਕ ਕਾ ਧਨੁ ਸੋਈ॥
  ਜੇ ਕੋ ਜੀਉ ਕਹੈ ਓਨ ਕਉ ਤਾ ਜਮ ਕੀ ਤਲਬ ਨ ਹੋਈ॥੪॥੩॥[35]

੬੫   ਜਾ ਕੈ ਰੂਪੁ ਨਾਹੀ ਜਾਤਿ ਨਾਹੀ ਨਾਹੀ ਮੁਖੁ ਮਾਸਾ॥. . .
  ਤੰਤ ਕਉ ਪਰਤੰਤੁ ਮਿਲਿਆ ਬਾਬਾ ਨਾਨਿਕਾ ਬੁਧਿ ਪਾਈ॥੪॥੪॥[36]

੬੬*   ਤਾ ਕਾ ਕਹਿਆ ਦਰਿ ਪਰਵਾਣੁ॥. . .
  ਕਥਨੀ ਬਦਨੀ ਨਾਨਿਕ ਜਲਿ ਜਾਇ॥੪॥੫॥

੬੬   ਅੰਮ੍ਰਿਤੁ ਨੀਰੁ ਗਿਆਨਿ ਮਨਿ ਮਜਨੁ ਅਠਿ ਸਠਿ ਤੀਰਥ ਸੰਗਿ ਗਹੇ॥. . .
  ਗੁਰਮੁਖਿ ਨਾਨਕ ਸਚਿ ਸਮਾਈਐ ਗੁਰਮੁਖਿ ਨਿਜ ਪਦੁ ਪਾਈਐ॥੪॥੬॥

੬੭   ਗੁਰਪਰਸਾਦੀ ਵਿਦਿਆ ਵੀਚਰੈ ਪੜਿ ਪੜਿ ਪਾਵੈ ਮਾਨੁ॥. . .
  ਭਗਤਿ ਸਰਮ ਕਾ ਕਪੜਾ ਮਾਗਉ ਹਰਿ ਗੁਣ ਨਾਨਿਕੁ ਰਵਤੁ ਰਹੈ॥੪॥੭॥[37]

੬੮*   ਆਵਤ ਕਿਨੈ ਨ ਰਾਖਿਓ ਜਾਵਤ ਕਿਉ ਰਖਿਆ ਜਾਈ॥. . .
  ਜਿਸ ਤੇ ਹੋਆ ਸੋਈ ਕਰਿ ਮਾਨਿਆ ਨਾਨਕ ਗਿਰਹੀ ਉਦਾਸੀ ਸੋ ਪਰਵਾਣੁ॥੪॥੮॥

੬੯*   ਦਿਸਟ ਵਿਕਾਰੀ ਬੰਧਨਿ ਬਾਧੈ ਹਉ ਤਿਸ ਕੈ ਬਲਿ ਜਾਈ॥. . .
  ਪਟਵਤਿ ਨਾਨਿਕੁ ਦਾਸਨਿ ਦਾਸਾ ਜਗਿ ਹਰਿਆ ਤਿਨਿ ਜੀਤਾ॥੪॥੯॥

੬੯   ਮਨੁ ਮਾਇਆ ਮਨੁ ਧਾਇਆ ਮਨੁ ਪੰਖੀ ਅਕਾਸੁ॥. . .
  ਜਨਮ ਮਰਣ ਦੁਖ ਕੰਟੀਐ ਨਾਨਕ ਛੂਟਸਿ ਨਾਇ॥੪॥੧੦॥[38]

ੂ੦----੭

ਰਾਗੁ ਪਰਭਾਤੀ ਦਖਣੀ [ਮਹਲਾ ੧]

੭੦   ਜਾਗਤੁ ਬਿਗਸੈ ਮੂਠੋ ਅੰਧਾ॥ ਗਲਿ ਫਾਹੀ ਸਿਰਿ ਮਾਰੇ ਧੰਧਾ॥. . .
  ਕਰਮਹੀਣੁ ਸਚੁ ਭੀਖਿਆ ਮਾਗੈ ਨਾਨਕ ਮਿਲੈ ਵਡਿਆਈ॥੪॥੧੧॥

੭੧*   ਮਸਟਿ ਕਰਉ ਮੂਰਖੁ ਜਗਿ ਕਹੀਓ॥
  ਅਧਿਕ ਬਕਉ ਤੇਰੀ ਲਿਵ ਰਹੀਓ॥. . .

ਤੂ ਬਕਸੇਹਿ ਜਾਤਿ ਪਤਿ ਹੋਇ॥

ਨਾਨਿਕ ਕਹੈ ਕਹਾਵੈ ਸੋਇ॥੫॥੭੨॥

ਰਾਗੁ ਪਰਭਾਤੀ [ਮਹਲਾ ੧]

੧੨ ਖਾਇਆ ਮੈਲੁ ਵਧਾਇਆ ਪੈਧੈ ਘਰ ਕੀ ਹਾਣਿ॥ . . .

ਨਾਨਿਕੁ ਜਲ ਕੋ ਮੀਨ ਸੈ ਥੇ ਭਾਵੈ ਰਾਖਹੁ ਪਰੀਤਿ॥੫॥੭੩॥

੧੩* ਗੀਤ ਸਾਦ ਹਰਖ ਚਤੁਰਾਈ॥

ਰਹਸ ਰੰਗ ਫੁਰਮਾਇਸਿ ਕਾਈ॥[39] . . .

ਜਿਨਿ ਚਾਖਿਆ ਪੂਰਾ ਪਦੁ ਹੋਇ॥

ਨਾਨਿਕੁ ਧ੍ਰਪਿਓ ਤਨਿ ਸੁਖੁ ਹੋਇ॥੫॥੭੪॥

੧੪* ਅੰਤਰੁ ਦੇਖਿ ਸਬਦਿ ਮਨੁ ਮਾਨਿਆ ਅਵਰੁ ਨ ਰਾਗੁਨਹਾਰਾ॥ . . .

ਨਾਨਕ ਰਸਨਿ ਰਸਾਏ ਕਰਤੇ ਰਵਿ ਰਹਿਆ ਪ੍ਰਭੁ ਸੋਈ॥੪॥੭੫॥[40]

੧੫* ਬਾਰਹ ਮਹਿ ਰਾਵਲ ਖਪਿ ਜਾਵਹਿ ਚਹੁ ਛਿਅ ਮਾਹਿ ਸਨਿਆਸੀ॥ . . .

ਨਾਨਿਕ ਸਤਗੁਰ ਮਿਲੈ ਮਿਲਾਇਆ ਦੁਖੁ ਪਰਛਤੁ ਕਾਲੁ ਨਸੈ॥੪॥੭੬॥

੧੬* ਸੰਤ ਕੀ ਰੇਨੁ ਸਾਧ ਜਨਾ ਸੰਗਤਿ ਹਰਿ ਕੀਰਤਿ ਤਰੁ ਤਾਰੀ॥ . . .

ਨਾਨਿਕੁ ਕਹੈ ਅਵਰੁ ਨਾਹੀ ਦੂਜਾ ਸਚਿ ਸਬਦਿ ਮਨੁ ਮਾਨਿਆ॥੫॥੭੭॥

ਰਾਗੁ ਪਰਭਾਤੀ ਮਹਲੁ ੩

੧੭* ਗੁਰਮੁਖਿ ਵਿਰਲਾ ਕੋਈ ਬੂਝੈ ਸਬਦੇ ਰਹਿਆ ਸਮਾਈ॥ . . .

ਨਾਨਕ ਨਾਮੁ ਧਿਆਇ ਸਦਾ ਤੂ ਸਤਗੁਰਿ ਦੀਆ ਦਿਖਾਈ॥੪॥੭੮॥

੭੭ ਨਿਰਗੁਣਿਆਰੇ ਨੋ ਬਕਸਿ ਲੈ ਸੁਆਮੀ ਆਪੇ ਲੇਹੁ ਮਿਲਾਈ॥ . . .

ਨਾਨਕ ਨਾਵੈ ਜੇਵਡੁ ਅਵਰੁ ਨਾ ਦਾਤਾ ਪੂਰੇ ਗੁਰ ਤੇ ਪਾਈ॥੪॥੭੯॥

੭੮ ਗੁਰਮੁਖਿ ਹਰਿ ਸਲਾਹਿਆ ਜਿਨਾ ਤਿਨਾ ਸਲਾਹਿ ਹਰਿ ਜਾਤਾ॥ . . .

ਨਾਨਕ ਨਾਮੁ ਮਿਲੈ ਵਡਿਆਈ ਗੁਰਸਬਦੀ ਸਚੁ ਪਾਏ॥੪॥੨੦॥

੭੯----੮

੭੯ ਜੋ ਤੇਰੀ ਸਰਟਾਈ ਹਰਿ ਜੀਉ ਤਿਨ ਤੂ ਰਖਟਜੋਗੁ॥ . . .

ਨਾਨਕ ਨਾਮੁ ਸਲਾਹਿ ਸਦਾ ਤੂ ਸਚੈ ਸਬਦਿ ਸਮਾਹਿ॥੪॥੨੧॥

੮੦* ਗੁਰਮੁਖਿ ਹਰਿ ਜੀਉ ਸਦਾ ਧਿਆਵਹੁ ਜਬ ਲਗਿ ਜੀਉ ਪਰਾਨੁ॥ . . .

ਨਾਨਕ ਨਾਮੁ ਮਿਲੈ ਵਡਿਆਈ ਪੂਰੈ ਭਾਗਿ ਧਿਆਇਆ॥੪॥੨੨॥

੧ਓ ਸਤਿਗੁਰ ਪਰਸਾਦੁ

ਰਾਗੁ ਪਰਭਾਤੀ ਲਲਤ

੮੩* ਕਵਣ ਤਰਾਜੀ ਕਵਣ ਤੋਲਾ ਤੇਰਾ ਕਵਣ ਸਰਾਫੁ ਬੁਲਾਵਾ॥

ਕਵਣੁ ਗੁਰੂ ਪਹਿ ਦੀਖਿਆ ਲੇਵਾ ਕੈ ਪਹਿ ਮੁਲੁ ਕਰਾਵਾ॥ . . .

ਅੰਧੁਲਾ ਨੀਚ ਜਾਤਿ ਪਰਦੇਸੀ ਖਿਨੁ ਆਵੈ ਤਿਲੁ ਜਾਵੈ॥

ਤਾਕੀ ਸੰਗਤਿ ਬਾਬਾ ਨਾਨਿਕੁ ਰਹਤਾ ਕਿਨ ਬਿਧਿ ਮੁੜਾ ਪਾਵੈ॥੪॥੧॥

੮੩ ਜੋਗੁ ਨ ਖਿਥਾ ਜੋਗੁ ਨਾਹੀ ਡੰਡੈ ਜੋਗੁ ਨਾਹੀ ਭਸਮ ਚੜਾਈਐ॥

ਜੋਗੁ ਨਾ ਮੁਦੀ ਮੂਡਿ ਮੁਡਾਇ ਐ ਜੋਗੁ ਨਾ ਸਿਧੀ ਵਾਈਐ॥ . . .

ਵਾਜੇ ਬਾਝਹੁ ਸਿੰਙੀ ਵਾਜੈ ਤਾ ਨਿਰਭਉ ਪਦੁ ਪਾਈਐ॥

ਅੰਜਨ ਮਾਹਿ ਨਿਰੰਜਨਿ ਰਹੀਐ ਜੋਗ ਜੁਗਤਿ ਇਵ ਪਾਈਐ॥੪॥੨॥[41]

੧ਓ ਸਤਿਗੁਰ ਪਰਸਾਦੁ ਸਚੁਨਾਮੁ ਕਰਤਾਰੁ ਨਿਰਭਉ

ਨਿਰੀਕਾਰੁ ਅਕਾਲ ਮੂਰਤਿ ਅਜੂਨੀ ਸੰਭਉ ਗੁਰਪਰਸਾਦੁ

ਰਾਗੁ ਪਰਭਾਤੀ ਦਖਣੀ ਅਸਟਪਦੀਆ [ਮਹਲਾ ੧][42]

੮੬* ਦੁਬਿਧਾ ਬਉਰੀ ਮਨੁ ਬਉਰਾਇਆ॥

ਝੂਠੈ ਲਾਲਚਿ ਜਨਮੁ ਗਵਾਇਆ॥. . .

ਰਾਮਿ ਨਾਮਿ ਉਤਮ ਗਤਿ ਹੋਈ॥

ਨਾਨਿਕ ਖੋਜਿ ਲਹੈ ਜਨੁ ਕੋਈ॥੮॥੧॥[43]

੮੮* ਮਾਇਆ ਮੋਹਿ ਸਗਲ ਜਗੁ ਛਾਇਆ॥

ਕਾਮਨਿ ਦੇਖਿ ਕਾਮਿ ਲੋਭਾਇਆ॥. . .

ਤਨੁ ਮਨੁ ਧਨੁ ਹਰਿ ਆਗੈ ਰਾਖਿਆ॥

ਨਾਨਿਕੁ ਕਹੈ ਮਹਾ ਰਸੁ ਚਾਖਿਆ॥੮॥੨॥

੯੦ ਨਿਵਲੀ ਕਰਮ ਭੁਅੰਗਮ ਭਾਠੀ ਰੇਚਕ ਪੂਰਕ ਕੁੰਭ ਕਰੈ॥. . .

ਮਨੁ ਮਾਰੇ ਜੀਵਤੁ ਮਰਿ ਜਾਣੁ॥   ਨਾਨਿਕ ਨਦਰੀ ਨਦਰਿ ਪਛਾਣੁ॥੮॥੩॥

੯੨----੬

੯੨ ਗੋਤਮ ਤਪਾ ਅਹਿਲਿਆ ਇਸਤਰੀ ਤਿਸੁ ਦੇਖਿ ਇੰਦੁ ਲੋਭਾਇਆ॥. . .

ਨਾਨਿਕ ਸਚਿ ਨਾਇ ਨਿਸਤਾਰਾ ਕੋ ਗੁਰਪਰਸਾਦਿ ਅਘੁਲੈ॥੮॥੪॥[44]

੯੪* ਆਖਣਾ ਸੁਨਟਾ ਨਾਮੁ ਆਧਾਰੁ॥

ਧੰਧਾ ਛੁਟਕਿ ਗਇਆ ਵੇਕਾਰੁ॥. . .

ਹਰਿ ਰਸੁ ਚਾਖਿਆ ਤਉ ਮਨੁ ਭੀਨਾ॥

ਪਤਿਵਤਿ ਨਾਨਿਕੁ ਅਵਰੁ ਨ ਦੂਜਾ॥੮॥੫॥

੯੫ ਰਾਮ ਨਾਮ ਜਪਿ ਅੰਤਰਿ ਪੂਜਾ॥

ਗੁਰਸਬਦੁ ਵੀਚਾਰਿ ਅਵਰੁ ਨ ਦੂਜਾ॥. . .

ਕਹੁ ਨਾਨਕ ਗੁਰਿ ਬੂਝ ਬੁਝਾਈ॥

ਨਾਮ ਬਿਨਾ ਗਤਿ ਕਿਨੈ ਨ ਪਾਈ॥੮॥੬॥

੯੬ ਇਕਿ ਧੁਰਿ ਬਕਸਿ ਲਏ ਗੁਰਿ ਪੂਰੈ ਸਚੀ ਬਣਤ ਬਣਾਈ॥. . .

ਨਾਨਿਕੁ ਤਿਨ ਕੇ ਚਰਨ ਪਖਾਲੇ ਜਿਨਾ ਗੁਰਮੁਖਿ ਸਚਾ ਭਾਇਆ॥੮॥੭॥

੯੯* ਆਪੇ ਭਾਂਤਿ ਬਣਾਏ ਬਹੁਰੰਗੀ ਸਿਸਟਿ ਉਪਾਈ ਪਰਭਿ ਖੇਲੁ ਕੀਆ॥. . .

ਨਾਨਕ ਗੁਰਮੁਖਿ ਮੇਲਿ ਮਿਲਾ ਗੁਰਮੁਖਿ ਹਰਿ ਹਰਿ ਜਾਇ ਰਲੇ॥੫॥੮॥[45]

੯੯*----੧੦

ਰਾਗੁ ਪਰਭਾਤੀ ਮਹਲੁ ੩

੯੯* ਗੁਰਪਰਸਾਦੀ ਵੇਖੁ ਤੂ ਹਰਿਮੰਦਰੁ ਤੇਰੈ ਨਾਲਿ॥. . .

ਨਾਨਕ ਗੁਰਮੁਖਿ ਵਣਜੀਐ ਸਚਾ ਸਉਦਾ ਹੋਇ॥੧॥੯॥

61

੧੦੧*   ਭੈ ਭਾਇ ਜਾਗੇ ਸੇ ਜਨ ਜਾਗਰਣੁ ਕਰਹਿ ਹਉਮੈ ਮੈਲੁ ਉਤਾਰਿ॥. . .

      ਨਾਨਕ ਨਾਮੁ ਨ ਵੀਸਰੈ ਜੋ ਕਿਛੁ ਕਰੇ ਸੁ ਹੋਗੁ॥੮॥੧੦॥

ੴ ਸਤਿਗੁਰ ਪਰਸਾਦਿ

ਰਾਗੁ ਪਰਭਾਤੀ ਗੁਲਾਮੁ

੧੦੨   ਸਹਜ ਭਾਇ ਮਿਲਾਇਆ ਗੁਰਿ ਪੂਰੈ ਵਿਚਹੁ ਹਉਮੈ ਖੋਈ॥. . .

      ਨਾਨਕੁ ਗੁਰੂ ਵਡਭਾਗੀ ਪਾਇਆ ਤਾ ਸਹਜੇ ਰਹਿਆ ਸਮਾਈ॥੪॥੧॥

੧੦੩*   ਆਪਣੈ ਵਸਿ ਕੀਤੋਨੁ ਸਭ ਕਿਛੁ ਹੋਰਸੁ ਹਥਿ ਕਿਛੁ ਨਾਹੀ॥. . .

      ਨਾਨਕ ਗੁਰਮੁਖਿ ਏਕੋ ਜਾਣੈ ਤਾ ਵਿਚਹੁ ਹਉਮੈ ਖੋਈ॥੩॥੨॥

ੴ ਸਤਿਗੁਰ ਪਰਸਾਦੁ ਸਚੁਨਾਮੁ ਕਰਤਾਰੁ ਨਿਰਭਉ

ਨਿਰੀਕਾਰੁ ਅਕਾਲ ਮੂਰਤਿ ਅਜੂਨੀ ਸੰਭਉ

ਰਾਗੁ ਪਰਭਾਤੀ ਲਲਤ ਕਬੀਰ ਨਾਮਦੇਉ

੧੦੫*   ਬਾਕੇ ਨੈਨ ਸਰਵਨ ਸੁਣਿ ਬਾਕੇ ਬਾਕੀ ਸੁੰਦਰਿ ਕਾਇਆ॥. . .

      ਕਹਤੁ ਕਬੀਰ ਤੇ ਜਨ ਕਬਹੁ ਨ ਹਾਰਨਿ ਢਾਲਿ ਜਿ ਜਾਨਨਿ ਪਾਸਾ॥੪॥੧॥[46]

ਰਾਗੁ ਪਰਭਾਤੀ ਕਬੀਰ

੧੦੬*   ਮਰਨ ਜੀਵਨ ਕੀ ਸੰਕਾ ਨਾਸੀ॥

      ਆਪਨ ਰੰਗਿ ਸਹਜਿ ਪਰਗਾਸੀ॥. . .

      ਕਹਤੁ ਕਬੀਰ ਕਿਲਵਿਖ ਭਏ ਖੀਨਾ॥

      ਮਨੁ ਭਇਆ ਜਗਜੀਵਨ ਲੀਨਾ॥੪॥੨॥

੧੦੬   ਮਨ ਕੀ ਬਿਰਥਾ ਮਨੁ ਹੂ ਜਾਨੈ ਕਿਆ ਬੂਝਲ ਅਗੈ ਕਹੀਐ॥. . .

      ਨਾਮਾ ਕਹੇ ਜਗਜੀਵਨੁ ਪਾਇਆ ਹਿਰਦੈ ਅਲਖ ਬਿਡਾਣੀ॥੪॥੩॥

੧੦੭   ਅਲਹੁ ਏਕੁ ਮਸੀਤਿ ਵਸਤੁ ਹੈ ਅਵਰੁ ਮੁਲਖੁ ਕਿਸੁ ਕੇਰਾ॥. . .

      ਕਹੁ ਕਬੀਰ ਸੁਨਹੁ ਨਰ ਨਰਵੈ ਪਰਹੁ ਏਕ ਕੀ ਸਰਨਾ॥

      ਕੇਵਲ ਨਾਮੁ ਜਪਹੁ ਰੇ ਪ੍ਰਾਨੀ ਤਾ ਨਿਹਚਉ ਹੋਸੀ ਤਰਨਾ॥੬॥੪॥

੧੦੮   ਅਵਲਿ ਅਲਹ ਨੂਰੁ ਉਪਾਇਆ ਕੁਦਰਤਿ ਕੇ ਸਭਿ ਬੰਦੇ॥. . .

      ਕਹਤੁ ਕਬੀਰ ਮੇਰੀ ਸੰਕਾ ਨਾਸੀ ਸਰਬ ਨਿਰੰਜਨ ਡੀਠਾ॥੪॥੫॥

੧੦੯*   ਵੇਦ ਕਤੇਬ ਕਹਹੁ ਮਤ ਝੂਠੇ ਝੂਠਾ ਜੋ ਨ ਵੀਚਾਰੈ॥. . .

      ਕਹੈ ਕਬੀਰ ਤੂ ਭਿਸਤ ਤੇ ਚੂਕਾ ਦੋਜਕ ਸਿਉ ਮਨੁ ਮਾਨਿਆ॥੪॥੬॥

੧੧੦*—–੧੧

੧੧੦*   ਆਦਿ ਜੁਗਾਦਿ ਜੁਗਾਦਿ ਜੁਗੋ ਜੁਗ ਤਾ ਕਾ ਅੰਤੁ ਨ ਜਾਨਿਆ॥. . .

      ਤੂ ਦੈਆਲੁ ਰਤਨ ਲਾਲੁ ਨਾਮਾ ਸਚਿ ਸਮਾਇਲਾ॥੩॥੭॥

੧੧੦   ਅਕੁਲਿ ਪੁਰਖਿ ਇਕੁ ਚਲਤੁ ਉਪਾਇਆ॥. . .

      ਪਟਵਤਿ ਨਾਮਦੇਉ ਇਤੁ ਜੀਉ ਚਿੰਤਾ ਵੈਸੁ ਲਹੈ॥

      ਅਮਰੁ ਹੋਇ ਸਦ ਹੀ ਆਕੁਲ ਪੁਰਖ ਚੈ॥੪॥੮॥

११११	ਤਿਨਿ ਚੰਦਨੁ ਮਸਤਕਿ ਪਾਤੀ॥

	ਰਿਦ ਅੰਤਰਿ ਕਰਤਲ ਕਾਤੀ॥. . .

	ਕਹੁ ਬੇਟੀ ਤ੍ਰਿਭਵਣੁ ਧਿਆਵੈ॥

	ਬਿਨੁ ਸਤਗੁਰ ਮੁਕਤਿ ਨਾ ਪਾਵੈ॥੫॥੧੯॥

१९२	ਸੁਨਿ ਸੰਧਿਆ ਤੇਰੀ ਦੇਵ ਦੇਵਾਕਰਿ ਅਧਪਤਿ ਆਦਿ ਸਮਾਈ॥. . .

	ਕਬੀਰ ਦਾਸਿ ਤੇਰੀ ਆਰਤੀ ਕੀਨੀ ਨਿਰੰਕਾਰ ਨਿਰਬਾਨੀ॥੩॥੧੦॥

ਰਾਗੁ ਪਰਭਾਤੀ ਲਲਤ

१९३*	ਏਕੁ ਕੋਟੁ ਪੰਚ ਸਿਕਦਾਰਾ ਪੰਚੇ ਮਾਗਹਿ ਹਾਲਾ॥

	ਜਿਮੀ ਨਾਹੀ ਮੈ ਕਿਸੈ ਕੀ ਬੋਈ ਐਸਾ ਦੇਨੁ ਦੁਖਾਲਾ॥. . .

	ਸੰਤਾ ਕਉ ਮਤੁ ਕੋਈ ਜੀਉ ਨਿ ਦੇਸਤੁ ਰਾਮੁ ਹੈ ਏਕੋ॥

	ਕਹਤ ਕਬੀਰੁ ਸੋਈ ਮੈ ਧਿਆਇਆ ਜਾ ਕਾ ਨਾਉ ਬਿਬੇਕੋ॥੪॥੧੧॥[47]

ੴ ਸਤਿਗੁਰੁ ਪਰਸਾਦੁ ਸਚੁਨਾਮੁ ਕਰਤਾਰੁ ਨਿਰਭਉ
ਨਿਰੀਕਾਰੁ ਅਕਾਲ ਮੂਰਤਿ ਅਜੂਨੀ ਸੰਭਉ ਗੁਰਪਰਸਾਦੁ

ਰਾਗੁ ਧਨਾਸਰੀ[48]

ਰਾਗੁ ਧਨਾਸਰੀ ਗੁਰੁ ਬਾਬੇ ਦੀ [ਮਹਲਾ ੧]

१२०*	ਜੀਉ ਡਰਤੁ ਹੈ ਆਪਣਾ ਕੈ ਸਉ ਕਰੀ ਪੁਕਾਰ॥. . .

	ਸਾਹਿਬ ਤੇਰੇ ਨਾਮ ਬਿਟਹੁ ਬਿਦ ਬਿਦ ਚੁਖ ਚੁਖ ਹੋਇ॥੧॥ ਰਹਾਉ॥੧॥[49]

१२१*	ਹਮਿ ਆਦਮੀ ਹਾ ਇਕ ਦਸੀ ਮੁਹਲਤਿ ਮੁਹਤਿ ਨ ਜਾਣਾ॥. . .

	ਜਬ ਲਗਿ ਦੁਨੀਆ ਜੀਵੀਐ ਨਾਨਿਕ ਕਿਛੁ ਸੁਣੀਐ ਕਿਛੁ ਕਹੀਐ॥

	ਭਾਲਿ ਥਕੇ ਹਮ ਰਹਣੁ ਨਾ ਪਾਇਆ ਜੀਵਦਿਆ ਮਰਿ ਰਹੀਐ॥੫॥੨॥[50]

१२२*	ਕਿਵ ਸਿਵਰੀ ਸਿਵਰਿਆ ਨਾਹੀ ਜਾਇ॥

	ਤਪੈ ਹਿਆਉ ਜੀਅੜਾ ਬਿਲਲਾਇ॥. . .

	ਜੇਹੀ ਨਦਰਿ ਕਰੇ ਤੈਸਾ ਹੋਇ॥

	ਵਿਣੁ ਨਦਰੀ ਨਾਨਿਕ ਨਾਹੀ ਕੋਇ॥੪॥੩॥[51]

ਰਾਗੁ ਧਨਾਸਰੀ ਮਹਲੁ ੩

१२३*	ਨਦਰਿ ਕਰੇ ਤਾ ਸਿਵਰਿਆ ਜਾਇ॥

	ਆਤਮਾ ਦਰਵੈ ਰਹੈ ਲਿਵ ਲਾਇ॥. . .

	ਭਨਥ ਨਾਨਿਕੁ ਜਨੁ ਕਰੇ ਵੀਚਾਰੁ ਸਾਚੀ ਬਾਣੀ ਸਉ ਧਰੇ ਪਿਆਰੁ॥

	ਤਾ ਕੋ ਪਾਵੈ ਮੋਖਦੁਆਰੁ॥ ਜਪੁ ਤਪੁ ਸਭੁ ਏਹੁ ਸਬਦੁ ਹੈ ਸਾਰੁ॥੫॥੪॥[52]

ਰਾਗੁ ਧਨਾਸਰੀ [ਮਹਲਾ ੧]

१२४*	ਜੀਉ ਤਪਤੁ ਹੈ ਬਾਰੋ ਬਾਰ॥

	ਤਪਿ ਤਪਿ ਖਪੈ ਬਹੁਤੁ ਵਿਕਾਰ॥. . .

ਜੇ ਕੋ ਡੂਬੈ ਫਿਰਿ ਹੋਵੈ ਸਾਰੁ॥

ਨਾਨਕ ਸਾਚਾ ਸਰਬ ਦਾਤਾਰੁ॥੪॥੫॥⁵³

੧੨੪————੧੨

੧੨੫* ਚੋਰੁ ਸਲਾਹੈ ਚਿਤੁ ਨ ਭੀਜੈ॥

ਜੇ ਬਦੀ ਕਰੇ ਤਾ ਤਸੁ ਨਾ ਛੀਜੈ॥. . .

ਤਿਸੁ ਭਾਵੈ ਆਪੀ ਪਰਵਾਣੁ॥

ਨਾਨਕ ਜਾਨੈ ਜਾਣੁ ਸੁਜਾਣੁ॥੪॥੬॥⁵⁴

੧੨੫ ਕਾਇਆ ਕਾਗਦੁ ਮਨੁ ਪਰਵਾਨਾ॥

ਸਿਰ ਕੇ ਲੇਖ ਨ ਪੜੈ ਇਆਣਾ॥. . .

ਪੜਿਆ ਬੂਝੈ ਸੋ ਪਰਵਾਣੁ॥

ਜਿਸੁ ਸਿਰਿ ਦਰਗਹ ਕਾ ਨੀਸਾਣੁ॥੪॥੭॥

੧੨੬ ਕਾਲੁ ਨਾਹੀ ਜੋਗੁ ਨਾਹੀ ਨਾਹੀ ਸਤ ਕਾ ਢਬੁ॥. . .

ਵਿਣੁ ਨਾਮ ਹਰਿ ਕੇ ਮੁਕਤਿ ਨਾਹੀ ਇਵ ਕਹੇ ਨਾਨਕੁ ਦਾਸੁ॥੪॥੮॥⁵⁵

ਰਾਗੁ ਧਨਾਸਰੀ ਮਹਲਾ ੩

੧੨੭* ਹਮ ਭੀਖਕ ਭੇਖਾਰੀ ਤੇਰੇ ਤੂ ਨਿਜਪਤਿ ਹੈ ਦਾਤਾ॥

ਹੋਹੁ ਦੈਆਲੁ ਨਾਮੁ ਦੇਹਿ ਮਾਂਗਤ ਜਨ ਕਉ ਸਦਾ ਰਹਾ ਰੰਗਿ ਰਾਤਾ॥. . .

ਭਨਤਿ ਨਾਨਕੁ ਭਰਮ ਪਟ ਖੁਲੇ ਗੁਰਪਰਸਾਦੀ ਜਾਨਿਆ॥

ਸਾਚੀ ਲਿਵ ਲਾਗੀ ਹੈ ਭੀਤਰਿ ਸਤਗੁਰ ਸਉ ਮਨੁ ਮਾਨਿਆ॥੩॥੮॥

੧੨੮* # ਕਾਮੁ ਕਰੋਧੁ ਮਾਇਆ ਮਦੁ ਮੀਠੇ ਦਲ ਬਦਲ ਜਿਉ ਉਨ ਵਿਰਹੇ॥. . .

ਨਾਨਕ ਮਾਨੁ ਨਿਮਾਨੇ ਸਾਚਾ ਰਿਦ ਅੰਤਰਿ ਹਰਿ ਹਰਿ ਗੁਰ ਧਿਆਨੇ॥੪॥੧੦॥⁵⁶

੧੨੮ ਇਹੁ ਧਨੁ ਅਖਟੁ ਨਾ ਨਿਖੁਟੈ ਨ ਜਾਇ॥

ਪੂਰੈ ਸਤਿਗੁਰਿ ਦੀਆ ਦਿਖਾਇ॥. . .

ਸਹਜੇ ਜਿਨਿ ਪ੍ਰਭੁ ਜਾਨਿ ਪਛਾਨਿਆ॥

ਨਾਨਕ ਨਾਮੁ ਮਿਲੈ ਮਨੁਮਾਨਿਆ॥੪॥੧੧॥

੧੨੯ ਹਰਿ ਨਾਮੁ ਧਨੁ ਨਿਰਮਲੁ ਅਤਿ ਅਪਾਰਾ॥

ਗੁਰ ਕੈ ਸਬਦਿ ਭਰੇ ਭੰਡਾਰਾ॥. . .

ਸਤਗੁਰੁ ਮਿਲੈ ਸਭ ਤਿਸਨਾ ਬੁਝਾਏ॥

ਨਾਨਕ ਨਾਮਿ ਸਾਤਿ ਸੁਖ ਪਾਏ॥੪॥੧੨॥

੧੩੦ ਸਦਾ ਧਨੁ ਅੰਤਰਿ ਨਾਮੁ ਸਮਾਲੇ॥

ਜੀਅ ਜੰਤ ਜਿਨੈ ਪਰਤਪਾਲੇ॥. . .

ਗੁਰਬਾਟੀ ਤੇ ਹਰਿਨਾਮੁ ਵਸਾਏ॥

ਨਾਨਿਕ ਸਚਿ ਰਤੇ ਪਰਭਿ ਆਪਿ ਮਿਲਾਏ॥੪॥੧੩॥

੧੩੧ ਜਗੁ ਮੈਲਾ ਮੈਲੋ ਹੋਇ ਜਾਇ॥

ਆਵੈ ਜਾਇ ਦੂਜੈ ਲੋਭਾਇ॥. . .

ਪ੍ਰਭ ਸਾਚੇ ਕੀ ਸਾਚੀ ਕਾਰ॥

ਨਾਨਿਕ ਨਾਮਿ ਸਵਾਰਣਹਾਰੁ॥੪॥੧੪॥

੧੩੨* ਜੋ ਹਰਿ ਸੇਵਹਿ ਤਿਨ ਬਲਿ ਜਾਉ॥
      ਤਿਨਾ ਹਿਰਦੈ ਸਾਚੁ ਸਚਾ ਮੁਖਿ ਨਾਉ॥. . .
      ਮਿਲਿ ਪ੍ਰੀਤਮ ਸਚੇ ਗੁਣ ਗਾਵਾ॥
      ਨਾਨਕ ਸਾਚੇ ਸਚਿ ਸਮਾਵਾ॥੪॥੧੫॥

੧੩੩*----੧੩

੧੩੩* ਮਨੁ ਮਰੈ ਧਾਤੁ ਮਰਿ ਜਾਇ॥
      ਬਿਨੁ ਮਨ ਮੂਏ ਕੈਸੇ ਹਰਿ ਪਾਇ॥. . .
      ਆਪਣੀ ਕਲਾ ਆਪੇ ਪ੍ਰਭੁ ਜਾਣੈ॥
      ਨਾਨਕ ਗੁਰਮੁਖਿ ਨਾਮੁ ਪਛਾਣੈ॥੪॥੧੬॥

੧੩੩   ਕਚਾ ਧਨੁ ਸੰਚਹਿ ਮੂਰਖ ਗਵਾਰ॥
      ਮਨਮੁਖ ਭੂਲੇ ਅੰਧ ਗਵਾਰ॥. . .
      ਸਚਾ ਸਚੁ ਆਪਿ ਦਿੜਾਏ॥
      ਨਾਨਕ ਆਪੇ ਵੇਖੈ ਆਪੇ ਸਚਿ ਲਾਏ॥੪॥੧੭॥

੧੩੪   ਨਾਵੈ ਕੀ ਕੀਮਤਿ ਮਿਤਿ ਕਹੀ ਨ ਜਾਇ॥. . .
      ਜਿਸੁ ਸਚਿ ਲਾਏ ਸੋਈ ਲਾਗੈ॥   ਨਾਨਕ ਨਾਮਿ ਸਦਾ ਸੁਖੁ ਆਗੈ॥੪॥੧੮॥

      ੴ ਸਤਿਗੁਰ ਪਰਸਾਦੁ

ਆਰਤੀ ਰਾਗੁ ਧਨਾਸਰੀ [ਮਹਲਾ ੧]
੧੩੫   ਗਗਨ ਮਹਿ ਥਾਲੁ ਰਵਿ ਚੰਦੁ ਦੀਪਕ ਬਨੇ ਤਾਰਿਕਾ ਮੰਡਲੋ ਜਨਕ ਮੋਤੀ॥. . .
      ਕਿਰਪਾ ਜਲੁ ਦੇਹੁ ਨਾਨਕ ਸਾਰੰਗ ਕਉ ਹੋਇ ਜਾਤੇ ਤੇਰੈ ਨਾਇ ਵਾਸਾ॥੪॥੧੯॥

ਰਾਗੁ ਧਨਾਸਰੀ ਪਸਤੋ ਮਾਰੂ ਗਡਾਓ[57]
੧੩੧* ਮੇਰੇ ਸਾਹਾ ਮੈ ਹਰਿ ਦਰਸਨਿ ਸੁਖੁ ਹੋਇ॥. . .
      ਜਿਵ ਭਾਵੈ ਤਿਵ ਰਖੁ ਤੂ ਮੇਰੇ ਪਿਆਰੇ ਸਚੁ ਨਾਨਕ ਕੇ ਪਤਿਸਾਹਾ॥੪॥੨੦॥[58]

੧੩੧   ਚੰਦਨ ਚੋਆ ਰਸ ਭੋਗ ਕਰਤ ਅਨੇਕ
      ਬਿਖਿਆ ਬਿਕਾਰ ਦੇਖੁ ਸਗਲ ਹੈ ਫੀਕੇ॥. . .
      ਪਾਇਓ ਰੇ ਪਰਮਨਿਧਾਨ ਚੁਕੋ ਹੈ
      ਅਧਮਾਨੁ ਏਕ ਨਿਰੰਕਾਰ ਨਾਨਕ ਮਨ ਲਗਨਾ॥੨॥[59]

      ੴ ਸਤਿਗੁਰ ਪਰਸਾਦੁ ਪੂਰਾ ਸਚੁਨਾਮੁ ਕਰਤਾਰੁ ਨਿਰਭਉ
         ਨਿਰੀਕਾਰੁ ਅਕਾਲ ਮੂਰਤਿ ਅਜੂਨੀ ਸੰਭਉ

ਰਾਗੁ ਧਨਾਸਰੀ ਛੰਦ [ਮਹਲਾ ੧]
੧੩੯* ਤੀਰਥਿ ਨਾਵਣਿ ਜਾਉ ਤੀਰਥੁ ਨਾਮੁ ਹੈ ਜੀਉ॥. . .
      ਨਾਨਕੁ ਸਚੁ ਕਹੈ ਬੇਨੰਤੀ ਮਨੁ ਮਾਂਜੈ ਸਚੁ ਸੋਈ॥੪॥੧੭॥[60]

੧੪੦   ਜੀਵਾ ਤੇਰੈ ਨਾਇ ਮਨਿ ਆਨੰਦੁ ਹੈ ਜੀਉ॥. . .
      ਨਾਨਕ ਨਾਮੁ ਮਹਾ ਰਸੁ ਮੀਠਾ ਤਿਸਨਾ ਨਾਮਿ ਨਿਵਾਰੀ॥੫॥੨॥

੧੪੩* ਪਿਰ ਸੰਗਿ ਮੂਠੜੀਏ ਤੈ ਖਬਰਿ ਨ ਪਾਈਆ ਜੀਉ॥. . .
ਨਾਨਕ ਸਚੁ ਮਿਲੈ ਵਡਿਆਈ ਪਿਰ ਘਰਿ ਸੋਹੈ ਨਾਰੀ॥੫॥੩॥

੧੪੫*----੧੪

ੴ ਸਤਿਗੁਰ ਪਰਸਾਦੁ

ਰਾਗੁ ਧਨਾਸਰੀ ਅਸਟਪਦੀਆ [ਮਹਲਾ ੧]

੧੪੬* ਗੁਰ ਸਰ ਸਾਗਰ ਰਤਨੀ ਭਰਪੂਰੇ॥
ਅੰਮ੍ਰਿਤੁ ਸੰਤ ਚੁਗਹਿ ਨਾਹੀ ਦੂਰੇ॥. . .
ਸੁਰਤਿ ਮੁਰਤਿ ਆਦਿ ਅਨੂਪ॥
ਨਾਨਕੁ ਜਾਚੈ ਸਾਚੁ ਸਰੂਪ॥੭॥੧॥[61]

ਰਾਗੁ ਧਨਾਸਰੀ ਦਖਣੀ [ਮਹਲਾ ੧]

੧੪੮ ਸਹਜਿ ਮਿਲੈ ਮਿਲਿਆ ਪਰਵਾਣੁ॥
ਨਾਹਿ ਤਿਸੁ ਮਰਣੁ ਨ ਆਵਣੁ ਜਾਣੁ॥. . .
ਜਿਉ ਤੁਧੁ ਭਾਵੈ ਤਿਉ ਰਾਖੁ ਰਜਾਇ॥
ਨਾਨਕਿ ਸਹਜਿ ਭਾਇ ਗੁਣ ਗਾਇ॥੮॥੨॥[62]

ੴ ਸਤਿਗੁਰੁ

ਰਾਗੁ ਧਨਾਸਰੀ ਸਦਾਸੇਵਕੁ

੧੫੦* ਗੁਰਮੁਖਿ ਨਾਮੁ ਜਪੈ ਜਨੁ ਕੋਈ॥
ਗੁਰਮੁਖਿ ਭਗਤਿ ਪਰਾਪਤਿ ਹੋਈ॥. . .
ਨਾਨਕ ਗੁਰਮੁਖਿ ਮਿਲੈ ਵਡਿਆਈ॥
ਗੁਰਮੁਖਿ ਸਹਜੇ ਰਹਿਆ ਸਮਾਈ॥੪॥੧॥

ੴ ਸਤਿਗੁਰ ਪਰਸਾਦੁ ਸਚੁਨਾਮੁ ਕਰਤਾਰੁ ਨਿਰਭਉ
ਨਿਰੀਕਾਰੁ ਅਕਾਲ ਮੂਰਤਿ ਅਜੂਨੀ ਸੰਭਉ॥੧॥

ਰਾਗੁ ਧਨਾਸਰੀ ਕਬੀਰ ਨਾਮੇ ਕੀ ਬਾਣੀ

੧੫੨* ਹਮ ਸਰਿ ਦੀਨ ਦੈਆਲ ਨਾ ਤੁਮ ਸਰਿ ਅਬ ਪਤੀਆਰ ਕਿਆ ਕੀਜੈ॥. . .
ਕਹਿ ਰਵਿਦਾਸ ਆਸ ਲਗਿ ਜੀਵਉ ਚਿਰ ਭਇਓ ਦਰਸਨੁ ਦੇਖੇ॥੨॥੧॥

੧੫੨ ਮਾਰਵਾੜਿ ਜੈਸੇ ਨੀਰੁ ਵਾਲਿਆ ਬੇਲਿ ਵਾਲਿਆ ਕਰਹਲਾ॥. . .
ਸਗਲ ਭਵਣ ਤੇਰੋ ਨਾਮ ਵਾਲਿਆ ਤਿਉ ਨਾਮੇ ਮਨਿ ਬੀਠਲਾ॥੫॥੨॥

੧੫੩ ਸਨਕ ਸਨੰਦਨ ਮਹੇਸ ਸਮਾਨਾ॥   ਸੇਖ ਨਾਗਿ ਤੇਰੋ ਮਰਮੁ ਨ ਜਾਨਾ॥. . .
ਕਹੁ ਕਬੀਰ ਜੋ ਭਰਮੈ ਨਾਹੀ॥   ਪਗ ਲਗਿ ਰਾਮ ਰਹੈ ਸਰਣਾਈ॥੫॥੩॥

੧੫੪ ਦਿਨ ਤੇ ਪਹਰ ਪਹਰ ਤੇ ਘੜੀਆ ਆਵ ਘਟੈ ਤਨੁ ਛੀਜੈ॥. . .
ਕਹਤੁ ਕਬੀਰ ਸੁਨਹੁ ਰੇ ਪ੍ਰਾਨੀ ਛੋਡਹੁ ਮਨ ਕੇ ਭਰਮਾ॥
ਕੇਵਲ ਨਾਮੁ ਜਪਹੁ ਰੇ ਪ੍ਰਾਨੀ ਪਰਹੁ ਏਕ ਕੀ ਸਰਨਾ॥੩॥੪॥

੧੫੫ ਜੋ ਜਨੁ ਭਾਉ ਭਗਤਿ ਕਛੁ ਜਾਨੈ ਤਾ ਕਾ ਅਚਰਜੁ ਕਾਹੋ॥. . .

66

ਕਹਤੁ ਕਬੀਰ ਸੁਨਹੁ ਰੇ ਲੋਈ ਭਰਮਿ ਨ ਭੂਲਹੁ ਕੋਈ॥

ਕਿਆ ਕਾਂਸੀ ਕਿਆ ਮਘਹਰੁ ਊਖਰੁ ਰਾਮੁ ਰਿਦੈ ਜੇ ਹੋਈ॥੨॥੫॥

੧੫੬* ਭੂਧੀ ਕਰਿ ਕੈ ਨੀਵ ਖੁਦਾਈ ਉਪਰਿ ਮੰਦਰ ਛਾਏ॥. . .

ਕਿਰਪਾ ਕਰੀ ਜਨ ਅਪੁਨੇ ਉਪਰਿ ਨਾਮਦੇਉ ਹਰਿ ਗੁਨ ਗਾਏ॥੪॥੬॥

੧੫੬----੧੫

੧੫੬ ਸੁਤ ਸੰਪਉ ਆ ਭਈ ਵਡਿਆਈ॥

ਖੋਜਿ ਰਹੇ ਕਿਛੁ ਸੰਗਿ ਨਿ ਜਾਈ॥. . .

ਕਹੁ ਕਬੀਰ ਮੇਰੈ ਅਵਰੁ ਨ ਕਾਮਾ॥

ਮਰਨ ਜੀਵਨੁ ਧਨੁ ਰਾਮ ਕੋ ਨਾਮਾ॥੪॥੭॥[63]

੧੫੭* ਪਤਿਤ ਪਾਵਨ ਮਾਧੋ ਬਿਰਦੁ ਤੇਰਾ॥

ਧਨਿ ਤੇ ਵੈ ਹਰਿ ਜਨ ਜਿਨਾ ਹਰਿ ਪ੍ਰਭੁ ਧਿਆਇਓ ਹੈ ਮੇਰਾ॥. . .

ਦੀਨਾ ਕਾ ਦੈਆਲ ਮਾਧੋ ਗਰਬਾ ਪਰਿਹਾਰੀ॥

ਚਰਨਿ ਸਰਨਿ ਨਾਮਾ ਬਲਿ ਤਿਹਾਰੀ॥੨॥੮॥

੧੫੮* ਦਸ ਬੈਰਾਗਨਿ ਮੋਹਿ ਬਸਿ ਕੀਨੀ ਪੰਚਹੁ ਕਾ ਮਿ[ਟ] ਨਾਵਉ॥. . .

ਕਹਤੁ ਨਾਮਦੇਉ ਬਾਹਰਿ ਕਿਆ ਭਰਮਹੁ ਇਤੁ ਮੰਦਰਿ ਸਹੁ ਪਾਈਐ॥੪॥੧੯॥

੧੫੮ ਚਿਤਿ ਸਿਮਰਨੁ ਕਰਉ ਨੈਨਿ ਅਲੋਵਉ ਸਰਵਨਿ ਬਾਨੀ ਬਲਿ ਪੂਰਿ ਰਾਖਉ॥. . .

ਕਹੈ ਰਵਿਦਾਸੁ ਇਕ ਬੇਨਤੀ ਹਰਿ ਸਿਉ ਪੈਜ ਰਾਖੁ ਰਾਜਾ ਰਾਮ ਮੇਰੀ॥੨॥੧੦॥

ਆਰਤੀ ਰਵਿਦਾਸ ਕੀ

੧੫੯* ਨਾਮੁ ਤੇਰਾ ਆਸਨੋ ਨਾਮੁ ਤੇਰਾ ਉਰਸਾ ਨਾਮੁ ਤੇਰਾ ਕੇਸਰੋ ਲੇ ਛਿਟਕਾਰੇ॥

ਨਾਮੁ ਤੇਰਾ ਅੰਭੁਲਾ ਨਾਮੁ ਤੇਰਾ ਚੰਦਨੋ ਘਸਿ ਜਪੇ ਨਾਮੁ ਤੁਝੈ ਕ ਉਚਾਰੇ॥. . .

ਦਸ ਅਠ ਅਠ ਸਠੇ ਚਾਰੇ ਖਾਣੀ ਏਹ ਵਰਤਣਿ ਹੈ ਸਗਲ ਸੈਸਾਰੇ॥

ਕਹੈ ਰਵਿਦਾਸੁ ਨਾਮੁ ਤੇਰੋ ਆਰਤੀ ਸਤਿ ਹਰਿਨਾਮੁ ਹਰਿਭੋਗ ਤੁਹਾਰੇ॥੪॥੧੧॥[64]

੧੬੦* # ਦੇਹੁਰੀ ਭੀਤਰਿ ਸਰੁਸਰਿਹ ਭੀਤਰਿ ਜਲੁਜਲਹਿ

ਭੀਤਰਿ ਆਛੈ ਨਿਜ ਕਵਲੰ॥. . .

ਬਦਿਤ ਤਿਲੋਚਨ ਗਹਿਓ ਹੈ ਉਜਲੁ ਥਾਉ

ਮੇਰਾ ਮਨੁ ਤੇਰੈ ਪਹਿ ਲਾਗੋ ਹੈ ਦੁਆਰਕੇ ਰਾਇ॥੩॥੧੨॥[65]

੧੬੦ ਜਿਨਿ ਮਾਤਾ ਕੇ ਉਦਕ ਉਦਰ ਮਹਿ ਕੀਆ ਦਸ ਦੁਆਰਾ॥

ਦੇ ਅਹਾਰੁ ਅਗਨਿ ਮਹਿ ਰਾਖੈ ਐਸਾ ਖਸਮੁ ਹਮਾਰਾ॥. . .

ਖਾਣ ਗੁਪਤ ਮਹਿ ਕੀਟੁ ਹੋਤੁ ਹੈ ਉਆ ਕਾ ਮਾਰਗ ਨਾਹੀ॥

ਕਹੈ ਧਨਾ ਪੂਰਨ ਤਾਹੁ ਕਾ ਮਤ ਮੇਰੇ ਜੀਅ ਡਰਾਨੀ॥੩॥੧੩॥[66]

੧੬੧* ਧੂਪ ਦੀਪ ਘ੍ਰਿਤੁ ਸਾਜਿ ਆਰਤੀ ਵਾਰਨੇ ਜਾਉ ਕਉਲਾਪਤੀ॥

ਮੰਗਲਾ ਹਰਿ ਮੰਗਲਾ॥ ਮੰਗਲੁ ਰਾਜੇ ਰਾਮ ਰਾਇ ਕੋ॥. . .

ਮਦਨ ਮੂਰਤਿ ਭੈ ਤਾਰਿ ਗੋਵਿੰਦੇ॥ ਸੈਨੁ ਭਣੈ ਭਜੁ ਪਰਮਨੰਦੇ॥੪॥੧੪॥

੧੬੧ ਸੰਕਰੋ ਸੁਰਸਰੀ ਵਸਤਾ ਸੁਰਸਰੀ ਇਸਨਾਨੁ ਰੇ॥

ਕੁਲ ਜਨ ਮੰਧੇ ਪਾਇਆ ਸਾਰਗ ਪ੍ਰਾਣੀ ਕਰਮਿ ਕਰਿ ਕਲੰਕ ਮਫੀਟੈਰੀ॥. . .

ਬਦਤਿ ਤਿਲੋਚਨ ਰਾਮ ਜੀਉ॥

ਨਾਰਾਇਨ ਨਿਦਸਿ ਕਾਹੇ ਰੀ ਭੂਲੀ ਗਵਾਰੀ॥੬॥੧੫॥[67]

੧੬੩ ਪਹਿਲ ਪੁਰੀਏ ਪੰਢਰਕ ਵਨਾ ਤਾਚੇ ਹੰਸਾ ਸਗਲੇ ਜਨਾ॥. . .
ਮਇ ਜੀ ਨਾਮਾ ਹੋ ਜੀਉ॥ ਆਏ ਕਿਤੁ ਕਾਰਟਾ॥
ਆਲਾ ਤ ਨਿਵਾਰਣਾ॥ ਜੀ ਮਕਾਰਣਾ॥੩॥੧੬॥[68]

ੴ ਸਤਿਗੁਰ ਪਰਸਾਦੁ ਸਚੁਨਾਮੁ ਕਰਤਾਰੁ ਨਿਰਭਉ

ਨਿਰੀਕਾਰੁ ਅਕਾਲ ਮੂਰਤਿ ਅਜੂਨੀ ਸੰਭਉ॥[69]

ਰਾਗੁ ਬਸੰਤੁ[70]

ਰਾਗੁ ਬਸੰਤੁ ਬਾਬੇ ਪਾਤਿਸਾਹ ਦਾ [ਮਹਲਾ ੧]

੧੬੯* ਮਾਹਾ ਮਾਹਿ ਭੁਮਾਰਖੀ ਚੜਿਆ ਸਦਾ ਬਸੰਤੁ॥. . .
ਨਾਨਿਕ ਹਰੇ ਨ ਸੂਕਨੀ ਜਿ ਗੁਰਮੁਖਿ ਰਹੇ ਸਮਾਇ॥੪॥੧॥

੧੭੦* ਰੁਤਿ ਆਈ ਲੇ ਸਰਸ ਬਸੰਤ ਮਾਹਿ॥
ਰੰਗਿ ਰਾਤੇ ਰਾਵਹਿ ਸਿ ਤੇਰੈ ਚਾਇ॥. . .
ਸਿਰੁ ਨਾਨਿਕ ਲੋਕਾ ਪਾਉ ਹੈ॥
ਬਲਿਹਾਰੀ ਜਾਉ ਜੇਤੇ ਤੇਰੇ ਨਾਵ ਹੈ॥੪॥੨॥

੧੭੧* ਸੁਇਨੇ ਕਾ ਚਉਕਾ ਕੰਚਨ ਕੁਆਰਿ॥
ਰੁਪੇ ਕੀਆ ਕਾਰਾ ਵਿਚਿ ਬਹਤੁ ਵਿਸਥਾਰ॥. . .
ਹੁਕਮੁ ਕਰਹਿ ਮੂਰਖ ਗਵਾਰ॥
ਨਾਨਿਕ ਸਾਚੇ ਕੇ ਸਿਫਤੀ ਭੰਡਾਰ॥੪॥੩॥[71]

੧੭੨* ਸਾਲਗਿਰਾਮ ਬਿਧ ਪੂਜਿ ਮਨਾਵਹੁ ਸੁਕਰਤ ਤੁਲਸੀ ਮਾਲਾ॥. . .
ਬਗੁਲੇ ਤੇ ਫੁਨਿ ਹੰਸਲਾ ਹੋਵੈ ਜੇ ਤੂ ਕਰਹਿ ਦੈਆਲਾ॥
ਪਟਵਤਿ ਨਾਨਕੁ ਦਾਸਨਿ ਦਾਸਾ ਦਇਆ ਕਰਹੁ ਦੈਆਲਾ॥੪॥੪॥

੧੭੨ ਸਹੁਰੜੀ ਵਥੁ ਸਭ ਕਿਛੁ ਸਾਝੀ ਪੇਵਕੜੈ ਧਨ ਵਖੇ॥. . .
ਪਟਵਤਿ ਨਾਨਿਕੁ ਏਕੁ ਲਘਾਏ ਜੇ ਕਰਿ ਸਚਿ ਸਮਾਵਾ॥੩॥੫॥

੧੭੩ ਰਾਜਾ ਬਾਲਿਕੁ ਨਗਰੀ ਕਾਚੀ ਦੁਸਟਾ ਨਾਲਿ ਪਿਆਰੋ॥. . .
ਪਟਵਤਿ ਨਾਨਿਕੁ ਦਾਸਨਿ ਦਾਸਾ ਖਿਨੁ ਤੋਲਾ ਖਿਨੁ ਮਾਸਾ॥੪॥੬॥

੧੭੪*----੧੬

੧੭੪* ਵਸਤ ਉਤਾਰਿ ਦਿਗੰਬਰੁ ਹੋਗੁ॥
ਜਟਾ ਧਾਰਿ ਕਿਆ ਕਮਾਵੈ ਜੋਗੁ॥. . .
ਨਾਨਕ ਮਿਲਿਆ ਸਤਗੁਰ ਸੰਗਿ॥
ਤਉ ਭਉਜਲ ਕੇ ਤੁਟਸਿ ਫੰਧਾ॥੫॥੭॥[72]

੧੭੫ ਸਾਹਿਬ ਭਾਵੈ ਸੇਵਕੁ ਸੇਵਾ ਕਰੇ॥
ਜੀਵਤੁ ਮਰੈ ਸਭਿ ਕੁਲ ਉਧਰੈ॥. . .

68

कहत नानिक सैसार के निहफलु कामा॥
गुरपरसादी को पावै अंब्रितु नामा॥४॥८॥⁷³

रागु बसंतु महलु ३

१८६* महा रुती माहि सदा बसंतु॥
जितु हरिआ सभ जीअ जंतु॥. . .
बिखिआ की बासना मनहि करेइ॥
अपना भाणा आपि करेइ॥४॥९॥⁷⁴

३८६ तेरा कीआ किरम जंतु॥
देहि ता जपी आदि मंतु॥. . .
ऊतम ऊचा सबदु कामु॥
नानिक वखाणै सचु नामु॥४॥१०॥

८८७ बनासपति मउली चड़िआ बसंतु॥
इहु मनु मउलिआ सतगुर संगि॥. . .
कहतु नानकु हउमै कहै न कोइ॥
आखणा वेखणा सभु साहिब ते होइ॥४॥११॥

१२८* राते सचि नामि हरि निहाला॥
दइआ करहु परभ दीन दैआला॥. . .
गुरि राखे वडभागी तारे॥
जन नानक कउ हरि अंब्रित धारे॥४॥१२॥⁷⁵

रागु बसंतु [महला १]

१२८ सगल भवण तेरी माइआ मोहि॥
मै अवरु न दीसै सरब तोहि॥. . .
लिवलागी राम तजि दूजा भाउ॥
नानिक हरि गुर मेलि मिलाउ॥४॥१३॥⁷⁶

३००⁷⁷ मेरी सखी सहेली सुनहु भाइ॥
मेरा पिरु रीसालू संगि साइ॥. . .
गुर संत सभा दुख मिटै रोगु॥
जन नानिक हरि वरु सहजि भोगु॥४॥१४॥

१८७ आपे कुदरति करे साजि॥
रचु आपि निबेड़ै राजु राजि॥. . .
फलु नामु परापति गुर तुसि देइ॥
कहु नानिक पावहि विरले केइ॥४॥१५॥⁷⁸

१८८ साचा सहु गुरु सुख दाता हरि मेले भुख गवाए॥. . .
पारसु भेटि भए से पारसु नानिक हरि रंगि संगि थीए॥४॥१६॥

१८९*----१२

रागु बसंतु महलु ३

69

੧੯੮* ਸਭਿ ਜੁਗ ਤੇਰੇ ਕੀਤੇ ਹੋਏ॥

ਸਤਗੁਰੁ ਭੇਟੈ ਬੁਧਿ ਮਤਿ ਹੋਏ॥. . .

ਨਾਨਕ ਇਹੁ ਤਨੁ ਬਿਰਖੁ ਰਾਮ ਨਾਮੁ ਫਲੁ ਪਾਏ ਸੋਇ॥੪॥੧੭॥

੧੯੯ ਤਿਨ ਬਸੰਤੁ ਜੋ ਹਰਿ ਗੁਣ ਗਾਇ॥

ਪੂਰੈ ਸਬਦਿ ਹਰਿ ਭਗਤਿ ਕਰਾਇ॥. . .

ਇਹੁ ਮਨੁ ਛੂਟਾ ਗੁਰਿ ਲੀਆ ਛਡਾਇ॥

ਨਾਨਕ ਮਾਇਆ ਮੋਹੁ ਗੁਰਸਬਦਿ ਜਲਾਇ॥੪॥੧੯॥[79]

੧੫੦ ਬਸੰਤੁ ਚੜਿਆ ਫੂਲੀ ਬਨਰਾਇ॥

ਏਹਿ ਜੀਅ ਜੰਤ ਫੂਲਹਿ ਹਰਿ ਸਉ ਚਿਤੁ ਲਾਇ॥. . .

ਆਪਿ ਬਸੰਤੁ ਜਗਤੁ ਸਭੁ ਵਾੜੀ॥

ਨਾਨਕ ਪੂਰੈ ਭਾਗਿ ਭਗਤਿ ਨਿਰਾਲੀ॥੪॥੧੯॥[80]

੧੫੧* ਗੁਰ ਕੀ ਬਾਣੀ ਵਿਟਹੁ ਹਉ ਵਾਰਿਆ ਭਾਈ ਸਬਦ ਵਿਟਹੁ ਬਲਿ ਜਾਈ॥. . .

ਨਾਨਕ ਤਿਨ ਮਨਿ ਸਦਾ ਸੁਖੁ ਵਸੈ ਭਾਈ ਸਬਦਿ ਮਿਲਾਵਾ ਹੋਇ॥੪॥੨੦॥[81]

੧੫੧ ਹਰਿ ਸੇਵੈ ਸੋ ਹਰਿ ਕਾ ਲੋਕੁ॥

ਸਦਾ ਸਹਜੁ ਕਦੇ ਨ ਹੋਵੈ ਸੋਕੁ॥. . .

ਦਰਿ ਸਾਚੈ ਪਤਿ ਸਉ ਘਰਿ ਜਾਇ॥

ਨਾਨਕ ਨਾਮਿ ਵਡਿਆਈ ਪਾਇ॥੪॥੨੧॥[82]

੧੫੨ ਅੰਤਰਿ ਪੂਜਾ ਮਨ ਤੇ ਹੋਇ॥

ਏਕੋ ਵੇਖੈ ਅਵਰੁ ਨ ਕੋਇ॥. . .

ਤਨੁ ਮਨੁ ਹਰਿਆ ਸਹਜਿ ਸੁਭਾਇ॥

ਨਾਨਕ ਨਾਮਿ ਰਹੇ ਲਿਵ ਲਾਇ॥੪॥੨੨॥

੧੫੩ ਭਗਤਿ ਵਛਲੁ ਹਰਿ ਵਸੈ ਮਨਿ ਆਇ॥

ਗੁਰਕਿਰਪਾ ਤੇ ਸਹਜਿ ਸੁਭਾਇ॥. . .

ਆਪਣਾ ਪ੍ਰਭੁ ਸੇਵੇ ਸਹਜਿ ਸੁਭਾਇ॥

ਨਾਨਕ ਨਾਮੁ ਵਸੈ ਮਨਿ ਆਇ॥੪॥੨੩॥

੧੫੪ ਮਾਇਆ ਮੋਹੁ ਸਬਦਿ ਜਲਾਏ॥

ਤਨੁ ਮਨੁ ਹਰਿਆ ਸਹਜਿ ਸੁਭਾਏ॥. . .

ਵਡਾ ਦਾਤਾ ਤਿਲੁ ਨ ਤਮਾਇ॥

ਨਾਨਕ ਮਿਲੀਐ ਸਬਦੁ ਕਮਾਇ॥੪॥੨੪॥[83]

੧੫੫* ਪੂਰੈ ਭਾਗਿ ਸਚੁ ਕਾਰ ਕਮਾਵੈ॥

ਏਕੋ ਚੇਤੈ ਫਿਰਿ ਜੂਨੀ ਨ ਆਵੈ॥. . .

ਜਿਨਿ ਸਚੁ ਸੇਵਿਆ ਤਿਨਿ ਰਸੁ ਪਾਇਆ॥

ਨਾਨਕ ਸਹਜੇ ਨਾਮਿ ਸਮਾਇਆ॥੪॥੨੫॥

੧੫੬* ਭਗਤਿ ਕਰਹਿ ਜਨ ਵੇਖਿਹ ਦੂਰਿ॥

ਸੰਤ ਜਨ ਕੀ ਪਗ ਪੰਕਜ ਮਹਿ ਧੂਰਿ॥. . .

ਹਰਿ ਰਸੁ ਚਾਖੈ ਤਾ ਸੁਧਿ ਹੋਇ॥

ਨਾਨਕ ਨਾਮਿ ਰਤੇ ਸਚੁ ਸੋਇ॥੪॥੨੬॥[84]

੧੯੭*----੧੯

੧੯੭* ਨਾਮਿ ਰਤੇ ਕੁਲ ਕਾ ਕਰਹਿ ਉਧਾਰੁ॥
ਸਚੀ ਬਾਣੀ ਨਾਮਿ ਪਿਆਰੁ॥ . .
ਸਚਾ ਸੇਵਹੁ ਸਚੀ ਬਾਣੀ॥
ਨਾਨਕ ਨਾਮੇ ਸਚਿ ਸਮਾਣੀ॥੪॥੨੭॥

੧੯੭ ਵਿਣੁ ਕਰਮਾ ਸਭ ਭਰਮਿ ਭੁਲਾਈ॥
ਮਾਇਆ ਮੋਹਿ ਬਹੁਤੁ ਦੁਖੁ ਪਾਈ॥ . .
ਜਿਨਿ ਇਕੁ ਜਾਤਾ ਸੇ ਜਨ ਪਰਵਾਣੁ॥
ਨਾਨਕ ਨਾਮਿ ਰਤੇ ਦਰਿ ਨੀਸਾਣੁ॥੪॥੨੮॥

੧੯੮ ਕਿਰਪਾ ਕਰੇ ਸਤਿਗੁਰੂ ਮੇਲਾਏ॥
ਆਪੇ ਆਪਿ ਵਸੈ ਮਨਿ ਆਏ॥ . .
ਤਿਸ ਤੇ ਨੇੜੇ ਕੋ ਨਾਹੀ ਦੂਰਿ॥
ਨਾਨਕੁ ਨਾਮਿ ਰਹਿਆ ਭਰਪੂਰਿ॥੪॥੨੯॥[85]

੧੯੯ ਗੁਰਸਬਦੀ ਹਰਿ ਚੇਤਿ ਸੁਭਾਇ॥
ਰਾਮ ਨਾਮਿ ਰਸਿ ਰਹੈ ਅਘਾਇ॥ . .
ਹਿਰਦੈ ਵਸਿਆ ਸਬਦ ਅਧਾਰਾ॥
ਨਾਨਕੁ ਜਾਣੈ ਸਭ ਉਪਾਵਣਹਾਰਾ॥੪॥੩੦॥

ੴ ਸਤਿਗੁਰ ਪਰਸਾਦੁ ਸਚੁਨਾਮੁ ਕਰਤਾਰੁ ਨਿਰਭਉ
ਨਿਰੀਕਾਰੁ ਅਕਾਲ ਮੂਰਤਿ ਅਜੂਨੀ ਸੰਭਉ॥੧॥[86]

ਰਾਗੁ ਬਸੰਤੁ ਅਸਟਪਦੀਆ ਬਾਬੇ ਦੀਆ [ਮਹਲਾ ੧]
੨੦੨* ਨਵ ਸਤ ਚਉਦਹ ਤੀਨਿ ਚਾਰਿ ਕਰਿ ਮਹਲਤਿ ਚਾਰਿ ਬਹਾਲੀ॥ . .
ਨਾਨਕ ਨਾਮੁ ਮਿਲੈ ਵਡਿਆਈ ਮੇਕਾ ਘੜੀ ਸਮਾਲੀ॥੮॥੧॥

ਰਾਗੁ ਬਸੰਤੁ ਦਖਣੀ [ਮਹਲਾ ੧]
੨੦੩ ਜਗੁ ਕਊਆ ਨਾਮੁ ਨਾਹੀ ਚੀਤਿ॥
ਨਾਮੁ ਨ ਵਿਸਰਿ ਗਿਰਹਿ ਦੇਖਹੁ ਭੀਤਿ॥ . .
ਨਾਨਕ ਠਾਢਾ ਚਾਹੈ ਪ੍ਰਭੁ ਦੁਆਰਿ॥
ਤੇਰੈ ਨਾਮਿ ਸੰਤੋਖੇ ਤੂ ਕਿਰਪਾਧਾਰਿ॥੮॥੨॥[87]

ਰਾਗੁ ਬਸੰਤੁ [ਮਹਲਾ ੧]
੨੦੪ ਮਨੁ ਭੂਲੋ ਭਰਮਸਿ ਆਇ ਜਾਇ॥
ਅਤਿ ਲੁਭਤੁ ਲੁਭਾਨਉ ਬਿਖਮ ਮਾਇ॥ . .
ਤੂ ਮੋਟੋ ਠਾਕੁਰ ਸਬਦ ਮਾਹਿ॥
ਮਨੁ ਨਾਨਕ ਮਨਿਆ ਸਚੁ ਸਲਾਹਿ॥੮॥੩॥[88]

੨੦੬*----੧੯

२०६* मतु भसमु अंधुले गरबि जाइ।।
इन विधि नागे जोगु नाहि।. . .
गुण नानक बोले भली बाटि।।
तुम होहु सुजाखे लेहु पछाटि।।१०।।५।।

२०७* दरसन की पिआस जिसु नर होई।।
एकतु राचै परहरि दोइ।. . .
नानिक हउमै सबदि जलाइआ।।
सतगुरि साचा दरसु दिखाइआ।।८।।५।।[89]

२०८ दुबिधा दुरमति अंधुली कार।।
मनमुखि भरमै मझ गुबार।. . .
नानिक भूले गुरु समझावै।।
एकु दिखावै सचि टिकावै।।८।।६।।

२०९* आपे भवरा फूल वेलि।।
आपे संगति मीत मेलि।. . .
नानिकु थापे हरि नामि सादि।।
बिनु हरि प्रीतम जनमु बादि।।८।।७।।

२१०* चंचलु चीतु न पावै पारा।।
आवतु जातु ना लागै वारा।. . .
दुख सुख ही ते गुरसबदि अतीता।।
नानिक रामु रवै हिति चीता।।८।।८।।

२११*----२०

१ੳ सतिगुर परसादु

रागु बसंतु सदासेवकु

२११ आपे ही संतु भगती लाइ आपे दैतु चिड़ाइआ।. . .
नानिक हरि जी नाही अंतरु जा हरि कै मनि भाइआ।।५।।१।।

२१२* जेता कपड़ा अंगि हढाइआ।।
भले भले तै भोजन खाइआ।. . .
तुध आपे ही सिरि दिता भारा।।
नानिक नाम बिना डुबि मूआ सैसारा।।५।।२।।

१ੳ सतिगुर

रागु बसंतु रामानंद

२१४* एकु दिविसि मंनि भइउ उमंग।।
चोआ चंदन प्रहपलीए संग।. . .
रामानंदु गावै ब्रहमु।।
राम नामु काटै कोट करम।।३।।१।।[90]

२२१* ਇਸ ਤਨ ਮਨ ਮਹਿ ਮਦਨ ਚੋਰ॥

ਜਿਨਿ ਗਿਆਨ ਧਿਆਨ ਹਿਰਿ ਲੀਨਾ ਮੋਰ॥. . .

ਮੇਰੋ ਮਰਨ ਜੀਵਨ ਦੁਖ ਆਥਿ ਧੀਰ॥

ਸੁਖ ਸਾਗਰ ਗੁਨ ਰਉ ਕਬੀਰ॥੩॥^{P1}

ੴ ਸਤਿਗੁਰੁ ਪਰਸਾਦੁ ਸਚੁਨਾਮੁ ਕਰਤਾਰੁ ਨਿਰਭਉ

ਨਿਰੀਕਾਰੁ ਅਕਾਲ ਮੂਰਤਿ ਅਜੂਨੀ ਸੰਭਉ ਗੁਰਪਰਸਤਿ

ਬਸੰਤੁ ਬਾਣੀ ਕਬੀਰ ਨਾਮੇ ਕੀ ਪੂਰੀ

२२२* ਮਉਲੀ ਧਰਤੀ ਮਉਲਿਆ ਅਕਾਸੁ॥

ਘਟਿ ਘਟਿ ਮਉਲਿਆ ਆਤਮ ਪਰਗਾਸੁ॥. . .

ਸੰਕਰੁ ਮਉਲਿਆ ਜੋਗਿ ਧਿਆਨਿ॥

ਕਬੀਰ ਏਕਾ ਸਭ ਸਮਾਨਿ॥੩॥੧॥

२२२ ਪੰਡਿਤ ਜਨ ਮਾਤੇ ਪੜਿ ਪੁਰਾਨ॥

ਜੋਗੀ ਜਨ ਮਾਤੇ ਹਰਿ ਧਿਆਨੁ॥. . .

ਇਸੁ ਦੇਹੀ ਕੇ ਅਧਿਕ ਕਾਮਾ॥

ਕਹੁ ਕਬੀਰ ਭਜੁ ਰਾਮ ਨਾਮਾ॥੩॥੨॥

२२३* ਮਾਤਾ ਜੂਠੀ ਪਿਤਾ ਭਿ ਜੂਠਾ ਜੂਠੇ ਹੀ ਫਲ ਲਾਗੇ॥. . .

ਕਹੁ ਕਬੀਰ ਸੋਈ ਨਰ ਸੂਚੇ ਜਿਨਿ ਸਾਚੀ ਪਾਈ ਵੀਚਾਰਾ॥੪॥੩॥

२२३ ਸਾਹਿਬੁ ਸੰਕਟਵੈ ਸੇਵਕੁ ਭਜੈ॥

ਚਿਰੰਕਾਲੁ ਨ ਜੀਵੈ ਦੋਵੈ ਕੁਲ ਲਾਜੈ॥. . .

ਗੰਗਾ ਗਇਆ ਗੋਦਾਵਰੀ ਸੈਸਾਰ ਕੇ ਕਾਮਾ॥

ਜੇ ਨਾਰਾਇਨੁ ਸੁ ਪਰਸਨ ਹੋਵੈ ਤਾ ਸੇਵਕੁ ਨਾਮਾ॥੩॥੪॥

२२४* ਲੋਭ ਲਹਰਿ ਅਤਿ ਨੀਝਰ ਵਾਜੈ ਕਾਇਆ ਡੂਬੈ ਕੇਸਵਾ॥. . .

ਨਾਮਦੇਉ ਕਹੈ ਹਉ ਤਰਿ ਭੀ ਨ ਜਾਨਾ ਬਾਹ ਦੇਹਿ ਬਾਹ ਦੇਹਿ ਬੀਠੁਲਾ॥੪॥੫॥

२२४ ਮਨ ਤੂਝੈ ਸੁਝੰਦਾ ਕਿਛੁ ਨਾਹਿ॥

ਤੂ ਦੇਖਿ ਪਹਿਰਾਵਾ ਭੂਲਿ ਜਾਹਿ॥. . .

ਕਹੁ ਰਵਿਦਾਸੁ ਜੋ ਜਪੈ ਨਾਮੁ॥

ਤਿਸੁ ਜਾਤਿ ਜਨਮੁ ਨਾਹੀ ਜੂਨਿ ਕਾਮੁ॥੪॥੬॥

२२५ ਦੇਖਹੁ ਲੋਕਾ ਕਲਿ ਕਾ ਭਾਉ॥

ਸੁਤਿ ਮੁਕਲਾਈ ਅਪਨੀ ਮਾਉ॥. . .

ਬਿਨੁ ਗੁਰ ਬਾਟ ਨ ਪਾਈ॥

ਕਹੁ ਕਬੀਰ ਸਮਝਾਈ॥੩॥੭॥^{P2}

२२६* ਪ੍ਰਿਹਲਾਦੁ ਸਿਧਾਰੇ ਪਤਨਸਾਲ॥

ਸੰਗਿ ਸਾਥਿ ਬਹੁ ਲੀਏ ਨਾਲਿ॥. . .

ਕਹੁ ਕਬੀਰ ਨਾਹੀ ਪਾਇਆ ਪਾਰੁ॥

73

ਪ੍ਰਹਿਲਾਦੁ ਉਧਾਰੇ ਨੇਕ ਬਾਰਾ॥੪॥

੨੨੧*   # ਕਿਸਨ ਬਸੰਤ ਭਲੇ ਤੁਮਿ ਆਏ ਦੁਆਦਸਿ ਬਨ ਤਨ ਫੂਲੇ॥. . .
        ਹਰਿ ਕੇ ਚਰਨ ਗਹੁ ਸਾਧ ਸੰਗਤਿ ਲਹੁ ਬਦਤਿ ਨਾਮਦੇਉ ਕਿਸਨਮਤੀ॥੩॥੪॥⁹³

੨੨੧----੨੧   [ਇਸੁ ਤਨ ਮਨ ਮਹਿ ਮਦਨ ਚੋਰੁ॥ ਵੇਖੋ ਪਤ੍ਰਾ ੨੨੧॥⁹⁴

ੴ ਸਤਿਗੁਰ ਪ੍ਰਸਾਦੁ ਸਚੁਨਾਮੁ ਕਰਤਾਰੁ ਨਿਰਭਉ ਨਿਰੀਕਾਰੁ
ਅਕਾਲ ਮੂਰਤਿ ਅਜੂਨੀ ਸੰਭਉ ਗੁਰਪ੍ਰਸਾਦੁ

ਰਾਗੁ ਭੈਰਉ⁹⁵

ਰਾਗੁ ਭੈਰਉ [ਮਹਲਾ ੧]

੨੨੯*   ਤੈ ਤੇ ਬਾਹਰਿ ਕਿਛੂਆ ਨ ਹੋਇ॥
        ਕਰਿ ਕਰਿ ਦੇਖੈ ਜਾਨੈ ਸੋਇ॥. . .
        ਕਰੇ ਕਰਾਏ ਜਾਨੈ ਆਪਿ॥
        ਨਾਨਕ ਦੇਖੈ ਥਾਪਿ ਉਥਾਪਿ॥੪॥੧॥

ਰਾਗੁ ਭੈਰਉ ਮਹਲੁ ੩

੨੨੯   ਜਾਤਿ ਕਾ ਗਰਬੁ ਨ ਕਰੀਅਹੁ ਕੋਈ॥
        ਬਰਹਮੁ ਬਿੰਦੇ ਸੋ ਬਿਰਹਮਣੁ ਹੋਈ॥. . .
        ਕਹਤੁ ਨਾਨਕੁ ਇਹੁ ਜੀਉ ਕਰਮਬਧੁ ਹੋਈ॥
        ਬਿਨੁ ਸਤਗੁਰ ਭੇਟੇ ਮੁਕਤਿ ਨ ਹੋਈ॥੫॥੨॥

੨੨੯*   ਜੋਗੀ ਗਿਰਹੀ ਪੰਡਿਤੁ ਭੇਖਿਆਧਾਰੀ॥
        ਏਹਿ ਸੁਤੇ ਅਪੁਨੈ ਅਹੰਕਾਰੀ॥. . .
        ਕਹਤੁ ਨਾਨਕੁ ਜਨੁ ਜਾਗੈ ਕੋਇ॥
        ਗਿਆਨੁ ਅੰਜਨੁ ਜਾ ਕੀ ਨੇਤੀ ਹੋਇ॥੬॥੩॥⁹⁶

੨੨੯   ਜਾ ਕਉ ਰਾਖੈ ਅਪੁਨੀ ਸਰਣਾਈ॥
        ਸਚੈ ਲਾਗੈ ਸਚਾ ਫਲੁ ਪਾਈ॥. . .
        ਕਹਤੁ ਨਾਨਕੁ ਮਾਰਿ ਜੀਵਾਲੇ ਸੋਇ॥
        ਐਸਾ ਬੁਝਹੁ ਭਰਮਿ ਭੁਲਹੁ ਮਤ ਕੋਇ॥੪॥੪॥⁹⁷

੨੩੦*   ਮੈ ਕਾਮਣਿ ਮੇਰਾ ਕੰਤੁ ਕਰਤਾਰੁ॥
        ਜੇਹਾ ਕਰਾਏ ਤੇਹਾ ਕਰੀ ਸੀਗਾਰੁ॥. . .
        ਭਨਥ ਨਾਨਕੁ ਕਰੇ ਕਿਆ ਕੋਇ॥
        ਜਿਸ ਨੋ ਆਪਿ ਮਿਲਾਵੈ ਸੋਇ॥੪॥੫॥

੨੩੦   ਸੋ ਮੁਨਿ ਜਿ ਮਨ ਕੀ ਦੁਬਿਧਾ ਮਾਰੇ॥
        ਦੁਬਿਧਾ ਮਾਰਿ ਬਰਹਮੁ ਬੀਚਾਰੇ॥. . .
        ਕਹਤੁ ਨਾਨਕੁ ਜੋ ਜਾਨੈ ਭੇਉ॥

74

आदि ਪੁਰਖੁ ਨਿਰੰਜਨ ਦੇਉ ॥੬॥੬॥

रागु ਭੈਰਉ ਦਖਣੀ [ਮਹਲਾ ੧]

੨੩੧ ਗੁਰ ਕੈ ਸਬਦਿ ਤਰੇ ਮੁਨਿ ਕੇਤੇ ਇੰਦ੍ਰਾਦਿਕ ਬ੍ਰਹਮਾਦਿਕ ਤਰੇ॥. . .
ਨਾਨਕ ਸਾਹਿਬੁ ਭਰਿ ਪੂਰਿ ਲੀਣਾ ਸਚਿ ਸਬਦਿ ਨਿਸਤਾਰਾ॥੪॥੭॥

੨੩੨* ਨੈਨੀ ਦਿਸਟਿ ਨਾਹੀ ਤਨ ਹੀਣਿਆ ਜਰਾ ਜੀਤਿਆ ਸਿਰਿ ਕਾਲੋ॥. . .
ਪਟਵਤਿ ਨਾਨਕ ਗੁਰਮੁਖਿ ਛੂਟਸਿ ਰਾਮਿ ਨਾਮਿ ਲਿਵ ਲਾਗੀ॥੪॥੮॥

੨੩੩* ਖੁੰਢੀ ਚਾਲ ਚਰਨ ਕਰ ਖਿਸਰੇ ਤੁਚਾ ਦੇਹ ਕੁਲਮਾਨੀ॥੯੮ . . .
ਗੁਰਪ੍ਰਸਾਦਿ ਪਰਮ ਪਦੁ ਪਾਇਆ ਨਾਨਕੁ ਕਹੈ ਵੇਚਾਰਾ॥੪॥੯॥

੨੩੩ ਸਗਲੀ ਰੈਣਿ ਸੋਵਤ ਗਲਿ ਫਾਹੀ ਦਿਨਸੁ ਜੰਜਾਲਿ ਗਵਾਇਆ॥. . .
ਸਬਦੁ ਵੀਚਾਰਿ ਰਾਮ ਰਸੁ ਚਾਖਿਆ ਨਾਨਕ ਸਚਿ ਪਤੀਨੇ॥੪॥੧੦॥

੨੩੪----੨੨

੨੩੪ ਗੁਰ ਕੈ ਸੰਗਿ ਰਤੇ ਦਿਨੁ ਰਾਤੀ ਰਾਮ ਰਸਨਿ ਰੰਗਿ ਰਾਤਾ॥. . .
ਸਗਲ ਦੁਖ ਮਿਟਹਿ ਗੁਰ ਸੇਵਾ ਨਾਨਕ ਨਾਮੁ ਸਖਾਈ॥੪॥੧੧॥

੨੩੫* ਹਿਰਦੈ ਨਾਮੁ ਸਰਬ ਧਨ ਧਾਰਨੁ ਗੁਰਪ੍ਰਸਾਦੀ ਪਾਈਐ॥. . .
ਅੰਤਰਿ ਬਾਹਰਿ ਏਕੋ ਜਾਨਿਆ ਨਾਨਕ ਅਵਰੁ ਨ ਦੂਆ॥੪॥੧੨॥

੨੩੬* ਜਗਿਨ ਹੋਮ ਪੁਨ ਤਪ ਪੂਜਾ ਦੇਹ ਦੁਖੀ ਨਿਤ ਦੂਖੁ ਸਹੇ॥. . .
ਗੁਰਪ੍ਰਸਾਦਿ ਰਾਖਿ ਲੇਹੁ ਜਨ ਕਉ ਹਰਿ ਰਸੁ ਨਾਨਿਕ ਝੋਲਿ ਪੀਆ॥੫॥੧੩॥

रागु ਭੈਰਉ ਮਹਲੁ ੩

੨੩੭* ਰਾਮੁ ਨਾਮੁ ਜਗਤਿ ਨਿਸਤਾਰਾ॥
ਭਵਜਲੁ ਪਾਰਿ ਉਤਾਰਨਹਾਰਾ॥. . .
ਨਦਰਿ ਕਰੇ ਸਤਿਗੁਰੁ ਮਿਲਾਏ॥
ਨਾਨਕ ਹਿਰਦੈ ਨਾਮੁ ਵਸਾਏ॥੪॥੧੪॥

੨੩੭ ਨਾਮੇ ਉਧਰੇ ਸਭਿ ਜਿਤਨੇ ਲੋਇ॥
ਗੁਰਮੁਖਿ ਜਿਨਾ ਪਰਾਪਤਿ ਹੋਇ॥. . .
ਆਪੇ ਕਰਤਾ ਦੇਵੈ ਸੋਇ॥
ਨਾਨਕ ਨਾਮੁ ਪਰਾਪਤਿ ਹੋਇ॥੪॥੧੫॥

੨੩੮* ਗੋਵਿਦ ਪ੍ਰੀਤਿ ਸਨਿਕਾਦਿਕ ਉਧਾਰੇ॥
ਰਾਮਿ ਨਾਮਿ ਸਬਦਿ ਵੀਚਾਰੇ॥. . .
ਆਪੇ ਵੇਖੈ ਵੇਖਣਹਾਰੁ॥
ਨਾਨਕ ਨਾਮੁ ਰਖਹੁ ਉਰਧਾਰਿ॥੪॥੧੬॥

੨੩੮ ਕਲਜੁਗ ਮਹਿ ਰਾਮ ਨਾਮੁ ਉਰਿਧਾਰੁ॥
ਬਿਨੁ ਨਾਵੈ ਮਾਥੈ ਪਾਵੈ ਛਾਰੁ॥. . .
ਸੋ ਸੇਵਹੁ ਜਿ ਕਲ ਰਹਿਆ ਧਾਰਿ॥
ਨਾਨਕ ਗੁਰਮਤਿ ਨਾਮਿ ਪਿਆਰਿ॥੪॥੧੭॥

੨੩੯* ਕਲਜੁਗ ਮਹਿ ਬਹੁ ਕਰਮ ਕਮਾਹਿ॥
ਨਰ ਤਿਨੀ ਕਰਮੀ ਥਾਇ ਨ ਪਾਹਿ॥੯੯ . . .

੭੫

कलजुग महि हरि जीउ एकु होर रुति न काई॥
नानक गुरमुखि राम नाम हिरदै लेहु जमाई॥४॥१८॥

२३९ दूबिआ मनमुखि रोगि विआपे तिसना जलहि अधिकाई॥. . .
नानक निहचलु साचा एकै ना ऊ मरै न जाइआ॥५॥१९॥

२४० मनमुखि दूबिआ सदा है रोगी [रोगी] सगल सैसारा॥. . .
नानक से पूरे वडभागी सतगुरि सेवा लाए॥
जो इछहि सोई फलु पावहि गुरबाणी सुखु पाए॥४॥२०॥

२४१*----२३

२४१* दुख विचि जंमै दुखि मरे दुख विचि कार कमाइ॥. . .
नानक तिनि की रेणु पूरै भागि पाईऐ
जिनी रामि नामि चितु लाइआ॥४॥२१॥

२४२* सबदु वीचारे सो जनु साचा जिन कै हिरदै साचा सोई॥. . .
नानक नामु जिना मनि वसिआ दरि साचै पति पाई॥४॥२२॥

२४२ मनमुखि भुख आसा नह उतरै दूजै भाइ खुआए॥. . .
नानक सतगुरि सोझी पाई सचि नामि निसतारा॥४॥२३॥[100]

२४३ कलि महि परेतु जिनी रामु न पछाता सतजुगि परमहंस वीचारी॥. . .
जो किछु करे सो भला करि मानै नानक नाउ वखाणै॥४॥२४॥

२४४* मनसा मनहि समाइ लै गुरसबदी वीचारि॥. . .
नानक हरि भगति परापति होई जोती जोति समाइ॥४॥२५॥

२४४ बाझु गुरू जगतु बउराना भूला चोटा खाई॥. . .
नानक गुरमुखि सबदि समाले रामि नामि वडिआई॥४॥२६॥

२४५ हउमै माइआ मोहि खुआइआ दुखु खाट दुखु खाइ॥. . .
आपे गुरमुखि दे वडिआई नानक नामि समाए॥४॥२७॥[101]

ੴ सतिगुर परसादु सचुनामु करतारु निरभउ
निरीकारु अकाल मूरति अजूनी संभउ गुरपरसादु

रागु भैरउ असटपदीआ [महला १]

२४८* आतम महि रामु रामु महि आतमु चीनसि गुर वीचारा॥. . .
हरिजन अनदिनु निरमल जिन कउ करमु नीसाणु पाइआ॥८॥१॥

रागु भैरउ महलु ३

२४९ गुर सेवा ते अंम्रित फलु पाइआ हउमै तिसना बुझाई॥. . .
नानक तिन कै सदा बलिहारे राम नामु उरिधारे॥८॥२॥

२५०----२४

२५१* तिनि करतै इकु चलतु उपाइआ॥
अनहत बाणी सबदु सुणाइआ॥. . .

76

ਕਹੈ ਨਾਨਕੁ ਸਭ ਕੋ ਕਰੈ ਕਰਾਇਆ।। . . .

ਕਰਤੈ ਆਪਣਾ ਰੂਪੁ ਦਿਖਾਇਆ।।੭੩।।੩।।

੨੫੩   ਮੇਰੀ ਪਟੀਆ ਲਿਖਹੁ ਹਰਿ ਗੋਵਿੰਦੁ ਗੋਪਾਲਾ।।

ਦੂਜੈ ਭਾਇ ਫਾਥੇ ਜਮਜਾਲਾ।। . . .

ਗੁਰ ਕੈ ਸਬਦਿ ਹਉਮੈ ਬਿਖੁ ਮਾਰੇ।।

ਨਾਨਕ ਰਾਮਨਾਮਿ ਸੰਤ ਨਿਸਤਾਰੇ।।੫।।੪।।102

੨੫੪   ਆਪੇ ਦੈਤ ਲਾਇ ਦਿਤੇ ਸੰਤ ਜਨਾ ਕਉ ਆਪੇ ਰਾਖਾ ਸੋਈ।। . . .

ਨਾਨਕ ਹਰਨਾਖਸੁ ਨਖੀ ਵਿਦਾਰਿਆ ਅੰਧੈ ਦਰ ਕੀ ਖਬਰਿ ਨ ਪਾਈ।।੫।।੫।।103

ਰਾਗੁ ਭੈਰਉ ਸਦਾਸੇਵਕੁ

੨੫੫   ਹਉਮੈ ਮਮਤਾ ਸਬਦੇ ਖੋਈ।।

ਗੁਰਪਰਸਾਦਿ ਸਦਾ ਸੁਖੁ ਹੋਈ।। . . .

ਨਾਨਕੁ ਗੁਰੁ ਪਾਇਆ ਪੂਰੈ ਭਾਗਿ।।

ਅਨਦਿਨੁ ਸਬਦੇ ਰਹਿਆ ਜਾਗਿ।।੪।।੧।।

੨੫੫   ਸੋਈ ਪੰਡਿਤੁ ਹਰਿ ਨਾਮੁ ਧਿਆਵੈ।।

ਸੋਈ ਪੰਡਿਤੁ ਹਉਮੈ ਸਬਦਿ ਜਲਾਵੈ।। . . .

ਭਨਥ ਨਾਨਕੁ ਜਨੁ ਕਰੇ ਕਰਾਇਆ।। . . .

ਤਿਸੁ ਵਿਣੁ ਦੂਜਾ ਅਵਰੁ ਨ ਕੋਈ।।੫।।੧।।104

੨੫੬   ਸਤਗੁਰਿ ਪੂਰੈ ਨਾਮੁ ਦਿੜਾਇਆ।।

ਅਉਗਣ ਮੇਟਿ ਗੁਣੀ ਬਕਸਾਇਆ।। . . .

ਅਨਹਤਿ ਰਾਤੇ ਸੇ ਬੈਰਾਗੀ।।

ਨਾਨਕ ਸੇਵਕਿ ਏਕ ਲਿਵ ਲਾਗੀ।।੫।।੨।।

ੴ ਸਤਿਗੁਰ ਪਰਸਾਦੁ ਸਚੁਨਾਮੁ ਕਰਤਾਰੁ ਨਿਰਭਉ
ਨਿਰੀਕਾਰੁ ਅਕਾਲ ਮੂਰਤਿ ਅਜੂਨੀ ਸੰਭਉ

ਰਾਗੁ ਭੈਰਉ ਕਬੀਰ ਨਾਮਦੇਉ ਭਗਤ

੨੫੭* ਨਾਗੇ ਆਵਣਾ ਨਾਗੇ ਜਾਵਨਾ।।

ਕੋਇ ਨ ਰਹੈਗਾ ਰਾਜਾ ਰਾਵਣਾ।। . . .

ਕਹੁ ਕਬੀਰ ਕਿਛੁ ਗੁਣੁ ਵੀਚਾਰਿ।।

ਚਲੇ ਜੁਆਰੀ ਹਾਥਿ ਦੁਇ ਝਾਰਿ।।੪।।੧।।

੨੫੭   ਸੋ ਮੁਲਾ ਜੁ ਮਨ ਸਉ ਲਰੈ।।

ਗੁਰ ਉਪਦੇਸਿ ਕਾਲ ਸਿਉ ਜੁਰੈ।।

ਮੁਸਲਮਾਨ ਕਾ ਏਕੁ ਖੁਦਾਇ।।

ਕਬੀਰੈ ਕਾ ਸੁਆਮੀ ਰਹਿਆ ਸਮਾਇ।।੪।।੨।।

੨੫੮* ਰੇ ਜਿਹਵਾ ਕਰਉ ਸਤ ਖੰਡਾ।।

ਜਾਮਿ ਨ ਉਚਰੈ ਸਿਰੀ ਗੋਵਿੰਦ।। . . .

ਪਟਵਤਿ ਨਾਮਦੇਉ ਏਹ ਕਾਰਨਾ॥

ਅਨੰਤ ਰੂਪ ਤੇਰੇ ਨਾਰਾਇਨਾ॥੪॥੩॥

੨੫੮ ਮੈਲਾ ਬ੍ਰਹਮਾ ਮੈਲਾ ਇੰਦੁ॥

ਰਵਿ ਮੈਲਾ ਮੈਲਾ ਹੈ ਚੰਦੁ॥. . .

ਕਹਤੁ ਕਬੀਰੁ ਤੇ ਜਨ ਪਰਵਾਨੁ॥

ਤੇ ਨਿਰਮਲ ਜੋ ਰਾਮੈ ਜਾਨੁ॥੬॥੪॥

੨੫੯*----੨੫

੨੫੯* ਪਰਧਨੁ ਪਰਦਾਰਾ ਪਰਹਰੀ॥

ਜਨ ਕੈ ਨਿਕਟਿ ਵਸੈ ਨਰਹਰੀ॥. . .

ਪਟਵਤਿ ਨਾਮਦੇਉ ਨਾ ਕੇ ਬਿਨਾ॥

ਨ ਸੋਹੇ ਬਤੀ ਸੁਲਖਨਾ॥੩॥੫॥

੨੫੯ ਸਿਵ ਕੀ ਪੁਰੀ ਵਸੈ ਬੁਧਿ ਸਾਰੁ॥

ਤਹ ਤੁਮ ਮਿਲਿ ਕੈ ਕਰਹੁ ਵੀਚਾਰੁ॥. . .

ਖਿੜਕੀ ਉਪਰਿ ਦਸਵਾ ਦੁਆਰੁ॥

ਕਹੁ ਕਮੀਰ ਤਾ ਕਾ ਅੰਤੁ ਨ ਪਾਰੁ॥੩॥੬॥

ਰਾਗੁ ਭੈਰਉ ਕਮੀਰੁ ਨਾਮਾ ਭਗਤ ਬਾਬੇ ਦੇ[105]

੨੬੦* ਜੈਸੀ ਭੂਖੇ ਪ੍ਰੀਤਿ ਅਨਾਦੀ॥

ਤਿਖਾਬੰਤੁ ਜਲ ਸੇਤੀ ਕਾਜੀ॥. . .

ਪ੍ਰਟਵਤਿ ਨਾਮਦੇਉ ਲਾਗੀ ਪ੍ਰੀਤਿ॥

ਗੋਬਿਦੁ ਵਸਿਆ ਨਾਮੈ ਕੈ ਚੀਤਿ॥੪॥੭॥

੨੬੦ ਬਿਨ ਦੇਖੇ ਨਾਹੀ ਉਪਜੈ ਆਸਾ॥

ਜੋ ਦੀਸੈ ਸੋ ਹੋਇ ਬਿਨਾਸਾ॥. . .

ਕਹੁ ਰਵਿਦਾਸ ਪਰਮ ਬੈਰਾਗੁ॥

ਰਿਦੈ ਰਾਮੁ ਕੀ ਨ ਜਪਹੁ ਅਭਾਗੁ॥੪॥੮॥

੨੬੧ ਆਗਮੁ ਦੁਰਗਮੁ ਗੜਿ ਰਚਿਓ ਵਾਸੁ॥

ਜਾ ਮਹਿ ਜੋਤਿ ਕਰੇ ਪਰਗਾਸੁ॥. . .

ਜੋਤਿ ਮਾਝਿ ਮਨੁ ਅਸਥਿਰੁ ਕਰੈ॥

ਕਹੁ ਕਬੀਰੁ ਸੋ ਪਰਾਨੀ ਤਰੈ॥੮॥੯॥

੨੬੨ ਮਨੁ ਕਰਿ ਮਕਾ ਕਿਬਲਾ ਕਰਿ ਦੇਹੀ॥

ਬੋਲਨਹਾਰੁ ਪਰਮ ਗੁਰੁ ਏਹੀ॥. . .

ਕਹੁ ਕਬੀਰ ਹਉ ਭਇਆ ਦੇਵਾਨਾ॥

ਮੁਸਿ ਮੁਸਿ ਮਨੂਆ ਸਹਜਿ ਸਮਾਨਾ॥੪॥੧੦॥

ਰਾਗੁ ਭੈਰਉ ਕਮੀਰੁ ਨਾਮਦੇਉ ਪੂਰੇ ਭਗਤ

੨੬੩* ਮੈ ਬਾਵਰੀ ਮੇਰਾ ਰਾਮੁ ਭਤਾਰੁ॥

ਰਚਿ ਰਚਿ ਤ ਕਉ ਕਰੀ ਸੀਗਾਰੁ॥. . .

ਉਸਤਤਿ ਨਿੰਦਾ ਕਰੈ ਜਨੁ ਕੋਈ॥

ਨਾਮੇ ਸ੍ਰਿ ਰੰਗੁ ਭੇਟੀਲੇ ਸੋਈ॥੪॥੧੧॥

ਰਾਗੁ ਭੈਰਉ ਕਬੀਰ ਨਾਮਾ ਭਗਤ ਬਾਬੇ ਦੇ

੨੬੩ ਸੰਡਾ ਮਰਕਾ ਜਾਇ ਪੁਕਾਰੇ॥ ਪੜੇ ਨਾਹੀ ਹਮ ਪਰੀਆਰੇ॥. . .
       ਨਾਮਦੇਉ ਕਹੈ ਹਮ ਨਰਹਰ ਧਿਆਵਹ ਰਾਮੁ ਅਡੈ ਪਦ ਦਾਤਾ॥੫॥੧੨॥

੨੬੪ ਨਾਉ ਮੇਰੈ ਖੇਤੀ ਨਾਉ ਮੇਰੈ ਵਾੜੀ॥
       ਭਗਤਿ ਕਰਾ ਜਨ ਸਰਨਿ ਤੁਮਾਰੀ॥. . .
       ਮਾਇਆ ਭੀਤਰਿ ਜੋ ਰਹੈ ਉਦਾਸੁ॥
       ਕਹੁ ਕਬੀਰ ਹਉ ਤਾਕਾ ਦਾਸੁ॥੪॥੧੩॥[106]

੨੬੪----੨੬

੨੬੫* ਗੁਰ ਸੇਵਾ ਤੇ ਭਗਤਿ ਕਮਾਈ॥
       ਤਾ ਏਹ ਮਾਨਸ ਦੇਹੀ ਪਾਈ॥. . .
       ਕਹੁ ਕਬੀਰ ਜੀਤਿ ਕੈ ਹਾਰਿ॥
       ਮੈ ਬਹੁ ਬਿਧਿ ਕਹਿਓ ਪੁਕਾਰਿ ਪੁਕਾਰਿ॥੫॥੧੪॥

੨੬੫ ਦੂਧੁ ਕਟੋਰੈ ਗਡਵੈ ਪਾਨੀ॥
       ਕਪਲ ਗਾਇ ਨਾਮੈ ਦੁਹਿ ਆਨੀ॥. . .
       ਦੂਧ ਪੀਆਇ ਭਗਤੁ ਘਰਿ ਗਇਆ॥
       ਨਾਮੈ ਹਰਿ ਕਾ ਦਰਸਨੁ ਪਇਆ॥੪॥੧੫॥

੨੬੬* ਕਬਹੁ ਖੀਰਿ ਖੰਡ ਘੀਰਤ ਭੋਜਨੁ ਨ ਭਾਵੈ॥
       ਕਬਹੁ ਰੁਰਾ ਚਨੇ ਬਨਾਵੈ॥. . .
       ਭਨਬ ਨਾਮਦੇਉ ਇਕੁ ਨਾਮੁ ਨਿਸਤਾਰੈ॥
       ਜਿਸੁ ਗੁਰ ਮਿਲੈ ਤਿਸੁ ਪਾਰਿ ਉਤਾਰੈ॥੪॥੧੬॥

੨੬੬ ਗੰਗਾ ਕੈ ਸੰਗਿ ਸਲਿਤਾ ਬਿਗਰੀ॥
       ਸੋ ਸਲਿਤਾ ਗੰਗਾ ਹੋਇ ਨਿਬਰੀ॥. . .
       ਸੰਤੁ ਕੇ ਸੰਗਿ ਕਬੀਰ ਵਿਗਰਿਆ॥
       ਸੋਈ ਕਬੀਰੁ ਰਾਮੁ ਹੋਇ ਨਿਬਰਿਆ॥੪॥੧੭॥

੨੬੭* ਮਾਥੈ ਤਿਲਕੁ ਹਾਥਿ ਮਾਲਾ ਬਾਨਾ॥
       ਲੋਗਨ ਰਾਮੁ ਖਿਲਉਨਾ ਜਾਨਾ॥. . .
       ਲੋਕੁ ਕਹੈ ਕਬੀਰੁ ਬਉਰਾਨਾ॥
       ਕਬੀਰ ਕਾ ਮਰਮੁ ਰਾਮੁ ਪਹਿਛਾਨਾ॥੪॥੧੮॥

੨੬੭* ਘਰ ਕੀ ਨਾਰਿ ਤਿਆਗੈ ਅੰਧਾ॥
       ਪਰਨਾਰੀ ਸਉ ਘਾਲੇ ਧੰਧਾ॥. . .
       ਕਹੈ ਨਾਮਦੇਉ ਇਹ ਵੀਚਾਰੁ॥
       ਇਨ ਵਿਧਿ ਸੰਤਹੁ ਉਤਰਹੁ ਪਾਰਿ॥੪॥੧੯॥

੨੬੭ ਜੋ ਪਾਥਰ ਕਉ ਕਹਤੇ ਦੇਵਾ॥
       ਤਿਸ ਕੀ ਬਿਰਥਾ ਹੋਵੈ ਸੇਵਾ॥. . .
       ਕਹਤੁ ਕਬੀਰ ਹਉ ਕਹਉ ਪੁਕਾਰਿ॥

ਸਮਝ ਦੇਖ ਸਾਕਤ ਗਵਾਰ॥

ਦੂਜੈ ਭਾਇ ਬਹੁਤੁ ਘਰਿ ਗਾਲੇ॥

ਰਾਮ ਭਗਤਿ ਹੈ ਸਦਾ ਸੁਖਾਲੇ॥੪॥੨੦॥

੨੬੮ ਜਲ ਮਹਿ ਮੀਨ ਮਾਇਆ ਕੇ ਬੇਧੇ॥

ਦੀਪਕ ਪਤੰਗ ਮਾਇਆ ਕੇ ਛੇਦੇ॥. . .

ਕਹੈ ਕਬੀਰ ਉਦਰੁ ਤਿਸੁ ਮਾਇਆ॥

ਤਉ ਛੂਟੈ ਜਉ ਸਾਧੂ ਪਾਇਆ॥੫॥੨੧॥

੨੬੯* ਜਉ ਗੁਰ ਦੇਉ ਤ ਮਿਲੈ ਮੁਰਾਰਿ॥

ਜਉ ਗੁਰ ਦੇਉ ਤਾ ਉਤਰੈ ਪਾਰਿ॥. . .

ਬਿਨੁ ਗੁਰਦੇਵ ਅਵਰੁ ਨਾਹੀ ਜਾਈ॥

ਨਾਮਦੇਉ ਗੁਰ ਕੀ ਸਰਣਾਈ॥੮॥੨੨॥[107]

੨੭੦*----੨੭

੨੭੦* ਬੇਗਮ ਪੁਰਾ ਸਹਰ ਕਾ ਨਾਉ॥

ਫਿਕਰੁ ਅਦੇਸੇ ਨਾਹੀ ਤਹ ਥਾਉ॥. . .

ਕਹੁ ਰਵਿਦਾਸ ਖਲਾਸ ਚਮਿਆਰਾ॥

ਜੋ ਹਮ ਸਹਰੀ ਸੋ ਮੀਤੁ ਹਮਾਰਾ॥੩॥੨੩॥[108]

੨੭੦ # ਸੰਤਨੁ ਕੈ ਇਕੁ ਰੋਟੁ ਜਾਚੁਲਾ

ਮੋ ਰੋਟ ਲੇ ਨਾਥੈ ਬੀਠੁਲਾ॥. . .

ਉਤਮ ਜਾਤਿ ਨ ਦੇਖ ਅਲੋਨੀ॥

ਨਾਮਦੇ ਕੈ ਹਬਿ ਘਿਰਤਾ ਕੀ ਭੋਨੀ॥੩॥੨੪॥[109]

੨੭੧* ਹਿਦੂ ਗਰਦਨਿ ਮਾਰਉ ਤੋਹਿ॥

ਮੁਈ ਗਾਇ ਜੀਵਾਇ ਦੇਹਿ ਮੋਹਿ॥. . .

ਧਨੁ ਰੇ ਨਾਮਾ ਧਨੁ ਤੇਰਾ ਰਾਮੁ॥

ਹਿਦੂ ਤੁਰਕ ਸਭਿ ਕਰਹਿ ਸਲਾਮੁ॥੧੫॥੨੫॥[110]

੨੭੨* # ਸੁਲਤਾਨੁ ਪੁਛੈ ਕਹੁ ਰੇ ਨਾਮਾ ਤੇਰਾ ਸੁਆਮੀ ਕੈਸਾ ਹੈ॥. . .

ਉਠੀ ਬਛਰੈ ਰੁਧੀ ਆਇ॥

ਨਾਮੈ ਭਗਤਿ ਕਰੀ ਲਿਵ ਲਾਇ॥੪॥੨੬॥[111]

੨੭੨ ਹਸਤ ਖੇਲਤ ਨਾਮਾ ਦੇਹੁਰੈ ਆਇਆ॥

ਭਗਤਿ ਕਰਤ ਨਾਮਾ ਮਾਰਿ ਉਠਾਇਆ॥. . .

ਜਿਉ ਜਿਉ ਨਾਮਾ ਹਰਿ ਉਚਰੈ॥

ਤਿਉ ਤਿਉ ਨਾਮੇ ਕਉ ਦੇਹੁਰਾ ਫਿਰੈ॥੪॥੨੭॥[112]

੨੭੩* ਜਉ ਲਗਿ ਮੈ ਮੇਰੀ ਕਰੈ॥

ਤਬ ਲਗਿ ਕਾਜੁ ਏਕੁ ਨਾਹੀ ਸਰੈ॥. . .

ਦਾਸੁ ਕਬੀਰੁ ਕਹੈ ਸਮਝਾਇ॥

ਕੇਵਲ ਰਾਮ ਰਹੁ ਲਿਵ ਲਾਇ॥੩॥੨੮॥[113]

ੴ ਸਤਿਗੁਰ ਪਰਸਾਦੁ ਸਚੁਨਾਮੁ ਕਰਤਾਰੁ ਨਿਰਭਉ

ਨਿਰੀਕਾਰੁ ਅਕਾਲ ਮੂਰਤਿ ਅਜੂਨੀ ਸੰਭਉ

ਰਾਗੁ ਮਾਰੂ[114]

ਰਾਗੁ ਮਾਰੂ ਬਾਬੇ ਪਾਤਿਸਾਹ ਕਾ [ਮਹਲਾ ੧]

੨੭੭* ਪਿਛਹੁ ਰਾਤੀ ਸਦੜਾ ਨਾਮੁ ਖਸਮ ਕਾ ਲੇਹੁ॥ . . .
        ਵਿਜੋਗੀ ਮਿਲਿ ਵੀਛੁੜੇ ਨਾਨਿਕ ਭੀ ਸੰਜੋਗੁ॥੧॥੧॥[115]

੨੭੭   ਮਿਲਿ ਮਾਤ ਪਿਤਾ ਪਿੰਡੁ ਕਮਾਇਆ ਤਿਨਿ ਕਰਤੈ ਲੇਖੁ ਲਿਖਾਇਆ॥ . . .
        ਭਉ ਬੇੜਾ ਜੀਉ ਚੜਾਉ॥   ਕਹੁ ਨਾਨਿਕ ਦੇਵੈ ਕਾਹੁ॥੪॥੨॥

ਰਾਗੁ ਮਾਰੂ-ਕੇਦਾਰਾ [ਮਹਲਾ ੧]

੨੭੮* ਕਰਣੀ ਕਾਗਦੁ ਮਨੁ ਮਸਵਾਨੀ ਬੁਰਾ ਭਲਾ ਦੁਇ ਲੇਖ ਪਏ॥ . . .
        ਏਕੁ ਨਾਮੁ ਭਰਿ ਅੰਮ੍ਰਿਤੁ ਦੇਵੈ ਤਉ ਨਾਨਿਕ ਤਿਸਟਸ ਦੇਹ॥੪॥੩॥

੨੭੮* ਬਿਮਰ ਮਝਾਰੰ ਬਸਸਿ ਨਿਰਮਲ ਜਲ ਪਦ ਮਨਿ ਜਾਵਲਰੇ॥ . . .
        ਪੂਰਬ ਲਿਖਿਆ ਪਾਵਸਿ ਨਾਨਿਕਾ ਰਸਨਾ ਨਾਮੁ ਜਪਿ ਰੇ॥੪॥੪॥

੨੭੯   ਸਖੀ ਸਹੇਲੀ ਗਰਬ ਗਹੇਲੀ॥
        ਤੂ ਸੁਣਿ ਪਿਆਰੇ ਕੀ ਬਾਤ ਸੁਹੇਲੀ॥ . . .
        ਭਨਥ ਨਾਨਿਕੁ ਅੰਦੇਸਾ ਏਹੀ॥
        ਬਿਨੁ ਦਰਸਨ ਕੈਸੇ ਰਵਾ ਸਨੇਹੀ॥੪॥੫॥[116]

੨੮੦* ਮੂਲ ਖਰੀਦੀ ਲਾਲਾ ਗੋਲਾ ਮੇਰਾ ਨਾਉ ਸਭਾਗਾ॥ . . .
        ਲੂਣ ਹਰਾਮੀ ਨਾਨਿਕੁ ਲਾਲਾ ਬਕਸੇਹਿ ਤੇ ਵਡਿਆਈ॥
        ਆਦਿ ਜੁਗਾਦਿ ਦਇਆ ਪਤਿ ਦਾਤਾ ਤੁਧੁ ਬਿਨੁ ਮੁਕਤਿ ਨ ਪਾਈ॥੪॥੬॥

੨੮੦   ਕੋਈ ਆਖੈ ਭੂਤਨਾ ਕੋ ਕਹੈ ਬੇਤਾਲਾ॥
        ਕੋਈ ਆਖੈ ਆਦਮੀ ਨਾਨਿਕੁ ਵੇਚਾਰਾ॥ . . .
        ਤਉ ਦੇਵਾਨਾ ਜਾਟੀਐ ਜਾ ਸਾਹਿਬ ਧਰੇ ਪਿਆਰੁ॥
        ਮੰਦਾ ਜਾਣੈ ਆਪ ਕਉ ਹੋਰ ਭਲਾ ਸੈਸਾਰੁ॥੪॥੭॥[117]

ਰਾਗੁ ਮਾਰੂ-ਕੇਦਾਰਾ ਬਾਬੇ ਦਾ ਮਹਲੁ ੩

੨੮੧* ਜਹ ਬੈਸਾਲੇਹਿ ਤਹ ਬੈਸਾ ਸੁਆਮੀ ਜਹ ਭੇਜੋਹਿ ਤਹ ਜਾਵਾ॥ . . .
        ਭਨਥ ਨਾਨਿਕ ਲੇਖਾ ਮੰਗੈ ਕਵਨਾ ਜਾ ਚੂਕਾ ਮਨਿ ਅਭਮਾਨਾ॥
        ਤਾਸੁ ਤਾਸੁ ਧਰਮਰਾਇ ਜਪਤੁ ਹੈ ਪਏ ਸਚੇ ਕੀ ਸਰਨਾ॥੫॥੮॥[118]

ਰਾਗੁ ਮਾਰੂ [ਮਹਲਾ ੧]

੨੮੨* ਇਹੁ ਧਨੁ ਸਰਬ ਰਹਿਆ ਭਰਪੂਰਿ॥
        ਮਨਮੁਖ ਫਿਰਹਿ ਸੇ ਜਾਨਹਿ ਦੂਰਿ॥ . . .
        ਭਨਥ ਨਾਨਿਕੁ ਅਕਥ ਕੀ ਕਥਾ ਸੁਟਾਏ॥
        ਸਤਗੁਰਿ ਮਿਲੈ ਤਾ ਇਹੁ ਧਨੁ ਪਾਏ॥੫॥੯॥

੨੮੨   ਸੂਰ ਸਰੁ ਸੋਸਿ ਲੈ ਸੋਮ ਸਰੁ ਪੋਖਿ ਲੈ ਜੁਗਤਿ ਕਰਿ ਮਰਤਸੁ ਸਨਬੰਧੁ ਕੀਜੈ॥ . . .

81

ਭਨਥ ਨਾਨਿਕ ਜਨੰ ਰਵੈ ਜੋ ਹਰਿ ਮਨੋ ਮਨ ਪਾਵਨ ਸਉ ਅੰਮ੍ਰਿਤੁ ਪੀਜੈ॥

ਮੀਨ ਕੀ ਚਪਲ ਸਉ ਜੁਗਤਿ ਮਨੁ ਰਾਖੀਐ ਉਡੈ ਨ ਹੰਸੁ ਨਾਹ ਕੰਧੁ ਛੀਜੈ॥੩॥੧੦॥[119]

੨੮੩----੧ [੨੮]

ਰਾਗੁ [ਮਾਰੂ] ਕੇਦਾਰਾ ਸਤਿਗੁਰ [ਦਾ] ਸਦਾਸੇਵਕੁ ਗੁਲਾਮੁ

੨੮੪* ਸਤਿਗੁਰ ਬਾਝਹੁ ਕਿਨੈ ਨ ਪਾਇਓ ਸਭ ਥਕੀ ਕਰਮ ਕਮਾਇ॥. . .

ਗੁਰ ਨਾਨਕੁ ਮਨ ਅੰਤਰਿ ਵਸਿਆ ਤਾ ਸਹਜੇ ਰਹਿਆ ਸਮਾਈ॥੫॥੧॥[120]

ਰਾਗੁ ਮਾਰੂ ਕਬੀਰ ਨਾਮਾ ਜੈਦੇਉ

੨੮੩* ਚੰਦੁ ਸਤਿ ਭੇਦਿਆ ਨਾਦੁ ਸਤਿ ਪੂਰਿਆ ਸੂਰਿ ਸਤੁ ਖੋੜਿ ਸਦਤੁ ਕੀਆ॥. . .

ਭਨਤਿ ਜੈਦੇਉ ਜੈਦੇ ਕਉ ਰਮਿਆ ਬ੍ਰਹਮ ਨਿਰਬਾਨ ਲਿਵਲੀਨੁ ਪਾਇਆ॥੨॥੧॥[121]

੨੮੫ ਦੇਹੀ ਗਾਵਾ ਜੀਉ ਧਰਿ ਮਹਤਾ ਬਸਹਿ ਕਿ ਪੰਚ ਕਿਰਸਾਨਾ॥. . .

ਕਹਤ ਕਬੀਰ ਸੁਨਹੁ ਰੇ ਸੰਤਹੁ ਖੇਤੈ ਕਰਹੁ ਨਿਬੇੜਾ॥

ਅਬ ਕੀ ਬਾਰ ਬਖਸਿ ਬੰਦੇ ਕਉ ਬਹੁਰਿ ਨ ਭਉਜਲ ਫੇਰਾ॥੩॥੨॥

੨੮੬* ਉਸਤਤਿ ਨਿੰਦਾ ਦੋਵੈ ਬਿਬਰਜਤ ਛੋਡਿ ਮਾਨੁ ਅਭਮਾਨਾ॥. . .

ਨਿਰਭਉ ਪੂਰਿ ਰਹਿਆ ਭਰਮੁ ਚੂਕਾ ਕਹੁ ਕਬੀਰ ਜਨ ਦਾਸਾ॥੪॥੩॥

੨੮੩ ਵੇਦ ਪੁਰਾਨ ਪੜੇ ਕਾ ਕਿਆ ਗੁਨੁ ਖਰ ਚੰਦਨ ਜੈਸੇ ਭਾਰਾ॥. . .

ਕਹੁ ਕਬੀਰ ਰਾਮੈ ਰਵਿ ਛੂਟਹੁ ਨਾਹਿ ਤ ਬੂਡਹੁ ਭਾਈ॥੪॥੪॥[122]

੨੮੫* ਬਨਹੁ ਬਸੇ ਕਿਆ ਹੋਈਐ ਜਾਤੇ ਮਨਹੁ ਨ ਜਾਹੁ ਵਿਕਾਰ॥. . .

ਕਹੁ ਕਬੀਰ ਅਬ ਜਾਨਿਆ ਗੁਰਿ ਗਿਆਨੁ ਦੀਆ ਸਮਝਾਇ॥

ਅੰਤਰਗਤਿ ਹਰਿ ਭੇਟਿਆ ਮੇਰਾ ਅਬ ਮਨੁ ਕਤਹੁ ਨ ਜਾਇ॥੪॥੫॥

੨੮੬ ਰਿਧਿ ਸਿਧਿ ਜਾ ਕਉ ਫੁਰੀ ਤਬ ਕਾਹੂ ਸਿਉ ਕਿਆ ਕਾਜਾ॥. . .

ਕਹੁ ਕਬੀਰ ਕੰਚਨ ਭਇਆ ਭਰਮੁ ਗਇਆ ਸਮੁਦੈ ਪਾਰਿ॥੪॥੬॥

੨੮੭* ਅਨਭਉ ਕਿਨੈ ਨ ਦੇਖਿਆ ਬੈਰਾਗੀਅੜੇ॥

ਬਿਨੁ ਭੈ ਅਨਭਉ ਨ ਹੋਇ ਵਣਾਹੰਬੈ॥. . .

ਕਹੁ ਕਬੀਰ ਇਕ ਬੇਨਤੀ ਬੈਰਾਗੀਅੜੇ

ਮੋਕਉ ਭਉਜਲ ਪਾਰਿ ਉਤਾਰਿ ਵਣਾਹੰਬੈ॥੮॥੭॥

੨੮੮* ਜਿਨਿ ਗੜ ਕੋਟ ਕੀਏ ਕੰਚਨ ਕੇ ਛੋਡਿ ਗਇਓ ਸੋ ਰਾਵਨੁ॥. . .

ਕਹੁ ਕਬੀਰ ਤੇ ਹਲਤਿ ਮੁਕਤੇ ਜਿਨਾ ਹਿਰਦੈ ਰਾਮ ਰਸਾਇਨੁ॥੩॥੮॥

੨੮੮* ਕਿਨ ਹੀ ਵਣਜਿਆ ਕਾਸੀ ਕਾਂਸਾ ਤਾਂਬਾ ਕਿਨ ਹੀ ਲਉਗ ਸੁਪਾਰੀ॥. . .

ਕਹਤ ਕਬੀਰ ਸੁਨਹੁ ਰੇ ਸੰਤਹੁ ਨਿਬਹੀ ਖੇਪ ਹਮਾਰੀ॥੪॥੮॥[123]

੨੮੮ ਖਟ ਕਰਮ ਕੁਲਿ ਸਉ ਜੁਗਤਿ ਹੈ ਹਰਿ ਭਗਤਿ ਹਿਰਦੈ ਨਾਹਿ॥. . .

ਐਸੇ ਦੁਰਮਤਿ ਨਿਸਤਰੇ ਤੂ ਕਿਵ ਨ ਤਰਹਿ ਰਵਿਦਾਸ॥੩॥੧੦॥

੨੮੯*----੨ [੨੯]

੨੮੯ ਉਦਕ ਸਮੁੰਦ ਸਲਲ ਕੀ ਸਾਖਿਆ ਨਦੀ ਤਰੰਗ ਸਮਾਵਹਿਗੇ॥. . .

ਕਹੁ ਕਬੀਰ ਜੋ ਨਾਮਿ ਸਮਾਨੇ ਸੁੰਨ ਰਹਿਆ ਲਿਵ ਸੋਈ॥੪॥੧॥

੨੯੦* ਰੇ ਕਲਵਾਲ ਗਵਾਰ ਮੂੜ ਮਤਿ ਉਲਟਿਆ ਪਵਨ ਫਿਰਾਵਉ॥. . .

ਅਬੈ ਪਦ ਪੂਰਿ ਤਾਪੁ ਤਹ ਨਾਸੀ ਕਹੁ ਕਬੀਰ ਵੀਚਾਰੀ॥

ਵਾਟ ਚਲੰਦੇ ਇਹੁ ਮਦੁ ਪਾਇਆ ਐਸਾ ਖੋਦ ਖੁਮਾਰੀ॥੪॥੭੨॥

੨੮੦ # ਚਾਲੀ ਅਚਲ ਭਈ ਥਿਤਿ ਪਾਈ ਜਹ ਕੀ ਤਹਾ ਸਮਾਈ॥. . .
ਕਹੁ ਕਬੀਰ ਮੈ ਅਵਸਰੁ ਪਾਇਆ ਬਹੁਰਿ ਨ ਫੇਰਿ ਬਜਾਵਉ॥੨॥੭੩॥[124]

੨੮੧* ਜੋ ਤੁਮ ਮੋਕਉ ਦੂਰਿ ਕਰਤ ਹਉ ਤਉ ਤੁਮ ਮੁਕਤਿ ਬਤਾਵਹੁ॥. . .
ਅਬ ਤਉ ਬਿਮਲ ਭਏ ਘਟ ਭੀਤਰਿ ਕਹੁ ਕਮੀਰ ਮਨੁ ਮਾਨਿਆ॥੨॥੭੪॥

ਕਮੀਰ ਨਾਮਾ ਬਾਬੇ ਦੇ ਭਗਤ

੨੮੨ ਕਾਮ ਕਰੋਧਿ ਤਿਸਨਾ ਕੇ ਲੀਨੇ ਗਤਿ ਨਾਹੀ ਏਕਾ ਜਾਨੀ॥. . .
ਕਹੁ ਕਮੀਰ ਜਿਨੀ ਰਾਮੁ ਨ ਚੇਤਿਆ ਸੋ ਡੂਬੇ ਖਰੇ ਸਿਆਨੇ॥੪॥੭੫॥

੨੮੩* ਚਾਰਿ ਮੁਕਤਿ ਚਾਰਿਉ ਸਿਧਿ ਮਿਲਿ ਕੈ ਦੂਲਹ ਪ੍ਰਭੁ ਕੀ ਸਰਨਿ ਪਰਿਉ॥. . .
ਕਹੈ ਨਾਮਾ ਗਤਿ ਵਸਿ ਕੇਸਵ ਅਜਹੁ ਬਲਿ ਕੈ ਦੁਆਰਿ ਖਰਿਉ॥੪॥੭੬॥

੨੮੩ ਤੇਡੀ ਪਾਗ ਤੇਡੇ ਚਾਲੇ ਲਾਗੇ ਬੀਰੇ ਖਾਨਿ॥. . .
ਕਹੈ ਕਮੀਰ ਅੰਤ ਕੀ ਵੇਲਾ ਆਇ ਲਗੌ ਕਾਲੁ ਨਿਦਾਨਿ॥੨॥੭੭॥[125]

ੴ ਸਤਿਗੁਰ ਪਰਸਾਦੁ ਬਾਬੇ ਪਾਤਿਸਾਹਿ ਕਾ
ਸਚੁਨਾਮੁ ਕਰਤਾਰ ਨਿਰਭਉ ਨਿਰੀਕਾਰੁ ਅਕਾਲ ਮੂਰਤਿ ਅਜੂਨੀ ਸੰਭਉ

ਰਾਗੁ ਤਿਲੰਗਾ[126]

ਰਾਗੁ ਤਿਲੰਗ ਬਾਬੇ ਪਾਤਿਸਾਹ ਕਾ ਬੋਲਣਾ [ਮਹਲਾ ੧]

੧੮੨* ਇਕ ਅਰਜ ਗੁਫਤੰ ਪੇਸਿ ਤੂ ਦਰਗੋਸ ਕੁ ਕਰਤਾਰ॥
ਹਕਾ ਕਬੀਰੁ ਕਰੀਮੁ ਤੂ ਬੇਐਬ ਪਰਬਦਗਾਰ॥. . .
ਬਦਿਬਖਤ ਹਮਹ ਬਖੀਲ ਗਾਫਿਲ ਬੇਨਜਰ ਬੇਬਾਕ॥
ਨਾਨਕੁ ਭੁਗੋਅੰ ਜਨ ਤੁਰਾ ਤੇਰਿਆ ਚਾਕਰਾ ਪਾਇ ਖਾਕ॥੪॥੧॥[127]

੧੮੨ ਭਉ ਤੇਰਾ ਭਾਗਾ ਖਲੜੀ ਮੇਰਾ ਚੀਤਾ॥
ਹਉ ਦੇਵਾਨਾ ਭਇਆ ਅਤੀਤਾ॥. . .
ਤੇਰੈ ਨਾਮਿ ਨਿਵੈ ਰਹੇ ਲਿਵਲਾਇ॥
ਨਾਨਕ ਤਿਨ ਦਰਿ ਭੀਖਿਆ ਪਾਇ॥੩॥੨॥[128]

੧੮੩* ਜਿਨਿ ਕੀਆ ਤਿਨਿ ਦੇਖਿਆ ਕਿਆ ਕਹੀਐ ਰੇ ਭਾਈ॥
ਆਪੇ ਜਾਣੈ ਕਰੇ ਆਪਿ ਜਿਨਿ ਵਾੜੀ ਹੈ ਲਾਈ॥. . .
ਅਪਿਓ ਪੀਵੈ ਜੋ ਨਾਨਕਾ ਭਰਮੁ ਭਰਮਿ ਸਮਾਵੈ॥
ਸਹਜੀ ਸਹਜੀ ਮਿਲਿ ਰਹੇ ਤਉ ਅਮਰਾਪਦੁ ਪਾਵੈ॥੧੦॥੩॥[129]

੧੮੩----੨੯

੧੮੩ ਜੈਸੀ ਮੈ ਆਵੈ ਖਸਮ ਕੀ ਬਾਣੀ ਤੈਸਾ ਕਰੀ ਗਿਆਨੁ ਵੇ ਲਾਲੋ॥. . .
ਸਚ ਕੀ ਬਾਣੀ ਨਾਨਕੁ ਆਖੈ ਸਚੁ ਸੁਣਾਇਸੀ ਸਚ ਕੀ ਵੇਲਾ॥੨॥੪॥[130]

੧੮੪ # ਅਲਹ ਏਕੁ ਕਰੀਮ ਕੁਦਰਤਿ ਸਚੁ ਕਾਦਰ ਪਾਕੁ॥. . .

ਅਰਦਾਸ ਬੰਦੇ ਬੁਗਉ ਨਾਨਿਕ ਤੂ ਮਿਹਰਵਾਨ ਖੁਦਾਇ॥
ਤੇਰਾ ਨਾਮੁ ਤਰਫੇ ਹਮ ਰਾਜੂ ਪਨਹ ਬੰਦੇ ਲਾਇ॥੩॥੫॥131

੩੦੦* ਬੇਦ ਕਤੇਬ ਇਫਤਰਾ ਜਿਤੁ ਦਿਲ ਕਾ ਫਿਕਰੁ ਨ ਜਾਇ॥
ਟੁਕ ਦਮੁ ਕਰਾਰੀ ਜੇ ਕਰਹੁ ਤਾ ਹਾਦਰਾ ਹਦੂਰਿ ਖੁਦਾਇ॥. . .
ਅਲਾਹ ਪਾਕ ਪਾਕ ਕੋਇ ਆਸ ਕਰਉ ਸਕ ਕਰਉ ਜੇ ਦੂਸਰ ਹੋਇ॥
ਕਮੀਰ ਕਰਮੁ ਕਰੀਮ ਕਾ ਉਹੁ ਕਰੈ ਜਾਨੈ ਸੋਇ॥੪॥੧॥132

2. 2. *Pothi at Sundar Kuṭia, Pinjore*

ਸੁੰਦਰ ਕੁਟੀਆ, ਪਿੰਜੌਰ, ਵਿਖੇ ਪਈ ਪੋਥੀ

੧ਓ ਸਤਿਗੁਰੁ ਪਰਸਾਦ ਸਚੁਨਾਮੁ ਕਰਤਾਰੁ
ਅਕਾਲ ਮੂਰਤਿ ਅਜੂਨੀ ਸੰਭਉ ਗੁਰ ਪੂਰੇ ਕਾ ਪਰਸਾਦੁ133

ਰਾਗੁ ਰਾਮਕਲੀ134

ਰਾਗੁ ਰਾਮਕਲੀ ਸਦੁ [ਮਹਲਾ ੧]

੨* ਕੋਈ ਪੜਤਾ ਸਹੰਸਾ ਕਿਰਤਾ ਕੋਈ ਪੜੈ ਪੁਰਾਣਾ॥. . .
ਪਟਵੰਤਿ ਨਾਨਿਕੁ ਜੇ ਤੂ ਦੇਵਹਿ ਤਾ ਹੋਵੈਹਿ ਅੰਤਿ ਸਖਾਈ॥੪॥੧॥

੩* ਸਰਬ ਜੋਤਿ ਤੇਰੀ ਪਸਰਿ ਰਹੀ॥ ਜਹ ਦੇਖਾ ਤਹ ਨਰਹਰੀ॥
ਪਟਵਤਿ ਨਾਨਿਕੁ ਦਾਸਨਿ ਦਾਸਾ ਪਰਤਾਪਹਿਗਾ ਪਰਾਨੀ॥੪॥੨॥

੩ ਜੇ ਦਰਿ ਵਸੈਹਿ ਕਵਨ ਦਰੁ ਕਹੀਐ ਦਰਾ ਭੀਤਰਿ ਦਰੁ ਕਵਨ ਲਹੈ॥. . .
ਇਨ ਵਿਧ ਸਾਗਰੁ ਤਰੀਐ ਜੀਵਤਿਆ ਇਵ ਮਰੀਐ॥੧॥ ਰਹਾਉ॥੩॥135

੪ ਸੁਰਤਿ ਸਬਦੁ ਸਾਖੀ ਮੇਰੀ ਸਿਧੀ ਵਾਜੈ ਲੋਕੁ ਸੁਟੈ॥. . .
ਐਸੇ ਭਗਤ ਮਿਲਹਿ ਜਨ ਨਾਨਕ ਤਿਨ ਜਮੁ ਕਾਹਿ ਕਰੈ॥੪॥੪॥

੫* ਸੁਣਿ ਮਾਛਿੰਦਾ ਨਾਨਿਕੁ ਬੋਲੈ॥
ਵਸਗਤਿ ਪੰਚ ਕਰੈਹਿ ਨਾਹੀ ਡੋਲੈ॥. . .
ਦੀਖਿਆ ਭੋਜਨੁ ਦਾਰੁ ਖਾਇ॥
ਤਾ ਛਿਅ ਦਰਸਨ ਕੀ ਸੋਝੀ ਪਾਇ॥੪॥੫॥

੬* ਹਮ ਡੋਲਤ ਬੇੜੀ ਪਾਪਿ ਭਰੀ ਹੈ ਪਵਣਿ ਲਗੈ ਮਤੁ ਜਾਈ॥. . .
ਪਰਸਤੁ ਪੈਰ ਸਿਝਤ ਤੇ ਸੁਆਮੀ ਅਖਰੁ ਜਿਨ ਕਉ ਆਇਆ॥੨॥੬॥136

੬ ਸੁਰਤੀ ਸੁਰਤਿ ਰਲਾਈਐ ਏਤੁ॥
ਤਨੁ ਕਰਿ ਤੁਲਹਾ ਲਾਘੈ ਜੇਤੁ॥. . .
ਐਸਾ ਦੀਵਾ ਬਾਲੇ ਕੋਈ॥ ਨਾਨਕ ਸੋ ਪਰਗਟਿ ਹੋਈ॥੪॥੭॥

੭* ਤੁਧਨੋ ਨਿਵਣੁ ਮਨਣੁ ਤੇਰਾ ਨਾਉ॥ ਸਚੁ ਭੇਟ ਬੈਸਣ ਕਉ ਥਾਉ॥. . .
ਸਹ ਕੀਆ ਗਲਾ ਦਰ ਕੀਆ ਬਾਤਾ ਤਾ ਤੇ ਕਹਣੁ ਕਹਾਇਆ॥੩॥੮॥

84

ੁ ਸਾਗਰ ਮਹਿ ਬੂਦ ਬੂਦ ਮਹਿ ਸਾਗਰੁ ਕਵਨੁ ਬੁਝੈ ਬਿਧਿ ਜਾਣੈ॥ . . .

ਨਾਨਕ ਤਿਨ ਕੈ ਸਦ ਬਲਿਹਾਰੀ ਜਿਨ ਏਕ ਸਬਦਿ ਲਿਵ ਲਾਈ ਰੇ॥੪॥੯॥

ੲ ਜਾ ਹਰਿ ਪ੍ਰਭਿ ਕਿਰਪਾ ਧਾਰੀ॥

ਤਾ ਹਉਮੈ ਵਿਚੋ ਮਾਰੀ॥ . . .

ਸਤਿਗੁਰਿ ਭਰਮੁ ਚੁਕਾਇਆ॥

ਕਹੁ ਨਾਨਕ ਸਬਦਿ ਮਿਲਾਇਆ॥੪॥੧੦॥

ੲ*----੧

ੲ* ਛਾਦਨੁ ਭੋਜਨੁ ਮਾਗਤੁ ਮਾਗੈ॥

ਖੁਧਿਆ ਦੁਸਟ ਜਲੈ ਦੁਖੁ ਆਗੈ॥ . . .

ਮਨ ਮਹਿ ਮੁਦਾ ਹਰਿ ਗੁਰ ਸਰਨਾ॥

ਨਾਨਕ ਰਾਮ ਭਗਤਿ ਜਨ ਤਰਨਾ॥੪॥੧੧॥

ਰਾਗੁ ਰਾਮਕਲੀ ਮਹਲਾ ੩

ੲ ਸਤਜੁਗਿ ਸਚੁ ਕਹੈ ਸਭੁ ਕੋਈ॥

ਘਰਿ ਘਰਿ ਭਗਤਿ ਗੁਰਮੁਖਿ ਹੋਈ॥ . . .

ਹਰਿਨਾਮੁ ਧਿਆਏ ਭਗਤੁ ਜਨੁ ਸੋਈ॥

ਨਾਨਕ ਜੁਗਿ ਜੁਗਿ ਨਾਮਿ ਵਡਿਆਈ ਹੋਈ॥੬॥੧੨॥[137]

ਰਾਗੁ ਰਾਮਕਲੀ ਅਸਟਪਦੀਆ [ਮਹਲਾ ੧]

੧੦ ਸੋਈ ਚੰਦੁ ਚੜਹਿ ਸੇ ਤਾਰੇ ਸੋਈ ਦਿਨੀਅਰੁ ਤਪਤ ਰਹੈ॥ . . .

ਨਾਨਕ ਨਾਮੁ ਮਿਲੈ ਵਡਿਆਈ ਏਦੂ ਉਪਰਿ ਕਰਮੁ ਨਹੀ॥

ਜੇ ਘਰਿ ਹੋਦਾ ਮੰਗਣਿ ਜਾਈਐ ਫੇਰਿ ਉਲਾਮਾ ਮਿਲੈ ਤਹੀ॥੮॥੧॥

ਰਾਗੁ ਰਾਮਕਲੀ ਦਖਣੀ [ਮਹਲਾ ੧]

੧੨* ਜਗੁ ਪਰਬੋਧਹਿ ਮੜੀ ਬਧਾਵਹਿ॥

ਆਸਣੁ ਤਿਆਗਿ ਕਾਹੇ ਸਚੁ ਪਾਵਹਿ॥ . . .

ਸਤਗੁਰ ਚਰਣੀ ਲਾਵੈ ਚੀਤੁ॥

ਨਾਨਿਕ ਜੋਗੀ ਤ੍ਰਿਭਵਣ ਮੀਤੁ॥੮॥੨॥

੧੩* ਘਟੁ ਮਟੁ ਦੇਹੀ ਮਨੁ ਬੈਰਾਗੀ॥

ਸੁਰਤਿ ਸਬਦੁ ਧੁਨਿ ਅੰਤਰਿ ਜਾਗੀ॥ . . .

ਗੁਰ ਚੇਲੇ ਅਪੁਨਾ ਮਨੁ ਮਾਨਿਆ॥

ਨਾਨਕ ਦੂਜਾ ਮੇਟਿ ਸਮਾਨਿਆ॥੮॥੩॥

੧੪ ਸਾਹਾ ਗਣਹਿ ਨ ਕਰਹਿ ਵੀਚਾਰੁ॥

ਸਾਹੇ ਉਪਰਿ ਏਕੰਕਾਰੁ॥

ਗੁਰ ਕੈ ਭਾਣੈ ਕਰਮੁ ਕਮਾਵੈ॥

ਨਾਨਕ ਸਚੇ ਸਚਿ ਸਮਾਵੈ॥੯॥੪॥

੧੫----੨

੧੬* ਹਠੁ ਨਿਗ੍ਰਹੁ ਕਰਿ ਕਾਇਆ ਛੀਜੈ॥

ਬਰਤੁ ਤਪਨੁ ਕਰਿ ਮਨੁ ਨਹੀ ਭੀਜੈ॥ . . .

85

ਗੁਰ ਕੀ ਸੇਵਾ ਰਾਮੁ ਰਵੀਜੈ॥

ਨਾਨਿਕ ਨਾਮੁ ਮਿਲੈ ਕਿਰਪਾ ਪਰਭ ਕੀਜੈ॥੮॥੫॥

੧੭* ਅੰਤਰਿ ਉਤਭੁਜ ਅਵਰੁ ਨ ਕੋਈ॥

ਜੋ ਕਹੀਐ ਸੋ ਪਰਭ ਤੇ ਹੋਈ॥. . .

ਬਿਨੁ ਗੁਰਸਬਦੁ ਨਾਹੀ ਘਰੁ ਬਾਰੁ॥

ਨਾਨਕ ਗੁਰਮੁਖਿ ਤੰਤੁ ਵੀਚਾਰੁ॥੮॥੬॥

੧੯ ਜਿਵ ਆਇਆ ਤਿਵ ਜਾਹਿਗਾ ਬਵਰੇ ਜਿਵ ਜਨਮੇ ਤਿਵ ਮਰਨ ਭਇਆ॥. . .

ਆਪੁ ਮਾਰਿ ਗੁਰਮੁਖਿ ਹਰਿ ਪਾਏ ਨਾਨਿਕੁ ਸਹਜਿ ਸਮਾਇ ਲਇਆ॥੧੨॥੭॥

ਰਾਗੁ ਰਾਮਕਲੀ ਮਹਲਾ ੩

੨੦ ਸਰਮੈ ਦੀਆ ਮੁਦਾ ਕੰਨੀ ਪਾਇ ਜੋਗੀ ਖਿਾ ਕਰਿ ਤੂ ਦਇਆ॥. . .

ਕਹੈ ਨਾਨਿਕੁ ਮੁਕਤਿ ਹੋਵੈਹਿ ਜੋਗੀ ਸਾਚੈ ਰਹਿ ਸਮਾਇ॥੧੨॥੮॥[138]

੨੨----੩

੧ਓ ਸਤਿਗੁਰ ਪਰਸਾਦੁ

ਰਾਗੁ ਰਾਮਕਲੀ ਦਖਣੀ [ਮਹਲਾ ੧]

੨੪* ਜਤੁ ਸਤੁ ਸੰਜਮੁ ਸਚੁ ਦਿੜਾਇਆ ਸਚਿ ਸਬਦਿ ਰਸਿ ਲੀਆ॥. . .

ਨਾਨਿਕ ਸਰਨਿ ਪ੍ਰਭੁ ਕੀ ਛੂਟੇ ਸਤਿਗੁਰ ਸਚੁ ਸਖਾਈ॥੧੦॥੧॥

੨੪ ਅਉਹਠਿ ਹਸਤ ਪੜੀ ਘਰੁ ਛਾਇਆ ਧਰਨਿ ਗਗਨਿ ਕਲ ਧਾਰੀ॥. . .

ਆਪੇ ਪਰਖੇ ਮਿਲੈ ਮਿਲਾਏ ਨਾਨਿਕੁ ਸਰਨਿ ਤੁਮਾਰੀ॥੨੫॥੨॥

ਰਾਗੁ ਰਾਮਕਲੀ ਮਹਲਾ ੩

੨੬* ਭਗਤਿ ਖਜਾਨਾ ਗੁਰਮੁਖਿ ਜਾਤਾ ਸਤਿਗੁਰਿ ਬੁਝਿ ਬੁਝਾਈ॥. . .

ਨਾਨਿਕ ਏਕੁ ਕਹੈ ਬੇਨੰਤੀ ਨਾਵਹੁ ਗਤਿ ਮਿਤਿ ਪਾਈ॥੨੭॥੩॥

੨੮* ਹਰਿ ਕੀ ਪੂਜਾ ਦੁਲੰਭੁ ਹੈ ਸੰਤਹੁ ਕਹਣਾ ਕਿਛੁ ਨ ਜਾਈ॥. . .

ਸਭ ਕਿਛੁ ਆਪੇ ਅਪਿ ਵਰਤੇ ਨਾਨਕ ਨਾਇ ਵਡਿਆਈ॥੨੯॥੪॥

੨੯* ਹਮ ਕੁਚੀਲ ਕੁਚੀਲ ਅੰਤਿ ਅਭਮਾਨੀ ਮਿਲਿ ਸਬਦੇ ਮੈਲੁ ਉਤਾਰੀ॥. . .

ਨਾਨਿਕ ਸੇ ਮੂਏ ਜਿਨਾ ਨਾਮੁ ਨ ਚੇਤਿਆ ਭਗਤ ਜੀਵੇ ਵੀਚਾਰੀ॥੩੦॥੫॥

੩੧ ਨਾਮੁ ਖਜਾਨਾ ਗੁਰ ਤੇ ਪਾਇਆ ਤ੍ਰਿਪਤਿ ਰਹੇ ਅਘਾਈ॥. . .

ਨਾਨਕ ਸੁਣਿ ਵੇਖਿਐ ਰਹਿਆ ਵਿਸਮਾਦੁ

ਮੇਰਾ ਪ੍ਰਭੁ ਰਵਿ ਰਹਿਆ ਹੈ ਸਭ ਥਾਈ॥੨੦॥੬॥[139]

੩੩*----੫

੧ਓ ਸਤਿਗੁਰ ਪਰਸਾਦਿ ਸਚੁਨਾਮੁ ਕਰਤਾਰੁ ਨਿਰਭਉ

ਨਿਰੀਕਾਰੁ ਅਕਾਲ ਮੂਰਤਿ ਅਜੂਨੀ ਸੰਭਉ॥੧॥[140]

ਓਅੰਕਾਰੁ ਰਾਗੁ ਰਾਮਕਲੀ [ਮਹਲਾ ੧]

੩੫* ਓਅੰਕਾਰਿ ਬ੍ਰਹਮਾ ਉਤਪਤਿ॥ ਓਅੰਕਾਰੁ ਜਿਨਿ ਕੀਆ ਚਿਤਿ॥. . .

ਨਾਨਕ ਸੋ ਪੜਿਆ ਸੋ ਪੰਡਿਤੁ ਬੀਨਾ ਜਿਨਾ ਰਾਮ ਨਾਮੁ ਗਲਿ ਹਾਰੁ॥੫੪॥੧॥

੫੩----੬

ੴ ਸਤਿਗੁਰ ਪਰਸਾਦਿ ਸਚੁਨਾਮੁ ਕਰਤਾਰੁ ਨਿਰਭਉ

ਨਿਰੀਕਾਰੁ ਅਕਾਲ ਮੂਰਤਿ ਅਜੂਨੀ ਸੰਭਉ

ਰਾਗੁ ਰਾਮਕਲੀ ਦਖਣੀ ਸਿਧ ਗੋਸਟਿ

੫੫* ਸਿਧ ਸਭਾ ਕਰਿ ਆਸਣਿ ਬੈਠੇ ਸੰਤ ਸਭਾ ਜੈਕਾਰੋ॥

ਤਿਸੁ ਆਗੈ ਰਹਰਾਸਿ ਹਮਾਰੀ ਸਾਚਾ ਅਪਰ ਆਪਾਰੋ॥. . .

ਸਤਿਗੁਰ ਤੇ ਨਾਉ ਪਾਈਐ ਅਵਰੁ ਜੋਗ ਜੁਗਤਿ ਤਾ ਹੋਈ॥

ਕਰਿ ਵੀਚਾਰੁ ਮਨਿ ਵੇਖਹੁ ਬਾਬਾ ਨਾਨਕ ਬਿਨੁ ਨਾਵੈ ਮੁਕਤਿ ਨ ਹੋਈ॥੭੨॥੨॥[141]

੭੪————੭

ੴ ਸਤਿਗੁਰ ਪਰਸਾਦਿ ਸਚੁਨਾਮੁ ਕਰਤਾਰੁ ਨਿਰਭਉ

ਨਿਰੀਕਾਰੁ ਅਕਾਲ ਮੂਰਤਿ ਅਜੂਨੀ ਸੰਭਉ॥੧॥

ਰਾਗੁ ਰਾਮਕਲੀ ਮਹਲੁ ੩[142]

੮੦* ਅਨਦੁ ਭਇਆ ਮੇਰੀ ਮਾਏ ਸਤਿਗੁਰੂ ਮੈ ਪਾਇਆ॥. . .

ਏਹੁ ਸਚੁ ਸਭਨਾ ਕਾ ਖਸਮੁ ਹੈ ਜਿਸੁ ਬਕਸੇ ਸੋ ਜਨੁ ਪਾਵਏ॥

ਇਵ ਕਹੈ ਨਾਨਕੁ ਸਚੁ ਸੋਹਿਲਾ ਸਚੇ ਘਰਿ ਗਾਵਹੈ॥੩੮॥੩॥[143]

੯੨————੮[144]

ੴ ਸਤਿਗੁਰ

ਰਾਗੁ ਰਾਮਕਲੀ[145]

੧੦੧* ਬਨਾਰਸੀ ਤਪੁ ਕਰਿ ਉਲਟੀ ਤੀਰਥ ਮਰਿ
ਅਗਨਿ ਦਹੈ ਕਾਇਆ ਕਲਸੁ ਕੀਜੈ॥. . .

ਅਸਥ ਰਾਇ ਨਦੁ ਰਾਜਾ ਮੇਰਾ ਰਾਮਚੰਦੁ
ਬਿਨਵੈ ਨਾਮਾ ਤਤ ਰਸੁ ਅੰਮ੍ਰਿਤ ਪੀਜੈ॥੪॥੧॥

੧੦੧ # ਮਦਰ ਚੁਨਤ ਮਾਸ ਦਸ ਲਾਗੇ ਦੁਇ ਬਮ ਦਸੇ ਦੁਆਰਾ॥
ਸੋਈ ਜੋਗੀ ਆਸਣਿ ਬੈਠਾ ਸੋਈ ਕਰਤ ਉਧਾਰਾ॥. . .

ਪਵਣ ਕਰਿ ਕੈ ਭਸਮ ਉਡਾਵਉ ਮਨ ਕੀ ਮੁਦ੍ਰਉ ਮਾਈ॥
ਮਨ ਪਟਵਤੇ ਉਪਰਿ ਆਸਣੁ ਤਹ ਕਸੀਰਿ ਲਿਵਲਾਈ॥੪॥੨॥[146]

੧੦੨ # ਦੁਪਰੀਤੇ ਸੁਪਰੀਤੇ ਅਨਿਕ ਕਰਮ ਕੀਤੇ
ਮਰਨ ਜੀਵਣ ਕੀ ਬੁਝਿ ਲੇ ਬਾਜੀ॥. . .

ਸੁਨ ਮੰਧੇ ਨਿਰੰਕਾਰੀ ਤੜਾ ਜੈਸੇ ਰਮਤਕਾਰੀ
ਧਨੁਖ ਕੀ ਰੇਖਿਆ ਅਨੂਪ ਬਾਣੀ॥

ਸਹਜ ਕੀ ਪੰਖੜੀ ਜਾਗੀ ਤਾ ਸੁਮੰਧੇ ਭਇਆ ਰਾਗੀ
ਭਨਥ ਬੇਣੀ ਤੇਰੀ ਜੁਗਤਿ ਐਸੀ॥੪॥੩॥[147]

੧੦੩* # ਨਾਰਦੁ ਕਹੈ ਸੁਨਹੁ ਨਰਾਇਣ ਬੈਕੁੰਠਿ ਵਸੈ ਕਿ ਕਉਲਾਸੰ॥
ਜਹ ਮਮ ਕਥਾ ਤਹੀ ਹਉ ਨਿਹਚਲ ਬਸਨ ਮਦਰਿ ਵਾਸੰ॥. . .

ਜੋ ਭਗਤ ਮੇਰਾ ਜਸੁ ਗਾਵਵਿ ਤੇ ਭਗਤਾ ਮਮ ਸਾਰੰ॥
ਉਨ ਕਉ ਜਿਵਾਏ ਮਇ ਜੇਵਾ ਉਨ ਕਉ ਪੀਆਏ ਮਇ ਪੀਆ
ਨਾਮਦੇਉ ਤਿਨ ਪਹਿ ਵਾਰੰ॥੪॥੪॥[148]

੧੦੪*　ਅੰਤਰਿ ਮਲੁ ਜੇ ਤੀਰਥ ਨਾਵੈ ਤਿਸੈ ਬੈਕੁੰਠਿ ਨ ਜਾਣਾ॥ . . .
　　　　ਕਹੈ ਕਮੀਰੁ ਤਿਸੈ ਸਰੇਵਹੁ ਬਾਵਰਿਆ ਸੈਸਾਰਾ॥੪॥੫॥[149]

੧੦੪　# ਰਾਜਾ ਰਾਵਣ ਸੁਨਹੁ ਬੇਨਤੀ ਕਹੈ ਮਦੋਦਰਿ ਰਾਣੀ॥
　　　　ਜਿਸ ਕੇ ਗੀਤੈ ਕਾਰਨ ਮੇਟੀ ਤਿਸੁ ਕੇ ਗੀਤੈ ਆਨੀਰੇ॥ . . .
　　　　ਰਿਖ ਬਾਦਰ ਮਿਲਿ ਭਏ ਇਕਠੇ ਤਾ ਕਾ ਅੰਤੁ ਨ ਪਾਇਆ॥
　　　　ਬਦਤਿ ਤਿਲੋਚਨੁ ਮੂਰਖ ਰਾਵਣ ਮਰਣ ਪਤਨੁ ਤੇਰਾ ਆਇਆ॥੪॥੬॥[150]

੧੦੫*　# ਧੰਧਾ ਕਰਤ ਚਰਨ ਕਰ ਬਾਕੇ ਜਨਮੁ ਗਇਆ ਤਨੁ ਛੀਨਾ॥
　　　　ਬਾਕੇ ਨੈਨ ਸਰਵਣ ਸੁਤਿ ਬਾਕੇ ਕਪਟ ਰਹਿਆ ਮਨ ਲੀਨਾ॥ . . .
　　　　ਕਹਤੁ ਕਮੀਰੁ ਸੁਨਹੁ ਮਨਾ ਮੇਰੇ ਕਰਿ ਲੇਹੁ ਜੋ ਕਿਛੁ ਕਰਨਾ॥
　　　　ਲਖ ਚਉਰਾਸੀ ਫੇਰੁ ਪੜੈਗਾ ਅੰਤਿ ਨਿਹਾਇਤ ਮਰਨਾ॥੩॥੭॥[151]

੧੦੬　# ਡਾਇਣ ਡਾਰੀ ਸੁਨਿ ਰੇ ਡੋਰਾ ਸਿੰਘ ਰਹਿਆ ਬਨੁ ਘੇਰੇ॥
　　　　ਪੰਚ ਕਟੰਬ ਗਿਰਹਿ ਮਹਿ ਜੂਝੇ ਤਾ ਵਜੇ ਸਬਦ ਘਨੇਰੇ॥ . . .
　　　　ਸੋਈ ਪੰਡਿਤ ਸੋਈ ਪੜਿਆ ਜੋ ਇਸ ਪਦੈ ਵੀਚਾਰੈ॥
　　　　ਕਹਤੁ ਕਮੀਰ ਸੋਈ ਗੁਰ ਮੇਰਾ ਜਿ ਆਪਿ ਤਰੈ ਮੋਹਿ ਤਾਰੈ॥੩॥੮॥[152]

੧ੴ ਸਤਿਗੁਰ ਪਰਸਾਦਿ ਸਚੁਨਾਮੁ ਕਰਤਾਰੁ ਨਿਰਭਉ
ਨਿਰੀਕਾਰ ਅਕਾਲ ਮੂਰਤਿ ਅਜੂਨੀ ਸੰਭਉ

ਰਾਮਕਲੀ ਕਬੀਰ ਕੀ[153]

੧੧੧*　ਕਾਇਆ ਕਲਾਲਨਿ ਲਾਹਨਿ ਮੇਲਉ ਗੁਰ ਕਾ ਸਬਦੁ ਗੁੜੁ ਕੀਨੁ ਰੇ॥ . . .
　　　　ਕਹੁ ਕਮੀਰ ਸਗਲੇ ਮਦ ਦੇਖੇ ਏਹੁ ਮਹਾਰਸੁ ਸਾਚੁ ਰੇ॥੪॥੧॥

੧੧੨*　ਆਨੀਲੇ ਕਾਗਦੁ ਕਾਟੀਲੇ ਗੁਡੀ ਅਕਾਸ ਮੰਧੇ ਭਰਮੀਅਲੈ॥ . . .
　　　　ਕਹਤ ਨਾਮਦੇਉ ਸੁਨਹੁ ਤਿਲੋਚਨ ਬਾਲਕੁ ਹਾਥ ਰਖਲੀਅਲੈ॥
　　　　ਆਪੁਨੇ ਮੰਦਰਿ ਕਾਜਿ ਬਿਰੁਧੀ ਚੀਤੁ ਸੁ ਬਾਲਕਿ ਰਾਖੀਲੈ॥੪॥੨॥

੧੧੨　ਵੇਦ ਪੁਰਾਨ ਸਾਸਤ ਅਨਰਾਗੀ ਗੀਤ ਕਵਿਤ ਨ ਗਾਉਗੋ॥ . . .
　　　　ਨਾਮਾ ਕਹੈ ਚਿਤੁ ਹਰਿ ਸਉ ਰਾਤਾ ਸੁਨਿ ਸਮਾਧ ਸਮਾਉਗੋ॥੪॥੩॥

੧੧੩　ਚੰਦੁ ਸੂਰਜੁ ਦੁਇ ਜੋਤਿ ਸਰੂਪੁ॥
　　　　ਜੋਤਿ ਅੰਦਰਿ ਬ੍ਰਹਮੁ ਅਨੂਪੁ॥ . . .
　　　　ਹੀਰਾ ਦੇਖਿ ਹੀਰੇ ਕਰਉ ਅਦੇਸ॥
　　　　ਕਹੁ ਕਬੀਰ ਨਿਰੰਜਨ ਅਲੇਖ॥੨॥੪॥

੧੧੪*　ਜੈ ਮੁਖਿ ਵੇਦੁ ਗਾਇਤੀ ਨਿਕਸੈ ਸੋ ਕਿਉ ਬ੍ਰਹਮਨੁ ਬਿਰਹੈ ਕਰੈ॥ . . . [ਕਬੀਰ]
　　　　ਹਮਰੇ ਰਾਮ ਨਾਮ ਕਹਿ ਉਬਰਹਿ ਬੇਦ ਭਰੋਸੇ ਪਾਡੇ ਤੁਮ ਡੂਬਿ ਮਰਹੁ॥੩॥੫॥

੧੧੪　ਬੰਧਚਿ ਬੰਧਨੁ ਪਾਇਆ॥
　　　　ਮੁਕਤੈ ਗੁਰਿ ਅਨਲੁ ਬੁਝਾਇਆ॥ . . .
　　　　ਕਰਿ ਕਰਤਾ ਉਤਰਸਿ ਪਾਰੰ॥
　　　　ਕਹਤੁ ਕਬੀਰਾ ਸਾਰੰ॥੪॥੬॥

88

ਪੜੀਐ ਗੁਨੀਐ ਭਉ ਸਭ ਸੁਨੀਐ ਅਨਭਉ ਭਾਉ ਨ ਦਰਸੈ॥

ਲੋਹਾ ਹਿਰਨ ਹੋਰ ਨ ਹੋਇ ਕੈਸੇ ਜਉ ਪਰਸਹਿ ਨ ਪਰਸੈ॥ . . .

ਕਹੁ ਰਵਿਦਾਸ ਸਭੇ ਨਹੀ ਸਮਝਸਿ ਭੂਲਿ ਪਰੇ ਸਭਿ ਬਉਰਾ॥

ਮੈ ਆਧਾਰੁ ਨਾਮੁ ਨਰਇਨ ਜੀਵਨ ਪਰਾਨ ਧਨੁ ਮੋਰਾ॥੮॥੧੭॥

੧੧੬* ਤਰਵਰੁ ਏਕੁ ਅਨੰਤ ਡਾਲ ਸਾਖ ਪਤ ਪੁਹਪ ਰਸਿ ਭਰਿਆ॥ . . .

ਕਹਤੁ ਕਬੀਰੁ ਹਉ ਤਾਕਾ ਸੇਵਕੁ ਜਿਨਿ ਏਹੁ ਬਿਰਵਾ ਦੇਖਿਆ॥੩॥੧੮॥

੧੧੬ ਗੁੜੁ ਕਰਿ ਗਿਆਨੁ ਧਿਆਨੁ ਕਰਿ ਮਹੂਆ ਭਉ ਭਾਠੀ ਮਨ ਧਾਰਾ॥

ਦਾਸੁ ਕਬੀਰ ਉਸੀ ਮਦਿ ਮਾਤਾ ਉਚ ਕਿਨਾ ਕਬਹੂ ਜਾਈ॥੩॥੧੯॥

੧੧੭* ਮਾਇਆ ਨ ਹੋਤੀ ਬਾਪੁ ਨ ਹੋਤਾ ਕਰਮੁ ਨ ਹੋਤੀ ਕਾਇਆ॥

ਨਾਮਾ ਪਰਟਵੈ ਪਰਮ ਤਤੁ ਹੈ ਸਤਿਗੁਰ ਹੋਇ ਲਖਾਇਆ॥੭॥੨੦॥

੧੧੭ ਮਦੁ ਮੋਨਿ ਦਇਆ ਕਰਿ ਝੋਲੀ ਪਤ ਕਾ ਕਰਹੁ ਵੀਚਾਰੁ ਰੇ॥ . . .

ਕਹਤੁ ਕਬੀਰ ਸੁਨਹੁ ਰੇ ਸੰਤਹੁ ਧਰਮ ਦਇਆ ਕਰਿ ਵਾੜੀ॥੩॥੨੧॥

੧੧੭----੪

੧੧੮* ਕਵਨਿ ਕਾਜ ਸਿਰੇ ਜਗ ਭੀਤਰਿ ਜਨਮਿ ਕਵਨੁ ਫਲੁ ਪਾਇਆ॥ . . .

ਕਹਤੁ ਕਬੀਰੁ ਭੀਰ ਜਨ ਰਾਖਹੁ ਸੇਵਾ ਕਰਉ ਤੁਮਾਰੀ॥੫॥੨੨॥

੧੧੯* ਐਸਾ ਸਿਮਰਨੁ ਕਰਿ ਮਨ ਮਾਹਿ॥ . . .

ਕਹੁ ਕਬੀਰ ਜਾ ਕਾ ਨਹੀ ਅੰਤੁ॥

ਤਿਸੁ ਆਗੇ ਕਿਛੁ ਤੰਤੁ ਨ ਮੰਤੁ॥੮॥੨੩॥

੧੨੦ ਤੂ ਮੇਰਾ ਮੇਰੁ ਪਰਬਤੁ ਸੁਆਮੀ ਓਟ ਗਹੀ ਮੁਖ ਤੇਰੀ॥ . . .

ਰਾਮ ਕਬੀਰਾ ਏਕ ਭਏ ਹੈ ਕੋਇ ਨ ਸਕੈ ਪਛਾਨੀ॥੬॥੨੪॥

੧੨੧* ਸਤਾ ਮਾਨਉ ਦੂਤਾ ਡਾਨਉ ਇਹ ਕੁਟਵਾਰੀ ਮੇਰੀ॥ . . .

ਗੁਰ ਦੀਨੀ ਵਸਤੁ ਕਬੀਰ ਕਉ ਲੇਵਹੁ ਵਸਤੁ ਸਮਾਲਿ॥੪॥੨੫॥[154]

ੴ ਸਤਿਗੁਰ ਪਰਸਾਦਿ ਸਚੁਨਾਮੁ ਕਰਤਾਰੁ ਨਿਰਭਉ

ਨਿਰੀਕਾਰ ਅਕਾਲ ਮੂਰਤਿ ਅਜੂਨੀ ਸਭਉ॥

ਰਾਗੁ ਸੋਰਠਿ[155]

ਰਾਗੁ ਸੋਰਠਿ [ਮਹਲਾ ੧]

੧੨੨* ਸਭਨਾ ਮਰਨਾ ਆਇਆ ਵੇਛੋੜਾ ਸਭਨਾ॥ . . .

ਨਾਨਿਕ ਅਵਗਣ ਜੇਤੜੇ ਏਤਲੇ ਗਲੀ ਜਜੀਰ॥ . .

ਆਗੈ ਗਏ ਨਿ ਮਨੀਅਨਿ ਸੇ ਮਾਰਿ ਕਢਹੁ ਵੇ ਪੀਰ॥੪॥੧॥

੧੨੩* ਮਨੁ ਹਾਲੀ ਕਿਰਸਾਣੀ ਕਰਣੀ ਸਰਮੁ ਪਾਣੀ ਤਨੁ ਖੇਤੁ॥ . . .

ਨਾਨਕ ਵੇਧੇ ਨਦਰਿ ਕਰਿ ਚੜੇ ਚਵਗਣ ਵਣੁ॥੪॥੨॥

੧੨੪* ਪੁਤੁ ਧਰਤੀ ਪੁਤੁ ਪਾਣੀ ਆਸਣੁ ਚਾਰਿ ਕੁਡ ਚਉਬਾਰਾ॥ . . .

ਪਟਵਤਿ ਨਾਨਕੁ ਸੁਣਹੁ ਮੇਰੇ ਦੈਆਲਰਾਇ ਡੁਬਤਾ ਪਥਰੁ ਲੀਜੈ॥੪॥੩॥

ਰਾਗੁ ਸੋਰਠਿ ਦਖਣੀ [ਮਹਲਾ ੧]

੧੨੪ ਜਾ ਤਿਸੁ ਭਾਵਾ ਤਦ ਹੀ ਗਾਵਾ ਤਾ ਜਨੁ ਗਾਵੈ ਕਾ ਫਲੁ ਪਾਵਾ॥. . .
ਕਹਤੁ ਨਾਨਿਕੁ ਬੁਝੈ ਕੋ ਵੀਚਾਰੀ॥ ਇਸੁ ਜੁਗ ਮਹਿ ਕਰਣੀ ਸਾਰੀ॥
ਕਰਣੀ ਕੀਰਤਿ ਹੋਈ॥ ਜਾ ਆਪੇ ਮਿਲਿਆ ਸੋਈ॥੪॥੪॥

੧੨੫––––੧੦

੧੨੫ ਮਾਇ ਬਾਧ ਕਉ ਬੇਟੋ ਨੀਕੋ ਸਸੁਰੈ ਚਤੁਰੁ ਜਵਾਈ॥. . .
ਨਾਨਿਕਾ ਗੁਰ ਬਿਨੁ ਭਰਮੁ ਨ ਭਾਗੈ ਸਚਿ ਨਾਮਿ ਵਡਿਆਈ॥੪॥੫॥

੧੨੬* ਹਉ ਪਾਪੀ ਪਤਿਤੁ ਪਰਮ ਪਾਖੰਡੀ ਤੂ ਨਿਰਮਲੁ ਨਿਰੰਕਾਰੀ॥. . .
ਪਰਣਵਤਿ ਨਾਨਕੁ ਦਾਸਨਿ ਦਾਸਾ ਗੁਰਮਤਿ ਜਾਨਿਆ ਸੋਈ॥੪॥੬॥

੧੨੭ ਅਲਖੁ ਅਪਾਰੁ ਅਗੰਮੁ ਅਗੋਚਰੁ ਨਾ ਤਿਸੁ ਕਾਲੁ ਨ ਕਰਮਾ॥. . .
ਤੰਤੈ ਕਉ ਪਰਮਤੰਤੁ ਮਿਲਾਇਓ ਨਾਨਿਕ ਸਰਨਿ ਤੁਮਾਰੀ॥੫॥੭॥

੧੨੮* ਜਿਉ ਮੀਨਾ ਬਿਨੁ ਪਾਣੀਐ ਤਿਉ ਸਾਕਤੁ ਮਰੈ ਪਿਆਸੁ॥. . .
ਸੁਖ ਦੁਖ ਦਾਤਾ ਗੁਰੁ ਮਿਲੇ ਕਹੁ ਨਾਨਕ ਸਿਫਤਿ ਸਮਾਇ॥੪॥੮॥

੧੨੯ ਆਪਨੋ ਘਰੁ ਮੂਸਤ ਰਖਿ ਨ ਸਾਕਹਿ ਕੀ ਪਰ ਘਰ ਜੋਹਨਿ ਲਾਗਾ॥. . .
ਨਾਨਿਕ ਰਾਮ ਨਾਮੁ ਜਪਿ ਗੁਰਮੁਖਿ ਹਰਿ ਪਾਏ ਮਸਤਕਿ ਭਾਗਾ॥੫॥੯॥

੧੨੯ ਤੂ ਪਰਭੁ ਦਾਤਾ ਦਾਨਿ ਮਤਿ ਪੂਰਾ ਹਮ ਥਾਰੇ ਭੇਖਾਰੀ ਜੀਉ॥. . .
ਨਾਨਕ ਗਿਆਨ ਰਤਨੁ ਪਰਗਾਸਿਆ ਹਰਿ ਮਨਿ ਵਸਿਆ ਨਿਰਕਾਰੇ॥੪॥੧੦॥

੧੩੦ ਸਰਬ ਜੀਆ ਸਿਰਿ ਲੇਖੁ ਧੁਰਹੁ ਲਿਖਿਆ ਹੋਈ॥. . .
ਅਪਰੰਪਰੁ ਪਾਰਬਰਹਮੁ ਪਰਮੇਸਰੁ ਨਾਨਿਕ ਗੁਰੁ ਮਿਲਿਆ ਸੋਈ॥੫॥੧੧॥

੧੩੨* ਜਿਸੁ ਨਿਧਿ ਜਲ ਕਾਰਿਟ ਤੁਮਿ ਜਗਿ ਆਏ ਸੋ ਅੰਮ੍ਰਿਤੁ ਗੁਰ ਪਾਹੀ॥. . .
ਜਿਵ ਭਾਵੈ ਤਿਵ ਰਾਖਹੁ ਹਰਿ ਜੀਉ ਜਨ ਨਾਨਿਕ ਸਬਦੁ ਸਾਲਾਹੀ॥੪॥੧੨॥

ਰਾਗੁ ਸੋਰਠਿ ਮਹਲੁ ੩

੧੩੨ ਸਤਗੁਰਿ ਮਿਲਿਐ ਉਲਟੀ ਭਈ ਭਾਈ ਜੀਵਤੁ ਮਰੈ ਤਾ ਬੁਝ ਪਾਇ॥. . .
ਨਾਨਕ ਨਾਉ ਹਰਿ ਪਾਈਐ ਭਾਈ ਗੁਰਸਬਦੀ ਮੇਲਾਇ॥੪॥੧੩॥[156]

੧੩੩ ਤਿਹੀ ਗੁਟੀ ਤ੍ਰੈਭਵਣ ਵਿਆਪਿਆ ਭਾਈ ਗੁਰਮੁਖਿ ਬੁਝ ਬੁਝਾਇ॥. . .
ਨਾਨਿਕ ਨਾਉ ਬੇੜਾ ਨਾਉ ਤੁਲਹੜਾ
ਭਾਈ ਜਿਤੁ ਲਗਿ ਪਾਰਿ ਜਨ ਪਾਇ॥੪॥੧੪॥

੧੩੩––––੧੧

੧੩੪* ਸਤਗੁਰੁ ਸੁਖ ਸਾਗਰ ਜੁਗ ਅੰਤਰਿ ਹੋਰ ਥੈ ਸੁਖ ਨਾਹੀ॥. . .
ਨਾਨਕ ਸਤਿਗੁਰ ਮਿਲੈ ਤਾ ਅੰਖੀ ਵੇਖੈ ਘਰੈ ਅੰਦਰਿ ਸਚੁ ਪਾਏ॥੪॥੧੫॥

੧੩੫* ਬਿਨੁ ਸਤਿਗੁਰ ਸੇਵੇ ਬਹੁਤੁ ਦੁਖ ਲਾਗਾ ਜੁਗ ਚਾਰੇ ਭਰਮਾਈ॥. . .
ਨਾਨਿਕ ਨਾਮਿ ਰਤੇ ਸੁਖ ਪਾਇਆ ਦਰਗਹ ਜਾਪਹਿ ਸੋਈ॥੪॥੧੬॥

੧੩੫ ਸਤਗੁਰ ਸੇਵੇ ਤਾ ਸਹਜ ਧੁਨਿ [ਉਪਜੈ] ਗਤਿ ਮਤਿ ਤਦ ਹੀ ਪਾਏ॥. . .
ਨਾਨਕ ਰਾਮਿ ਨਾਮਿ ਨਿਸਤਾਰਾ ਸਬਦੇ ਹਉਮੈ ਖੋਈ॥੪॥੧੭॥[157]

੧੩੬ ਸੇਵਕ ਸੇਵ ਕਰਹਿ ਸਭਿ ਤੇਰੀ ਜਿਨ ਸਬਦੈ ਸਾਦੁ ਆਇਆ॥. . .

ਨਾਨਕ ਨਾਵਹੁ ਗਤਿ ਮਤਿ ਪਾਈ ਏਹ ਰਾਸਿ ਹਮਾਰੀ॥੪॥੧੯॥

੧੩੭ ਭਗਤਿ ਖਜਾਨਾ ਭਗਤਾ ਕਉ ਦੀਆ ਨਾਉ ਹਰਿ ਧਨੁ ਸਚੁ ਸੋਈ॥ . . .
ਨਾਨਕ ਰਾਮਿ ਨਾਮਿ ਨਿਸਤਾਰਾ ਸਬਦਿ ਰਤੇ ਹਰਿ ਪਾਗਾ॥੪॥੧੯॥

੧੩੮ ਸਾਚੀ ਭਗਤਿ ਸਤਿਗੁਰ ਤੇ ਹੋਵੈ ਸਾਚੀ ਹਿਰਦੈ ਬਾਣੀ॥ . . .
ਨਾਨਕ ਨਾਮੁ ਸਾਲਾਹਨਿ ਸੇ ਜਨ ਸੋਹਨਿ ਦਰਿ ਸਾਚੈ ਪਤਿ ਪਾਈ॥੪॥੨੦॥

੧੪੦* ਦਾਸਨਿ ਦਾਸੁ ਹੋਵੈ ਤਾ ਹਰਿ ਪਾਏ ਵਿਚਹੁ ਆਪੁ ਗਵਾਈ॥ . . .
ਨਾਨਕ ਨਾਮਿ ਰਤਾ ਇਕ ਰੰਗੀ ਸਬਦਿ ਸਵਾਰਣਹਾਰਾ॥੪॥੨੧॥

੧੪੧* ਹਰਿ ਜੀ ਤੁਧਨੋ ਸਦਾ ਸਲਾਹੀ ਪਿਆਰੇ ਜਿਚਰੁ ਘਟ ਅੰਤਰਿ ਹੈ ਸਾਸਾ॥ . . .
ਨਾਨਕ ਨਾਮੁ ਵਸਿਆ ਮਨ ਅੰਤਰਿ ਭਾਈ ਅਵਰੁ ਨ ਦੂਜਾ ਕੋਈ॥੪॥੨੨॥

੧੪੨* ਗੁਰਮੁਖਿ ਭਗਤਿ ਕਰਹਿ ਪ੍ਰਭ ਭਾਵਹਿ ਅਨਦਿਨੁ ਨਾਮੁ ਵਖਾਣੇ॥ . . .
ਨਾਨਕੁ ਦਾਸੁ ਕਹੈ ਬੇਨੰਤੀ ਹਉ ਲਾਗਾ ਤਿਨ ਕੈ ਪਾਏ॥੪॥੨੩॥

੧੪੩ ਸੋ ਸਿਖੁ ਸਾਖੀ ਬੰਧਪੁ ਹੈ ਭਾਈ ਜਿ ਗੁਰ ਕੇ ਭਾਣੇ ਵਿਚਿ ਆਵੈ॥ . . .
ਨਾਨਕ ਨਾਮ ਵਸੈ ਮਨ ਅੰਤਰਿ ਵਿਚੇ ਆਪੁ ਗਵਾਈਐ॥੪॥੨੪॥

੧੪੪----੧੨

ੴ ਸਤਿਗੁਰ ਪਰਸਾਦਿ ਸਚੁਨਾਮੁ ਕਰਤਾਰੁ ਨਿਰਭਉ
ਨਿਰੀਕਾਰ ਅਕਾਲ ਮੂਰਤਿ ਅਜੂਨੀ ਸੰਭਉ॥੧॥

ਰਾਗੁ ਸੋਰਠਿ ਅਸਟਪਦੀਆ [ਮਹਲਾ ੧]

੧੪੫ ਦੁਬਿਧਾ ਨ ਪੜਉ ਹਰਿ ਬਿਨੁ ਹੋਰ ਨ ਪੂਜਾ ਮੜੈ ਮਸਾਣਿ ਨ ਜਾਈ॥ . . .
ਪੂਰਾ ਬੈਰਾਗੀ ਸਹਜਿ ਸੁਭਾਗੀ ਸਚੁ ਨਾਨਕ ਮਨੁ ਮਾਨੈ॥੧॥੧॥158

੧੪੮* ਆਸਾ ਮਨਸਾ ਬੰਧਨੀ ਭਾਈ ਕਰਮ ਧਰਮ ਬੰਧਕਾਰੀ॥ . . .
ਧਨੁ ਵਪਾਰੀਆ ਨਾਨਕਾ ਭਾਈ ਮੇਲਿ ਕਰੇ ਵਪਾਰੁ॥੨॥

੧੫੦* ਤੂ ਗੁਣ ਦਾਤਾ ਉਜਲੋ ਭਾਈ ਨਿਰਮਲ ਮੈਲੁ ਨ ਹੋਇ॥ . . .
ਖਿਨ ਪਲੁ ਰਾਮੁ ਰਿਦੈ ਵਸੈ ਭਾਈ ਨਾਨਕ ਮਿਲਣੁ ਸੁਭਾਇ॥੧੦॥੩॥159

੧੫੨* ਜਿਨੀ ਸਤਿਗੁਰ ਸੇਵਿਆ ਪਿਆਰੇ ਤਿਨਕੇ ਸਾਥ ਤਰੇ॥ . . .
ਧਨੁ ਲੇਖਾਰੀ ਨਾਨਕਾ ਪਿਆਰੇ ਸਚੁ ਲਿਖੈ ਉਰਧਾਰਿ॥੮॥੪॥

ਰਾਗੁ ਸੋਰਠਿ ਮਹਲੁ ੩

੧੫੪* ਨਿਗੁਣਿਆ ਨੋ ਆਪੇ ਬਖਸਿ ਲਏ ਭਾਈ ਸਤਿਗੁਰ ਕੀ ਸੇਵਾ ਲਾਇ॥ . . .
ਨਾਨਕ ਨਾਮੁ ਹਰਿ ਮਨਿ ਵਸੈ ਭਾਈ ਤਿਸੁ ਬਿਘਨੁ ਨ ਲਾਗੈ ਕੋਇ॥੮॥੫॥

੧੫੪----੧੩

੧੫੫ ਹਰਿ ਜੀਉ ਸਬਦੇ ਜਾਪਦਾ ਭਾਈ ਪੂਰੈ ਭਾਗਿ ਮਿਲਾਇ॥ . . .
ਨਾਨਕ ਨਾਮੁ ਸਮਾਲਿ ਤੂ ਭਾਈ ਅਪਰੰਪਰੁ ਗੁਣੀ ਗਹੀਰੁ॥੮॥੬॥

੧੫੭* ਭਗਤਾ ਦੀ ਸਦਾ ਤੂ ਰਖਦਾ ਪ੍ਰਭ ਜੀਉ ਧੁਰਿ ਤੂ ਰਖਦਾ ਆਇਆ॥ . . .
ਨਾਨਕ ਤਿਨ ਕੈ ਹਉ ਸਦਾ ਬਲਿਹਾਰੈ ਜਿਨਾ ਹਰਿ ਰਖਿਆ ਉਰਿਧਾਰਾ॥੮॥੭॥

੧੫੯* ਸਤਿਗੁਰਿ ਮਿਲਿਐ ਉਲਟੀ ਭਈ ਭਾਈ ਜੀਵਤ ਮਰੈ ਤਾ ਬੂਝ ਪਾਈ॥ . . .
ਨਾਨਕ ਨਾਉ ਬੇੜਾ ਨਾਉ ਤੁਲਹੜਾ ਭਾਈ ਜਿਤੁ ਲਗਿ ਪਾਰਿ ਜਨ ਪਾਇ॥੪॥੮॥160

੧੬੦* ਨਾ ਬੇੜੀ ਨਾ ਤੁਲਹੜਾ ਭਾਈ ਕਿਨ ਵਿਧਿ ਪਾਰਿ ਪਾਇ॥. . .
      ਨਵ ਨਿਧਿ ਨਾਮੁ ਪਲੈ ਪਵੈ ਭਾਈ ਤਾ ਸਹਜੇ ਰਹੈ ਸਮਾਇ॥੪॥੧॥

੧੬੦   ਮਨ ਰੇ ਸਾਚੀ ਲਿਵ ਰਹੁ ਤੂ ਲਾਗਾ॥. . .
      ਆਪੁ ਗਇਆ ਤਾ ਸਤਗੁਰ ਮਿਲਿਆ ਨਾਨਿਕ ਹਰਿ ਗੁਣ ਗਾਇ॥੪॥੨॥

        ੧ਓ ਸਤਿਗੁਰ ਪਰਸਾਦਿ ਸਚੁਨਾਮੁ ਕਰਤਾਰੁ ਨਿਰਭਉ
           ਨਿਰੀਕਾਰ ਅਕਾਲ ਮੂਰਤਿ ਅਜੂਨੀ ਸੰਭਉ

ਰਾਗੁ ਸੋਰਠਿ ਕਬੀਰ ਨਾਮੇ ਕੀ

੧੬੧* ਜਾ ਕਾ ਠਾਕੁਰੁ ਨੀਕਾ ਹੋਵੈ॥   ਸੋ ਜਨੁ ਪਰ ਘਰਿ ਜਾਤੁ ਨ ਸੋਹੈ॥. . .
      ਕਹਤੁ ਕਬੀਰੁ ਈਸਰੁ ਜਗਿ ਸੋਈ ਜਾ ਕੈ ਹਿਰਦੇ ਅਵਰੁ ਨ ਕੋਈ॥੫॥੧॥[161]

੧੬੧   ਦੁਇ ਦੁਇ ਲੋਚਨ ਪੇਖਾ॥
      ਮੈ ਹਰਿ ਬਿਨੁ ਅਵਰੁ ਨ ਵੇਖਾ॥. . .
      ਕਹੁ ਕਬੀਰ ਰੰਗਿ ਰਾਤਾ॥
      ਮਿਲਿਆ ਜਗਜੀਵਨੁ ਦਾਤਾ॥੪॥੨॥

੧੬੩* ਬੁਤ ਪੂਜਿ ਪੂਜਿ ਹਿੰਦੂ ਮੂਏ ਤੁਰਕ ਮੂਏ ਸਿਰੁ ਨਿਵਾਈ॥. . .
      ਹਰਿ ਕੇ ਨਾਮ ਬਿਨੁ ਕਿਨਿ ਗਤਿ ਪਾਈ ਕਹੁ ਉਪਦੇਸੁ ਕਬੀਰਾ॥੪॥੩॥

੧੬੩   ਦੁਲੰਭੁ ਜਨਮੁ ਪੁਨਿ ਫਲ ਪਾਇਆ ਬਿਰਥਾ ਜਾਤੁ ਹੈ ਅਬਥੇਕੀ॥. . .
      ਕਾਹੁ ਰਵਿਦਾਸੁ ਉਦਾਸੁ ਦਾਸ ਮਤਿ ਪਰਹਰੁ ਕਰੋਹੁ ਕਰਹੁ ਜੀਅ ਦਇਆ॥੩॥੪॥

੧੬੩----੧੪

੧੬੪   ਜਬ ਹਮ ਹੋਤੇ ਤਬ ਤੂ ਨਾਹੀ ਜਬ ਤੂ ਹੈ ਹਮਿ ਨਾਹੀ॥. . .
      ਕਹੁ ਰਵਿਦਾਸ ਹਾਥ ਪੈ ਨੇੜਾ ਸਹਜੇ ਹੋਇ ਸੁ ਹੋਈ॥੪॥੫॥

੧੬੫   ਜਬ ਦੇਖਾ ਤਬ ਗਾਵਾ॥
      ਤਉ ਜਨ ਧੀਰਕ ਪਾਵਾ॥. . .
      ਗੁਰਪ੍ਰਸਾਦਿ ਮੈ ਨਿਜ ਘਰਿ ਜਾਨਿਆ॥
      ਜਨ ਨਾਮਾ ਸਹਜ ਸਮਾਨਿਆ॥੪॥੬॥

੧੬੬   ਰਿਦੈ ਕਪਟੁ ਸੁਧੁ ਮਨਿ ਗਿਆਨੀ॥
      ਕਾਹੇ ਬਿਰੋਲਹੁ ਪਾਨੀ॥. . .
      ਕਹੈ ਕਬੀਰ ਵੀਚਾਰੀ॥
      ਭਉ ਸਾਗਰ ਤਾਰ ਮੁਰਾਰੀ॥੨॥੭॥[162]

੧੬੧* ਸੁਖ ਸਾਗਰੁ ਸੁਰਤਰੁ ਚਿੰਤਾਮਨਿ ਕਾਮਧੇਨੁ ਵਸਿ ਜਾ ਕੇ॥. . .
      ਕਹੁ ਰਵਿਦਾਸ ਪਰਗਾਸੁ ਰਿਦੈ ਹਰਿ ਜਨਮ ਮਰਨ ਭਉ ਭਾਗੀ॥੩॥੮॥[163]

੧੬੧   ਤਿਸੁ ਬਾਝੁ ਨ ਜੀਵਿਆ ਜਾਈ॥
      ਸੋ ਮਿਲੈ ਤ ਘਾਲ ਅਘਾਈ॥. . .
      ਕਬੀਰੈ ਸੋ ਧਨੁ ਪਾਇਆ॥

92

ਹਰਿ ਭੇਟਤ ਆਪੁ ਗਵਾਇਆ॥੪॥੮॥

੧੬੭* ਐਸਾ ਇਕੁ ਨਾਮੁ ਰਤਨੁ ਨਿਰਮੋਲਕੁ ਪੁਨਿ ਪਦਾਰਥੁ ਪਾਇਆ॥. . .
ਕਹੁ ਭੀਖਨ ਦੁਇ ਨੈਨ ਸੰਤੋਖੇ ਜਹ ਦੇਖਾ ਤਹ ਸੋਈ॥੨॥੧੦॥

੧੬੮ ਨੈਨੀ ਨੀਰੁ ਵਹੈ ਤਨੁ ਖੀਨਾ ਭਏ ਕੇਸ ਦੁਧਵਾਨੀ॥. . .
ਗੁਰਪ੍ਰਸਾਦਿ ਕਹੈ ਜਨੁ ਭੀਖਨੁ ਪਾਵਉ ਮੋਖ ਦੁਆਰਾ॥੩॥੧੧॥

੧੬੯ ਜਉ ਹਮ ਬਾਧੇ ਮੋਹ ਫਾਸ ਹਮ ਪ੍ਰੇਮ ਬੰਧਨਿ ਤੁਮ ਬਾਧੇ॥. . .
ਕਹੁ ਰਵਿਦਾਸ ਭਗਤਿ ਇਕ ਬਾਢੀ ਅਬ ਇਹ ਕਾਸਉ ਕਹੀਐ॥
ਜਾ ਕਾਰਨਿ ਹਮ ਤੁਮ ਸੇਵਹਉ ਸੋ ਦੁਖੁ ਅਜਹੁ ਸਹੀਐ॥੪॥੧੨॥

੧੭੦* ਜਾ ਕੇ ਨਿਗਮ ਦੂਧ ਕੇ ਬਾਟਾ॥
ਸਮੁੰਦ ਵਲੋਵਨ ਕਉ ਮਾਟਾ॥. . .
ਸੁ ਰਸੁ ਕਬੀਰੈ ਜਾਨਿਆ॥
ਮੇਰਾ ਗੁਰਪ੍ਰਸਾਦੀ ਮਨੁ ਮਾਨਿਆ॥੪॥੧੩॥

੧੭੦ ਕਿਆ ਪੜੀਐ ਕਿਆ ਗੁਨੀਐ॥
ਕਿਆ ਵੇਦ ਪੁਰਾਨੀ ਸੁਨੀਐ॥. . .
ਕਹੁ ਕਬੀਰ ਜਬਿ ਜਾਨਿਆ॥. . .
ਨ ਪਤੀਜੈ ਤਾ ਕਹਾ ਕਰੀਜੈ॥੪॥੧੪॥

੧੭੦----੧੫

੧੭੧ ਜਬ ਜਾਰੀਐ ਤਬ ਹੋਇ ਭਸਮੁ [ਤਨ] ਕਿਰਮ ਦਲ ਖਾਈ॥. . . [ਕਬੀਰ]
ਝੂਠੀ ਮਾਇਆ ਆਪੁ ਬੰਧਾਇਆ ਜਿਉ ਨਲਨੀ ਭਰਮਿ ਸੂਆ॥੪॥੧੫॥

੧੭੨ ਪਾੜ ਪੜੋਸਨਿ ਪੂਛਿ ਲੇ ਨਾਮਾ ਕੈ ਪਹਿ ਛੰਨਿ ਛਵਾਈ॥. . .
ਨਾਮੇ ਕੇ ਸੁਆਮੀ ਸੀਅ ਬਹੋਰੀ ਲੰਕ ਭਭੀਖਨ ਆਪਿਓ॥੪॥੧੬॥

੧੭੩* ਜੇ ਤੁਮ ਨ ਤੋਰਹੁ ਤਾ ਹਮ ਨਹੀ ਤੋਰਾ॥. . .
ਰਾਮ ਭਜਨਿ ਕਟਹਿ ਜਮ ਫਾਸਾ॥   ਭਗਤਿ ਹੇਤੁ ਗਾਵੈ ਰਵਿਦਾਸਾ॥੪॥੧੭॥

੧੭੩ ਬੇਦ ਪੁਰਾਨ ਸਭੈ ਮਤਿ ਸੁਨਿ ਕੈ ਕਰੀ ਕਰਮ ਕੀ ਆਸਾ॥. . .
ਕਹੈ ਕਮੀਰ ਨਰ ਭਏ ਖਾਲਸੈ ਰਾਮ ਭਗਤਿ ਜਿਹ ਜਾਨੀ॥੪॥੧੮॥[164]

੧੭੪* # ਜੋ ਪੂਜਾ ਹਰਿ ਭਲ ਮਾਨੈ ਸਾ ਪੂਜਨਹਾਰ ਨਾ ਜਾਨੈ॥
ਗੁਸਈਆ ਭਈ ਬਿਕਲ ਮਤਿ ਮੇਰੀ॥. . .
ਕਹੁ ਕਮੀਰੈ ਸੁ ਗਾਵਾ ਮੈ ਨ ਗਾਵਾ ਆਪੁ ਲਖਾਵਾ॥
ਜੋਇ ਸੁਖ ਦੁ[ਖ] ਮਾਹਿ ਸਮਾਨਾ ਸੋਈ ਪੂਜਨਹਰੁ ਸਿਆਨਾ॥੩॥੧੯॥[165]

੧੭੪ # ਤੂ ਦੈਆਲੁ ਮੈ ਦਮ ਦ ਮੰਦਰੁ ਵਾਜਉ ਜੈਸੇ ਵਜਾਵੈ॥. . .
ਰਾਮ ਜਪਤ ਜਨ ਕਹਾ ਸਮਾਏ ਕੋਈ ਹੈ ਕਮੀਰ ਸਮਝਾਵੈ॥੨॥੨੦॥[166]

੧੭੫* ਸੁਖ ਸਾਗਰ ਸੁਰਤਰਿ ਚਿੰਤਾਮਨਿ ਕਾਮਧੇਨੁ ਵਸਿ ਜਾ ਕੈ॥
ਕਹੁ ਰਵਿਦਾਸ ਪਰਗਾਸੁ ਰਿਦੈ ਹਰਿ ਜਨਮ ਮਰਨ ਭਉ ਭਾਗੀ॥੩॥੨੧॥[167]

੧੭੫* # ਮਾਟੀ ਖੋਦਿ ਕੇ ਭੀਤਿ ਉਸਾਰੀ ਪਸੂ ਕਹੈ ਘਰੁ ਮੇਰਾ॥. . . [ਕਬੀਰ]
ਗਏ ਪਖੰਡੀਆ ਬਾਜੀ ਨ ਪਾਟੀ ਕਵਨ ਕਾਹੂ ਕੈ ਆਵੈ॥੩॥੨੨॥[168]

੧੭੫ ਆਰ ਨਹੀ ਜਿਤੁ ਤੂਆ ਰਬੀ ਹੋਵੈ ਤਾ ਠਾਉ ਅਰੂਆ॥. . .

93

ਰਵਿਦਾਸ ਭਣੈ ਸਿਰੀ ਰਾਮਾ ਮਏ ਨਾਹੀ ਜਮ ਸਿਉ ਕਾਮਾ॥

ਹਉ ਗਢਿ ਗਢਿ ਬਹਤੁ ਵਿਗੁਤਾ ਵਿਣੁ ਗਢੇ ਧੁਰੇ ਪਹੁਤਾ॥੨॥੨੩॥[169]

ੴ ਸਤਿਗੁਰ ਪਰਸਾਦੁ ਸਚੁਨਾਮੁ ਕਰਤਾਰੁ ਨਿਰਭਉ

ਨਿਰੀਕਾਰ ਅਕਾਲ ਮੂਰਤਿ ਅਜੂਨੀ ਸੰਭਉ॥੧॥

ਰਾਗੁ ਮਲਾਰ[170]

ਰਾਗੁ ਮਲਾਰ ਗੁਰੂ ਬਾਬੇ ਦਾ [ਮਹਲਾ ੧]

੧੮੩* ਖਾਣਾ ਪੀਅਣਾ ਹਸਣਾ ਸਵਣਾ ਵਿਸਰਿ ਗਇਆ ਹੈ ਮਰਣਾ॥. . .

ਨਾਨਿਕ ਰੁਤਿ ਸੁਹਾਵੀ ਸਾਈ ਵਿਣੁ ਨਾਵੈ ਰੁਤਿ ਕੇਹਿ॥੪॥੧॥

੧੮੩ ਪਵਣੈ ਪਾਣੀ ਜਾਣੈ ਜਾਤਿ॥

ਕਾਇਆ ਅਗਨਿ ਕਰੇ ਨਿਭਰਾਤਿ॥. . .

ਵਿਚ ਸਨਾਤੀ ਸੇਵਕੁ ਹੋਇ॥

ਨਾਨਿਕ ਪਾਣੀਆ ਪਹਿਰੈ ਸੋਇ॥੪॥੨॥

੧੮੪ ਇਕੁ ਦੁਖੁ ਵੇਛੋੜਾ ਇਕ ਦੁਖ ਭੁਖ॥

ਇਕ ਦੁਖ ਸਕਤਵਾਰ ਜਮਦੂਤ॥. . .

ਦੁਖ ਰੋਗ ਸਭਿ ਗਇਆ ਹੈ ਗਵਾਇ॥

ਨਾਨਕ ਛੁਟਿਐ ਸਾਚੈ ਨਾਇ॥੪॥੩॥

੧੮੫* ਦੁਖ ਮਹੁਰਾ ਮਾਰਣੁ ਹਰਿ ਕਾ ਨਾਮੁ॥. . .

ਤੇ ਧਨਵੰਤੁ ਦਿਸਹਿ ਘਰ ਜਾਇ॥

ਨਾਨਿਕ ਜਨਨੀ ਧੰਨੀ ਮਾਇ॥੪॥੪॥

੧੮੫ ਬਾਗੇ ਕਾਪੜ ਬੋਲੈ ਬੈਣ॥

ਲੰਮਾ ਨੰਕੁ ਕਾਲੇ ਤੇਰੇ ਨੈਣ॥. . .

ਨਾਨਿਕ ਨਦਰਿ ਕਰੇ ਤਾ ਜਪੀ ਕਰਿ ਗੁਰੁ ਪੀਰੁ॥

ਸਚਿ ਸਮਾਵੈ ਏਹੁ ਸਰੀਰੁ॥੪॥੫॥

ਰਾਗੁ ਮਲਾਰ ਮਹਲ ੩

੧੮੬ ਕਿ ਇਹੁ ਮਨੁ ਗਿਰਹੀ ਕਿ ਇਹ ਮਨ ਉਦਾਸੀ॥. . .

ਕਹਤੁ ਨਾਨਿਕ ਕਵਨ ਬਿਧਿ ਕਰੇ ਕਿਆ ਕੋਇ॥. . .

ਸਾਸਤ ਵੇਦ ਕੀ ਫਿਰਿ ਕੂਕ ਨ ਹੋਇ॥ ੫॥੬॥

੧੮੬————੧੬

ਰਾਗੁ ਮਲਾਰ ਬਾਬੇ ਦਾ ਮਹਲ ੩

੧੮੭ ਨਿਰੰਕਾਰੁ ਅਕਾਰੁ ਹੈ ਆਪੇ ਆਪੇ ਭਰਮੁ ਭੁਲਾਏ॥. . .

ਕਹਿਤੁ ਨਾਨਿਕ ਗੁਰਪਰਸਾਦੀ ਬੁਝੈ ਕੋਈ ਐਸਾ ਕਰੇ ਵੀਚਾਰਾ॥. . .

ਜਿਉ ਜਲ ਉਪਰਿ ਫੇਨ ਬੁਦਬਦਾ [ਤੈਸਾ ਇਹ ਸੰਸਾਰਾ]॥

94

जिस ते होआ तिसै समाना चूकि गइआ पसारा॥४॥७॥

रागु मलार दखणी [महला १]

१८८ साची सुरति नामि नाही तिपते हउमै करत गवाइआ॥ . . .
भगति हीनु नानकु हरि देखहु इकु नाम मिलै उरिधारा॥४॥८॥

१८९ जिनि धन पिर का साद न जानिआ सा बिलख बदनि कुलखानी॥¹⁷¹ . . .
नानक राम नामु रिद अंतरि गुरमुखि मेलि मिलाई॥५॥९॥

१९१* पर दारा पर धन तजि लोभा हउमै बिखै बिकारा॥ . . .
नानक गुरमुखि महलि बुलाईऐ हरि मेलै मेलनहारा॥४॥१०॥

१९१----१९६¹⁷²

रागु मलार महलु ३

१९२ जिनी हुकमु पछाणिआ से हरि मिले हउमै सबदि जलाइ॥ . . .
नानक नामु समालि तू हरि दरि सदा सोभा पाइ॥४॥११॥

१९३* सतगुर ते पावै घरु दरु महलु सु बाणु॥ . . .
नानक नामु धिआइ सदा तू भउ सागर जितु पावहि पारि॥४॥१२॥

१९३ बेदु बाणी जग वरतदा त्रै गुण करे वीचारु॥ . . .
नानक नामे ही पति ऊपजै हरि नामे रहा समाइ॥८॥१३॥

१९५ जीउ पिंड पराण सभि तिसदे घटि घटि रहिआ समाई॥ . . .
तनु मनु प्रान धरी तिसु आगे नानक आपु गवाए॥४॥१४॥

१९६ मेरा प्रभु सचा दुख निवारणु सबदे पाइआ जाई॥ . . .
नानक नाम बिना कोई किछु नाही नामे दे वडिआई॥४॥१५॥

१९७* गुर सलाही सदा सुख दाता प्रभु नराइणु सोई॥ . . .
नानक नामु प्रभु ते पाईऐ जिन कउ धुरि लिखिआ होई॥५॥१६॥

१९८*----१७

१९८* गुण गावह नामे सभि ऊधरे गुर का सबदु वीचारि॥ . . .
नानक जिसु भावै तिसु आपे देवै भावै तिवै चलाई॥८॥१७॥

१९९* हरि किरपा करे गुर की कारै लाए॥ . . .
गुरकिरपा ते इहु रोगु जाइ॥
नानक सचे सचि समाइ॥८॥१८॥

२०० भरमि भरमि जोनि मनमुख भरमाई॥
जमकालु मारे नित पति गवाई॥ . . .
हादरु हदूरि हरि वेपरवाहा॥
नानक गुरमुखि नामि समाहा॥४॥१९॥

२०१ हउमै बिखु मनु मोहिआ लदिआ अजगरि भारी॥ . . .
नानक सतगुर पूरा पाइआ मनि जपिआ नाम मुरारि॥४॥२०॥

२०१----१७

२०२ जीवत मुकत गुरमंती लागे॥

ਹਰਿ ਕੀ ਭਗਤਿ ਅਨਦਿਨੁ ਸਦਾ ਜਾਗੇ॥. . .

ਜੋ ਹਰਿ ਮਿਲਿਆ ਵਿਛੁੜਿ ਨ ਜਾਇ॥

ਨਾਨਕ ਹਰਿ ਹਰਿਨਾਮਿ ਸਮਾਇ॥੪॥੨੧॥

੨੦੩*   ਰਸਨਾ ਨਾਮੁ ਸਭੁ ਕੋਈ ਕਹੈ॥

ਸਤਗੁਰੁ ਸੇਵੇ ਤਾ ਨਾਮੁ ਲਹੈ॥. . .

ਚਹੁ ਜੁਗਿ ਸੋਭਾ ਨਿਰਮਲ ਜਨੁ ਸੋਇ॥

ਨਾਨਕ ਗੁਰਮੁਖਿ ਵਿਰਲਾ ਕੋਇ॥੫॥੨੨॥

ਰਾਗੁ ਮਲਾਰ ਦਖਣੀ [ਮਹਲਾ ੧]

੨੦੪*   ਕਰਉ ਬਿਨਉ ਗੁਰ ਅਪੁਨੇ ਪ੍ਰੀਤਮ ਹਰਿ ਵਰੁ ਆਨਿ ਮਿਲਾਵੈ॥. . .

ਨਾਨਕ ਰਾਮ ਨਾਮੁ ਜਪਿ ਗੁਰਮੁਖਿ ਧਨੁ ਸੋਹਾਗਨਿ ਸਚਿ ਸਹੀ॥੪॥੨੩॥

ਰਾਗੁ ਮਲਾਰ ਅਸਟਪਦੀਆ ਦਖਣੀ [ਮਹਲਾ ੧]

੨੦੫   ਚਕਵੀ ਨੈਨ ਨੀਦ ਨਾਹੀ ਚਾਹੈ ਬਿਨੁ ਪਿਰ ਨੀਦ ਨਾ ਪਾਈ॥. . .

ਗੁਰਪਰਸਾਦੀ ਘਰ ਹੀ ਪਿਰੁ ਪਾਇਆ ਤਉ ਨਾਨਕ ਤਪਤਿ ਬੁਝਾਈ॥੮॥੧॥

੨੦੬*   ਅਖਲੀ ਊਡੀ ਜਲੁ ਭਰ ਨਾਲਿ॥

ਡੂਗਰੁ ਊਚਾ ਗੜੁ ਤਪਤਾਲਿ॥. . .

ਜਮਣਾ ਮਰਣਾ ਦੀਸੈ ਸਿਰਿ ਊਭੇ ਖੁਧਿਆ ਨਿੰਦਾ ਕਾਲੰ॥

ਨਾਨਕ ਨਾਮੁ ਮਿਲੈ ਮਨਿ ਭਾਵੈ ਸਚੀ ਨਦਰਿ ਰੀਸਾਲੰ॥੮॥੨॥[173]

੨੦੭   ਮਰਨ ਮੁਕਤਿ ਗਤਿ ਸਾਰ ਨ ਜਾਨੈ॥

ਕੰਠੇ ਬੈਠਾ ਗੁਰਸਬਦੁ ਪਛਾਨੈ॥. . .

ਸੇ ਦੁਖ ਆਗੈ ਜਿ ਭੋਗ ਬਿਲਾਸੇ॥

ਨਾਨਕ ਮੁਕਤਿ ਨਾਹੀ ਬਿਨੁ ਨਾਵੈ ਸਾਚੇ॥੮॥੩॥

੨੦੮*   ਜਾਗਤੁ ਜਾਗਿ ਰਹੈ ਗੁਰ ਸੇਵਾ ਬਿਨੁ ਹਰਿ ਮੈ ਕੋ ਨਾਹੀ॥. . .

ਨਾਨਕ ਸੋ ਪ੍ਰਭੁ ਜਿ ਪ੍ਰਭੁ ਦਿਖਾਵੈ ਬਿਨੁ ਸਾਚੇ ਜਗੁ ਸੁਪਨਾ॥੯॥੪॥

੨੦੮----੧੯

੨੦੯*   ਚਾਤਕਿ ਮੀਨ ਜਲ ਹੀ ਤੇ ਸੁਖ ਪਾਵਹਿ ਸਾਰਿੰਗ ਸਬਦੁ ਸੁਹਾਈ॥. . .

ਭਨਥ ਨਾਨਕ ਤੁਝ ਹੀ ਤੇ ਮਨੁ ਮਾਨਿਆ ਕੀਮਤਿ ਕਹਨੁ ਨ ਜਾਈ॥੧੦॥੫॥

ਰਾਗੁ ਮਲਾਰ ਮਹਲੁ ੩

੨੧੦*   ਕਰਮੁ ਹੋਵੈ ਸਤਗੁਰੁ ਪਾਈਐ ਵਿਣੁ ਕਰਮੈ ਪਾਇਆ ਨ ਜਾਇ॥. . .

ਨਾਨਕ ਸੇ ਜਨ ਬਾਇ ਪਏ ਜਿਨਾ ਹਰਿ ਭਾਣਾ ਭਾਇ॥੮॥੬॥[174]

ੴ ਸਤਿਗੁਰ ਪਰਸਾਦਿ ਸਚੁਨਾਮੁ ਕਰਤਾਰੁ ਨਿਰਭਉ

ਨਿਰੀਕਾਰ ਅਕਾਲ ਮੁਰਤਿ ਅਜੂਨੀ ਸੰਭਉ॥

ਰਾਗੁ ਮਲਾਰ ਕਬੀਰ ਨਾਮਾ ਕੀ ਬਾਨੀ

੨੧੧   ਜਾਚੈ ਘਰਿ ਦਰਗਦਗਾ ਸਰਾਇਚਾ॥ ਬੈਕੁੰਠ ਭਵਨ ਚਿਤੁਸਾਲ॥. . .

ਨਾਮਾ ਪਠਵੈ ਤਾਰੀ ਆਤਿ॥ ਸਗਲ ਭਗਤ ਜਾਚੈ ਨੀਸਾਣਿ॥੫॥੧॥[175]

੨੧੩ ਅਲਾਵੰਤੀ ਏਹਿ ਭਰਮ ਜੋ ਹੈ ਮੈ ਉਪਰਿ ਸਭਿ ਕੋਪਲਾ॥ . . .
        ਫੇਰਿ ਦੇਹੁਰਾ ਨਾਮੇ ਕਉ ਦੀਆ ਪੰਡਿਤ ਕਉ ਪਿਛਵਾੜਲਾ॥੩॥੨॥

੨੧੪* ਸੁਰਸਰੀ ਸਲਲ ਕਿਰਤ ਬਾਰੁਨੀ ਰੇ ਸੰਤ ਜਨ ਕਰਤ ਨਾਹੀ ਪਾਨੰ॥ . . .
        ਬਿਪੁ ਪਰਧਾਨ ਡੰਡਉਤਿ ਕਰਹਿ
        ਤੇਰੈ ਨਾਇ ਸਰਨਾਇ ਪਏ ਦਾਸ ਰਵਿਦਾਸਾ॥੩॥੩॥

੨੧੪ # ਗਗਨਿ ਅਮਰੁ ਛਾਇਆ ਆਪੁਨੇ ਰੰਗੇ॥
        ਅਲਖ ਨਿਰੰਜਨ ਰਾਮਈਆਂ ਰਵਿ ਰਹਿਆ ਸੰਗੇ॥ . . .
        ਪਟਵਤਿ ਨਾਮਾ ਸੁਆਮੀ ਹਰਿ ਕੀਨੀ ਦਇਆ॥
        ਜਨਮ ਮਰਣ ਕਾ ਭਰਮੁ ਮਿਟਿ ਗਇਆ॥੨॥੪॥[176]

੨੧੫ ਸੋਹਿ ਲਾਗੀ ਲੇ ਤਾਲਾ ਮੇਲੀ॥   ਜਿਉ ਵਛਰੇ ਬਿਨੁ ਗਊ ਦੁਹੇਲੀ॥ . . .
        ਨਾਮਦੇਇ ਨਰਾਇਨੁ ਪਾਇਲੋਗ ਸਤਗੁਰ ਭੇਟਲਾ ਅਲਖ ਲਖਾਇਲੋ॥੩॥੫॥[177]

੨੧੫----੧੯

੧ਓ ਸਤਿਗੁਰ ਪਰਸਾਦੁ
ਬਾਬੇ ਨਾਨਕ ਵੇਦੀ ਪਾਤਿਸਾਹੁ [ਦੀ] ਦੀਨ ਦੁਨੀਆ ਕੀ ਟੇਕ[178]

ਰਾਗੁ ਸਾਰਗ[179]

ਰਾਗੁ ਸਾਰਗ ਦਖਣੀ [ਮਹਲਾ ੧]

੨੧੬* ਪੂਰਨ ਪਰਾਨ ਜੋਤਿ ਪਰਮੇਸਰ ਪ੍ਰੀਤਮ ਪਰਾਨ ਹਮਾਰੇ॥ . . .
        ਹਰਿ ਕੈ ਨਾਮਿ ਰਤੀ ਸੋਹਾਗਨਿ ਨਾਨਕ ਨਾਮੁ ਤੁਮਾਰਾ॥੪॥੧॥[180]

੨੧੬ ਜਬ ਲਗਿ ਦਰਸ ਨ ਪਰਸੇ ਪ੍ਰੀਤਮੁ ਤਬ ਲਗਿ ਭੁਖ ਪਿਆਸੀ॥ . . .
        ਨਾਨਿਕ ਪਰਭ ਤੇ ਸਾਚਿ ਸੁਹੇਲੀ ਪ੍ਰਭੁ ਦੇਖਤ ਮਨੁ ਧੀਰੈ॥੪॥੨॥

੨੧੭* ਇਨ ਵਿਧਿ ਹਰਿ ਮਿਲੀਐ ਵਰ ਕਾ ਮਨਿ ਧਨ ਸੋਹਾਗੁ ਪਿਆਰੀ॥ . . .
        ਨਾਨਕ ਗੁਰਮੁਖਿ ਨਾਮੁ ਅਮੋਲਕੁ ਜੁਗ ਜੁਗ ਅੰਤਰਿ ਧਾਰੀ॥੪॥੩॥

੧ਓ ਸਤਿਗੁਰ ਪਰਸਾਦ

ਰਾਗੁ ਸਾਰਗ ਦਖਣੀ ਅਸਟਪਦੀਆ [ਮਹਲਾ ੧]

੨੧੮ ਹਰਿ ਕੀ ਪਿਆਸ ਪਿਆਸੀ ਕਾਮਨਿ ਦੇਖਉ ਰੈਨਿ ਸਬਾਈ॥ . . .
        ਨਾਨਿਕ ਹਰਿ ਬਿਨੁ ਘਰੀ ਨ ਜੀਵਾ ਹਰਿ ਕਾ ਨਾਮੁ ਵਡਾਈ॥੮॥੧॥

੨੧੯ ਕਰੋਧੁ ਨਿਵਾਰਿ ਜਲੇ ਹਉ ਮਮਤਾ ਪ੍ਰੇਮ ਸਦਾ ਨਵ ਰੰਗੀ॥ . . .
        ਨਾਨਿਕ ਸਾਚੇ ਸਚਿ ਸਮਾਣੇ ਹਰਿ ਕਾ ਨਾਮੁ ਵਖਾਣੀ॥੮॥੨॥

ਰਾਗੁ ਸਾਰਗ ਮਹਲੁ ੩

੨੨੦ ਕੋਟ ਕੁਟੰਤਰ ਕੇ ਦੁਖ ਬਿਨਾਸਨ ਹਰਿ ਸਾਚਾ ਮਨਿ ਭਾਇਆ॥ . . .
        ਨਾਨਕ ਨਾਮਿ ਰਤੇ ਸਦਾ ਬੈਰਾਗੀ ਏਕ ਸਬਦਿ ਲਿਵ ਲਾਈ॥੮॥੩॥

੨੨੧ ਹਰਿ ਗਹਿਰ ਗਭੀਰੁ ਗੁਨੀ ਗਹੀਰੁ ਗੁਰ ਕੈ ਸਬਦਿ ਪਛਾਨਿਆ॥ . . .
        ਨਾਨਿਕ ਸੇ ਜਨ ਬਾਇ ਪਏ ਹੈ ਜਿਨ ਕੀ ਪਤਿ ਪਾਵੈ ਲੇਖੈ॥੮॥੪॥

            ੧ਓ ਸਤਿਗੁਰ ਪਰਸਾਦਿ ਸਚੁਨਾਮੁ ਕਰਤਾਰੁ ਨਿਰਭਉ
                ਨਿਰੀਕਾਰ ਅਕਾਲ ਮੂਰਤਿ ਅਜੂਨੀ ਸੰਭਉ

ਰਾਗੁ ਸਾਰਗ ਕਬੀਰੁ ਨਾਮਾ ਭਗਤਾ [ਦੀ ਬਾਣੀ]
੨੨੩ ਆਪੁਨਾ ਦੇਹੁ ਦੇਹੁਰਾ ਅਪੁਨਾ ਆਪਿ ਲਗਾਵੈ ਪੂਜਾ॥ . . .
        ਕਹਤ ਨਾਮਦੇਉ ਤੂ ਮੇਰਾ ਠਾਕੁਰੁ ਜਨੁ ਉਰਾ ਤੂੰ ਪੂਰਾ॥੨॥੧॥
੨੨੪* ਬਹਤੁ ਪਰਤਾਪੁ ਗਾਵ ਸਉ ਪਾਏ ਟਕਾ ਲਖ ਦੁਇ ਬਰਾਤਾ॥
        ਕਹਾ ਨਰ ਗਰਬਸਿ ਥੋਰੀ ਬਾਤ॥ . . .
        ਕਹਤ ਕਬੀਰ ਰਾਮੁ ਭਜੁ ਬਵਰੇ ਤੇਰਾ ਜਨਮੁ ਇਕਾਰਥ ਜਾਤ॥੪॥੨॥
੨੨੪ ਜੈਸੇ ਮੀਨੁ ਪਾਨੀ ਮਹਿ ਰਹੈ॥
        ਓਹ ਕਾਲ ਜਾਲ ਕੀ ਸੁਧਿ ਨਾ ਲਹੈ॥ . . .
        ਕਹਤ ਨਾਮਦੇਉ ਤਾਚੀ ਆਣਿ॥
        ਨਿਰਭਉ ਬੀਰਹਿ ਅਸੰਖ ਖਾਣਿ॥੪॥੩॥

੨੨੪––––੨੦

                    98

3

Non-canonical Compositions in the Extant Goindval Pothis

There are thirty-six compositions in the two extant Goindval Pothis, which are not available in the Kartarpur Pothi/Adi Granth. Since these compositions did not become part of Sikh scripture, and access to the Goindval Pothis has long been restricted, there is no information pertaining to their existence available in Sikh tradition.

Among these compositions, three are attributed to the Sikh Gurus, two appear in *rag* Suhi and *rag* Tilang under the name of Guru Nanak, and the third one is assigned *rag* Dhanasri and is recorded under the authorship of Guru Amardas. The composition in *rag* Suhi under Guru Nanak's name in the Goindval Pothis is also present in a recently surfaced manuscript, Ms. 1245 (folios 748-749) at the Guru Nanak Dev University library, Amritsar, but the other two in *rag* Tilang, and in *rag* Dhanasri are not to be found in any other known collection of early Sikh writings.

Fourteen compositions from this group in the Goindval Pothis are attributed to Gulam Sadasevak. As discussed in Chapter 1 in some detail, this name seems to have been used by Guru Ramdas before his actual ascendance to Sikh Guruship in 1574. These compositions are recorded in both the extant pothis and appear in *rags*: Suhi, Prabhati, Dhanasri, Basant, Bhairo, Maru, and Sorathi. None of these compositions are found in any other available collection of early Sikh writings.

In addition, there are nineteen compositions attributed to non-Sikh saints in various *rags* in both the extant Goindval Pothis. Nine of these compositions are assigned to Kabir, six to Namdev, two to Trilochan, and one each to Beni and Sharaf. Seven of these compositions under the name of Kabir and Namdev, the texts of which are marked with an asterisk in this chapter, are to my knowledge not found in any other available source of their hymns.

I take delight in introducing this set of hitherto unknown compositions to scholars interested in medieval Indian literature, and look forward to an interesting discussion about the possible reasons for their being dropped from the Sikh canon.

3. 1. Compositions attributed to the Gurus

੩. ੧. ੧. ਰਾਗੁ ਸੂਹੀ ਛੰਦ ਦਖਣੀ [ਮਹਲਾ ੧]

ਕਰਿ ਲਾਲਚ ਮਨੁ ਲੋਭਾਣਾ ਕਿਉ ਕਰਿ ਛੁਟੀਐ ਜੀ॥
ਇਹੁ ਸਾਕਤੁ ਕਰਮਿ ਭੁਲਾਣਾ ਦਰਗਹ ਚੁਟਿ ਸੁਟੀਐ ਜੀ॥
ਦਰਗਹ ਪਤਿ ਜਾਵੈ ਚੋਟਾ ਖਾਵੈ ਜਿਸੁ ਮਨਮੁਖਿ ਨਾਮੁ ਨ ਹੋਈ॥
ਧਰਮਰਾਇ ਸਿਰਿ ਲੇਖਾ ਮਾਗੈ ਜਮੁ ਪਕੜੈ ਦੁਖੁ ਦੇਈ॥
ਕਰਨ ਪਲਾਵ ਕਰੇ ਬਿਲਲਾਵੈ ਧਿਗੁ ਜੀਵਣੁ ਸੈਸਾਰੇ॥
ਨਾਨਕ ਮੁਕਤਿ ਹੋਇ ਗੁਰਸਬਦੀ ਹਰਿ ਜਪੀਐ ਪ੍ਰੀਤਿ ਪਿਆਰੇ ਜੀ॥੧॥
ਲਾਲਚ ਛੋਡਿ ਮਨਾ ਮਹਲੁ ਨ ਪਾਇਸੀ ਜੀ॥
ਛੁਟਹਿ ਗੁਰ ਕੀ ਸੇਵਾ ਜਿ ਨਾਮੁ ਧਿਆਇਸੀ ਜੀ॥
ਹਰਿ ਨਾਮੁ ਧਿਆਵਹਿ ਗਤਿ ਪਤਿ ਪਾਵਹਿ ਹਰਿ ਜਨ ਕੈ ਸੰਗੈ॥
ਜਿਨਿ ਤਨੁ ਮਨੁ ਸਾਜਿ ਕੀਆ ਗੜੁ ਮੰਦਰੁ ਸੋ ਰੰਗਨਹਾਰਾ ਰੰਗੇ॥
ਹਰਿ ਨਾਮਿ ਰਤੇ ਇਕਾਦਿਕ ਮੁਨਿ ਜਨ ਤੇਤੀਸ ਕਰੋੜੀ ਪਾਰਿ ਤਰੇ॥
ਸਾਧਿਕ ਸਿਧ ਸੇਵਹਿ ਗੁਰ ਆਪੁਨੇ ਨਾਨਕ ਊਤਮੁ ਸੰਗਿ ਹਰੇ॥੨॥
ਕੂੜ ਕਲ ਰੁਖੈ ਕਾਲੁ ਮਨਮੁਖਿ ਲਦਿਆ ਜੀ॥
ਜਗੁ ਸਾਗਰੁ ਖਾਰਾ ਅਸਗਾਹੁ ਗਰਬਿ ਗਰਬਿਆ ਜੀ॥
ਪੰਚਿ ਪਚਿ ਮੁਏ ਅਚੇਤ ਨ ਚੇਤਹਿ ਜਿਉ ਹਰਣਾਖਸ ਦੁਰਜੋਧਨ ਗਇਆ॥
ਕੁੰਭਕਰਨੁ ਮਹਿ ਰਾਵਣੁ ਦਹਸਿਰੁ ਲੰਕਾ ਸਮੇਤੀ ਭਸਮ ਭਇਆ॥
ਜਨ ਕੀ ਪਤਿ ਰਾਖੀ ਰਖਣਹਾਰੈ ਗੁਰਿ ਗੋਪਾਲਿ ਮੁਰਾਰੇ॥
ਨਾਨਕ ਰਾਮਿ ਨਾਮਿ ਮਨੁ ਰਤਾ ਸਤਗੁਰ ਸਬਦੁ ਵੀਚਾਰੇ॥੩॥
ਹਰਿ ਭਗਤਾ ਨਾਮੁ ਅਧਾਰੁ ਸੋ ਪ੍ਰੀਤਿ ਭਾਇਆ ਜੀ॥
ਅੰਤਰਿ ਸਚੁ ਵੀਚਾਰੁ ਸਤਗੁਰ ਤੇ ਪਾਇਆ ਜੀ॥
ਗੁਰਸਬਦ ਕਮਾਇਆ ਪੂਰਾ ਪਾਇਆ ਅੰਮ੍ਰਿਤੁ ਪੀ ਤ੍ਰਿਪਤਾਸ ਭਏ॥
ਅਵਨਾ ਗਵਨਾ ਦੋਊ ਮੇਟੇ ਹਉਮੈ ਲੋਭਾ ਸਬਦਿ ਦਹੈ॥
ਸਾਸਿ ਗਿਰਾਸਿ ਕਬਹੁ ਨ ਵਿਸਰੈ ਜਾ ਕੇ ਜੀਅ ਪਰਾਣਾ॥
ਨਾਨਕ ਸਤਗੁਰਿ ਟੇਕ ਟਿਕਾਈ ਗੁਰਸਬਦੀ ਮਨੁ ਮਾਨਾ॥੪॥੧॥੨੨॥

ਅਲਹ ਏਕੁ ਕਰੀਮੁ ਕੁਦਰਤਿ ਸਚੁ ਕਾਦਰੁ ਪਾਕੁ॥

ਸਰਗਸਤ ਬਾਜੀ ਖਲਕ ਸਾਜੀ ਹਮੁ ਹੋਸੀ ਖਾਕੁ॥੧॥

ਦੁਨੀਆ ਮੁਕਾਮੀ ਫਨਾਹਿ॥

ਅਲਮਉਤ ਅਜਰਾਈਲੁ ਹਾਜਰੁ ਕਬਜ ਕਰਿ ਲੇ ਜਾਹਿ॥੧॥ ਰਹਾਉ॥

ਜਨ ਮਾਦਰਿ ਪਿਦਰਿ ਫਰਜੰਦ ਬਿਰਾਦਰ ਮਹਲ ਮੰਡਿਪ ਊਚ॥

ਚੰਦਨ ਅਲਮ ਜਾਇਸੀ ਮੁਕਾਮੁ ਖਾਨੇ ਕੂਚ॥੨॥

ਅਰਦਾਸ ਬੰਦੇ ਭੁਗਉ ਨਾਨਿਕ ਤੂ ਮਿਹਰਵਾਨੁ ਖੁਦਾਇ॥

ਤੇਰਾ ਨਾਮੁ ਤਰਫੇ ਹਮੁ ਰਾਜੁ ਪਨਹ ਬੰਦੇ ਲਾਇ॥੩॥੫॥

ਕਾਮੁ ਕਰੋਧ ਮਾਇਆ ਮਦੁ ਮੀਠੇ ਦਲ ਬਦਲ ਜਿਉ ਉਨ ਵਿਰਹੇ॥
ਗੁਰਵੀਚਾਰਿ ਅਚਾਰੁ ਕਮਾਇਆ ਮੈ ਅੰਧਲੇ ਨਾਮੁ ਸੁ ਤਨੁ ਲਹੇ॥੧॥
ਆਤਮਾ ਰਾਮ ਕਉ ਹਰਿ ਹਰਿ ਜਪੁ ਪੂਜਾ॥
ਗੁਰਮੁਖਿ ਆਪੁਨੋ ਠਾਕੁਰੁ ਜਾਨਿਆ ਹਉ ਮੈ ਕਇਆ ਭਉ ਦੂਜਾ॥੧॥ ਰਹਾਉ॥
ਪ੍ਰਿਉ ਪ੍ਰਿਉ ਕਰੇ ਬਾਬੀਹਾ ਬੋਲੈ ਇਕ ਨਿਸ ਬੁਦ ਸਹੇਰੈ॥
ਉਨਵਿ ਘਨਿਹਾਰੁ ਵਾਰਸਿ ਗਰਜੈ ਬਿਨੁ ਜਲ ਪਿਆਸ ਨ ਟਾਰੈ॥੨॥
ਮਨੁ ਪੰਖੀ ਤਨੁ ਤਰਵਰੁ ਕਹੀਐ ਪੰਚ ਭੂਤ ਸਚਿ ਰੰਗਿ ਵਸੇ॥
ਸਤਗੁਰ ਸਬਦਿ ਤਤੁ ਲੇ ਸੰਗ ਰਹਿ ਹਰਿ ਭਜੁ ਕਾਲੁ ਬਿਕਾਲੁ ਨਸੇ॥੩॥
ਕੀਰਤਿ ਕਰਨੀ ਹਰਿ ਗੁਰ ਰਸੁ ਚਰਨੀ ਅਹਿਨਿਸਿ ਮਜਨੁ ਗੁਰਗਿਆਨੇ॥
ਨਾਨਿਕ ਮਾਨੁ ਨਿਮਾਨੇ ਸਾਚਾ ਰਿਦ ਅੰਤਰਿ ਹਰਿ ਹਰਿ ਗੁਰਧਿਆਨੇ॥੪॥੧੦॥

3. 2. *Gulam Sadasevak*

੩. ੨. ੧. ਰਾਗੁ ਸੂਹੀ ਗੁਲਾਮੁ ਸਦਾਸੇਵਕੁ

ਮੈ ਅਵਗਣਿਆਰੀ ਕੋ ਗੁਣੁ ਨਾਹੀ॥
ਬਿਨੁ ਗੁਰ ਭੇਟੇ ਮਿਲਣੁ ਨ ਪਾਹੀ॥੧॥
ਨਾ ਮੈ ਰੂਪੁ ਅਚਾਰੁ ਨ ਕੋਈ॥
ਕਿਉ ਕਰਿ ਸਾਹਿਬ ਮਿਲਣਾ ਹੋਈ॥੧॥ ਰਹਾਉ॥
ਮੈ ਸੀਗਾਰ ਬਹੁ ਰੂਪ ਅਚਾਰ॥
ਬਿਨੁ ਗੁਰ ਭੇਟੇ ਜਮੁ ਕਰੇ ਖੁਆਰ॥੨॥
ਨਾ ਮੈ ਰੂਪੁ ਨ ਰੰਗੁ ਨ ਕੋਈ॥
ਸਹਜੇ ਹਰਿ ਪ੍ਰਭੁ ਰਵੈ ਨ ਸੋਈ॥੩॥
ਖਰੀ ਸਿਆਣਪ ਬਹੁਤੁ ਚਤੁਰਾਈ॥
ਦੂਜੈ ਲਾਗੀ ਭਰਮਿ ਭੁਲਾਈ॥
ਕਾਮਨਿ ਕੰਤਿ ਚਿਤਿ ਨਾ ਪਾਈ॥੪॥
ਤਿਸਨਾ ਅਗਨਿ ਬੁਡੇ ਬਹੁ ਮਾਇਆ॥
ਤਾ ਕਾਮਣਿ ਸੇਜੇ ਸਿਰੀਰ ਗੁਆਇਆ॥੫॥
ਭਨਥ ਨਾਨਕੁ ਪ੍ਰਭੁ ਅਲਖੁ ਅਬਿਨਾਸੀ॥
ਗੁਰਪਰਸਾਦੀ ਧਨ ਸੋਹੈ ਜਿਨਿਸੀ॥੬॥੧॥

103

ਪਿਰ ਕੈ ਰੰਗਿ ਰਤੀ ਸੋਹਾਗਣਿ ਅਨਦਿਨੁ ਰਲੀਆ ਮਾਣੈ॥
ਹਰਿ ਕੈ ਨਾਇ ਰਤੀ ਸਦਾ ਬੈਰਾਗਣਿ ਹਰਿ ਕਾ ਨਾਮੁ ਵਖਾਣੈ॥੧॥
ਹਰਿ ਹਰਿ ਨਾਮੁ ਜਪਹੁ ਮੇਰੀ ਮਾਈ॥
ਦਰਸਨ ਬਿਨੁ ਮੈ ਰਹਣੁ ਨ ਜਾਈ॥੧॥ ਰਹਾਉ॥
ਤੂ ਦੈਆਲ ਕਿਰਪਾ ਕਰਿ ਮੇਰੇ ਸੁਆਮੀ ਮੈ ਦੀਜੈ ਨਾਮੁ ਵਡਾਈ॥
ਨਾਮੁ ਦਾਨੁ ਦੇਹਿ ਭਗਤ ਜਨ ਕਉ ਭਾਜਿ ਪਇਆ ਸਰਣਾਈ॥੨॥
ਜਿਨਿ ਹਰਿ ਕਾ ਪ੍ਰੇਮੁ ਨ ਚਾਖਿਆ ਸੇ ਡੂਬਿ ਮੁਏ ਬਿਨੁ ਪਾਣੀ॥
ਜਮ ਦਰਿ ਬਧਾ ਚੋਟਾ ਖਾਵੈ ਅਬ ਕਿਆ ਕਰੇ ਪਰਾਣੀ॥੩॥
ਜਿਸੁ ਤੂ ਦੇਹਿ ਸੋਈ ਜਨੁ ਪਾਵੈ ਇਕ ਤਿਲੁ ਤੇਰੀ ਵਡਿਆਈ॥
ਨਾਨਿਕ ਨਾਮੁ ਵਸੈ ਘਟ ਅੰਤਰਿ ਤਾ ਸਹਜੇ ਹਰਿ ਗੁਣ ਗਾਈ॥੪॥੨॥

104

३. २. ३.   ਰਾਗੁ ਸੂਹੀ ਗੁਲਾਮੁ ਸਦਾਸੇਵਕੁ

ਪਕੇ ਮਡਪ ਮਹਲ ਹਜਾਰਾ॥
ਖਿਨ ਮਹਿ ਜਾਤ ਨ ਲਾਗੈ ਬਾਰਾ॥੧॥
ਇਹੁ ਧਨੁ ਐਸਾ ਜੈਸੇ ਬਿਰਖ ਕੀ ਛਾਇਆ॥
ਬਿਨਸਿ ਜਾਇਗਾ ਨ ਰਹੈਗੀ ਮਾਇਆ॥੧॥ ਰਹਾਉ॥
ਪੁਤ੍ਰ ਕਲਤ੍ਰ ਮੋਹੁ ਝੂਠ ਪਸਾਰਾ॥
ਨਾਲਿ ਨ ਚਲਿਆ ਅੰਤ ਕੀ ਬਾਰਾ॥੨॥
ਇਸਤਰੀ ਪੁਰਖੈ ਬਹਤੁ ਪਿਆਰਾ॥
ਓਹ ਭੀ ਛੋਡਿ ਗਏ ਘਰੁ ਬਾਰਾ॥੩॥
ਭਨਥ ਨਾਨਿਕ ਜਗੁ ਸਗਲਾ ਸੋਇਆ॥
ਗੁਰਪਰਸਾਦੀ ਜਨੁ ਮੁਕਤੁ ਹੋਆ॥੪॥੩॥

३. २. ੪.   ਰਾਗੁ ਪ੍ਰਭਾਤੀ ਗੁਲਾਮੁ ਸਦਾਸੇਵਕੁ

ਸਹਜ ਭਾਇ ਮਿਲਾਇਆ ਗੁਰਿ ਪੂਰੈ ਵਿਚਹੁ ਹਉਮੈ ਖੋਈ॥
ਸਦਾ ਅਲਿਪਤੁ ਰਹੈ ਦਿਨੁ ਰਾਤੀ ਪੂਰਨੁ ਕਿਰਪਾ ਹੋਈ॥੧॥
ਜਪਿ ਮੇਰੇ ਮਨ ਨਾਮੁ ਨਿਧਾਨੁ॥
ਗੁਰਿ ਪੂਰੈ ਹਰਿ ਨਾਮੁ ਦਿੜਾਇਆ ਸਹਜ ਭਾਇ ਜਪੀ ਹਰਿ ਨਾਮੁ॥੧॥ ਰਹਾਉ॥
ਏਕ ਨਾਮ ਤੇ ਸਭੁ ਜਗੁ ਉਪਜਿਆ ਜਿਸੁ ਭਾਵੈ ਤਿਸੁ ਦੇਈ॥
ਮਨਮੁਖਿ ਮੂਲੁ ਗਵਾਇਆ ਆਪਣਾ ਦੂਜੈ ਭਾਇ ਤਿਖੋਈ॥੨॥
ਗੁਰਪਰਸਾਦੀ ਉਲਟੀ ਭਈ ਤਾ ਮਨੁ ਨਿਜ ਘਰਿ ਆਇਆ॥
ਪਰਿ ਘਰਿ ਜਾਤਾ ਘਰਿ ਮਹਿ ਆਇਆ ਤਾ ਸਹਜੇ ਹਰਿ ਗੁਣ ਗਾਇਆ॥੩॥
ਅਉਗਣ ਮਹਿ ਗੁਣੁ ਗੁਰੁ ਦਿਖਾਇਆ ਤਾ ਮਨੁ ਰਹਿਆ ਠਾਈ॥
ਨਾਨਕੁ ਗੁਰੁ ਵਡਭਾਗੀ ਪਾਇਆ ਤਾ ਸਹਜੇ ਰਹਿਆ ਸਮਾਈ॥੪॥੧॥

106

ਅਪਨੈ ਵਸਿ ਕੀਤੋਨੁ ਸਭ ਕਿਛੁ ਹੋਰਸੁ ਹਥਿ ਕਿਛੁ ਨਾਹੀ॥
ਗੁਰਮੁਖਿ ਹੋਵੈ ਸੁ ਚਰਨੀ ਲਾਗੈ ਮਨਮੁਖ ਆਵੈ ਜਾਹੀ॥੧॥
ਮਨ ਮੇਰੇ ਪਉ ਤੂ ਸਤਿਗੁਰ ਕੀ ਪਾਈ॥
ਸਤਿਗੁਰ ਮਿਲਿਐ ਨਵ ਨਿਧਿ ਪਾਵੈ ਸਹਜੇ ਹਰਿ ਗੁਣ ਗਾਈ॥੧॥ ਰਹਾਉ॥
ਆਪੇ ਦੇਵੈ ਆਪੇ ਲੇਵੈ ਆਪੇ ਦੇ ਵਡਿਆਈ॥
ਆਪੇ ਕਰੇ ਕਰਾਏ ਕਰਤਾ ਆਪੇ ਰਹੈ ਸਮਾਈ॥੨॥
ਜਹ ਦੇਖਾ ਤਹ ਏਕੋ ਪਸਰਿਆ ਦੂਜਾ ਅਵਰੁ ਨ ਕੋਈ॥
ਨਾਨਿਕ ਗੁਰਮੁਖਿ ਏਕੋ ਜਾਨੈ ਤਾ ਵਿਰਹੁ ਹਉਮੈ ਖੋਈ॥੩॥੨॥

ਗੁਰਮੁਖਿ ਨਾਮੁ ਜਪੈ ਜਨੁ ਕੋਈ॥

ਗੁਰਮੁਖਿ ਭਗਤਿ ਪਰਪਤਿ ਹੋਈ॥

ਗੁਰਮੁਖਿ ਵਿਰਲਾ ਬੁਝੈ ਕੋਈ॥

ਨਾਮਿ ਰਤੇ ਸਦਾ ਸੁਖੁ ਹੋਈ॥੧॥

ਜਪਿ ਮਨ ਮੇਰੇ ਏਕੋ ਨਾਮੁ॥

ਗੁਰਿ ਪੂਰੈ ਦਿਤਾ ਏਹੁ ਨਿਧਾਨੁ॥੧॥ ਰਹਾਉ॥

ਗੁਰਮੁਖਿ ਇਹੁ ਧਨੁ ਪਲੈ ਪਾਇ॥

ਗੁਰਮੁਖਿ ਸਹਜੇ ਰਹਿਆ ਸਮਾਇ॥

ਗੁਰਮੁਖਿ ਜਾ ਤੋ ਘਰ ਮਹਿ ਆਨੈ॥

ਗੁਰਮੁਖਿ ਹਿਰਦੈ ਨਾਮੁ ਪਛਾਨੈ॥੨॥

ਗੁਰਮੁਖਿ ਲੋਹ ਭਏ ਹੈ ਕੰਚਨੁ॥

ਗੁਰਮੁਖਿ ਦੋਖ ਸਗਲੇ ਭਉ ਭੰਜਨੁ॥

ਗੁਰ ਮਿਲਿਐ ਘੰਨੁ ਪਾਇਆ ਸੋਈ॥

ਜਾਮ ਕੰਕਰ ਕੀ ਫਿਰਿ ਚਿਤ ਨ ਹੋਈ॥੩॥

ਗੁਰਮੁਖਿ ਮਸਤਕਿ ਲਿਖਿਆ ਲੇਖੁ॥

ਗੁਰਮੁਖਿ ਪਾਰਿ ਉਤਾਰੈ ਏਕੁ॥

ਨਾਨਿਕ ਗੁਰਮੁਖਿ ਮਿਲੈ ਵਡਿਆਈ॥

ਗੁਰਮੁਖਿ ਸਹਜੇ ਰਹਿਆ ਸਮਾਈ॥੪॥੧॥

३. २. ੧.   ਰਾਗੁ ਬਸੰਤੁ ਗੁਲਾਮੁ ਸਦਾਸੇਵਕੁ

ਆਪੇ ਹੀ ਸੰਤੁ ਭਗਤੀ ਲਾਇ ਆਪੇ ਦੈਤੁ ਚਿੜਾਇਆ॥

ਆਪੇ ਹੀ ਸੰਤ ਕੀ ਕਰਹਿ ਤੂ ਰਖਿਆ ਆਪੇ ਦੁਸਟ ਪਚਾਇਆ॥੧॥

ਤੂ ਆਪਣਾ ਖੇਲੁ ਆਪੇ ਹੀ ਕਰਦਾ ਆਇਆ॥

ਹਉ ਹੋਰਸੁ ਕਿਸੁ ਆਖਾ ਜਾ ਕੋਇ ਨ ਦੀਸੈ

ਤੂ ਆਪੇ ਰਹਿਆ ਸਮਾਇਆ॥੧॥ ਰਹਾਉ॥

ਆਪੇ ਹੀ ਤੂ ਭਗਤੀ ਲਾਏ ਆਪਿ ਕਰਾਵਹਿ ਸੇਵਾ॥

ਤੂ ਆਪੇ ਆਪਿ ਵਰਤਹਿ ਸੁਆਮੀ ਹੋਰੁ ਨ ਕੋਈ ਦੇਵਾ॥੨॥

ਤੂ ਦੀਨ ਦੈਆਲ ਕਿਰਪਾਲ ਮੇਰੇ ਸੁਆਮੀ

ਤੂ ਭਗਤਾ ਕੀ ਪੈਜ ਰਖਦਾ ਆਇਆ॥

ਭਗਤ ਤੇਰੇ ਤੂ ਭਗਤਾ ਕਾ ਪ੍ਰੀਤਮੁ ਭਗਤ ਪਏ ਤੇਰੀ ਸਰਣਾਇਆ॥੩॥

ਸੰਤ ਜਨ ਕੀ ਜੇ ਕੋ ਨਿੰਦਾ ਕਰੇ ਸੋ ਪਰਭਿ ਆਪਿ ਭੁਲਾਇਆ॥

ਨਾਨਿਕ ਹਰਿ ਜੀ ਨਾਹੀ ਅੰਤਰੁ ਜਾ ਹਰਿ ਕੈ ਮਨਿ ਭਾਇਆ॥੪॥੧॥

109

ਜੇਤਾ ਕਪੜੁ ਅੰਗਿ ਹਢਾਇਆ॥

ਭਲੇ ਭਲੇ ਤੈ ਭੋਜਨ ਖਾਇਆ॥

ਤਾ ਬੁਰਾ ਕਰੇਦੇ ਅਗੈ ਆਇਆ॥੧॥

ਮੇਰਾ ਗੋਵਿੰਦੁ ਗਰਬਾ ਪਰਹਾਰੀ॥

ਜੋ ਨਰੁ ਗਰਬੁ ਕਰੇਗਾ ਤ ਕਉ ਹੋਗਿ ਖੁਆਰੀ॥੧॥ ਰਹਾਉ॥

ਕਬਹੁ ਚੜਿ ਘੋੜੈ ਧਾਵੈ॥

ਕਬਹੁ ਪੈ ਪਾਸ ਡਰਾਵੈ॥

ਅੰਤ ਕੀ ਵੇਲਾ ਚਿਤਿ ਨ ਆਵੈ॥੨॥

ਹੁਣਿ ਤੇਰਾ ਕਾਲੁ ਨੇੜੈ ਆਇਆ॥

ਕਿਹੁ ਨ ਚਲੈ ਜਮਿ ਪਕੜਿ ਚਲਾਇਆ॥

ਪੂਰਬਿ ਲਿਖਿਆ ਸੋ ਫਲੁ ਪਾਇਆ॥੩॥

ਸਤਗੁਰ ਨਾਲਿ ਚਿਤੁ ਨਿਮਖ ਨ ਲਾਇਆ॥

ਅੰਤ ਕਾਲਿ ਤੁਧ ਹੋਇ ਸਖਾਇਆ॥

ਆਪਣਾ ਕੀਤਾ ਆਪੇ ਪਾਇਆ॥੪॥

ਇਹੁ ਜੰਤੁ ਕਿਆ ਕਰੇ ਵੇਚਾਰਾ॥

ਤੁਧ ਆਪੇ ਹੀ ਸਿਰਿ ਦਿਤਾ ਭਾਰਾ॥

ਨਾਨਿਕ ਨਾਮ ਬਿਨਾ ਡੂਬਿ ਮੋਆ ਸੈਸਾਰਾ॥੫॥੨॥

ਹਉਮੈ ਮਮਤਾ ਸਬਦੇ ਖੋਈ॥

ਗੁਰਪਰਸਾਦਿ ਸਦਾ ਸੁਖੁ ਹੋਈ॥੧॥

ਨਾਨਿਕ ਹਉਮੈ ਸਬਦਿ ਜਲਾਏ॥

ਗੁਰਪਰਸਾਦੀ ਪਰਮਪਦ ਪਾਏ॥੧॥ ਰਹਾਉ॥

ਜਿਸੁ ਉਪਰਿ ਕਿਰਪਾ ਕਰੇ ਕਰਤਾਰੁ॥

ਸੋ ਗੁਰਪਰਸਾਦੀ ਪਾਵੈ ਪਾਰੁ॥੨॥

ਮੈ ਮੂਰਖ ਹੋਰ ਟੇਕ ਨ ਕਾਈ॥

ਜਿਉ ਭਾਵੈ ਤਿਉ ਰਾਖਿ ਲੇਹੋ ਗੁਸਾਈ॥੩॥

ਨਾਨਿਕੁ ਗੁਰੁ ਪਾਇਆ ਪੂਰੈ ਭਾਗਿ॥

ਅਨਦਿਨੁ ਸਬਦੇ ਰਹਿਆ ਜਾਗਿ॥੪॥੧॥

111

ਸੋਈ ਪੰਡਿਤੁ ਹਰਿ ਨਾਮੁ ਧਿਆਵੈ॥

ਸੋਈ ਪੰਡਿਤੁ ਜਿ ਹਉਮੈ ਸਬਦ ਜਲਾਵੈ॥

ਹਉਮੈ ਮਾਰਿ ਰਹੈ ਨਿਰਬਾਣੁ॥

ਸੋ ਪੰਡਿਤੁ ਦਰਗਹ ਪਰਵਾਣੁ॥੧॥

ਪੜ ਰੇ ਪੰਡਿਤ ਹਰਿ ਹਰਿ ਨਾਮਾ॥

ਸਦ ਹੀ ਲਾਗੈ ਤੈਨੋ ਸਹਜ ਧਿਆਨੁ॥੧॥ ਰਹਾਉ॥

ਸੋਈ ਪੰਡਿਤੁ ਜਿ ਪੰਚਾ ਮਾਰੈ॥

ਸੋਈ ਪੰਡਿਤੁ ਜਿ ਹਰਿ ਨਾਮੁ ਸਮਾਰੈ॥

ਸੋਈ ਪੰਡਿਤੁ ਜਿ ਮਾਇਆ ਤੇ ਦੂਰਿ॥

ਸੋਈ ਪੰਡਿਤੁ ਸਦਾ ਹਦੂਰਿ॥੨॥

ਸੋਈ ਪੰਡਿਤੁ ਜਿਨਿ ਬ੍ਰਹਮ ਪਛਾਤਾ॥

ਸੋਈ ਪੰਡਿਤੁ ਜਿ ਹਰਿ ਰੰਗਿ ਰਾਤਾ॥

ਸੋਈ ਪੰਡਿਤੁ ਜਿਨਿ ਹਉਮੈ ਮਾਰੀ॥

ਤਿਸੁ ਪੰਡਿਤੁ ਰਿਦੈ ਵਸੈ ਮੁਰਾਰੀ॥੩॥

ਸਤਗੁਰ ਮਿਲਿਐ ਹਉਮੈ ਖੋਈ॥

ਸਤਗੁਰ ਮਿਲੀਐ ਲੋਹ ਕੰਚਨ ਹੋਈ॥

ਸਤਗੁਰ ਮੇਰਾ ਪ੍ਰਾਨ ਅਧਾਰਾ॥

ਸਤਗੁਰ ਕੈ ਹਉ ਸਦਾ ਬਲਿਹਾਰਾ॥੪॥

ਭਨਥ ਨਾਨਕੁ ਜਨੁ ਕਰੇ ਕਰਾਇਆ॥

ਸੋਈ ਮੁਕਤੁ ਜਿਨਿ ਹਰਿ ਨਾਮੁ ਧਿਆਇਆ॥

ਕਰਣ ਕਾਰਣੁ ਆਪੇ ਪਰਭੁ ਸੋਈ॥

ਤਿਸੁ ਵਿਣੁ ਦੂਜਾ ਅਵਰੁ ਨ ਕੋਈ॥੫॥੧॥

112

ਸਤਗੁਰਿ ਪੂਰੈ ਨਾਮੁ ਦਿੜਾਇਆ॥
ਅਉਗਣ ਮੇਟਿ ਗੁਣੀ ਬਕਸਾਇਆ॥
ਸਤਗੁਰ ਤੇ ਮੈ ਨਵਨਿਧਿ ਪਾਈ॥
ਸਤਗੁਰ ਸਹਜੇ ਰਹਿਆ ਸਮਾਈ॥੧॥
ਸਤਗੁਰ ਮੋ ਕਉ ਭਏ ਦੈਆਲਾ॥
ਸਤਗੁਰ ਕੇ ਹਮ ਬਾਲ ਗੁਪਾਲਾ॥੧॥ ਰਹਾਉ॥
ਸਤਗੁਰ ਵਿਚਿ ਵਡੀ ਵਡਿਆਈ॥
ਸਤਗੁਰ ਕੀ ਕੀਮ ਕਿਨੈ ਨ ਪਾਈ॥
ਤਿਸੁ ਸਤਗੁਰ ਤੇ ਇਕੁ ਸੇਵਕੁ ਭਇਆ॥
ਤਿਨਿ ਸੇਵਕਿ ਸਭੁ ਜਗੁ ਉਧਰਇਆ॥੨॥
ਤਿਸੁ ਸੇਵਕ ਕਉ ਸਦ ਬਲਿਹਾਰੀ॥
ਜਿਨਿ ਡੂਬਤ ਜੀਉ ਲੀਆ ਉਬਾਰੀ॥
ਓਹੁ ਸੇਵਕੁ ਓਹੁ ਸਤਗੁਰੁ ਪੂਰਾ॥
ਸਰਬ ਕਲਾ ਸਾਚੇ ਭਰਪੂਰਾ॥੩॥
ਆਪੇ ਸੇਵਕੁ ਸਤਗੁਰ ਪੂਰਾ॥
ਅਨਹਤ ਸਬਦੁ ਵਜਾਵੈ ਤੂਰਾ॥
ਅਨਹਤਿ ਰਾਤੇ ਸੇ ਬੈਰਾਗੀ॥
ਨਾਨਕ ਸੇਵਕਿ ਏਕ ਲਿਵ ਲਾਗੀ॥੪॥੨॥

113

ਸਤਗੁਰ ਬਾਝਹੁ ਕਿਨੈ ਨ ਪਾਇਓ ਸਭ ਥਕੀ ਕਰਮ ਕਮਾਇ॥

ਜੇ ਬਹੁਤੇਰਾ ਲੋਚਹਿ ਪਰਾਨੀ ਬਿਨੁ ਸਚੈ ਬਾਇ ਨ ਪਾਇ॥੧॥

ਤੂ ਸਤਗੁਰ ਕੀ ਚਰਨੀ ਲਾਗੁ ਮਨਾ॥

ਸਾਧ ਸੰਗਤਿ ਬਿਨੁ ਕਿਨੈ ਨ ਪਾਇਓ ਤੂ ਭਜਿ ਪਉ ਸਰਨਾ॥੧॥ ਰਹਾਉ॥

ਜੋ ਜੋ ਸਰਨਿ ਪਏ ਪ੍ਰਭ ਤੇਰੀ ਤਿਨ ਕੀ ਮੈ ਓਟ ਗਹੀ॥

ਚਰਨ ਕਵਲ ਹਿਰਦੈ ਰਾਖੁ ਏਹ ਗਾਠਿ ਦੇਹੁ ਮਨ ਮਹੀ॥੨॥

ਮੇਰੀ ਮੇਰੀ ਕਰਤ ਮੂਏ ਤੁਮ ਪਰਾਨੀ ਮੇਰੀ ਸੰਗਿ ਨ ਜਾਈ॥

ਜਿਨ ਕਾਰਨਿ ਤੂ ਸੰਚਹਿ ਮਾਇਆ ਤੇ ਫੁਨਿ ਕਾਮਿ ਨ ਆਈ॥੩॥

ਧਰਮਰਾਇ ਜਬ ਲੇਖਾ ਮਾਗੈ ਤਬਿ ਕਿਆ ਕਰਹਿ ਪਰਾਨੀ॥

ਜਮ ਡੰਡੁ ਸਿਰ ਊਪਰਿ ਕੜਕੈ ਦਰ ਕੀ ਖਬਰਿ ਨ ਜਾਨੀ॥੪॥

ਭਜਿ ਪਉ ਤੂ ਸਤਿਗੁਰ ਕੀ ਸਰਨਾ ਜੋ ਹੋਵੈ ਅੰਤਿ ਸਖਾਈ॥

ਗੁਰੁ ਨਾਨਕੁ ਮਨ ਅੰਤਰਿ ਵਸਿਆ ਤਾ ਸਹਜੇ ਰਹਿਆ ਸਮਾਈ॥੫॥੧॥

ਨਾ ਬੇੜੀ ਨਾ ਤੁਲਹੜਾ ਭਾਈ ਕਿਨ ਵਿਧਿ ਪਾਰਿ ਪਾਇ॥

ਨਾ ਜਪ ਨਾ ਤਪੁ ਸੰਜਮਾ ਭਾਈ ਕਿਉ ਕਰਿ ਲੰਘਿਆ ਜਾਇ॥੧॥

ਮਨ ਰੇ ਸਤਗੁਰ ਕੀ ਪਉ ਸਰਟਾਇ॥

ਸਤਗੁਰੁ ਬੇੜਾ ਨਾਮ ਕਾ ਭਾਈ ਸੋ ਤੁਧ ਲਏਗਾ ਲਘਾਇ॥੧॥ ਰਹਾਉ॥

ਜਿਨੀ ਚਲਣ ਜਾਨਿਆ ਭਾਈ ਸੇ ਦੂਜੈ ਕਿਉ ਲਗੈ ਜਾਇ॥

ਰਤਨੁ ਜਨਮੁ ਗਵਾਇਆ ਭਾਈ ਗਏ ਨੀ ਪਛੋਤਾਇ॥੨॥

ਸਤਗੁਰ ਸਉ ਚਿਤੁ ਲਾਈਐ ਭਾਈ ਸਤਗੁਰ ਲਏ ਲਘਾਇ॥

ਸਤਗੁਰ ਸਉ ਜੋ ਗਹਿ ਰਹੈ ਭਾਈ ਸੋ ਅੰਤਿ ਨ ਪਛੋਤਾਇ॥

ਨਾਨਿਕ ਗੁਰ ਕੀ ਚਰਨੀ ਲਾਗੁ ਭਾਈ ਅੰਤੇ ਲਏ ਛਡਾਇ॥

ਨਵ ਨਿਧਿ ਨਾਮੁ ਪਲੈ ਪਵੈ ਭਾਈ ਤਾ ਸਹਜੇ ਰਹੈ ਸਮਾਇ॥੪॥੧॥

ਰਾਗੁ ਸੋਰਠਿ ਗੁਲਾਮੁ ਸਦਾਸੇਵਕੁ

ਮਨ ਰੇ ਸਾਚੀ ਲਿਵ ਰਹੁ ਤੂ ਲਾਗਾ॥
ਸਾਚੀ ਲਿਵ ਲਾਗੀ ਸਾਚੋ ਉਪਜੈ ਦੂਜਾ ਭਰਮੁ ਭਉ ਭਾਗਾ॥੧॥ ਰਹਾਉ॥
ਸਤਗੁਰ ਮਿਲਿਐ ਸਚੁ ਪ੍ਰਗਾਸਿਆ ਜਿਨ ਕਉ ਧੁਰਿ ਲਿਖਿਆ ਭਾਈ॥
ਸਤਗੁਰ ਤੇ ਨਵਨਿਧਿ ਪਾਈ ਤਿਸਦਾ ਕਹਟਾ ਕਿਛੁ ਨ ਜਾਈ॥੧॥
ਇਹੁ ਰਸ ਸਾਚਾ ਤਿਨ ਕਉ ਆਇਆ ਜਿਨਾ ਇਕ ਮਨਿ ਸਤਗੁਰ ਧਿਆਇਆ॥
ਸਤਗੁਰਿ ਸਾਚੀ ਬੂਝ ਬੁਝਾਈ ਤ ਅਲਖੁ ਨਿਰੰਜਨੁ ਪਾਇਆ॥੨॥
ਸਤਗੁਰ ਛਡਿ ਜੋ ਦੂਜੈ ਲਾਗੈ ਤਿਨੀ ਆਪਨਾ ਜਨਮੁ ਗਵਾਇਆ॥
ਜਮੁ ਦਰਿ ਬਧੇ ਚਪਟਾ ਖਾਵਹਿ ਫਿਰਿ ਫਿਰਿ ਜੋਨੀ ਪਾਇਆ॥੩॥
ਸਤਗੁਰ ਕੀ ਸਰਣਾਈ ਪਵੈ ਤਾ ਜੂਨਿ ਕਟੀਐ ਵਿਚਹੁ ਆਪੁ ਗਵਾਇ॥
ਆਪੁ ਗਇਆ ਤਾ ਸਤਗੁਰ ਮਿਲਿਆ ਨਾਨਿਕ ਹਰਿ ਗੁਣ ਗਾਇ॥੪॥੨॥

3. 3. Kabir

੩. ੩. ੧.   ਰਾਗੁ ਸੂਹੀ ਕਬੀਰ

* ਜੈਸੇ ਰੰਗੁ ਸੁਪਨੈ ਨਿਧਿ ਪਾਈ ਮਨ ਹੀ ਮਨ ਸਮਾਨਾ॥
ਨਾਹੀ ਓਹੁ ਰੰਗੁ ਨਾਹੀ ਸੋਈ ਧੰਨੁ ਫਿਰਿ ਪਾਛੈ ਪਛੁਤਾਨਾ॥੧॥
ਬਾਵਰੇ ਤੈ ਮਤੁ ਜਾਨਿਆ ਤਨੁ ਧਨੁ ਹੈ ਮੇਰਾ ਮਾਤ ਪਿਤਾ ਸੁਤ ਭਾਈ॥
ਖਿਨ ਭੰਹਨ ਪਾਨੀ ਪਾਖਾਨ ਜਿਵ ਨਾਵੈ ਨਾਵ ਬਿਲਾਈ॥੧॥ ਰਹਾਉ॥
ਪੂਤ ਕਲਤੁ ਗਿਰਹੁ ਸਗਲ ਬਿਥਾਰਾ ਤੈ ਮਤੁ ਜਾਣਹਿ ਸਾਰਾ॥
ਕੈ ਕਿਰਮੁ ਹੋਹਿ ਕੈ ਬਿਸਟਾ ਮੂਏ ਹੋਹਿ ਸਭ ਛਾਰਾ॥੨॥
ਜਮੁ ਕਾਹੂ ਕੀ ਸੰਕ ਨ ਮਾਨੈ ਕਰ ਗਹ ਚੋਟੀ ਮਾਰੇ॥
ਅਜੈ ਨ ਚੇਤਿਆ ਮੂੜ ਮਨ ਮੇਰੇ ਵੇਦ ਪੁਰਾਨ ਪੁਕਾਰੇ॥੩॥
ਇਹੁ ਸੈਸਾਰੁ ਅਧ ਕੀ ਜੇਵੜੀ ਭੂਲਿ ਪੜੇ ਜਮ ਫਾਹੀ॥
ਕਹੁ ਕਬੀਰ ਸੋਈ ਜਨ ਉਬਰੇ ਇਕੁ ਰਾਮੁ ਜਿਨਾ ਮਨ ਮਾਹੀ॥੪॥੧॥

117

੩. ੩. ੨. ਰਾਗੁ ਸੂਹੀ ਕਬੀਰ

ਕੁਸਲੁ ਕੁਸਲੁ ਕਰ ਸਭ ਜਗ ਬਿਨਸਿਆ ਪਰਿਓ ਕਾਲ ਕੀ ਫਾਸੀ॥
ਏਕੁ ਅਲਖੁ ਨ ਜਾਈ ਲਖਿਆ ਪੂਰਨੁ ਸਰਬ ਨਿਵਾਸੀ॥੧॥
ਕੁਸਲ ਖੇਮ ਅਰੁ ਸਹੀ ਸਲਾਮਤਿ ਏਹ ਕਤ ਕਾਰਨਿ ਕੀਨੇ॥
ਆਵਤ ਜਾਤ ਦੋਉ ਪਦ ਲੂਟੇ ਸਰਬ ਸੰਗਿ ਹਰਿ ਲੀਨੇ॥੧॥ ਰਹਾਉ॥
ਸੁਰਿ ਨਰਿ ਮੁਨਿ ਜਨ ਪੀਰ ਅਉਲੀਏ ਤਹ ਆਦਿ ਪਰਮਪਦ ਚੀਨੇ॥
ਕੋਟ ਅਸੰਖ ਕਹ ਲਉ ਬਰਨਉ ਤਿਨੀ ਪੈਆਨੇ ਦੀਨੇ॥੨॥
ਧਰਨਿ ਅਕਾਸੁ ਪਉਣ ਫੁਨਿ ਜਾਈ ਹ ਚਦ ਸੂਰਜੁ ਫੁਨਿ ਜਾਸੀ॥
ਕਹੁ ਕਬੀਰ ਫੁਨਿ ਹਮ ਤੁਮ ਜਾਈ ਹੈ ਰਹੈ ਰਾਮੁ ਅਬਿਨਾਸੀ॥੩॥੧੦॥

118

੩. ੩. ੩. ਰਾਗੁ ਮਾਰੂ ਕਬੀਰ

* ਚਾਲੀ ਅਚਲ ਭਈ ਥਿਤਿ ਪਾਈ ਜਹ ਕੀ ਤਹਾ ਸਮਾਈ॥

ਅਬ ਮੋਹਿ ਹਰਿਓ ਰੇ ਭਾਈ॥੧॥ ਰਹਾਉ॥

ਕਰਤ ਭੇਖ ਭਰਮ ਅਰੁ ਪਾਖੰਡਾ ਲੇ ਲੇ ਸੰਖ ਉਘਾਈ॥

ਗਿਆਨ ਅੰਜਨ ਜਰਿ ਭਏ ਭਸਮ ਸਰਿ ਦੇਤ ਦੋਤਿ ਮਿਲਾਈ॥੧॥

ਨਾਹੀ ਉਰਵਾਰੁ ਪਾਰੁ ਨਾਹੀ ਪਰ ਮਿਤਿ ਕਤ ਅਵਓ ਕਤ ਜਾਵਓ॥

ਕਹੁ ਕਬੀਰ ਮੈ ਅਵਸਰੁ ਪਾਇਆ ਬਹੁੜਿ ਨ ਫੇਰਿ ਬਜਾਵਓ॥੨॥੧੩॥

119

੩. ੩. ੪.   ਰਾਗੁ ਰਾਮਕਲੀ ਕਬੀਰ

* ਮਦਰੁ ਚੁਨਤ ਮਾਸ ਦਸ ਲਾਗੇ ਦੁਇ ਬਮ ਦਸੇ ਦੁਆਰਾ॥

ਸੋਈ ਜੋਗੀ ਆਸਣਿ ਬੈਠਾ ਸੋਈ ਕਰਤ ਉਧਾਰਾ॥੧॥

ਮੈ ਕਿਆ ਜਾਨਾ ਐਸਾ ਜੋਗੀ॥

ਰਹੈ ਅਲਿਪਤੁ ਸਰ ਬਰ ਸਭੋਗੀ॥੧॥ ਰਹਾਉ॥

ਆਵਤ ਜੋਗੀ ਸਭੁ ਜਗੁ ਦੇਖਿਆ ਜਾਤੁ ਨ ਲਖਿਆ ਕੋਇ॥

ਆਸਣੁ ਛੋਡਿ ਚਲਿਆ ਜਬ ਜੋਗੀ ਪਾਛੈ ਮੁਦਰਾ ਮਾਤਾ ਰੋਈ॥

ਆਪੇ ਜੋਗੀ ਆਪੇ ਭੋਗੀ ਆਪੇ ਪੁਰਖ ਅਕੇਲਾ॥

ਤੀਨਿ ਭਵਟ ਮਹਿ ਸਿਧੀ ਵਾਜੈ ਆਪਿ ਗੁਰੂ ਆਪਿ ਚੇਲਾ॥੩॥

ਪਵਟ ਕਰਿ ਕੈ ਭਸਮ ਉਡਾਵਉ ਮਨ ਕੀ ਮੁੰਡਉ ਮਾਈ॥

ਮਨ ਪਟਵਤੇ ਉਪਰਿ ਆਸਣੁ ਤਹਾ ਕਬੀਰਿ ਲਿਵ ਲਾਈ॥੪॥੨॥.

120

ਧੰਧਾ ਕਰਤ ਚਰਨ ਕਰ ਥਾਕੇ ਜਨਮੁ ਗਇਆ ਤਨੁ ਛੀਨਾ॥

ਥਾਕੇ ਨੈਟ ਸਰਵਣ ਸ੍ਰੁਤਿ ਥਾਕੇ ਕਪਟ ਰਹਿਆ ਮਨ ਲੀਨਾ॥੧॥

ਜਾਹਿ ਜਾਦੀ ਨਾਉ ਨਾ ਲੀਆ॥੧॥ ਰਹਾਉ॥

ਜਾਗੁ ਜਾਗੁ ਜਾਗ ਮਨ ਮੇਰੇ ਸੋਇ ਰਹਿਆ ਕਦਿ ਜਾਗਹਿਗਾ॥

ਜਾ ਘਟ ਭੀਤਰਿ ਚੋਰੁ ਪੜੈਗਾ ਤਾ ਕਿਸ ਕੈ ਅੰਜਲਿ ਲਾਗਹਿਗਾ॥੨॥

ਕਹਤ ਕਬੀਰ ਸੁਨਹੁ ਮਨਾ ਮੇਰੇ ਕਰਿ ਲੈਹੁ ਜੋ ਕਿਛੁ ਕਰਣਾ॥

ਲਖ ਚਉਰਾਸੀ ਫੇਰੁ ਪੜੈਗਾ ਅੰਤਿ ਨਿਹਾਇਤਿ ਮਰਣਾ॥੩॥੭॥

ਡਾਇਣ ਡਾਰੇ ਸੁਨਹੇ ਡੋਰਾ ਸਿੰਧ ਰਹਿਆ ਬਨੁ ਘੇਰੇ॥
ਪੰਚ ਕੁਟੰਬ ਗਿਰਹਿ ਮਹਿ ਜੂਝੇ ਤਾ ਵਾਜੇ ਸਬਦ ਘਨੇਰੇ॥੧॥
ਤਬ ਨਾਮੁ ਜਪਹੁ ਰੇ ਪ੍ਰਾਨੀ ਬੁਝਹੁ ਅਕਥ ਕਹਾਨੀ॥੧॥ ਰਹਾਉ॥
ਰੋਹਿਆ ਮਿਰਗ ਸਸੈ ਬਨੁ ਘੇਰਿਆ ਪਾਰਬਿ ਬਾਨੁ ਨ ਮੇਲੈ॥
ਜੇ ਜਲੁ ਜਲੈ ਸਗਲ ਬਨ ਠਾਟਾ ਮਛ ਅਹੇੜੈ ਖੇਲੈ॥੨॥
ਸੋਈ ਪੰਡਤਿ ਸੋਈ ਪੜਿਆ ਜੋ ਇਸ ਪਦੈ ਵੀਚਾਰੈ॥
ਕਹਤੁ ਕਬੀਰੁ ਸੋਈ ਗੁਰੁ ਮੇਰਾ ਜਿ ਆਪ ਤਰੈ ਮੋਹਿ ਤਾਰੈ॥੩॥੮॥

ਜੋ ਪੂਜਾ ਹਰਿ ਭਲ ਮਾਨੈ ਸਾ ਪੂਜਨਹਾਰ ਨਾ ਜਾਨੈ।।੧।।
ਗੁਸਈਆ ਭਈ ਬਿਕਲ ਮਤਿ ਮੇਰੀ।।
ਨਾ ਜਾਨਾ ਦੁਨੀ ਦਿਵਾਨੀ ਤੇਰੀ।।੧।। ਰਹਾਉ।।
ਕਹਿ ਭਓ ਭਗਤੀ ਕੀ ਪੂਜਾ ਕਿਉ ਭਇਆ ਦੇਵ ਤੇ ਦੂਜਾ।।
ਕਿਆ ਕੀਚੈ ਝੂਠੁ ਪਸਾਰਾ ਪੂਜੀਐ ਪੂਜਨਹਾਰਾ।।੨।।
ਕਹੁ ਕਬੀਰੈ ਸੁ ਗਾਵਾ ਮੈ ਨ ਗਾਵਾ ਆਪੁ ਲਖਾਵਾ।।
ਜੋਇ ਸੁਖ ਦੁਖ ਮਾਹਿ ਸਮਾਨਾ ਸੋਈ ਪੂਜਨਹਾਰੁ ਸਿਆਨਾ।।੩।।੧੯।।

३. ३. ੮.   ਰਾਗੁ ਸੋਰਠਿ ਕਬੀਰ

* ਤੂ ਦੈਆਲੁ ਮੈ ਦਮ ਦ ਮੰਦਰੁ ਵਾਜਉ ਜੇਸੇ ਵਜਾਵੈ॥
ਕਰਮਬੰਧੁ ਮੈ ਰਮ ਕ ਪੁਤਰਾ ਨਾਚਉ ਜੈਸੇ ਨਚਾਵੈ॥੧॥
ਤ੍ਰਿਗੁਣ ਕਾਛਿ ਕਾਛਿ ਆਵੈ॥
ਨਾਨਾ ਵਿਧਿ ਸੁਆਗ ਦਿਖਾਵੈ॥੧॥ ਰਹਾਉ॥
ਜੈਸੇ ਕਾਚਾ ਭਾਡਾ ਬਿਨਸਿ ਫੂਟਿ ਜਾਇ ਬਹੁਰਿ ਕਾਮਿ ਨਾਹੀ ਆਵੈ॥
ਰਾਮ ਜਪਤ ਜਨ ਕਹਾ ਸਮਾਏ ਕੋਈ ਹੈ ਕਮੀਰ ਸਮਝਾਵੈ॥੨॥੨੦॥

124

ਮਾਟੀ ਖੋਦਿ ਕੈ ਭੀਤਿ ਉਸਾਰੀ ਪਸੂ ਕਹੁ ਘਰੁ ਮੇਰਾ॥

ਘੜਿ ਛੋਡਿ ਹੰਸਿ ਕੀਆ ਪੈਆਨਾ ਬਹੁੜਿ ਨ ਕਰਸੀ ਫੇਰਾ॥੧॥

ਮਨ ਰੇ ਤਨੁ ਕਾਗਦ ਕਾ ਪੁਤਰਾ॥

ਊਪਜੈ ਬਿਨਸਿ ਜਾਇ ਛਿਨ ਭੀਤਰਿ ਗਰਬੁ ਨਾ ਛੋਡੈ ਬਪੁਰਾ॥੧॥ ਰਹਾਉ॥

ਤਿਲ ਤਿਲੁ ਕਰ ਕੈ ਇਹੁ ਧਨੁ ਜੋੜਿਆ ਲਇ ਮਾਟੀ ਮੈ ਗਾਡਿਆ॥

ਰੁਧਾ ਕੁੰਭ ਸਬਦੁ ਨਾਹੀ ਉਚਰੈ ਜਹ ਗਾਡਿਆ ਤਹ ਛਾਡਿਆ॥੨॥

ਕਹੁ ਕਬੀਰ ਨਟ ਨਾਟਿਕਾ ਬਾਕੇ ਸਿਆਮ ਜੀਉ ਬੇਨੁ ਬਜਾਵੈ॥

ਗਏ ਪਖੰਡੀਆ ਬਾਜੀ ਨ ਪਾਟੀ ਕਵਨ ਕਾਹੁ ਕੈ ਆਵੈ॥੩॥੨੨॥

3. 4. *Namdev*

੩. ੪. ੧.   ਰਾਗੁ ਸੂਹੀ ਨਾਮਦੇਵ

ਮਾਤ ਕਹੈ ਮੇਰੇ ਪੁਤਰਾ ਘਰਿ ਅੰਨਿ ਕਿਉ ਸਰਸੀ॥
ਜਿਨਿ ਏਹੁ ਜਗਤੁ ਉਪਾਇਆ ਸੋ ਚਿੰਤਾ ਕਰਸੀ॥੧॥
ਕਰਮ ਕਰ ਕੋਕਰਮ ਕਰਾ ਤਾ ਬਰਜੁ ਰੀ ਮਾਈ॥
ਆਦਿ ਪੁਰਖੁ ਮਇ ਸੇਵਿਆ ਜਿਨੀ ਸਿਸਟਿ ਉਪਾਈ॥੧॥ ਰਹਾਉ॥
ਦੀਪ ਕੈ ਬਿਨੁ ਮੰਦਰੁ ਕੈਸਾ ਸਿਸਿਅਰ ਬਿਨੁ ਰੈਣੀ॥
ਬਿਨੁ ਮਾਤਾ ਬਾਲਿਕੁ ਕੈਸਾ ਤਿਉ ਨਾਮ ਵਿਹੂਣੀ॥੨॥
ਕਾਹੂ ਕੈ ਮਨਿ ਕੋਉ ਵਸੈ ਕਾਉ ਕਿਛੁ ਸੁਹਾਈ॥
ਨਾਮਦੇ ਕੈ ਮਨਿ ਰਾਮਈਆ ਛੀਪਾ ਹਰਿ ਗੁਨ ਗਾਈ॥੩॥੧੧॥

੩. ੪. ੨.   ਰਾਗੁ ਬਸੰਤੁ ਨਾਮਦੇਵ

* ਕਿਸਨ ਬਸੰਤ ਭਲੇ ਤੁਮਿ ਆਏ ਦੁਆਦਸਿ ਬਨ ਤਨ ਫੂਲੇ॥

ਨਾਭਿ ਕਵਲ ਤੇ ਬ੍ਰਹਮਾ ਉਪਜੇ ਤ ਤੁਮਿ ਕੈਸੇ ਭੂਲੇ॥੧॥

ਮਨ ਭਵਰਰੇ ਪੀਉ ਰਾਮੁ ਨਾਮੁ ਰਸੁ॥

ਬਹੁਰਿ ਨ ਭਵਹਿ ਸੁਟਹਿ ਹਰਿ ਜਸੁ॥੧॥ ਰਹਾਉ॥

ਜੁਗ ਜੁਗ ਸਿਆਮ ਅਬਰ ਬਟ ਫੂਲੇ ਗਲਤ ਭਈ ਸਭਿ ਧਰਤੀ॥

ਅਮਰ ਵੇਲਿ ਸੁਖ ਨਾਰਦ ਪੀਵਦੇ ਤੂ ਕਿਉ ਨ ਪੀਵਹਿ ਉਧਰੰਤੀ॥੨॥

ਸਹਜਿ ਮੂਲ ਗੁਰੁ ਅਡੋਲ ਭਗਤਿ ਕਰਿ ਪੰਚ ਤਤੁ ਕੁਲ ਜੋਤੀ॥

ਹਰਿ ਕੇ ਚਰਨ ਗੁਰੁ ਸਾਧ ਸੰਗਤਿ ਲਹੁ ਬਦਤਿ ਨਾਮਦੇਉ ਕਿਸਨਮਤੀ॥੩॥੪॥

127

३. ४. ३.   ਰਾਗੁ ਭੈਰਉ ਨਾਮਦੇਵ

* ਸੰਤਨ ਕੈ ਇਕੁ ਰੋਟੁ ਜਾਚੁਲਾ ਮੋ ਰੋਟੁ ਲੇ ਨਾਠੋ ਬੀਠੁਲਾ॥੧॥

ਘਿਰਤੁ ਲੇਹੁ ਜੀਉ ਤੁਮਿ ਘਿਰਤੁ ਲੇਹੁ॥

ਘਿਰਤੁ ਲੇਹੁ ਮੋਕਉ ਦਰਸਨੁ ਦੇਹੁ॥੧॥ ਰਹਾਉ॥

ਕੂਕਰੁ ਹੋਇ ਨ ਵਸੈ ਉਜਾੜਿ॥

ਘਿਰਤ ਸੰਗਿ ਰੋਟ ਖਾਹੁ ਮੁਰਾਰਿ॥੨॥

ਉਤਮ ਜਾਤਿ ਨ ਦੇਖੁ ਅਲੋਨੀ॥

ਨਾਮਦੇ ਕੈ ਹਥਿ ਘਿਰਤਾ ਕੀ ਡੋਨੀ॥੩॥੨੪॥

੩. ੪. ੪.   ਰਾਗੁ ਭੈਰਉ ਨਾਮਦੇਵ

ਸੁਲਤਾਨੁ ਪੂਛੈ ਕਹੁ ਰੇ ਨਾਮਾ ਤੇਰਾ ਸੁਆਮੀ ਕੈਸਾ ਹੈ॥
ਸੁਕੀ ਸੇਜ ਜਲੈ ਮਹਿ ਨਿਕਸੈ ਤੜਦੀ ਬਾਟਿ ਅਮੜਾਵੈ॥੧॥
ਰੇ ਘਰਿ ਜਾਹੁ ਨਾਮਾ ਗਾਵੈ ਰਾਮਾ॥
ਭਗਤ ਜਨ ਕੇ ਪੂਰੇ ਕਾਮਾ॥੧॥ ਰਹਾਉ॥
ਤ੍ਰਿਭਵਣ ਧਨੀ ਪੀਤ ਪਿਤਬਰੁ ਬਸੁਲੇ ਨਾਮਾ ਗਾਵੈ॥
ਸੁਕੀ ਸੇਜ ਜਲੈ ਤੇ ਨਿਕਸੈ ਖੜਿਦੀ ਬਾਨਿ ਪਹੁਚਾਵੈ॥੨॥
ਜੇ ਨ ਜੀਵਾਵਹਿ ਮੁਈ ਗਾਇ॥
ਤਾ ਨਾਮਾ ਪਕੜਿ ਮਾਰਹੁ ਠਾਇ॥੩॥
ਉਠੀ ਬਛਰੈ ਚੁਧੀ ਮਾਇ॥
ਨਾਮੇ ਭਗਤਿ ਕਰੀ ਲਿਵ ਲਾਇ॥੪॥੨੬॥

३. ४. ५.   ਰਾਗੁ ਰਾਮਕਲੀ ਨਾਮਦੇਵ

ਨਾਰਦੁ ਕਹੈ ਸੁਨਹੁ ਨਰਾਇਨ ਬੈਕੁੰਠਿ ਵਸੈ ਕਿ ਕਉਲਾਸੰ॥

ਜਹ ਮਮ ਕਥਾ ਤਹੀ ਹਉ ਨਿਹਚਲੁ ਬਸਨ ਮੰਦਰਿ ਵਾਸੰ॥੧॥

ਵੈਸਨੋ ਤੇ ਮੈ ਮੈ ਤੇ ਵੈਸਨੋ ਸੁਨਿ ਨਾਰਦ ਮੁਨਿ ਸਾਚੰ॥

ਜੋ ਭਗਤਾ ਗੀਤਾ ਗੁਨ ਗਾਵੈ ਤਾ ਕੈ ਰਿਦੈ ਤਕਤ ਹੋਇ ਨਾਚੰ॥੧॥ ਰਹਾਉ॥

ਜੋਗੀ ਜਤੀ ਤਪੀ ਸਨਿਆਸੀ ਇਕ ਟਕਿ ਧਿਆਨਿ ਬਹੀਠਾ॥

ਜਜਹਿ ਜਗ ਵੇਦਾ ਅਉਰੁ ਉਚਰਹਿ ਤਿਨ ਹਉ ਕਬਹੁ ਨ ਡੀਠਾ॥੨॥

ਗੰਗਾ ਆਦਿ ਸਗਲ ਤੀਰਥ ਕਰਿ ਉਨ ਜਾਸ ਕ ਕੋਟ ਭਰਮਿ ਆਵਹਿ॥

ਸਭਿ ਵਰਤ ਵਰਤ ਸਾਧਨ ਕਰੇ ਸੋ ਮੈ ਕਬਹੁ ਨ ਪਾਵੈ॥੩॥

ਜੋ ਭਗਤ ਮੇਰਾ ਜਸੁ ਗਾਵਵਿ ਤੇ ਭਗਤਾ ਮਮ ਸਾਰੰ॥

ਉਨ ਕਉ ਜਿਵਾਏ ਮਇ ਜੇਵਾ ਉਨ ਕਉ ਪੀਆਏ ਮਇ ਪੀਆ

ਨਾਮਦੇਉ ਤਿਨ ਪਹਿ ਵਾਰੰ॥੪॥੪॥

੩. ੪. ੬.   ਰਾਗੁ ਮਲਾਰ ਨਾਮਦੇਵ

* ਗਗਨਿ ਅਮਰੁ ਛਾਇਆ ਆਪੁਨੈ ਰੰਗੇ॥
ਅਲਖ ਨਿਰੰਜਨ ਰਾਮਈਆ ਰਵਿ ਰਹਿਆ ਸੰਗੇ॥੧॥
ਤੇਰੀ ਨ ਜਾਨੀ ਮਾਇਆ॥
ਰਾਮ ਨਾਮੈ ਜੀਅੜਾ ਵੇਖਿਆ ਭਰਮੁ ਚੁਕਾਇਆ॥੧॥ ਰਹਾਉ॥
ਪਟਵਤਿ ਨਾਮਾ ਸੁਆਮੀ ਹਰਿ ਕੀਨੀ ਦਇਆ॥
ਜਨਮ ਮਰਣ ਕਾ ਭਰਮੁ ਮਿਟਿ ਗਇਆ॥੨॥੪॥

131

3. 5. Trilochaṇ

੩. ੫. ੧.   ਰਾਗੁ ਧਨਾਸਰੀ ਤ੍ਰਿਲੋਚਨ

ਦੇਹੁਰੀ ਭੀਤਰਿ ਸਰੁਸਰਹਿ ਭੀਤਰਿ
ਜਲੁ ਜਲਹਿ ਭਤਿਰਿ ਆਛੈ ਨਿਜ ਕਵਲੰ॥
ਸੋਈ ਰੀ ਸੀਤਲ ਸਰੁ ਸੋਈ ਹੈ
ਨਿਰਮਲੁ ਜਲੁ ਜਾਗਤੁ ਸੋਵਤੁ
ਮੋ ਕਉ ਮਿਲਿਆ ਹੈ ਸਾਰਗਧਰੁ॥੧॥
ਮੋਰੈ ਮੋਰੈ ਅਹਨੇ ਰਾਮੁ ਰਵਿ ਜਾਇ॥
ਹਰਿ ਕਾ ਚਲਿਤੁ ਮੋਰੈ ਹੀਅਰੈ ਵਸਿਓ ਰੀ ਮਾਇ॥੧॥ ਰਹਾਉ॥
ਨੈਨ ਨਿਵਾਰਉ ਤ ਸਰਵਣ ਨ ਰਹਨੀ
ਸਰਵਨ ਨਿਵਾਰਉ ਤਾ ਮਨ ਰਹੈ ਨ ਠਾਇ॥
ਠਗ ਚੇ ਲਡੂ ਖਾਏਦੀ ਨੇਰੀ ਜਾਦਮ ਰਾਏ
ਜਤ ਬੀਠਲੁ ਤਤ ਜਾਉਰੀ ਬਹਿ ਨ ਮਾਇ॥੨॥
ਲੋਹੇ ਚੇ ਸੰਗਲ ਪਾਏ ਤੋੜੇ ਰੀ ਘਟ ਚ ਘਾਏ
ਅਸਨੇਹ ਕੇ ਸੰਗਲ ਤਿਸ ਨਾ ਤੋੜੇ ਨ ਜਾਹੀ॥
ਬਦਿਤ ਤਿਲੋਚਨੁ ਗਹਿਓ ਹੈ ਉੂਜਲ ਠਾਉ
ਮੇਰਾ ਮਨੁ ਤੇਰੈ ਪਹਿ ਲਾਗੋ ਹੈ ਦੁਆਰਕੇ ਰਾਇ॥੩॥੧੨॥

३. ੫. ੨.   ਰਾਗੁ ਰਾਮਕਲੀ ਤ੍ਰਿਲੋਚਨ

ਰਾਜਾ ਰਾਵਣ ਸੁਨਹੁ ਬੇਨਤੀ ਕਹੈ ਮਦੋਦਰਿ ਰਾਣੀ॥
ਜਿਸੁ ਕੇ ਰੀਤੈ ਕਾਰਨ ਮੇਟੀ ਤਿਸੁ ਕੇ ਰੀਤੈ ਆਨੀਰੇ॥੧॥
ਸੀਆ ਫੇਰਿ ਨ ਕਰਿ ਸਾਗ ਰਾਮ॥
ਪਗਿ ਲਗਿ ਕੰਤੁ ਮਨਾਵਹੁ ਰਾਜਾ ਰਾਮੁ॥੧॥ ਰਹਾਉ॥
ਦਸ ਸਿਰ ਬੀਸ ਭੰਡ ਭੁਜ ਮੇਰੇ ਕੁਭਕਰਣੁ ਮੇਰਾ ਭਾਈ॥
ਮੇਘਨਾਥੁ ਗੁ ਭੀਤਰਿ ਗਾਜੈ ਮਦੁ ਸਾਗਰੁ ਮੇਰੀ ਖਾਈ॥੨॥
ਰਿਛ ਬੰਦਰ ਮਿਲਿ ਭਏ ਇਕਠੇ ਉਹ ਦੇਖੁਸ ਇਰੁ ਬੰਧ॥
ਦੂਹੁ ਦੂਹੁ ਲੋਚਨ ਸਭ ਕਿਛੁ ਸੂਝੇ ਬੀਸ ਲੈਨ ਹੇ ਅੰਧ॥੩॥
ਰਿਛ ਬਾਦਰ ਮਿਲਿ ਭਏ ਇਕਠੇ ਤਾ ਕਾ ਅੰਤੁ ਨ ਪਾਇਆ॥
ਬਦਤਿ ਤਿਲੋਚਨ ਮੂਰਖ ਰਾਵਣ ਮਰਣੁ ਪਤਨੁ ਤੇਰਾ ਆਇਆ॥੪॥੬॥

133

3. 6. Beṇi

3. ੬. ੧. ਰਾਗੁ ਰਾਮਕਲੀ ਬੇਣੀ

ਦੁਪਰੀਤੇ ਸੁਪਰੀਤੇ ਅਨਿਕ ਕਰਮ ਕੀਤੇ
ਮਰਨ ਜੀਵਣ ਕੀ ਬੁਝਿ ਲੇ ਬਾਜੀ॥
ਤਿਹ ਗੁਣਾ ਤੇ ਰਹੈ ਵਧਿ ਬਰਹਮ ਲਖੇ
ਬਹੜਿ ਬਹੜਿ ਨਾਹੀ ਤੇਰੀ ਸੁਦਰੀ ਸਾਜੀ॥੧॥
ਐਸੇ ਖਾਇ ਮਨੁ ਲਾਗਾ ਰਹਣੁ ਨ ਜਾਇ॥
ਦੁਕਰਤੁ ਸੁਕਰਤੁ ਮੇਰਾ ਗਇਆ ਹੀ ਗਵਾਇ॥੧॥ ਰਹਾਉ॥
ਬਿਚਰਿ ਲੇ ਮਾਇਆ ਬਿਆਪੀ ਨਾਹੀ ਰੇ ਫਨੈ ਸਮਾਧੀ
ਗੁਰਿ ਤਤੁ ਗਿਆਨੁ ਨਿਜਰ ਅੰਬ੍ਰਿਤੁ ਦੀਆ॥
ਸਬਦੁ ਕਾ ਕਲਸ ਕੀਆ ਤਾ ਸੁਲੇ ਅੰਬ੍ਰਿਤੁ ਪੀਆ
ਦੇਖੀ ਬਾਜੀ ਉਲਟੀ ਤਾ ਗਵਣੁ ਕੀਆ॥੨॥
ਅਖਬ ਨਾ ਕਿਆ ਕਬੀਐ ਤੇਰਾ ਕਉਣੁ ਬਾਨੁ
ਜਿ ਮਬੀਐ ਰੂਪ ਅਨੇਕ ਅਨੰਤ ਮਾਇਆ॥
ਸਹਜ ਅੰਤਰਿ ਕਿਰਨਿ ਵਿਗਾਸੀ ਆਤਮਾ ਪਰਗਾਸੀ
ਖਜਿਤ ਖੋਜਤ ਅਚਿਤ ਭਇਆ॥੩॥
ਸੁਨ ਮੰਧੇ ਨਿਰੰਕਾਰੀ ਤੜਾ ਜੈਸੇ ਚਮਤਕਾਰੀ
ਧਨਖ ਕੀ ਰੇਖਿਆ ਅਨੂਪ ਬਾਣੀ॥
ਸਹਜ ਕੀ ਪੰਖੜੀ ਜਾਗੀ ਤਾ
ਸੁਮੰਧੇ ਭਇਆ ਰਾਗੀ ਭਨਥ ਬੇਣੀ ਤੇਰੀ ਜੁਗਤਿ ਐਸੀ॥੪॥੩॥

134

3. 7. Sharaf

੩. ੭. ੧.   ਰਾਗੁ ਸੂਹੀ ਸ਼ਰਫ਼

ਜਿਸੁ ਕਾਰਨਿ ਤਨੁ ਮਨੁ ਜਾਲਿਆ॥
ਤਿਨਿ ਸਰਜਨਿ ਕਉਲੁ ਨ ਪਾਲਿਆ॥੧॥
ਮੇਰੀ ਡਾਲ ਨ ਮੋੜਿ ਮਸਤਾ ਮਾਲੀਆ॥
ਕਚੀ ਕਲੀ ਨ ਤੋੜ ਮਸਤਾ ਮਾਲੀਆ॥੧॥ ਰਹਾਉ॥
ਜਿਸੁ ਕਾਰਨਿ ਦੁਖੁ ਸੁਖੁ ਹਉ ਸਹਾ॥
ਢੁਢੇਦੀ ਮਾਟਕੁ ਨਾ ਲਹਾ॥੨॥
ਛਿਟਕਾਇਨ ਵੰਗਾ ਚੂੜੀਆ॥
ਸਹ ਵਾਝਹੁ ਗਾਲੀ ਕੂੜੀਆ॥੩॥
ਕਿਵ ਫਹਿ ਆਪਿ ਗਰਬਿਆ॥
ਤਨੁ ਖਾਕੁ ਸੇਤੀ ਗਡਿਆ॥੪॥
ਕਿਵ ਤਹਿ ਆਵਲ ਬਾਵਲਾ॥
ਦੀਬਾਣੁ ਨ ਸੇਵਹਿ ਰਾਵਲਾ॥੫॥
ਜੋ ਦਿਸੈ ਸੋਇ ਵਖਾਣੀਐ॥
ਕੁਦਰਤੀ ਸਾਹਿਬੁ ਜਾਟੀਐ॥੬॥
ਢੁਢੇਦੀ ਮਾਟਕੁ ਪਾਇਆ॥
ਇਕੁ ਪੁਨੀ ਸਹੁ ਘਰਿ ਆਇਆ॥੭॥
ਸੇਖ ਸਰਫ਼ ਨ ਹੋਹੁ ਉਤਾਵਲਾ॥
ਇਕਤੁ ਸਟ ਨ ਥੀਵਹਿ ਚਾਵਲਾ॥੮॥੧੨॥

Notes

Chapter 1

1. Note that the traditional identification of the manuscript prepared during Guru Arjan's time with the Kartarpur Pothi, a manuscript presently in the custody of Guru Amarjit Singh Sodhi, in Kartarpur, has been open to controversy. The Kartarpur Pothi is dated "Samat 1661, *miti* Bhadon *vadi* 1 (1604 C. E.)," which indeed falls during Guru Arjan's period, and my research confirms the traditional position; for a detailed discussion, see my "The Making of Sikh Scripture" (Ph. D. diss., Columbia University, 1993), pp. 94-113; Harbhajan Singh, *Gurbani Sampadan Nirnai* (Chandigarh: Satnam Prakashan, 1989), pp. 81-91; Daljeet Singh, *Essay on the Authenticity of Kartarpuri Bir and the Integrated Logic and Unity of Sikhism* (Patiala: Punjabi University, 1987); Sahib Singh, *Adi Bir bare* (Amritsar: Singh Brothers, 1987), pp. 121-122; Bhai Jodh Singh, "Sri Kartarpur vali Pavitar 'Adi' Bir," in Piar Singh, ed., *Bhai Jodh Singh Gadd Saurabh* (Patiala: Punjabi University, 1986), pp. 487-496; Giani Mahan Singh, *Param Pavitar Adi Bir da Sankalna Kal*, (Amritsar: Khalsa Samachar, 1952), pp. 3, 33, and 50; Bhai Vir Singh, *Sri Asht Gur Chamatkar, Bhag 1 te 2* (Amritsar: Khalsa Samachar, 1990), pp. 2: 66-67. For scholars who do not accept the Kartarpur Pothi as the document prepared during Guru Arjan's time, see Piar Singh, *Gatha Sri Adi Granth* (Amritsar: Guru Nanak Dev University, 1992), pp. 174-209; Piara Singh Padam, *Sri Guru Granth Prakash* (Patiala: Kalam Mandir, 1990), p. 100; Sant Inder Singh Chakarvarti, "Sri Guru Granth Sahib dian Biran de Bhed," in Jeet Singh Sital, ed., *Gurmat Sahitt* (Patiala: Punjab Language Department, 1989), p. 212; Pritam Singh, "Bhai Banno Copy of the Sikh Scripture," *Journal of Sikh Studies* 11: 2 (1984), p. 99; Giani Gurdit Singh, "Adi Bir da Rachna Kal," *Prakash*, June 30, 1952; G. B. Singh, *Sri Guru Granth Sahib dian Prachin Biran* (Lahore: Modern Publications, 1944), pp. 247-273. See also Surjit Hans, *A Reconstruction of Sikh History from Sikh Literature* (Jalandhar: ABS Publications, 1988), pp. 251, and 261, notes 72-73. Hans refers to a passage in Sukha Singh's *Gurbilas Dasvin Patishahi* written in 1797, which questions the authenticity of the manuscript at Kartarpur. Harnamdas Udasi, however, interprets this same eighteenth-century passage as referring to the manuscript

presently at Bhai ki Droli, a village near Moga, Faridkot; see his *Adi Shri Guru Granth Sahib Ji dian Puratani Biṛan te Vichar* (Kapurthala: Kantesh Ayurvedic Pharmacy, n. d. 1969?), pp. 116-119. Regarding the tradition of the turning of the Kartarpur Pothi into the Adi Granth by the mere addition of Guru Tegh Bahadur's compositions, see "The Making of Sikh Scripture," pp. 108-113. For a discussion of the arrangement of the text in the Adi Granth, see Mohinder Kaur Gill, *Guru Granth Sahib di Sampadan-kala* (Delhi: Rabbi Prakashan, 1974)

2. For another early source of the text of the saints, see Gopal Narayan Bahura, ed., *The Padas of Surdas* (Jaipur: Maharaja Savai Man Singh 2 Museum, 1982). According to the colophon, this manuscript was prepared in 1582. The text includes 411 hymns, which belong to Surdas, Kabir, Namdev, Ravidas, Parmanand, etc., placed under 22 different *rags*.

3. On the basis of information available in the Goindval Pothis, the question of the time of admittance of the non-Sikh saints' compositions into the Sikh sacred text can be resolved in a cogent manner. Three views about this particular issue are available in Sikh literature. Starting with Sarupdas Bhalla, traditional sources place the entry of the hymns of the saints into Sikh scripture during Guru Arjan's time. See Sarupdas Bhalla, *Mahima Prakash, Bhag Duja* (Patiala: Punjab Language Department, 1971), pp. 369-371.

Writing at the beginning of the twentieth century, Teja Singh and Sahib Singh located the inclusion of the saints' hymns in Sikh sacred literature in Guru Nanak's time. See Teja Singh, "Sri Guru Granth Sahib da Sampadan," in Giani Lal Singh, ed., *Guru Arjan: Jivan te Rachna* (Patiala: Punjab Language Department, 1985). pp. 138-140; Sahib Singh, *Adi Biṛ bare*, pp. 85-108 (some of the essays in this book had been published by 1954, in Punjabi journals, and thus had become part of scholarly discussion much before the publication of the book), and *Sri Guru Granth Sahib Darpaṇ* (Jalandhar: Raj Publishers, 1961-1964), pp. 3: 841-916.

Scholars of the third opinion link the inclusion of the non-Sikh saints' hymns in Sikh literature with Guru Amardas' period: G. B. Singh, *Sri Guru Granth Sahib dian Prachin Biṛan*, p. 24; Mohan Singh Dewana, *A History of Punjabi Literature* (Jalandhar: Bharat Prakashan, 1971), pp. 37, and 46; Balbir Singh Dil, *Amar Kavi Guru Amardas* (Patiala: Punjab Language Department, 1975), pp. 52-53; Giani Gurdit Singh, *Itihas Sri Guru Granth Sahib, Bhagat*

Baṇi Bhag (Chandigarh: Sikh Sahitt Sansathan, 1990), p. 481. I find this scholarly position most convincing.

For an important discussion of medieval collections of religious poetry, see John Stratton Hawley, "The *Nirguṇ/Saguṇ* Distinction in Early Manuscript Anthologies of Hindu Devotion," in David N. Lorenzen, ed., *Bhakti Religion in North India* (Albany: State University of New York Press, 1995). pp. 160-180.

4. Sarupdas Bhalla, *Mahima Prakash, Patishahi* 3, *Sakhi* 18, p. 208:

ਜਨਮੇ ਪ੍ਰਭੂ ਸੁੰਦਰ ਸੁਖਧਾਮ। ਸੰਸਰਾਮ ਰਾਧਾ ਗੁਰ ਨਾਮ। . . .

ਸਤਿਗੁਰ ਕੀ ਬਾਣੀ ਸੋ ਲਿਖੇ। ਜਿ ਸਰਧਾ ਹੋਇ ਸੋ ਇਨ ਸੇ ਸਿਖੇ।

Patishahi 5, *Sakhi* 11, pp. 358-359, and 361:

ਏਕ ਦਿਵਸ ਪ੍ਰਭ ਪ੍ਰਾਤਹਕਾਲ। ਦਇਆ ਭਰੇ ਪ੍ਰਭ ਦੀਨ ਦਿਆਲ।

ਯਹ ਮਨ ਉਪਜੀ ਪ੍ਰਗਟਿਓ ਜਗ ਪੰਥ। ਤਿਹ ਕਾਰਨ ਕੀਜੇ ਅਬ ਗ੍ਰੰਥ।੨। . . .

ਤਬ ਗੁਰਦਾਸ ਕਰੀ ਅਰਦਾਸ। ਸਭ ਪੋਥੀ ਸੰਸਰਾਮ ਕੇ ਪਾਸ।

ਮੋਹਨ ਮਸਤਾਨ ਸਾਹਿਬ ਕਾ ਪੂਤੂ। ਵੇ ਤਪ ਭਗਤ ਜੋਗ ਕਾ ਸੂਤੂ।੪।

ਪ੍ਰਥਮੇ ਤਾ ਸੋ ਪੋਥੀ ਲੀਜੇ। ਪੁਨ ਬਾਣੀ ਅਵਰ ਇਕਤੂ ਕੀਜੇ।

ਤਬ ਬੰਧੇਜ ਗ੍ਰੰਥ ਕਾ ਹੋਇ। ਜੋ ਭਾਵੈ ਸਤਿਗੁਰ ਸੋ ਹੋਇਆ। . . .

ਹਸ ਮੋਹਨ ਸੰਸਰਾਮ ਬੁਲਾਏ। ਪੋਥੀ ਗੁਰ ਅਰਜਨ ਦੇਵ ਦਿਵਾਏ।

ਅਵਰੁ ਬਾਣੀ ਜਹਾ ਕਹਾ ਜੁ ਆਈ। ਠੌਰ ਠੌਰ ਸੋ ਸਗਲ ਮੰਗਾਈ।੧੩।

5. In popular Sikh thinking, this writing is linked with the name of the preeminent eighteenth century Sikh, Bhai Mani Singh (d. 1738), but in recent research this is not accepted. For a brief discussion of its attribution and time of writing, see Piar Singh, *Gatha Sri Adi Granth*, pp. 13-14; Piar Singh believes it was prepared between 1785 and 1790, and was written by Giani Surat Singh. For reference to the compilation of the Adi Granth, see Tarlochan Singh Bedi, ed., *Sikhan di Bhagatmala* (Patiala: Punjabi University, 1994), pp. 122-123.

6. Giani Inder Singh Gill, ed., *Sri Gur Bilas Patishahi 6* (Amritsar: Vazir Hind Press, 1977), pp. 52-55. Sohan Kavi, the name with which this source is traditionally linked, is difficult to identify. Bhai Kahn Singh Nabha attributes this document to Bhai Gurmukh Singh and Bhai Darbara Singh, both of Amritsar, and assumes that it was written around 1833-1843, see his *Gurmat Sudhakar* (Patiala: Punjab Language Department, 1970), p. 217. For the standard edition of Bhai Santokh Singh's work, see Bhai Vir Singh, ed., *Sri Gur Pratap Suraj Granth* (Amritsar: Khalsa Samachar, 1963). The issue of the compilation of the scriptural text appears on pp. 6: 2044-2059.

7. *Adi Sri Guru Granth Sahib Ji Saṭik (Faridkot vala Ṭika)* (Patiala: Punjab Language Department, 1970), p. 1: 430. The Faridkot commentary resulted from Sikh communal effort to explain the text of the Adi Granth in an authoritative manner. The original draft completed in 1883 by Giani Badan Singh Sekhvan was reviewed by a committee of eight scholars under the leadership of Bawa Sumer Singh of Patna. The preparation of this commentary was a result of the discomfort of Sikhs with the translation of the Adi Granth by the German scholar Ernest Trumpp, in 1877; see Ernest Trumpp, *The Adi Granth or the Holy Scripture of the Sikhs* (Delhi: Munshiram Manoharlal, 1978). This hymn's association with the Goindval Pothis is now fully accepted by Sikh tradition; see Bhai Vir Singh, *Santhaya Sri Guru Granth Sahib* (Amritsar: Khalsa Samachar, 1981), p. 3: 1188.

8. Giani Gian Singh, *Tvarikh Guru Khalsa* (Patiala: Punjab Language Department, 1970), pp. 1: 393-396. This discussion is under the heading "*Sri Guru Granth Sahib Ji di Rachna.*"

9. Giani Gian Singh, *Tvarikh Guru Khalsa*, pp. 1: 393-396.

10. See Gurbachan Singh Talib, *Bani of Sri Guru Amar Das* (New Delhi: Sterling Publishers, 1979), p. vi; Harbans Singh, *The Heritage of the Sikhs* (Delhi: Manohar, 1983), p. 43.

11. In *Sri Gur Bilas Patishahi 6* and *Sri Gur Pratap Suraj Granth* the details of the treatment given by Guru Arjan to the Goindval Pothis has a very deep resonance of the ceremonial respect offered to the Adi Granth in the nineteenth century Sikh community. *Sri Gur Bilas Patishahi 6*, p. 69:

> ਨਗਨ ਚਰਨ ਸ੍ਰੀ ਗੁਰ ਚਲੇ ਖਾਸਾ ਕੰਧ ਉਠਾਇ।
> ਪੰਥ ਚਰਿਤ ਸੁੰਦਰ ਅਧਿਕ ਕਹੋ ਗ੍ਰੰਥ ਬਢ ਜਾਇ੧੮੦। . .
> ਫੂਲ ਪ੍ਰਸਾਦਿ ਲਏ ਸਿੱਖ ਸੰਗਤ ਆਵਤ ਭੇ ਮਨ ਹਰਖ ਧਰਾਈ।
> ਆਇ ਪ੍ਰਣਾਮ ਕਰੀ ਗੁਰ ਕੋ ਗੁਰ ਪੋਥੀਅਨ ਫੂਲ ਪ੍ਰਸਾਦਿ ਚੜਾਈ੧੮੪।

Bhai Santokh Singh, *Sri Gur Pratap Suraj Granth*, p. 6: 2073:

> ਸੁਨਿ ਧੀਰਜ ਸਤਿਗੁਰ ਦਈ ਹੁਇ ਤਜਾਰ ਚਲੇ ਹੈ।
> ਖਾਸੇ ਪਰ ਪੁਸਤਕ ਸੁਭਤਿ ਸੁਭ ਚਮਰ ਝੁਲੇ ਹੈ।
> ਰਾਗੀ ਕਰਤੇ ਕੀਰਤਨ ਬਹੁ ਸਾਜ ਬਜਾਏ।
> ਤਬ ਸੰਧਨਿ ਕੀ ਧੁਨਿ ਭਈ ਸੁਮਨਸ ਬਰਸਾਏ।੩੮।

References to the ceremonial treatment of the Adi Granth begin in the mid-eighteenth century writings, see W. H. McLeod, ed., *The Chaupa Singh Rahit-nama* (Otago: University of Otago Press, 1987), p. 38. See also Bhagat Singh, *Maharaja Ranjit Singh and his Times* (New Delhi: Sehgal, 1990), pp.

285-286. Bhagat Singh's account is built on Ali-ud-Din Mufti's *Ibaratnama* written in 1854, and the reports of the early British visitors to the Punjab.

12. Sarupdas Bhalla, *Mahima Prakash, Patishahi 5, Sakhi 11*, p. 359:

ਪ੍ਰੋਹਤ ਕੋ ਸਤਿਗੁਰ ਕਹਾ ਜਾਰੁ ਸੰਸਰਾਮ ਕੇ ਪਾਸ।

ਕਰਿ ਦਇਆ ਪੋਥੀ ਸਭ ਦੀਜੀਐ ਤਬ ਲਿਖੇ ਗ੍ਰੰਥ ਗੁਰਦਾਸ।

13. Tarlochan Singh Bedi, ed., *Sikhan di Bhagatmala* , pp. 122-123.

14. *Sri Gur Bilas Patishahi 6*, pp. 52-71. Bhai Santokh Singh, *Sri Gur Pratap Suraj Granth*, pp. 6: 2044-2057.

15. *Sri Gur Bilas Patishahi 6*, p. 55. Bhai Santokh Singh, *Sri Gur Pratap Suraj Granth*, p. 6: 2057.

16. Giani Gian Singh, *Tvarikh Guru Khalsa*, pp. 1: 393-396.

17. Piar Singh argues that the declaration of the author of *Mahima Prakash* concerning the Goindval Pothis' being the sole source of the Kartarpur Pothi was primarily to enhance their importance and consequently that of the Bhalla family, their custodians; see *Gatha Sri Adi Granth*, p. 415. This thinking echoes Surjit Hans' argument that the main point of *Mahima Prakash* was to glorify the Bhalla family and, as a result, increase the stature of the author, himself a Bhalla. Hans places the claim presented in the *Mahima Prakash* that Bhai Gurdas--another Bhalla--was given the responsibility of differentiating between genuine and false hymns of the Gurus in the context of this family agenda, see Surjit Hans, *A Reconstruction of Sikh History from Sikh Literature*, pp. 285-287.

My view is different from that of these two scholars. First, the tradition of the use of the Goindval Pothis in the making of the Kartarpur Pothi seems fairly popular in the Sikh community and all writers who addressed this theme took it up. Second, I think by the time *Mahima Prakash* was written, the precise details of the role of the Goindval Pothis in the evolution of the Sikh sacred text had become rather hazy. Consequently, Sarupdas Bhalla is not able to understand the Goindval Pothis as an important precursor of the Kartarpur Pothi, nor does he know that these pothis contained the complete text of the hymns of the Gurus and those of the saints. Instead of having a very specific family agenda, Bhalla simply affirms the popular Sikh tradition, according to which Guru Arjan collected the hymns of Guru Nanak for the first time.

18. According to some of these accounts, hymns of the first four Gurus were available in the Goindval Pothis; to these Guru Arjan added his hymns

and got the Kartarpur Pothi prepared. Universally accepting that the Goindval Pothis were in the custody of Baba Mohan, these writers apparently have not thought through the ramifications of the break between Baba Mohan and the fourth Guru, Guru Ramdas. *Sri Gur Bilas Patishahi 6*, pp. 52, and 73:

ਮੋਹਨ ਮੋਹਰੀ ਨਾਮ ਸੁ ਮੋਹਨਿ ਬਸੈ ਚੁਬਾਰੇ।

ਚਾਰ ਗੁਰੁ ਜੋ ਆਦਿ ਪੋਥੀਆਂ ਤਿਹ ਨਿਕਟਾਰੇ।

ਕੋਉ ਜਤਨ ਕਰ ਸੋਇ ਪੋਥੀਆਂ ਲਿਆਇ ਹੈ।

ਕਹਿਓ ਭਾਈ ਗੁਰਦਾਸ ਹਮੋ ਪ੍ਰਭ ਜਾਇ ਹੈ।੭੧। . . .

ਮੈ ਭਾਖੋ ਤੁਮ ਲਿਖੋ ਬਨਾਏ।

ਚਾਰ ਗੁਰੁ ਬਾਣੀ ਸੁਖ ਪਾਏ।

ਪੋਥੀਆਂ ਇਹੁ ਗੁਰ ਬੇਦ ਸੁ ਬਾਣੀ।

ਹਮ ਲਜਾਏ ਤੁਮ ਪਹਿ ਇਕਠਾਣੀ। . . . ।੨੧੬।

See also Bhai Santokh Singh, *Sri Gur Pratap Suraj Granth*, pp. 6: 2085-2086.

19. For changes in Punjab educational system, see Ganda Singh, ed., *Punjab, 1849-1960* (Ludhiana: Punjabi Sahitt Academy, 1962), pp. 359-379; G. W. Leitner, *Indigenous Education in the Punjab Since Annexation* (Patiala: Punjab Language Department, 1970).

For history of the printed text of the Adi Granth, see Harveen Kaur Randhawa, "Early Printing History of *Guru Granth Sahib*" (M. Phil. term paper, Guru Nanak Dev University, 1985). I am grateful to Harsharan Singh Ahluwalia of Guru Nanak Dev University for arranging to send this important piece of research to me.

20. Teja Singh and Sahib Singh argued emphatically for the origin of the Sikh scripture as being during Guru Nanak's time. They made special use of two passages from seventeenth century writings:

ਤਿਤੁ ਮਹਲਿ ਜੋ ਸਬਦੁ ਹੋਇਆ ਸੋ ਪੋਥੀ ਅੰਗਦ ਜੋਗ ਮਿਲੀ;

ਬਾਬਾ ਫਿਰਿ ਮਕੇ ਗਇਆ ਨੀਲ ਬਸਤ੍ਰ ਧਾਰੇ ਬਨਵਾਲੀ।

ਆਸਾ ਹਥਿ ਕਿਤਾਬ ਕਛਿ ਕੂਜਾ ਬਾਗ ਮੁਸਲਾ ਧਾਰੀ।

These were used to support the existence of a book compiled by Guru Nanak. See "Vilayat vali Janam Sakhi," in Kirpal Singh, ed., *Janam Sakhi Prampra* (Patiala: Punjabi University, 1987), p. 57; For the *vars* of Bhai Gurdas, see Gursharan Kaur Jaggi, ed., *Varan Bhai Gurdas* (Patiala: Punjabi University, 1987), p. 71. The thematic and linguistic relationship between the hymns of the Guru Nanak and his successors were presented as a further proof that the later Gurus had the writings of the earlier ones with them when they composed their hymns; see Sahib Singh, *Gurbani te Itihas bare* (Amritsar: Singh Brothers, 1986), pp. 20-39.

21. Sahib Singh, *Gurbani te Itihas bare*, pp. 9-19.

22. For the importance assigned to the Goindval Pothis in the compilation of the Sikh sacred text, see Bhai Kahn Singh Nabha, *Gurushabad Ratanakar Mahan Kosh* (Patiala: Punjab Language Department, 1981), pp. 427, and 996; Bhai Vir Singh, *Sri Asht Gur Chamatkar, Bhag 1 te 2*, pp. 2: 48-51; Teja Singh, *Shabadarth Sri Guru Granth Sahib Ji*, p. 248; Bhai Jodh Singh, *Sri Kartarpuri Bir de Darshan*, pp. 123-125; Piara Singh Padam, *Sri Guru Granth Prakash*, pp. 55-56, and *Sri Guru Amardas Ji di Bani* (Patiala: Punjabi University, 1979), pp. 23-24; Giani Gurdit Singh, *Itihas Sri Guru Granth Sahib*, pp. 562-565. Although Piara Singh Padam and Giani Gurdit Singh are not willing to accept the Kartarpur Pothi as the manuscript prepared during Guru Arjan's period, they do not raise any suspicion as to the tradition of the use by Guru Arjan of the Goindval Pothis.

In the beginning of the twentieth century, the task of understanding the evolution of the Sikh sacred text commenced, but finding solutions to the difficulties presented were not so easy. On the one hand no clarity seemed to be emerging concerning manuscripts prepared in the sixteenth century; on the other, according to Sikh tradition the original volume of the Adi Granth had been lost in the eighteenth century in a bloody battle with the forces of Ahmad Shah Abdali. In these debates the Kartarpur Pothi came to be recognized as the *textus receptus* for the Adi Granth. For a discussion of this issue, see Harbhajan Singh, *Gurbani Sampadan Nirnai*, pp. 173-180.

23. G. B. Singh, *Sri Guru Granth Sahib dian Prachin Biran*, pp. 12-79.

24. For information about the Guru Harsahai Pothi, see Giani Gurdit Singh, *Itihas Sri Guru Granth Sahib*, pp. 560-561. For the history of the Sodhi family at Guru Harsahai, see Lepel H. Griffin and Charles Francis Massy, *Chiefs and Families of Note in the Punjab* (Lahore: Government Press, 1909), pp. 234-236. According to my research, there appears to be no doubt about the authenticity of this pothi. In 1970, the pothi was stolen from the railway compartment, when the family was bringing it back from a visit to their followers in Faridabad. The theft was reported in the Nirvana police station, but nothing could be done to retrieve the text. Haresh Singh Sodhi is presently the Guru at this seat; according to the family's lineage chart (*kursinama*), he is in the sixteenth generation from Guru Ramdas. The

information in this note was related to me by Guru Haresh Singh himself, in Guru Harsahai, January 1994, during my visit with the family.

25. Sahib Singh, *Gurbaṇi te Itihas bare,* pp. 20-39. The practice of giving the pothi as part of the succession ceremony (*dastarbandi*) is referred to in the literature produced by Miharban's family in the seventeenth century. See Govindnath Rajguru, ed., *Goshṭi Guru Miharvanu* (Chandigarh: Panjab University, 1974), pp. 175-179. In that case the pothi must have been the one, which was present at Guru Harsahai until 1970.

26. Sahib Singh, *Gurbaṇi te Itihas bare,* p. 30; *Adi Biṛ bare,* pp. 34-81.

27. Sahib Singh, *Gurbaṇi te Itihas bare,* p. 34-39; *Adi Biṛ bare,* pp. 82-84.

28. For a detailed discussion on this point see Giani Gurdit Singh, *Itihas Sri Guru Granth Sahib,* pp. 479-481.

29. According to Giani Gurdit Singh, the first reference to the Bahoval Pothi came in 1946, in the debate about the *Ragmala;* see his *Itihas Sri Guru Granth Sahib,* p. 568; and Mahan Singh, "Bahoval vali Pothi Sahib," *Kheṛa* (March 1980). For further information see Piar Singh, *Gatha Sri Adi Granth,* pp. 120-129. For discussion of Ms. 1245 at Guru Nanak Dev University, Amritsar, see Pashaura Singh, "The Text and Meaning of the Adi Granth" (Ph. D. diss., University of Toronto, 1991), pp. 24-28, and "An Early Sikh Scriptural Tradition: The Guru Nanak Dev University Manuscript 1245," *International Journal of Punjab Studies* 1: 2 (1994), pp. 197-222. Piar Singh further extended the information about this manuscript in *Gatha Sri Adi Granth,* pp. 135-173. For this discussion's interesting continuation, see Bachittar Singh Giani, ed., *Planned Attack on Aad Sri Guru Granth Sahib* (Chandigarh: International Centre of Sikh Studies, 1994). For information on manuscript 1192 at Panjab University, see Piar Singh, *Gatha Sri Adi Granth,* pp. 305-308. In my view, this is an extremely important manuscript, a fact which Piar Singh has not been able to properly determine.

30. For some examples of the stories Sahib Singh refuted, see *Sri Guru Granth Sahib Darpaṇ,* pp. 1: 146, 602-604, and 2: 495-496. For the stories linked with these hymns see *Adi Sri Guru Granth Sahib Ji Saṭik (Faridkot vala Ṭika),* pp. 1: 32, 255-256, and 549-551.

Shabadarth Sri Guru Granth Sahib Ji includes notes by Teja Singh that shed very important light on contemporary issues in Guru Arjan's hymns: see pp. 96, 198, 199, 200, 248, 371, 396, 495, 500, 618, 619-625, 673, 674, 677-678,

714, 723, 781, 806, 807, 817, 818-819, 821, 825, 927, and 1137-1138. For more on this debate see Surjit Hans, *A Reconstruction of Sikh History from Sikh Literature*, pp. 137-144. Here one need only to mention that many of these hymns were composed in thanks for God's grace (for example, at Guru Hargobind's birth, his recovery from illness, etc.). Verses of the *chhant*, in *rag* Gauṛi, Adi Granth, p. 248, clearly fit into Baba Mohan's familial context:

ਮੋਹਨ ਤੇਰੇ ਬਚਨ ਅਨੂਪ ਚਾਲ ਨਿਰਾਲੀ।

ਮੋਹਨ ਤੂੰ ਮਾਨਹਿ ਏਕੁ ਜੀ ਅਵਰ ਸਭ ਰਾਲੀ।. . .

ਮੋਹਨ ਤੂੰ ਸੁਫਲੁ ਫਲਿਆ ਸਣੁ ਪਰਿਵਾਰੇ।

ਮੋਹਨ ਪੁਤੁ ਮੀਤ ਭਾਈ ਕੁਟੰਬ ਸਭਿ ਤਾਰੇ।

31. Two preeminent Sikh scholars of this century believe that this *chhant* was composed in praise of God, but feel no discomfort with the tradition of Guru Arjan having sung it at Goindval: Bhai Vir Singh, *Santhaya Sri Guru Granth Sahib*, pp. 4: 1583-1587; Teja Singh, *Shabadarth Sri Guru Granth Sahib Ji*, p. 248.

32. For an exception to this general attitude, see J. S. Grewal's brilliant essay "Dissent in Early Sikhism," in *From Guru Nanak to Maharaja Ranjit Singh: Essays in Sikh History* (Amritsar: Guru Nanak Dev University, 1982).

33. According to the date entered in the Kartarpur Pothi, it was prepared in 1604. Because the center of the community at this time was Amritsar, there appears to be no room for doubt that the pothi was prepared there. In the third decade of the seventeenth century, when Guru Hargobind left Amritsar under pressure from Mughal administration in Lahore and came to Kartarpur, the pothi also arrived in Kartarpur with him. As he was unable to come to an agreement with the Mughals, Guru Hargobind went into the Shivalik Hills and established the town of Kiratpur. The Guru left the pothi at Kartarpur with the intent of returning there or else he took it with him to Kiratpur and it was later brought back: on this phase of the pothi's history there is no consensus among scholars. See Bhai Jodh Singh, "Prachin Biṛan bare Bhullan di Sodhan," in Piar Singh, ed., *Bhai Jodh Singh Gadd Saurabh*, p. 425; G. B. Singh, *Sri Guru Granth Sahib dian Prachin Biṛan*, pp. 99-100; Gopal Singh, "Adi Granth te usda Prabhav Punjabi Boli ute," in Surinder Singh Kohli, ed., *Punjabi Sahitt da Itihas, Bhag Paila* (Chandigarh: Panjab University, 1973), p. 292. During this time, the pothi somehow came into Dhirmal's possession, and in the middle decades of the

seventeenth century it proved beneficial to his claim to authority within the Sikh community.

Three earliest manuscripts of Sikh scripture, the Guru Harsahai Pothi, the Goindval Pothis, and the Kartarpur Pothi, remained in the custody of families that were involved in the struggle for the Guruship during the sixteenth and seventeenth centuries. They were, respectively, with Prithi Chand at Amritsar, the Bhallas at Goindval, and Dhirmal at Kartarpur (where the latter text still resides). In the background of prevalent Sikh thinking there is varied degree of apathy toward these families, who are supposed to have challenged the Gurus at one time or another. As a result of this thinking, scholars such as Sahib Singh have been unprepared to address the importance of these early manuscripts.

34. There are two important reasons for giving such a detailed account of Sahib Singh's views on this subject. First, his thinking has left a deep impression upon the twentieth century Sikh religious imagination, and in institutions such as Gurmat College, Patiala, Sikh Missionary College, Amritsar, Sikh Missionary Society, Ludhiana, etc., his reconstruction of the compilation of the Adi Granth is considered authoritative. See, for example, Harbhajan Singh, *Gurbani Sampadan Nirnai,* pp. 18-20; Sadhu Singh, "Utri Amrika vich Sikh Adhiain da Sarvekhan," *Watan* (Vancouver) 5: 3 (1994).

Second, in this decade an attempt has been made to challenge the authenticity of the Goindval Pothis on the basis of information from Sahib Singh's investigation. According to those who hold this opinion, the Goindval Pothis are not a foundational source of Sikh scripture. They place the preparation of these pothis some time after 1595. For details of this argument see Daljeet Singh and Kharak Singh, "Goindval Pothis-A Post 1595 Production," in Bachittar Singh Giani, ed., *Planned Attack on Aad Sri Granth Sahib,* pp. 115-121; as a background to the essays in this book, a translation into English of a section of Sahib Singh's *Adi Bir bare* has been provided, pp. 287-290. In a conference held by supporters of this line of thought at the gurdwara in Glen Rock, New Jersey, Balwant Singh Dhillon pushed the dating of the Goindval Pothis even further forward to Guru Tegh Bahadur's period, that is, after 1664. In support of this argument, Dhillon quoted Gulam Sadasevak's composition recorded on folio 284 of the pothi at Jalandhar. According to Dhillon, the first verse of this composition: ਸਤਗੁਰ ਬਾਝਹੁ ਕਿਨੈ ਨ ਪਾਇਓ ਸਭ ਥਕੀ ਕਰਮ ਕਮਾਇ॥ (No one can attain the Lord without the Satguru, I

146

am tired of doing all things), is found in the compositions of Hariji (1639-1696), a descendant of Prithi Chand (for the text of this composition, see Chapter 3, p. 114). This strong proof, according to his view, not only takes the writing period to Hariji's time but clearly joins the Goindval Pothis with the followers of Prithi Chand. Dhillon's argument is not convincing. The verse's particular relationship with Hariji is unclear since the thought expressed here often appears in the hymns of the Gurus; see Guru Nanak's verse: ਸਤਿਗੁਰ ਬਾਝੁ ਨਾ ਪਾਇਓ ਸਭ ਥਕੀ ਕਰਮ ਕਮਾਇ ਜੀਓ॥, *rag* Sri, Adi Granth, p. 72. There seems to be no historical evidence in support of the argument that associates the Goindval Pothis with the family of Prithi Chand. The attempt to draw this connection is apparently aimed at undermining the authority of the Goindval Pothis.

The degree of consensus on the Goindval Pothis among scholars associated with the International Centre of Sikh Studies, Chandigarh, is not entirely clear. In 1994, along with *Planned Attack on Aad Sri Granth Sahib* in which several authors took the position mentioned above, the I. C. S. S. also published Trilochan Singh's *Ernest Trumpp and W. H. McLeod: As Scholars of Sikh History Religion and Culture*, which fully supports the traditional position on this issue, see pp. 232, and 349-350.

35. Gursharan Kaur Jaggi, *Babe Mohan valian Pothian* (Delhi: Arsi Publishers, 1987). According to Jaggi's introduction, this account was not prepared in a methodical manner, but regardless of its shortcomings, was the only one available. For example of the usage of the information about the pothis provided by Bawa Prem Singh, see G. B. Singh, *Sri Guru Granth Sahib dian Prachin Biṛan*, pp. 27-29; Bhai Vir Singh, *Santhaya Sri Guru Granth Sahib*, pp. 4: 1585-1586.

36. Bhai Jodh Singh, *Sri Kartarpuri Biṛ de Darshan*, p. *kaka* and for Bawa Prem Singh's letters to the author, see pp. 123-125.

37. Giani Gurdit Singh took these photographs in 1976. With time, the photographs in the set left with the Punjabi University library decreased, and now only go up to folio 210. I saw one complete copy of the primary set with Giani Gurdit Singh (56 Sector 4, Chandigarh). I also have a copy of the complete set of photographs originally available at the Punjabi University, the permission for which was granted by the university's Vice-Chancellor, H. K. Manmohan Singh. I am indebted to him for this kindness.

38. Nirbhai Singh used these photographs in a very effective manner in his investigation. See "The Collection of the Hymns of the Guru Granth," *Journal of Sikh Studies* 8: 1 (1981), pp. 9-22, and *Bhagata Namdeva in the Guru Grantha* (Patiala: Punjabi University, 1981). It is bit surprising that after 1981 Nirbhai Singh has written nothing more on this theme.

39. Giani Gurdit Singh, *Itihas Sri Guru Granth Sahib*, pp. 550-586. On 24 February, 1991, this book was declared to be an eminently important work by the Shiromani Gurdwara Prabandhak Committee. See *Giani Gurdit Singh* (Amritsar: Dharam Prachar Committee, 1991).

40. Piar Singh, *Gatha Sri Adi Granth*, pp. 71-112.

41. Pritam Singh gave this information to Satnam Singh Bhugra of East Lansing, in a letter dated November 16, 1992. It seems that the Guru Nanak Dev University Press suggested some major revisions in the work he had submitted at that time. In a recent telephone conversation (January 1996), however, Pritam Singh told Joginder Singh Ahluwalia of Richmond, California, that his work on the Goindval Pothis has been completed, and submitted to the Press. I have no information as to the precise nature of Pritam Singh's research. In 1993, during my trip to Pinjore to gather remaining information about the pothi there, the Bhalla family told me that he had been coming there to study the pothi as well. For some reason, our ways have never crossed and my efforts to meet him, never materialized.

42. W. H. McLeod, "The Study of Sikh Literature," in John Stratton Hawley and Gurinder Singh Mann, eds., *Studying the Sikhs: Issues for North America* (Albany: State University of New York Press, 1993), pp. 53-55. For an earlier essay on this theme, see "The Sikh Scriptures," in his *The Evolution of the Sikh Community: Five Essays* (Oxford: Clarendon Press, 1976), pp. 59-82. See also W. Owen Cole and Piara Singh Sambhi, *The Sikhs: Their Religious Beliefs and Practices* (Brighton: Sussex Academic Press, 1995), pp. 44-52; Mark Juergensmeyer and N. Gerald Barrier, eds., *Sikh Studies: Comparative Perspectives on a Changing Tradition* (Berkeley: Berkeley Religious Studies Series, 1979), pp. 97-124; Max Arthur Macauliffe, *The Sikh Religion: Its Gurus, Sacred Writings and Authors* (New Delhi: S. Chand and Company, 1985), pp. 3: 55-63.

43. See my article in Indu Banga, ed., *Five Punjabi Centuries: Polity, Economy, Society, and Culture* (Delhi: Manohar, forthcoming). The article was written in 1993, and my research has further expanded since then.

44. For a picture of this palanquin, see Trilochan Singh, *Ernest Trumpp and W. H. McLeod*, p. 350; see also Madanjit Kaur, "Goindval," in Krishan Lal Sharma, ed., *Guru Amar Das: Jivan ate Chintan* (Amritsar: Guru Nanak Dev University, 1986), pp. 41-42; Bhai Vir Singh, *Santhaya Sri Guru Granth Sahib*, pp. 4: 1585-1586.

45. See Giani Gian Singh, *Tvarikh Guru Khalsa*, p. 1: 394. Some decades earlier, at the invitation of the ruling family of Patiala, the Sodhis of Kartarpur also took the pothi in their custody to Patiala. See Gopal Singh, "Adi Granth te usda Prabhav Punjabi Boli ute," p. 295.

46. Kahn Singh Nabha, *Mahan Kosh*, p. 427; G. B. Singh, *Sri Guru Granth Sahib dian Prachin Biṛan*, pp. 27-29; Bhai Vir Singh, *Santhaya Sri Guru Granth Sahib*, p. 4: 1586. During this period, the Shiromani Gurdwara Prabandhak Committee made an unsuccessful attempt to obtain the pothis present in the custody of the Sodhi families at Harsahai and Kartarpur. After long and protracted litigation, these families were successful in establishing their personal ownership of the pothis. This information was given to me by the families at Harsahai and Kartarpur during my visits to these places. For information on the activities of the Shiromani Gurdwara Prabandhak Committee, see Surjit Singh Gandhi, *Perspectives on Sikh Gurdwaras Legislation* (New Delhi: Atlantic Publishers, 1993); Shamsher Singh Ashok, *Shiromani Gurdwara Prabandhak Committee da Punjab Sala Itihas* (Amritsar: Sikh Itihas Research Board, 1982).

47. No neighbors of the Bhalla house in Lajpat Nagar even know that there is such an important manuscript in their vicinity. In the past few years, the Bhalla family has very kindly permitted me to examine the pothi on several *sangrand* days.

48. Bhai Gurdas, *Varan*, 26: 33, p. 232. Bhai Gurdas writes about the seats of authority established by the sons of the early Gurus.

> ਬਾਲ ਜਤੀ ਹੈ ਸਿਰੀ ਚੰਦੁ ਬਾਬਾਣਾ ਦੇਹੁਰਾ ਬਣਵਾਇਆ।
> ਲਖਮੀ ਦਾਸਹੁ ਧਰਮ ਚੰਦੁ ਪੋਤਾ ਹੁਇ ਕੇ ਆਪੁ ਗਣਾਇਆ।
> ਮੰਜੀ ਦਾਸੁ ਬਹਾਲਿਆ ਦਾਤਾ ਸਿਧਾਸਣਿ ਸਿਧਿ ਆਇਆ।
> ਮੋਹਣੁ ਕਮਲਾ ਹੋਇਆ ਚਉਬਾਰਾ ਮੋਹਰੀ ਬਣਵਾਇਆ।
> ਮੀਣਾ ਹੋਆ ਪਿਰਥੀਆ ਕਰਿ ਕਰਿ ਤੋਡਕ ਬਰਲੁ ਚਲਾਇਆ।
> ਮਹਾਦੇਉ ਅਹੰਮੇਉ ਕਰਿ ਕਰਿ ਬੇਮੁਖ ਪੁਤਾ ਭਉਕਾਇਆ।
> ਚੰਦਨ ਵਾਸੁ ਨ ਵਾਸ ਬੋਹਾਇਆ॥੩੩॥

49. For a discussion of this issue, see G. B. Singh, *Gurmukhi Lippi da Janam te Vikas* (Chandigarh: Panjab University, 1981); and Piara Singh Padam, *Gurmukhi Lippi da Itihas* (Patiala: Kalam Mandir, 1988).

50. Pritam Singh, "Punjabi Boli," in Mohinder Singh Randhawa, ed., *Punjab* (Patiala: Punjab Language Department, 1960), p. 387, and *Khoj Patrika* 36 (September 1992), pp. 110-133.

51. Gursharan Kaur Jaggi, *Babe Mohan valian Pothian*, p. 2; Piar Singh, *Gatha Sri Adi Granth*, pp. 109-112. There is no reference available either to *Sakhian Guru Amardas Bhalle kian* or *Sakhian Guru Bans kian*, in Shamsher Singh Ashok, *Punjabi Hathlikhatan di Suchi* (Patiala: Punjab Language Department, 1961-1963).

52. Teja Singh, "Sri Guru Granth Sahib da Sampadan," pp. 135-136; Piara Singh Padam, *Sri Guru Amardas ji di Bani*, pp. 23-24 (Padam appears to place the date for the writing of the pothi at Jalandhar later than that of the one at Pinjore); Giani Gurdit Singh, *Itihas Sri Guru Granth Sahib*, p. 565. This date is accepted by several scholars I have spoken to.

53. Gursharan Kaur Jaggi, *Babe Mohan valian Pothian*, p. 2.

54. Piar Singh, *Gatha Sri Adi Granth*, p. 71.

55. Piar Singh, *Gatha Sri Adi Granth*, p. 112.

56. Bhai Kahn Singh Nabha, *Mahan Kosh,* p. 76.

57. The date recorded in the blessing is less than six months after the birth of Guru Hargobind, the only son of Guru Arjan; see Bhai Kahn Singh Nabha, *Mahan Kosh*, p. 265. It is not entirely clear if there was any relationship between these two occurrences. According to Sikh tradition, in the circumstances of there being no son in Guru Arjan's home until 1595, the Guru's elder brother, Prithi Chand, expected the Guruship to go to his son, Miharban; but after Guru Hargobind was born, this hope was lost and Prithi Chand increased his opposition to Guru Arjan. If the Bhalla family had any connection with this uproar, Sikh traditions are completely silent about it. Here it must be remembered that there is an alternative tradition that places Guru Hargobind's birth in 1590; see Ratan Singh Jaggi, ed., *Kesar Singh Chhibbar da Bansavlinama Dasan Patishahian ka* (Chandigarh: Punjab University, 1972), pp. 47, and 56.

58. Piar Singh, *Gatha Sri Adi Granth*, pp. 82-83, and 112.

59. The following hymns have problems in their attribution:

Rag Dhanasri,   ਨਦਰਿ ਕਰੇ ਤਾ ਸਿਮਰਿਆ ਜਾਇ॥

Goindval Pothis	Kartarpur Pothi	Adi Granth, p. 661
Mahala 3	Mahala 3	Mahala 1

Rag Suhi,   ਜਪ ਤਪ ਕਾ ਬੰਧੁ ਬੇੜੁਲਾ ਜਿਤੁ ਲੰਘਹਿ ਵਹੇਲਾ॥

Goindval Pothis	Kartarpur Pothi	Adi Granth, p. 729
Mahala 3	Mahala 3	Mahala 1

Rag Basant,   ਬਸਤੁ ਉਤਾਰਿ ਦਿਗੰਬਰੁ ਹੋਗੁ॥

Goindval Pothis	Kartarpur Pothis	Adi Granth, p. 1169
Mahala 1	Mahala 1	Mahala 3

Rag Basant,   ਸਾਹਿਬ ਭਾਵੈ ਸੇਵਕੁ ਸੇਵਾ ਕਰੈ॥

Goindval Pothis	Kartarpur Pothi	Adi Granth, p. 1170
Mahala 1	Mahala 1/3	Mahala 3

Rag Prabhati,   ਆਪੇ ਭਾਂਤਿ ਬਣਾਇ ਬਹੁਰੰਗੀ ਸਿਸਟਿ ਉਪਾਇ ਪ੍ਰਭਿ ਖੇਲ ਕੀਆ॥

Goindval Pothis	Kartarpur Pothis	Adi Granth, p. 1334
Mahala 1	Mahala 1/3	Mahala 3

Note that in the original writing of the Kartarpur Pothi the hymns in *rag* Basant and *rag* Prabhati were attributed to Mahala 1 but later changed to Mahala 3; in the pothi's table of contents, written later, both hymns were recorded under the heading of Mahala 3, the attribution that appears in the Adi Granth. It is important to remember that such variations of attributions continue to appear in later manuscripts. On several of these changes, see Teja Singh's notes, *Shabadarth Sri Guru Granth Sahib Ji*, pp. 661, 1169, and 1170.

60. Bhai Jodh Singh, *Sri Kartarpuri Biṛ de Darshan*, p. 85. I examined this detail myself, and Bhai Jodh Singh's observation is accurate.

61. Regarding the inscribing of this hymn in the pothi at Jalandhar, it is necessary to mention that after its heading the phrase "*mahala panjavan 5*," referring to Guru Arjan is added, in a pen with a slightly thicker tip (see photograph, p. 200). Mahala plus a number is the standard designation in Sikh scripture for the authorship by a particular Guru. When and why did someone make this irrelevant addition to the original heading? There is, however, no doubt that the change of attribution from Guru Nanak to Guru Ramdas was made very early and then continued. I have carefully examined Ms. 1245, Amritsar; the Banno Pothi (1642), Kanpur; the Seva-panthi Pothi (1653), Patiala; the Buṛa Sandhu Pothi (1654), Amritsar; etc. I did not find this hymn under Guru Nanak's title anywhere.

151

62. Giani Gurdit Singh, *Itihas Sri Guru Granth Sahib*, p. 563. See also Gursharan Kaur Jaggi, *Babe Mohan valian Pothian*, p. 30.

63. Piar Singh, *Gatha Sri Adi Granth*, p. 108.

64. According to Sikh tradition, Guru Ramdas' hymn in *rag* Gujri, which opens with the verse: ਹਰਿ ਕੇ ਜਨ ਸਤਿਗੁਰ ਸਤਪੁਰਖਾ ਬਿਨਉ ਕਰਉ ਗੁਰ ਪਾਸਿ॥, is associated with the period before he became Guru; see Teja Singh, *Shabadarth Sri Guru Granth Sahib Ji*, pp. 10, and 492; *Adi Sri Guru Granth Sahib Ji Saṭik (Faridkot vala Ṭika)*, p. 1: 32; Sahib Singh, *Sri Guru Granth Sahib Darpaṇ*, p. 1: 146. Guru Arjan's hymn in *rag* Majh, which opens with: ਮੇਰਾ ਮਨੁ ਲੋਚੈ ਗੁਰਦਰਸਨ ਤਾਈ॥, is thought to have been composed before he took the Guruship; see *Adi Sri Guru Granth Sahib Ji Saṭik (Faridkot vala Ṭika)*, p. 1: 255; Teja Singh, *Shabadarth Sri Guru Granth Sahib Ji*, p. 96.

65. Among the group of known Sikhs of this approximate period, other candidates for authorship of these hymns may be ruled out. Baba Mohan, in whose custody the pothis remained, can be taken to be the foremost candidate, but there is little basis for an argument that might identify him with Gulam Sadasevak. Neither in Sikh tradition nor in Bhalla family memory, is there any reference to his having composed any text at all. Furthermore, if the writings attributed to Gulam Sadasevak were actually Baba Mohan's, then, in the situation of the pothis being in the care of the Bhalla family, both before and after Baba Mohan's time, there would have been no sense to their having been crossed out.

Of the other Gurus' living children, Baba Sri Chand, son of Guru Nanak, could have been a candidate; but in the context of numerous traditions about the special respect assigned to him, the recording of his compositions after those of the Gurus does not appear likely. Also, as is found in his extant writings, instead of the signature of "Nanak," he used the signature "Nanak *puta*." See Piar Singh, "Solvhin Sadi de Hor Kavi," in Surinder Singh Kohli, ed., *Punjabi Sahitt da Itihas, Bhag Paila*, pp. 273-282. Besides in the hymns of the Gurus, the signature "Nanak" appears only in three couplets attributed to Mardana, a disciple of Guru Nanak, Adi Granth, p. 553, who had long since died by this time.

Among leading Sikhs of the time, the name of Baba Buddha is preeminent, but there is no tradition about his having created any hymns. At the time the pothis were written, Bhai Gurdas' must have yet been very young: in the absence of strong proof, his birth can only be placed in the

152

second half of the sixteenth century. In his writings, there is no effort to use the authoritative signature of Nanak. For an important study on the issue of the signature, see John Stratton Hawley, "Author and Authority in the *Bhakti Poetry of North India*," *The Journal of Asian Studies* 47: 2 (1988), pp. 269-290.

66. Such a collection may have been later appended in the second section of the Guru Harsahai Pothi: see Giani Gurdit Singh, *Itihas Sri Guru Granth Sahib*, p. 560-561. This pothi stayed with Guru Ramdas' descendants until recently, see above, note 24.

67. This principle is not applicable to the Kartarpur Pothi. After this pothi's original writing, additional hymns of Guru Arjan have been added to it. For example, the last hymns in *rag* Devgandhari (folio 415), the *var* in *rag* Basant (folio 854), etc., were in all likelihood composed after the compilation of the pothi and recorded in it later. There is no such instance in the writing of the Goindval Pothis.

68. Giani Gian Singh, *Tvarikh Guru Khalsa*, p. 1: 394.

69. In fact, neither has actually written on this subject; but it has arisen quite a few times in my conversations with them.

70. The issue of the precise number of the Goindval Pothis came up accidentally during my stay with Dr. and Mrs. Nirankari in December 1994. I am deeply obliged to them both for their affection and encouragement. Dr. Nirankari has several early Sikh scriptural manuscripts in his custody and he graciously permitted me to photograph the oldest one prepared in 1676. I am grateful for this kindness.

71. Keeping in mind the close affinity of the text of the Goindval Pothis with that of the Adi Granth, I have attempted to count the number of pages in the standard edition of the Adi Granth that correspond to the hymns in the four pothis. The following estimate emerges from this correspondence:

	pages in the Adi Granth
Pothi at Jalandhar	104
Pothi at Pinjore	86
Pothi referred to by Giani Gian Singh	180
Remaining text of the Gurus' and saints' hymns	125

As expected, the 125-page count is too small for its contents to have been recorded in two pothis instead it is just the right amount to constitute one additional pothi.

72. The acceptance of this distinction is obvious in the titles recorded in the Goindval Pothis. For example, titles such as "Suhi Babe di" and "Tilang Babe Patishah da" show that Suhi is being treated as feminine while Tilang is masculine.

73. In the interest of separating *rags* from *raginis*, I have altered the sequence of *rags* of this pothi from that given in the *Tvarikh Guru Khalsa*: Sri, Asa, Gauri, Vadhans. It is difficult to say whether the pothi seen by Giani Gian Singh actually had the arrangement outlined in his book or whether his editors conformed the sequence to that available in the Adi Granth. The original manuscript of Giani Gian Singh's book might, perhaps, shed light on this point. I examined one such manuscript in Moti Bagh, Patiala, in January 1990, but because I did not then know of this complication, I could make no study regarding it.

74. The opening *rag* section of the pothi at Jalandhar is *rag* Suhi, which is known as having been the favorite *rag* of the Sufis (much as *rag* Ramkali, the opening *rag* section of the pothi at Pinjore, is the favorite *rag* of the Nath Yogis); see Taran Singh, *Sri Guru Granth Sahib Ji da Sahitak Itihas* (Amritsar: Faqir Singh and Sons, n. d. 1963?), pp. 76, and 80. *Rag* Tilang was probably appended to the first pothi on account of it, too, having an affinity with the Sufis; hymns in this section employ a large number of Persian words. The same explanation may work for the appending of Namdev's hymns in *rag* Kanra in the pothi containing the section on *rag* Sri. They both seem to be favorite *rags* of the Vaishnavas. By placing these *rags* at the opening of the Goindval Pothis, Guru Amardas may have been attempting to address the strongest religious sects of his contemporary Punjab.

75. For further discussion of this issue, see my "The Making of Sikh Scripture," pp. 134-137. See also, O. C. Gangoly, *Rags and Raginis* (Bombay: Nalanda Publications, 1935), pp. 83-89.

76. Guru Nanak sees himself as a singer (ਢਾਡੀ) and bard (ਸ਼ਾਇਰ) involved in spreading the name of God. See the following in the Adi Granth:

> ਹਉ ਢਾਢੀ ਵੇਕਾਰੁ ਕਾਰੇ ਲਾਇਆ॥ . . .
> ਢਾਢੀ ਸਚੈ ਮਹਿਲ ਖਸਮਿ ਬੁਲਾਇਆ॥ . . .
> ਢਾਢੀ ਕਰੇ ਪਸਾਉ ਸਬਦੁ ਵਜਾਇਆ॥, p. 150;
> ਕਰੇ ਕਰਾਏ ਸਭ ਕਿਛੁ ਜਾਣੈ ਨਾਨਕ ਸਾਇਰ ਇਵ ਕਹਿਆ॥, p. 434;
> ਨਾਨਕੁ ਸਾਇਰੁ ਏਵ ਕਹਤੁ ਹੈ ਸਚੇ ਪਰਵਦਗਾਰਾ॥, p. 660.

In Guru Nanak's hymns interesting images of actual writing surface; these can be associated with his effort to commit to writing his own compositions; see Adi Granth:

ਜਾਲਿ ਮੋਹੁ ਘਸਿ ਮਸੁ ਕਰਿ ਮਤਿ ਕਾਗਦੁ ਕਰਿ ਸਾਰੁ॥

ਭਾਉ ਕਲਮ ਕਰਿ ਚਿਤੁ ਲੇਖਾਰੀ ਗੁਰ ਪੁਛਿ ਲਿਖੁ ਬੀਚਾਰੁ॥

ਲਿਖੁ ਨਾਮੁ ਸਾਲਾਹੁ ਲਿਖੁ ਲਿਖੁ ਅੰਤੁ ਨ ਪਾਰਾਵਾਰੁ॥, p. 16;

ਕਾਇਆ ਕਾਗਦੁ ਜੇ ਥੀਐ ਪਿਆਰੇ ਮਨੁ ਮਸਵਾਣੀ ਧਾਰਿ॥

ਲਲਤਾ ਲੇਖਣਿ ਸਚ ਕੀ ਪਿਆਰੇ ਹਰਿ ਗੁਣ ਲਿਖਹੁ ਵੀਚਾਰਿ॥

ਧਨੁ ਲੇਖਾਰੀ ਨਾਨਕਾ ਪਿਆਰੇ ਸਾਚੁ ਲਿਖੇ ਉਰਧਾਰਿ॥, p. 636;

ਸੁਟਿ ਪਾਡੇ ਕਿਆ ਲਿਖਹੁ ਜੰਜਾਲਾ॥

ਲਿਖੁ ਰਾਮਨਾਮ ਗੁਰਮੁਖਿ ਗੋਪਾਲਾ॥, p. 930;

ਧਨੁ ਸੁ ਕਾਗਦੁ ਕਲਮ ਧਨੁ ਧਨੁ ਭਾਂਡਾ ਧਨੁ ਮਸੁ॥

ਧਨੁ ਲੇਖਾਰੀ ਨਾਨਕਾ ਜਿਨਿ ਨਾਮੁ ਲਿਖਾਇਆ ਸਚੁ॥, p. 1291.

In addition, images from reading (ਪੜਨਾ) appear also in Guru Nanak's hymns, see Akali Kaur Singh, *Guru Shabad Ratan Prakash* (Patiala: Punjab Language Department, 1986), p. 491. It is certain that Guru Nanak was literate, knowing both the local language and Persian.

77. Here it may be worth noting that in Islam great emphasis is put on the unique revelation of Qur'an in Arabic. The adoption of the Gurmukhi script for the Sikh sacred writings may be viewed in this context. For brief information on the issue of the *ahl-i-kitab*, see K. A. Nizami, *Some Aspects of Religion and Politics in India during the Thirteenth Century* (Delhi: Idarah-i-Adabiyat-i Delli, 1974), pp. 308-309.

78. The background to the Sikhs' belief in the existence of four sacred books in Judaism, Christianity, and Islam is necessarily Islamic. The Punjabi word "Jambur" is the local version of the Arabic "Zabur" used for the Psalms in the Qur'an (*sura* 4, 161; 17, 57; 21, 105). The origin of the word goes back to Hebrew "Zimrah." I am grateful to Jeanette Wakin of Columbia University for this information. The common phrase used to refer to the scriptural texts in Sikh literature is *ved-kateb*, and for Bhai Gurdas the Sikh revelation is distinct from the earlier ones enshrined in Hindu and Semitic texts. He writes: ਵੇਦੁ ਕਤੇਬਹੁ ਬਾਹਰਾ ਅਨਹਦ ਸਬਦ ਅਗੰਮ ਅਲਾਪੇ, and ਵੇਦ ਕਤੇਬਾ ਚਾਰਿ ਚਾਰਿ ਚਾਰ ਵਰਨ ਚਾਰਿ ਮਜਹਬ ਚਲਾਏ, Bhai Gurdas, *Varan*, 23: 19, p. 209, and 33: 2, p. 268.

79. This information was given to me by Bibi Agya Kaur, head of the Bhalla family at Pinjore, but she was unable to assist me in my attempts to find out more about their whereabouts in Phagwara. Regarding the claim of

Mohan Singh Dewana to have seen pothis of this set in 1933, at Goindval, and in 1960, at Amritsar, see G. B. Singh, *Sri Guru Granth Sahib dian Prachin Biṛan*, pp. 456-457; Giani Gurdit Singh, *Itihas Sri Guru Granth Sahib*, p. 567. The information provided by Dewana about the text of the *mulmantar* used in the documents he saw seems to be important; unlike Giani Gurdit Singh, I am not willing to dismiss lightly Dewana's claim to have seen the pothis belonging to the Goindval set.

80. In the following chart, column 1 gives the number of gathering in the pothi, column 2 indicates the folios in that gathering. The folio numbers recorded in these six gatherings include discrepancies resulting from incorrect folding of the folios at the time of their framing.

Pothi at Jalandhar

no.	folios
14	105-113
19	147-155
30	235-243
36	283-291

Pothi at Pinjore

10	73-81

In the pothi at Jalandhar, this confusion in the folios is due to their dislocation. In the pothi at Pinjore, the closing verses of the *Siddh Gosht* and the opening stanzas of the *Anand,* which appear on these folios, run smoothly, but the folio number is entered incorrectly. The number of the ninth gathering appears on the bottom corner of folio 76* (actually folio 73*), and this is followed by a gathering that has six folios. Folios numbering 78 and 77 are turned in the reverse direction and have become part of the following gathering.

81. The pothi at Jalandhar is constructed of thirty-seven gatherings of eight folios each. There are, however, ten folios in gathering 18, and two loose folios, which are left over from originally the last gathering in the pothi, are attached at the end. In my assessment, at the time of the framing of the folios and the rebinding of the pothi, the last gathering got dislocated, two folios remain at their initial position at the end, three got attached in the *rag* Basant section, and the other three perhaps got lost. In any case, with thirty-seven gatherings and four extra folios, the total number of folios of this pothi comes to 300. The pothi at Pinjore has twenty-eight gatherings and a total of

224 folios. There are discrepancies: in gatherings 10 and 14 there are six folios, but the loss of four folios is covered by gatherings 11 and 26, which contain ten folios each. The gathering's numbers have been written with extreme care in the lower right-hand corner of the last folio of each gathering. In the pothi at Jalandhar these numbers appear on the left-hand side page of the following folios: 9, 17, 25, 33, 41, 49, 57, 65, 73, 81, 89, 97, 105, 113, 121, 129, 137, 147, 155, 163, 171, 179 (some extra folios with hymns in *rag* Tilang from the last gathering have been shifted and attached here, and the number of the twenty-fifth gathering is printed on folio 203). After this the series' numbering runs correctly: 211, 219, 227, 235, 243, 251, 259, 267, 275, 283, 291, 298. In the pothi at Pinjore, the gatherings' number appear on the following folios: 9, 17, 25, 33, 41, 49, 57, 65, 76, 79, 89, 97, 105, 111, 119, 127, 135, 143, 151, 159, 167, 175, 183, 191, 199, 209, 217, 225 (the last half page). The number entered on folio 76 is a mistake: this is actually folio 73.

82. For an important discussion of Islamic book making, see Gulnar K. Bosch, John Carswell, and Guy Petherbridge, *Islamic Bindings and Book Making* (Chicago: Oriental Institute, University of Chicago, 1981), pp. 45-47. In addition, it is possible that the services of Muslim scribes were used in the preparation of Sikh manuscripts. I have seen one very elaborately illustrated eighteenth-century manuscript of the Adi Granth in which a scene of a city, with a mosque at the center, is depicted on the last folio of the text. There is little doubt that this manuscript was prepared by a professional scribe of the Qur'an.

In all this, it is appropriate to point out that among Punjabi Hindus, folios tended to be simply gathered and pressed together between two pieces of cardboard or wood. This type of binding can be seen even today in the making of *vahis* ("account books"), and it reaches far back into the manuscript tradition.

83. It is not easy to read the writing of the third scribe. Proof of this difficulty is that a scholar of Bawa Prem Singh's caliber was not successful in deciphering this handwriting. See Gursharan Kaur Jaggi, *Babe Mohan valian Pothian*, p. 31.

84. Gursharan Kaur Jaggi, *Babe Mohan valian Pothian*, p. 44. Bhai Jodh Singh, *Sri Kartarpuri Biṛ de Darshan*, p. kaka.

85. Bhai Jodh Singh, "Sri Kartarpur vali Pavitar 'Adi' Biṛ," in Piar Singh, ed., *Bhai Jodh Singh Gadd Saurabh*, p. 491. Whether Bhai Jodh

Singh's view was based upon examination of the Kartarpur Pothi itself or offered as an impressive explanation, that fit well into the traditional understanding of the slow collection of the hymns of the Gurus and their editing by Guru Arjan cannot now be discerned. One problem, however, becomes immediately evident. Bhai Jodh Singh argued that each gathering consisted of eight folios. Why, then, did the actual text of the Kartarpur Pothi begin on folio 45? According to Bhai Jodh Singh's own argument, if five gatherings were set aside for a table of contents, then the text should have begun on folio 41; if six, then it should have begun on folio 49; see *Sri Kartarpuri Biṛ de Darshan*, p. 46. It is clear that Bhai Jodh Singh's neat scheme does not seem to conform to the basic structure of the Kartarpur Pothi.

86. In the pothi at Jalandhar this numbering begins with 1 and continues successively to 29, notation and number being written on the following folios: 9, 18*, 27, 38, 45, 54*, 70, 79, 92, 99*, 110*, 124, 133*, 145*, 156, 174*, 189*, 197*, 206*, 211*, 227, 234, 241*, 250, 259*, 264, 270*, 283, 289. An additional example of the notation numbered 29, was entered on folio 183, but later struck out: this has to do with the fact that folio 183 was initially toward the end of the pothi (see above, note 81); when the pothi was rebound it was somehow moved forward. An implied notation number 30 is to be assumed at the end of the pothi. In the pothi at Pinjore, this sign is found on folios 9*, 15, 22, (?), 33*, 53, 74, 92, 117*, 125, 133, 144, 154, 163, 170, 186, 191, 201, 208, 215, and 224.

87. In the pothi at Jalandhar the first time this notation appears, it is at the end of Guru Nanak's *chaupadas*. On the basis of this particular placement, Bawa Prem Singh was misled into believing that this sign had been meant to mark the end of the groups of hymns of Guru Nanak. See Gursharan Kaur Jaggi, *Babe Mohan valian Pothian*, p. 15. Such an interpretation is not, however, applicable elsewhere in the text.

88. Piar Singh, *Gatha Sri Adi Granth*, pp. 99-100.

89. Under the title of *rag* Maru in the pothi at Jalandhar, there are only ten hymns by Guru Nanak and Guru Amardas, but in the corresponding *rag* section in the Kartarpur Pothi, seventy-six hymns are recorded. In the original writing of the pothi, *rag* Maru is combined with *rag* Kedara. The principle of combining these two *rags* later appears to have been revised and in all likelihood some hymns recorded under *rag* Kedara; but as the text of

rag Kedara is not available in the extant pothis, we cannot say anything as to what was recorded in it. Therefore, reference to hymns in *rag* Maru in the Goindval Pothis will be omitted from the following discussion.

90. See Chapter 2 below, *rag* Suhi, note 18; *rag* Dhanasri, note 56; and *rag* Tilang, note 131.

91. Here it is also appropriate to note that of the three compositions that appear in the extant Goindval Pothis but not in the Kartarpur Pothi, one is also listed under the heading of *rag* Tilang. Thus three of the total eight compositions at issue are in *rag* Tilang. This further increases the likelihood evidence that some discrepancies between the Goindval Pothis and the Kartarpur Pothi are to be traced to disturbances in the folios of the pothi now at Jalandhar.

92. See Chapter 2 below, *rag* Prabhati, notes 46, 47; *rag* Bhairo, note 108; *rag* Ramkali, note 149; *rag* Sorathi, note 161; and *rag* Malar, note 177.

93. Studies done in this century on the issues related to the non-Sikh saints' hymns in the Adi Granth have not yet been able to elucidate the subject fully and scholars have not been able to overcome the effect of traditional Sikh thought, which links Guru Arjan with the selection and editing of these hymns. Almost all the hymns of the non-Sikh saints written in the hand of the primary scribe of the Goindval Pothis are present in the Kartarpur Pothi. Without giving this information its due importance, Pashaura Singh presents a long discussion of the process of Guru Arjan's selection of the saints' hymns, see his "The Text and Meaning of the Adi Granth," p. 175-195.

94. Sikh tradition itself has forgotten the memory of *ghar*. Teja Singh associates it with *gah*, a category found in Iranian music; see *Shabadarth Sri Guru Granth Sahib Ji*, p. 14. According to Charan Singh, however, it is a variation of *tal*; see *Sri Guru Granth Bani Biaura* (Amritsar: Khalsa Tract Society, 1945), pp. 21-22. I have questioned various experts on Sikh sacred music, but no one was able to give me much information on this subject.

95. During the writing of the Kartarpur Pothi, despite the care with which the hymns were entered, there were cases of duplication. As it was detected the duplicated hymns were crossed out. See Bhai Jodh Singh's notes, *Sri Kartarpuri Bir de Darshan*, pp. 57, 82, and 87. For the remaining case of duplication among the hymns of the Gurus, see Guru Amardas' *chaupada* ਗੁਰਮੁਖਿ ਕ੍ਰਿਪਾ ਕਰੇ ਭਗਤਿ ਕੀਜੇ ਬਿਨੁ ਗੁਰ ਭਗਤਿ ਨਾ ਹੋਈ॥, Kartarpur Pothi, folio 65, Adi

Granth, p. 32. This hymn, later reappears as part of Guru Amardas' first *ashṭpadi* in the same *rag*, (stanzas 1-3, and 8), Kartarpur Pothi, folio 93, Adi Granth, pp. 64-65. (With the exception of Ms. 1245, this duplication reoccurs in all early manuscripts). For such an example in the writings of the saints, see Ravidas' hymn in *rag* Sorathi: ਸੁਖਸਾਗਰੁ ਸੁਰਤਰ ਚਿੰਤਾਮਨਿ ਕਾਮਧੇਨੁ ਬਸਿ ਜਾ ਕੈ॥, Kartarpur Pothi, folio 498, Adi Granth, p. 658. This hymn later appears in *rag* Maru, Kartarpur Pothi, folio 810, Adi Granth, p. 1106. There are also few *shaloks* that appear twice in the text.

96. I am very grateful to Giani Gurdit Singh for this information. Some photographs of this pothi are in his care and these are being used in his research for the book he will soon be publishing on the early Sikh texts.

97. At the time of addition of the hymns of Guru Tegh Bahadur, no change was made to the order in which the text had been recorded in the Kartarpur Pothi. In manuscripts beginning with this period, there are two traditions as to where the hymns of Guru Tegh Bahadur in *rag* Jaijavanti (a newly employed *rag*) should be included: at the end of the *rag* sequence as in the Adi Granth itself, or in the middle of the text. The variation is not, however, instrumental to the present argument.

98. See note 48.

99. For information about the 1659 manuscript, see G. B. Singh, *Sri Guru Granth Sahib dian Prachin Biṛan*, pp. 167-177. No other scholar appears to have seen this manuscript; it is G. B. Singh's information that is being repeated by everyone. According to my research, this manuscript may now be in the Singh Sabha Gurdwara in Dehra Dun. I had planned to go there in December 1994, with the sole purpose of locating this important manuscript, but because of time constraints was unable to do so.

100. Once a year, a fair is held at these seats, to which devotees flock from great distances to see their Guru. Guru Harsahai's festival is held in the beginning of the summer (in the months of Chet and Vaisakh), and at its closing, a *mala* ("rosary") and a *padam* (a precious stone), traditionally associated with Guru Nanak, are put up for public display. Originally, the display included the Guru Harsahai Pothi, but since its loss it has been replaced by another small manuscript of hymns of the Gurus.

The annual gathering at Kartarpur takes place on the occasion of Vaisakhi, when the followers of the Sodhi family gather there in large numbers. The manuscript in the custody of the family is at the center of this festival. At some point, this family also began to celebrate Guru Nanak's birthday. The tradition of these two annual fairs continues till this day and many of their followers come to Kartarpur to participate in the festivities.

The problem of the Dehra Dun seat is different. As Ramrai was childless, this seat fell under the control of the Udasis, whose leader is called a mahant. The center of the seat is a cot and a flagpole from Ramrai's period. At the annual festival, held toward the end of the summer (in the months of Saon-Bhadon), the cot is put up for ceremonial display and the flagpole is covered with a new cloth. See Bhai Kahn Singh Nabha, *Mahan Kosh*, pp. 649, and 1035-1036. As I have said, the seat also had the manuscript prepared in 1659, which has been recently shifted to the Singh Sabha Gurdwara in Dehra Dun. The circumstances that resulted in this shift are not clear to me.

101. In literature related to Sikh *rahit*, keeping any familial or social relationship with the followers of Prithi Chand, Dhirmal, or Ramrai is prohibited. Written reference to this proscription goes back to the first decade of the eighteenth century; see Ganda Singh, ed., *Kavi Sainapati Rachit Sri Guru Sobha* (Patiala: Punjabi University, 1988), p. 81. Sainapati writes:

ਕੀਏ ਜਦਿ ਬਚਨਿ ਸਤਿਗੁਰੂ ਕਾਰਨ ਕਰਨ
ਸਰਬ ਸੰਗਤਿ ਆਦਿ ਅੰਤਿ ਮੇਰਾ ਖਾਲਸਾ।
ਮਾਨੇਗਾ ਹੁਕਮੁ ਸੋ ਤੇ ਹੋਵੇਗਾ ਸਿਖ ਸਹੀ
ਨਾ ਮਾਨੇਗਾ ਹੁਕਮ ਸੋ ਤੇ ਹੋਵੇਗਾ ਬਿਹਾਲਸਾ।
ਪਾਂਚ ਕੀ ਕੁਸੰਗਤਿ ਤਜਿ ਸੰਗਤਿ ਸੋ ਪ੍ਰੀਤਿ ਕਰੇ
ਦਯਾ ਔਰ ਧਰਮ ਧਾਰ ਤਿਆਗੇ ਸਭ ਲਾਲਸਾ।
ਹੁੱਕਾ ਨਾ ਪੀਵੇ ਸੀਸ ਦਾੜੀ ਨਾ ਮੁੰਡਾਵੇ
ਸੋ ਤੇ ਵਾਹਿਗੁਰੂ ਵਾਹਿਗੁਰੂ ਗੁਰੂ ਜੀ ਕਾ ਖਾਲਸਾ।

The reference to "the five to be boycotted" is found in other literature as well; this group includes, in addition to the three mentioned above, masands (Gurus' deputies in the early Sikh community) and *kuṛimars* ("killers of daughters," referring to the Rajputs of the Shivalik hills). This sentiment still exists within the Sikh community and appears in the authoritative version of *Sikh Rahit Maryada*, compiled by the Shiromani Gurdwara Prabandhak Committee, in the middle decades of this century; see *Sikh Rahit Maryada* (Amritsar: Shiromani Gurdwara Prabandhak Committee, 1978), p. 33.

102. Kesar Singh Chhibbar, *Bansavlinama Dasan Patishahian ka*, pp. 42-44.

103. For discussion on this point see Miriam Levering, ed., *Rethinking Scripture: Essays from a Comparative Perspective* (Albany: State University of New York Press, 1989), pp. 1-17. The accepted scholarly definition of scripture as a written book, which according to the contributors to this collection is not comprehensive, fits the Adi Granth perfectly. Unfortunately, the collection includes no essay on the Sikh sacred text. For comparative study of the issues related to the scripture, see Wilfred Cantwell Smith, *What is Scripture?* (Minneapolis: Fortress Press, 1993).

104. The word *damdama* linked with this sacred manuscript is traditionally associated with Damdama, Bhatinda, where Guru Gobind Singh stayed for a short while after leaving Anandpur in December 1704. Recent researches, however, link this version with another Damdama, near Anandpur, and this explanation seems far more convincing than the traditional view. For this discussion, see Piara Singh Padam, *Sri Guru Granth Prakash*, p. 112, and Harbhajan Singh, *Gurbani Sampadan Nirnai*, pp. 199-236. For the earliest extant manuscript of this version, see Harbhajan Singh, *Gurbani Sampadan Nirnai*, pp. 95-96.

105. In my view, the controversy that developed around Piar Singh's *Gatha Sri Adi Granth*, in 1993, is closely associated with this particular issue. In common thinking, scholars related with International Centre of Sikh Studies in Chandigarh were held responsible for this whole episode: as Piar Singh does not accept the authenticity of the Kartarpur Pothi, this group blocked the sale of his book. I believe, however, that criticism that proved more damaging to Piar Singh in the eyes of Sikh leadership came from scholars like Giani Gurdit Singh, who perceived in Piar Singh's book a suggestion that the text of the Adi Granth needed revision in light of his research; see Giani Gurdit Singh's letter on this point, *World Sikh News*, (January 15, 1993). The issue of the closed nature of the Sikh canon is extremely crucial and any scholar working in this area needs to be aware of it.

106. In the opening decades of the twentieth century, however, controversy about the presence of the *Ragmala* in the Adi Granth took a very different turn. Babu Teja Singh, head of the Panch Khalsa Divan at Bhasaur, was not content raising questions regarding the validity of the *Ragmala*, but his followers went ahead and dropped it from the text of the Adi Granth, published under the title of *Gurmukhi Courses*. It is not surprising that on July 15, 1927, he and his wife, Bibi Niranjan Kaur, were expelled from the

Sikh community by a resolution passed in the general meeting of the Shiromani Gurdwara Prabandhak Committee. This resolution was later issued under the seal of the Akal Takhat. For an elaborate discussion of this controversy see Balbir Singh, *Ragmala da Saval te Jodh Kavi ate Alam* (Amritsar: Khalsa Samachar, 1969); Shamsher Singh Ashok, *Shiromani Gurdwara Prabandhak Committee da Punjah Sala Itihas*, pp. 49, 53-57, and 228; Giani Gurdit Singh, *Itihas Sri Guru Granth Sahib*, pp. 460-463.

For general discussion of the issue of *Ragmala*, see *Ragmala bare Vichar* (Amritsar: Sura Masak Patar, 1986); and Surinder Singh Kohli, *A Critical Study of Adi Granth* (Delhi: Motilal Banarsidass, 1961), pp. 100-114. Eminent scholars such as Bhai Kahn Singh Nabha, Bhai Vir Singh, G. B. Singh, Piara Singh Padam, Randhir Singh, and Shamsher Singh Ashok have given their views on the *Ragmala*. This issue cannot be dismissed lightly: this debate is on, and different positions are taken by Sikh forums, such as the Shiromani Gurdwara Prabandhak Committee, the Damdami Taksal, the Akhaṇḍ Kirtani Jatha, and the Sant Samaj. The Sant Samaj decided against participating in the World Sikh Meet-1995, organized by the Shiromani Gurdwara Prabandhak Committee and held at Amritsar on September 21-25, 1995, for the simple reason that the Committee was not ready to take a firm stand on the "inclusion of the *Ragmala* for a complete *paṭh* ("reading") of Guru Granth Sahib." See *World Sikh News* (September 22, 1995).

107. See note 34.

108. See Pashaura Singh, "The Text and Meaning of the Adi Granth," pp. 92-100, 113-117, 140-141.

109. Piar Singh, *Gatha Sri Adi Granth*, pp. 437-438. According to Piar Singh, loose gatherings containing hymns in separate *rags* were in circulation in the early Sikh community and were being copied in distant congregations. For proof of this type of compilation, he presents the Bahoval Pothi and the manuscript associated with Bhai Painda; see his *Gatha Sri Adi Granth*, pp. 437-438. There is no doubt that the Bahoval Pothi and the manuscript of Bhai Painda do not conform to the standard texts prepared in the seventeenth century, but I think that other reasons can be found for the existence of anomalies in them. It is necessary to do further study on these two manuscripts to work out their relationship with major sources such as the Goindval Pothis and the Kartarpur Pothi. Furthermore, there are flaws in Piar Singh's description of the Bahoval Pothi that need to be pointed out.

According to his information, this pothi does not contain hymns in *rags* Kalian, Toḍi, Berari, and Mali Gaura; see *Gatha Sri Adi Granth*, p. 122. In actuality, hymns in these *rags* are found there: *rag* Kalian (folios 603-607), *rag* Toḍi (folios 637-644), *rag* Berari (folios 586-587), *rag* Mali Gaura (folios 587-590). For a discussion of this period in Sikh history, see Fauja Singh, *Guru Amardas: Life and Teachings* (Delhi: Sterling, 1979), and J. S. Grewal, *Guru Nanak in History* (Chandigarh: Panjab University, 1979), pp. 287-313.

110. I think that the view presented by Pashaura Singh is not convincing in light of the data he himself presents. Even if one does not go into the dating and history of Ms. 1245, the main manuscript he uses to make this point, the examples Pashaura Singh offers in his "The Text and Meaning of the Adi Granth," p. 103-107, to show the changes made between the text of Ms. 1245 and the Kartarpur Pothi are as follows:

Ms. 1245: "ਜੋਇ," "ਉਤਰੈ," "ਬਨਾ," "ਸਹਸ," "ਹੋਨਿ," "ਕਿਉ"

K. Pothi: "ਜੇ," "ਉਤਰੀ," "ਬੰਨਾਂ," "ਸਹਸ," "ਹੋਹਿ," "ਕਿਵ"

On the basis of these changes, Pashaura Singh argues that Guru Arjan was editing the earlier text. I think, rather, that the issue of variants in these texts is related to evolution in the writing of a new script in early Sikh sources. Some examples of variants between the Goindval Pothis and the Kartarpur Pothi are as follows:

G. Pothis: "ਦੁਬਿਧਾ,' "ਮੁਧਧ," "ਕਸੁਭ," "ਰਗ," "ਪਰਗਾਸ," "ਪਰਸਾਦਿ"

K. Pothi: "ਦੁਬਿਧਾ," "ਮੁਗਧ," "ਕਸੁੰਭ," "ਰੰਗ," "ਪ੍ਰਗਾਸ," "ਪ੍ਰਸਾਦਿ"

These changes suggest that in the Kartarpur Pothi an attempt has been made to record words as accurately as possible according to their Punjabi pronunciation. There are also other groups of standard variants in these manuscripts:

The following groups of words in the Goindval Pothis:

1. "ਅੰਬ੍ਰਿਤ," "ਸੰਬਤ," "ਸਿਫਤ," "ਸੈਸਾਰ," "ਹਾਜਿਰਾ ਹਜੂਰ," "ਬਕਸਿਸ"

2. "ਅਵਹੁ," "ਕਵਡੀ," "ਕਿਵ," "ਪਵੜੀ"

3. "ਵਿਹੁਟਾ," "ਵਿਨਾਸ," "ਵਿਚਾਰ," "ਵਿਟੁ," "ਵੇਖ"

4. "ਕਾਮਨੀ," "ਕਰਨੀ," "ਚਰਨੀ"

appear in their variant forms in the Kartarpur Pothi:

1. "ਅੰਮ੍ਰਿਤ," "ਸੰਮਤ," "ਸਿਫਤ," "ਸੰਸਾਰ," "ਹਾਦਿਰਾ ਹਦੂਰ," "ਬਖਸਿਸ"

2. "ਅਉਹੁ," "ਕਉਡੀ," "ਕਿਉ," "ਪਉੜੀ"

3. "ਬਿਹੁਟਾ," "ਬਿਨਾਸ," "ਬਿਚਾਰ," "ਬਿਨੁ," "ਦੇਖ"

4. "ਕਾਮਟੀ," "ਕਰਟੀ," "ਚਰਟੀ"

I do not think that such variants can offer a basis for establishing that a serious editorial effort was underway in the preparation of the later manuscripts, and that the changes are the direct result of that concerted effort.

There is another fundamental difficulty in Pashaura Singh's argument about Guru Arjan's editing policy. If Guru Arjan was editing the available hymns of the Gurus, does it mean that he deliberately left out writings that did not conform to Sikh theology? Pashaura Singh's answer seems to be in the affirmative. In the context of the text found in the Goindval Pothis, and the way it was copied into the Kartarpur Pothi, there is no basis to construct this argument.

111. Bhai Jodh Singh, *Sri Kartarpuri Bir de Darshan*, pp. 10, 22, 33, 37, 62, 69, 73, 76, 80, 83, 93, 99, 103, 105.

112. For the critique of Piar Singh's and Pashaura Singh's research works done by the scholars associated with the International Centre of Sikh Studies, and their manifesto regarding the study of textual variants, see the editorial essay in *Abstract of Sikh Studies* (Chandigarh: Institute of Sikh Studies, January 1993), pp. 1-46. They have continued to maintain this position, see Gurtej Singh, "Guru Granth Sahib bare Kur Kahanian nun Thal Pai Jave," *Punjabi Tribune* (September 22, 1995), p. 6; for an interesting response to this, see Jatinder Pannu, "Vidvana de Sanghin Bing Den da Silsila ate 'Professor of Sikhism'," *Navan Zamana* (September 24, 1995), p. 6.

113. The leadership of the Shiromani Gurdwara Prabandhak Committee has, as a matter of principle, avoided interfering in academic discussion; instead it has encouraged research on Sikhism and has made major contribution toward the textual studies of the Adi Granth. In the 1930s, the Shiromani Gurdwara Prabandhak Committee published Teja Singh's *Shabadarth Sri Guru Granth Sahib Ji* in four volumes. In the middle decades of this century, because of its patronage of Piara Singh Padam, Randhir Singh, and Giani Gurdit Singh, the Committee had to face severe criticism from institutions such as the Chief Khalsa Divan; see Giani Mahan Singh, *Param Pavitar Adi Bir da Sankalna Kal*, pp. 31-32, and 49-52. Nevertheless, the Committee went on to support scholarship, and published another major work in the area of textual studies of the Adi Granth; see Randhir Singh, Giani Kundan Singh, Bhai Gian Singh Nihang, eds., *Sri Guru Granth Sahib dian Santha-sainchian ate Puratan Hathlikhatan de praspar Path-bhedan di Suchi* (Amritsar: Shiromani Gurdwara Prabandhak Committee, 1977).

I believe that the concern of the authorities of the Shiromani Gurdwara Prabandhak Committee in the controversy around Piar Singh's *Gatha Sri Adi Granth* was related to the difficult political circumstances through which the Sikh leadership had to pass in the last decade. From speeches made at a large Sikh gathering in Chandigarh on January 28, 1993, it almost appeared that the Shiromani Gurdwara Prabandhak Committee might reverse its earlier position of openness to research and oppose any textual work on the Adi Granth. In the aftermath of Piar Singh's problem, however, steps have been slowly taken toward softening such a hard stance. In the summer of 1994, while a group of scholars made a very strong attempt to have Pashaura Singh expelled from the Sikh community, *Chardi Kala* (June 24 and 25, 1994), the Akal Takhat gave him a nominal punishment, *World Sikh News* (July 1, 1994). This change in attitude also surfaced during controversy surrounding Amarjit Singh Grewal's editorial essay in *Vismad Nad* 3: 1 (January 1994). Grewal was not given any penance whatsoever, *World Sikh News* (June 24, 1994).

Another example of the changing winds came during my visit to the Punjab in last winter. I was treated very affectionately by Gurcharan Singh Tohra, president of the Shiromani Gurdwara Prabandhak Committee, during my ninety minutes meeting with him at his home in January 1995, in which I read to him the last section of this chapter. His satisfaction about my position on the role of early Sikh scriptural manuscripts and his approval of my work at Columbia University resulted in my being honored publicly at the Manji Sahib, Amritsar, on January 7, 1995. The citation given to me on that occasion read: Gurinder Singh Mann is honored for presenting an authentic picture of Sikhism in its contemporary context, and for his role in the development of Punjabi language at Columbia University. I was very thankful for this recognition. For later developments on this issue, see *Ajit* (February 3, 1995), *India West* (May 19, 1995), and *The Sikh Review* (August 1995), pp. 73-74.

There is no reference whatsoever to the controversy related to the textual studies of the Adi Granth in the messages of both Jathedar Manjit Singh, the acting Jathedar of the Akal Takhat, and Gurcharan Singh Tohra, released on the occasion of the World Sikh Meet. See *World Sikh Meet-1995* (Amritsar: Shiromani Gurdwara Prabandhak Committee, September 1995), pp. 5-11.

114. Here it is necessary to remember that the Kartarpur Pothi was chosen to play the role of *textus receptus* after much thought, in the absence of the earliest historically known manuscript of the Damdama version. This decision is absolutely appropriate: the authenticity of the Kartarpur Pothi can be effectively established and its history at Kartarpur reconstructed with reasonable certainty; see Harbhajan Singh, *Gurbani Sampadan Nirnai*, p. 162.

115. According to this view there are variants still present in the Kartarpur Pothi and the authoritative text of the Adi Granth. For examples, see Sant Gurbachan Singh Ji Khalsa, *Gurbani Path Darshan, Bhag Duja*, (Bhindar Kalan: Gurdwara Akhand Prakash, 1990), pp. 36-40. The problem of the placement of the text of the *mulmantar* is also not completely resolved, see Harbhajan Singh, *Gurbani Sampadan Nirnai*, pp. 134-198.

Chapter 2

2. 1. The Pothi at Jalandhar

Rag Suhi

1. The text of the *mulmantar* seems to have gone through a process of evolution. The earliest version of the *mulmantar* (ੴ ਸਚਨਾਮ ਕਰਤਾਰ) is available in the Guru Harsahai Pothi; see Giani Gurdit Singh, *Itihas Sri Guru Granth Sahib*, p. 8. It is important to point out that Giani Gurdit Singh was unable to read this text accurately and transcribed it in his appended note as: ੴ ਸਤਿਨਾਮ. Evolving through the Goindval Pothis, the *mulmantar* attained its canonical form in the Kartarpur Pothi, and was exactly copied into later manuscripts as it appears there.

Pashaura Singh has argued that the variation in the text of the *mulmantar* between the Goindval Pothis and the Kartarpur Pothi resulted from doctrinal modifications made by Guru Arjan; see his "The Text and Meaning of the Adi Granth," pp. 95-97. I do not find this argument very convincing, except that it fits well in Pashaura Singh's line of thought that Guru Arjan did a major editorial job on the existing text to give it its canonical form. The contemporary Sikh understanding of the role and the status of the *mulmantar* in Sikh scripture is constructed around its

167

interpretations presented by nineteenth-century Nirmala and Udasi scholars. For the complex interpretations of the *mulmantar*, see Pritam Singh, ed., *Sikh Concept of the Divine* (Amritsar: Guru Nanak Dev University, 1985), pp. 1-23. For background of Sikh scholarly traditions, see Taran Singh, *Gurbani dian Viakhia Pranalian* (Patiala: Punjabi University, 1980).

The scribe of the Goindval Pothis often drops *kanna* in the following words: ਅਕਲ, ਅਤਮ, ਅਵਤ, ਸਚੁਨਮੁ, ਕਰਤਰੁ, ਜਹਿਗਾ, ਜਤਾ, ਡਾਲ, ਤਿਸਨ, ਧਨਸਰੀ, ਨਨਕ, ਨਿਰੀਕਰ, ਪਟੀ, ਪਰਸਦੁ, ਪਰਭਤੀ, ਬੇੜ, ਬਬ, ਮਹੀ, ਮੰਗਤ, ਰਖਿਆ, ਰਗੁ, ਰਮੁ, ਰਮਕਲੀ. I have added the required *kanna* and the words read: ਅਕਾਲ, ਆਤਮ, ਆਵਤ, ਸਚੁਨਾਮੁ, ਕਰਤਾਰੁ, ਜਾਹਿਗਾ, ਜਾਤਾ, ਡਾਲ, ਤਿਸਨਾ, ਧਨਾਸਰੀ, ਨਾਨਕ, ਨਿਰੀਕਾਰ, ਪਾਟੀ, ਪਰਸਾਦੁ, ਪਰਭਾਤੀ, ਬੇੜਾ, ਬਾਬਾ, ਮਾਹੀ, ਮਾਂਗਤ, ਰਾਖਿਆ, ਰਾਗੁ, ਰਾਮੁ, ਰਾਮਕਲੀ. The use of the *tippi* has not yet stabilized in these early writings and the following words which need it often appear without it: ਸੁਦਰੀ, ਹਿਦੁ, ਕੁਭ, ਖਿਭਾ, ਤਰਗ, ਨਦ, ਨਿਦਾ, ਨਿਰਕਾਰ, ਪਿਡ (ਸੁੰਦਰੀ, ਹਿੰਦੁ, ਕੁੰਭ, ਖਿੰਭਾ, ਤਰੰਗ, ਨੰਦ, ਨਿੰਦਾ, ਨਿੰਰਕਾਰ, ਪਿੰਡ), and other words unnecessarily include it: ਅੰਤਿ, ਖੰਟ, ਤੰਤ, ਦੰਖਟੀ, ਲੰਦਿਆ (ਅਤਿ, ਖਾਟ, ਤਤ, ਦਖਟੀ, ਲਦਿਆ). In this case I have not made any change and have kept the original text.

2. In this *rag* section, there are thirty-one hymns attributed to Guru Nanak and Guru Amardas. In its corresponding section, the Adi Granth contains thirty-two hymns recorded under their names. Two of these hymns, by Guru Nanak are actually present in the *rag* Prabhati section of the Goindval Pothis (see below, note 41). Meanwhile, one *chhant* in this *rag* in the Goindval Pothis, attributed to Guru Nanak, is not available in the Adi Granth (see below, note 18).

Also regarding comparison of the Goindval Pothis and the Adi Granth with regards to hymns in *rag* Suhi: the *Suhi ki Var* of Guru Amardas recorded in the Adi Granth is not available in the Goindval Pothis. It is likely that the couplets and stanzas that constitute this *var* were present, but not all connected, in a pothi not extant. These stanzas and couplets seem to have been brought together during the period of the compilation of the Kartarpur Pothi. For a review of this argument, see Sahib Singh, *Sri Guru Granth Sahib Darpan*, pp. 1: 534-535; Piara Singh Padam, *Punjabi Sahitt di Rup Rekha* (Patiala: Kalam Mandir, 1971), pp. 170-171.

3. The word "Suhbi" is also used for *rag* Suhi. At the head of the hymns of Guru Nanak, sometimes "Guru Baba," and "Baba Patishah" appear, instead of the standard title "Mahala 1." Sometimes only the name of the *rag* is recorded; the layout of the hymns is considered indication enough of their

attribution to Guru Nanak. It is important to point out that the word "Mahala," when it appears, is spelt "Mahal" or "Mahalu" in the Goindval Pothis, which affirms its masculine form and etymological source in Arabic or Persian. Traditional Sikh scholarly thinking relates this title to the Sanskrit *mahila* (women); this is incorrect. For a discussion of this term, see, Sahib Singh, *Sri Guru Granth Sahib Darpaṇ*, p. 1: 24.

4. The word ਸਾਰਾ does not appear in this verse as recorded in the Adi Granth, p. 728. By dropping this word the meter of the verse is made to conform to the rest of the stanza. In the Goindval Pothis, the most frequent forms of the signature of Nanak are: ਨਾਨਿਕ or ਨਾਨਿਕੁ, whereas in the Adi Granth, the more common forms are: ਨਾਨਕ or ਨਾਨਕੁ.

5. This hymn is entitled ਅਸਟਪਦੀਆ ਮਹਲਾ ੧ ਘਰ ੧, and appears in the Adi Granth, p. 750. The following two verses recorded in the Adi Granth are not available in the pothi:

ਸੁਰਤਿ ਮਤਿ ਨਾਹੀ ਚਤੁਰਾਈ॥   ਕਰਿ ਕਿਰਪਾ ਪ੍ਰਭ ਲਾਵਹੁ ਪਾਈ॥੪॥. . .

ਅਨਿਕ ਜਨਮ ਬਿਛੁਰਤ ਦੁਖ ਪਾਇਆ॥   ਕਰੁ ਗਹਿ ਲੇਹੁ ਪ੍ਰੀਤਮ ਪ੍ਰਭ ਰਾਇਆ॥੭॥

6. The titles of ਸੁਰਜੀ and ਕੁਰਜੀ, which appear with this and the following hymn in the Adi Granth, p. 762, are not found in pothi.

7. The words ਇਹੁ ਤਨੁ in this verse do not appear in the verse recorded in the Adi Granth, p. 730. By dropping these words the meter of the verse is harmonized with the rest of the stanza.

8. In the Adi Granth, p. 751, ਜੀਉ appears at the end of the verse.

9. At this point, the scribe has drawn three lines and written "1" underneath them. For a discussion of this notation, see Chapter 1, p. 34.

10. These three hymns (9-11) are recorded under the title ਮਹਲਾ ੧ ਘਰ ੬ in the Adi Granth, pp. 729-730. In the case of the tenth and eleventh hymns, the original title in the pothi seems to have been "Suhi." This normally would mean that these were hymns of Guru Nanak; however, at a later time "Mahala 2," and "Mahala 3" were added at the beginning of hymns 10, and 11, respectively. This attribution also appears in the Janam-sakhi of Guru Nanak created by Hariji, see *Janam Sakhi Sri Guru Nanak Dev Ji* (Amritsar: Khalsa College, 1969), pp. 2: 67-68. For problems in attribution see above, Chapter 1, note 59; and below, *rag* Prabhati, note 45; *rag* Dhanasri, notes 52, and 58; *rag* Basant, notes 72, and 73.

11. The word ਜਿਸੁ does not appear in this verse in the Adi Granth, p. 729.

12.   The text of this hymn in the Adi Granth, p. 730, includes the following verses which are not recorded in the pothi:

ਏਤੁ ਦੁਆਰੇ ਧੋਇ ਹਛਾ ਹੋਇਸੀ॥   ਮਤੁ ਕੋ ਜਾਣੈ ਜਾਇ ਅਗੈ ਪਾਇਸੀ॥

13.   Instead of the word *chhant*, which is used in the Adi Granth for hymns of this type, the Goindval Pothis use *chhand*.   Regarding *chhants*, there is a basic difference in organization between the Goindval Pothis and the Adi Granth.   In the Goindval Pothis the *chhants* are placed before the *ashṭpadis*, but in the Adi Granth they follow them.   The explanation for this change is not entirely clear.   *Chhants* sometime contain six stanzas of six verses each, thus becoming longer compositions than *ashṭpadis*, which normally have eight stanzas of four verses each.   In a general system of organization constructed around the increasing length of hymns, this may be the reason for placing the *chhants* after the *ashṭpadis*.

14.   The use of filler ਰਾਮ is frequently employed in the Goindval Pothis, but in the Adi Granth it is dropped at many places.

15.   In the titles of these *chhants* there is an interesting addition: "the *chhant* is to be sung to the tune of ਆਵਹੋ ਸਾਜਨਾ.   This type of instructions appear in the Adi Granth as well.   For example, a hymn recorded in Adi Granth, p. 91, is to be sung to the tune of another hymn (ਏਕੁ ਸੁਆਨੁ ਕੈ ਘਰ ਗਾਵਣਾ).   There are also references to prevalent tunes of popular Punjabi ballads, to which the eight *vars* in the Adi Granth are to be sung.

16.   The word ਕੀ in this verse does not appear in the Adi Granth, p. 771.

17.   This verse in the Adi Granth, p. 772, contains ਦਿਨੁ ਰਾਤੀ, instead of ਵਡਭਾਗੀ, found in the pothi.

18.   This *chhant* (number 11) does not appear in the Adi Granth.   In the pothi at Jalandhar, there are six *chhants* (1, 2, 3, 11, 12, and 13) attributed to Guru Nanak.   The *chhants* numbered 4 to 10 belong to Guru Amardas.   In the Adi Granth, pp. 763-767, five of Guru Nanak's *chhants* a(1, 2, 3, 12, and 13) are recorded together and are organized according to their *ghar* placement. It is possible that at the time of the compilation of the Kartarpur Pothi, the *chhant* in question, being the only one to be in *rag* Suhi-Dakhṇi, was separated out by the scribe, to be recorded at the end of the sequence of Guru Nanak's *chhants*.   In the complex process of bringing together two scattered segments (1-3, and 11-13) of Guru Nanak's *chhants* and their rearrangement according to the new category of *ghar*, this *chhant* was somehow missed.   For problems like this, see below, *rag* Dhanasri, note 56; *rag* Tilang, note 131.

170

19. This *chhant* is completed on folio 38. The scribe leaves some folios blank before starting the *ashtpadis,* on folio 40. On the folios left blank, the following hymn in *rag* Vaḍhans, Mahala 1, is recorded:

ਕਾਇਆ ਕੂੜ ਵਿਗਾੜ ਕਾਹੇ ਬਾਬਾ ਨਾਯਓ॥. . .

ਬਾਬਾ ਨਾਨਕ ਜਿਨ ਨਾਉ ਮਿਲਿਆ ਕਰਮ ਹੋਏ ਗੁਰ ਕਦੇ॥

ਸਭਓ ਪੇ ਸਾਅਬ ਪੇ ਆਪੇ ਏਕ ਨਦਰਿ ਕਰੇ॥੪॥

20. The word ਜਿਗੁਰ only appears in the text of *rag* Suhi. According to Piar Singh this word is either a distortion of the Persian word ਦੀਗਰ ("other") or is indicative of some region like Dakhṇi; see his *Gatha Sri Adi Granth*, pp. 78-80. I think this word is somehow related to the *ashtpadis*: it appears in the title of the three *ashtpadis* at this point in the pothi at Jalandhar and once more in the writing of Shaikh Sharaf, which also contains eight stanzas (folio 62). The exact nature of the relationship is not clear, however.

21. An additional verse with ਰਹਾਉ appears in this hymn in the Adi Granth, p. 752. The verse is as follows:

ਬਿਨੁ ਬੂਝੇ ਸਭ ਦੁਖ ਦੁਖ ਕਮਾਵਟਾ॥   ਹਉਮੈ ਆਵੈ ਜਾਇ ਭਰਮਿ ਭੁਲਾਵਟਾ॥੧॥

22. In this *rag* section, the computation regarding the hymns includes three columns. The first column records the number of stanzas in the hymn, the second indicates the number of the hymn in the subsection to which it belongs, and the third indicates the hymn's number in the overall sequence of the *rag* section. For example, this particular hymn contains eight stanzas, is fourth in the sequence of *ashtpadis*, and is thirty-first in the section on *rag* Suhi. An examination of the extant Goindval Pothis indicates that the scribe has left blank folios at the ends of groups of hymns of different types to separate them from one another. These blank folios could also be used to record new hymns composed by the living Guru. I believe that the scribe discontinued the third column of computation after completing the *rag* Suhi section because the addition of fresh composition on the blank folio would be likely to disturb the sequence of the column. Only the two-column computation is found in the pothi at Pinjore.

23. For a discussion of the writings of Gulam Sadasevak, see Chapter 1, pp. 22-24.

24. At the end of the first and the third compositions of this section only the number of stanzas is recorded.

25. Under any given *rag*, the subsection devoted to the hymns of the non-Sikh saints always follows that comprising the hymns of the Gurus. No

concerted effort is made to separate hymns under the names of individual saints, although usually the subsection of hymns of the non-Sikh saints begins with the title "Kabir Nama."

26. This composition by Kabir is not present in the Adi Granth, nor to my knowledge is it available in any other collection of his compositions.

27. There is a mistake in the computation of hymns at this point: this hymn is counted as number 4, instead of number 5. The scribe is generally extremely careful and mistakes of this nature are rare in the extant Goindval Pothis.

28. The three stanzas of this hymn are recorded and then crossed out. The complete hymn, however, is recorded on folio 60. After crossing out the hymn, the scribe did not subtract it from the count, with the result that this second mistake rectifies the problem referred to in the previous note.

29. This hymn appears in the Adi Granth, p. 792, with the following additional verses:

ਕੁਆਰ ਕੰਨਿਆ ਜੈਸੇ ਕਰਤ ਸੀਗਾਰਾ॥   ਕਿਉ ਰਲੀਆ ਮਾਨੈ ਬਾਝੁ ਭਤਾਰਾ॥

30. The last three compositions in *rag* Suhi are recorded in the hand of the second scribe, and none of them are present in the Adi Granth. For a discussion of this particular hymn of Kabir, see Giani Gurdit Singh, *Itihas Sri Guru Granth Sahib*, pp. 574-575; Gursharan Kaur Jaggi, *Babe Mohan valian Pothian*, p. 52, note 60; Piar Singh, *Gatha Sri Adi Granth*, pp. 80-81. All scholars associate this hymn with the one found in the Adi Granth, p. 332:

ਜੀਵਤ ਪਿਤਰ ਨਾ ਮਾਨੈ ਕੋਊ ਮੂਏ ਸਿਰਾਧ ਕਰਾਹੀ॥
ਪਿਤਰ ਭੀ ਬਪੁਰੇ ਕਹੁ ਕਿਉ ਪਾਵਹਿ ਕਊਆ ਕੂਕਰ ਖਾਹੀ॥
ਮੋਕਉ ਕੁਸਲੁ ਬਤਾਵਹੁ ਭਾਈ॥
ਕੁਸਲ ਕੁਸਲ ਕਰਤੇ ਜਗ ਬਿਨਸੈ ਕੁਸਲੁ ਭੀ ਕੈਸੇ ਹੋਈ॥

This connection is not correct. The hymn recorded in the pothi at Jalandhar is a different one and is found in other collections that contain the hymns of Kabir; see Winand M. Callewaert and Bart Op de Beeck, eds., *Devotional Hindi Literature* (New Delhi: Manohar, 1991), p. 1: 319; Mataprasad Gupta, ed., *Kabir Granthavali* (Alahabad: Lokbharati Prakashan, 1969), p. 364; Bhagavatsvarup Mishra, ed., *Kabir Granthavali* (Agra: Vinod Pustak Mandir, 1969), 478; L. B. Ram 'Anant', ed., *Kabir Granthavali* (Delhi: Regal Book Depot), p. 512.

31. This composition of Namdev is not present in the Adi Granth, but does appear with slight variations in other collections of his hymns. See

Gopal Narayan Bahura, ed., *The Padas of Surdas*, pp. 140-141; Winand M. Callewaert and Bart Op de Beeck, eds., *Devotional Hindi Literature*, p. 1: 419; Winand M. Callewaert and Mukund Lath, eds., *The Hindi Padavali of Namdev* (New Delhi: Motilal Banarsidass, 1989), p. 375.

32. This composition does not appear in the Adi Granth, nor does the Adi Granth include any other hymn under the name of Shaikh Sharaf. One stanza of the composition recorded in the pothi at Jalandhar is available in other sources, see Kirpal Singh, ed., *Janam Sakhi Prampra*, p. 344. For more compositions of Shaikh Sharaf, see Sant Singh Sekhon, ed., *Shabad Shalok* (Patiala: Punjab Language Department, 1969), pp. 253-257. There is tomb of Shaikh Sharaf at Panipat, popularly known as the tomb of Bu Shah Ali Qalandar. A large fair is held there annually, as it seems to have been for centuries. For a late seventeenth-century reference to this fair, see Sujan Rai Bhandari, *Khulastut Tvarikh* (Patiala: Punjabi University, 1972), pp. 36-37. See also Bruce B. Lawrence, *Notes from a Distant Flute: The Extant Literature of pre-Mughal Indian Sufism* (Tehran: Imperial Iranian Academy of Philosophy, 1978), pp. 79-81.

Rag Prabhati

33. In this *rag* section there are thirty-four hymns of the Gurus. In the Adi Granth, however, there are only thirty-three hymns in the corresponding section. Two hymns of Guru Nanak that appear under the combined *rag* Prabhati-Lalat in the pothi at Jalandhar are recorded in the Adi Granth, in the *rag* Suhi section, pp. 730-731; see above, note 1, and below, note 41. Meanwhile, one hymn of four stanzas by Guru Amardas found in the Adi Granth, pp. 1334-1335 (ਮੇਰੇ ਮਨ ਗੁਰ ਅਪਣਾ ਸਾਲਾਹਿ॥), is not available in the pothi at Jalandhar, but we can infer that this particular hymn may have come from some other *rag* section in the Goindval Pothis. Since not all the Goindval Pothis are extant, it is hard to give a final word on this particular issue. The notable feature in the writing of the name of *rag* Prabhati in the Goindval Pothis is that it does not employ the conjunct form /r/ later found in the Adi Granth.

34. The sequence of hymns from 1 through 22 is the same in both the pothi at Jalandhar and the Adi Granth. This particular hymn is recorded in *rag* Prabhati-Bibhas in the Adi Granth, p. 1327.

35. The words ਲੇ in the opening verse, and ਤਾ in the final verse do not appear in the Adi Granth, p. 1328.

36. ਬਾਬਾ in the final verse is not present in the Adi Granth, p. 1328, and ਪਰਤੰਤੁ in the pothi appears as ਪਰਮਤੰਤੁ, in the Adi Granth, p. 1328.

37. The final verse of this hymn in the Adi Granth, p. 1329, opens with ਸਿਫਤਿ ਸਰਮ, instead of ਭਗਤਿ ਸਰਮ, found in the pothi.

38. The incomplete opening verse of the third stanza in the pothi appears in the Adi Granth, p. 1329, as follows:

ਘਟਿ ਘਟਿ ਏਕੁ ਵਖਾਣੀਐ ਕਹਉ [ਨਾ ਦੇਖਿਆ ਜਾਇ]॥

39. The word ਸਾਦ in the pothi appears as ਨਾਦ in the Adi Granth, p. 1331.

40. A verse in this hymn in the Adi Granth, p. 1331, reads:

ਉਪਰਿ ਕੂਪੁ ਗਗਨ ਪਨਿਹਾਰੀ ਅੰਮ੍ਰਿਤੁ ਪੀਵਣਹਾਰਾ॥

In the pothi, the verse, however, appears as:

ਉਪਰਿ ਕੂਪੁ ਗਾਗਰਿ ਪਨਿਹਾਰੀ ਅੰਮ੍ਰਿਤੁ ਪੀਵਣਹਾਰਾ॥

The word ਗਾਗਰਿ of the pothi seems to fit in better in the context. One needs to check this point with the text in the Kartarpur Pothi.

41. These two hymns appear in the Adi Granth, pp. 730-731, in the *rag* Suhi section. Pashaura Singh accounts for the change of *rag* by relating it to the subject matter of the hymns; see his "The Text and Meaning of the Adi Granth," p. 115. To me, however, this change seems to be related to the *rag* combination of Prabhati and Lalat that is found in the pothi at Jalandhar. To combine these two *rags* was acceptable at the time of the compilation of the Goindval Pothis, but for some reason it was not thought to work when the Kartarpur Pothi was compiled; thus, the shifting of these hymns along with two other hymns that had also been recorded in *rag* Prabhati-Lalat in the Goindval Pothis (see below, notes 46 and 47). There are other examples of this sort of change in the hymns of the non-Sikh saints; see *rag* Dhanasri, note 66; *rag* Bhairo, note 108; *rag* Ramkali 149; *rag* Sorathi 161; *rag* Malar, note 177.

42. This hymn is recorded in the Adi Granth, p. 1342, in *rag* Prabhati-Bibhas.

43. The sequence of the opening two verses of the last stanza in the pothi is reversed in the Adi Granth, p. 1342. They appear in the Adi Granth as follows:

ਸਾਚਾ ਆਪਿ ਅਨੂਪੁ ਅਧਾਰੋ॥ ਅਵਰ ਨਾਹੀ ਕਰਿ ਦੇਖਣਹਾਰੋ॥

44. Instead of ਨਾਇ in the pothi, ਨਾਮਿ appears in the Adi Granth, p. 1344. The sequence of *ashṭpadis* 1 through 7 is identical in both the pothi and the Adi Granth, pp. 1342-1345.

45. This hymn of five stanzas in the pothi is clearly attributed to Guru Nanak, while in the Adi Granth, p. 1334, it is recorded under the name of Guru Amardas.

46-47. Both these hymns are recorded in the *rag* Suhi section in the Adi Granth, p. 793.

Rag Dhanasri

48. In the pothi, twenty-five hymns of the Gurus are found in this *rag*. In the Adi Granth, however, twenty-three hymns appear under their names. *Chaupada* number 10 attributed to Guru Amardas in the pothi is not available in the Adi Granth (see below, note 56), and *chaupada* number 20 attributed to Guru Nanak in the pothi is present in the Adi Granth, p. 670, but is recorded under the name of Guru Ramdas (see below, note 58).

49. The refrain is used after all four stanzas of this hymn. This feature continues in the Adi Granth, p. 660. (For another example of use of the refrain verse more than once in a given hymn, see below *rag* Ramkali, note 135. The count of stanzas of this hymn is continuos (1-4) in the pothi at Jalandhar, but in the Adi Granth each stanzas is counted separately.

50. The words ਜੀਵੀਐ and ਥਕੇ appear as ਰਹੀਐ and ਰਹੈ, respectively, in the Adi Granth, p. 661.

51. This hymn in the Adi Granth, p. 661, begins with ਕਿਉ ਸਿਮਰੀ and the last verse contains ਜੈਸੀ ਨਦਰਿ.

52. This hymn is recorded in the Adi Granth, p. 661, under the name of Guru Nanak. In all the early manuscripts--Ms. 1245, folio 566; the Kartarpur Pothi, folio 499; the Banno Pothi, Kanpur--this hymn is attributed to Guru Amardas. There seems to be little doubt that this hymn is the creation of Guru Amardas. On the basis of its appearance among the hymns of Guru Nanak, later scribes mistakenly attributed it to Guru Nanak.

53. The meaning of the strange instruction recorded on folio 124, ਚਉਬਾਰੈ ਗਾਵੈ ਪਹਿਲਾ ਰਾਗੁ ਧਨਾਸਰੀ ("*Rag* Dhanasri should be sung first at the balcony"), is not clear.

54. Instead of ਤਿਸੁ, the Adi Granth, p. 662, records ਤੁਹ.

55. This sequence of hymns 1-8 is identical in the pothi and the Adi Granth.

56. This *chaupada* is not present in the Adi Granth. In the pothi the section on *rag* Dhanasri opens with a set of eight hymns by Guru Nanak, which appears in exactly the same way in the Adi Granth. Subsequently, there is a difference in sequence between the two texts. In the Adi Granth, the set of hymns of Guru Nanak is followed by his *arti* (prayer), which in the pothi is recorded as number 19 in the *rag*, and appears after the hymns of Guru Amardas. This change in sequence may be accounted for by the scribe's understandable effort to bring the hymns of Guru Nanak together. Having brought the *arti* to the section of Guru Nanak's hymns, the scribe continued to the next group of hymns, by Guru Amardas. Here, the introduction of *ghar,* in the Kartarpur pothi/Adi Granth organization, demanded further change. The original sequence of the hymns by Guru Amardas, numbered 9-18 in the pothi, appears in the Adi Granth as follows:

11-13 in *ghar* 2; 14-18 in *ghar* 3; 9 in *ghar* 4

It is probable that in this restructuring, hymn number 10 in the pothi was missed. Guru Nanak's *arti* had already been inscribed earlier, making the total number of hymns in the pothi and the Adi Granth match at the end; the scribe would therefore have been likely to overlook the omission.

57. The meaning of the statement ਧਨਾਸਰੀ ਪਸਤੋ ਮਾਰੂ ਗੜਓ, recorded on folio 137, is not clear.

58. This hymn is recorded in the section devoted to Guru Nanak's compositions. The handwriting and the pen are the same as in the earlier portion of the text and this hymn is counted in the regular sequence. "Mahala 5" has been added to the title later. In the Adi Granth, p. 670, this hymn is recorded in the name of Guru Ramdas. For a discussion of this issue, see Chapter 1, pp. 21-22.

59. This hymn is recorded in the folios originally left blank between the *chaupadas* and the *chhants* in the pothi; it is not written in the hand of the primary scribe of the Goindval Pothis, nor is it introduced in the column of computation of hymns. In the Adi Granth, pp. 678-679, this hymn appears in the name of Guru Arjan, and begins with what in the pothi is the second stanza. For detailed discussion, see Chapter 1, pp. 21-22.

60. In the Adi Granth, p. 687, the opening verse does not contain the word ਜੀਉ, although later verses include it, as in the text of the pothi.

61. In the Adi Granth, p 685, the opening verse of this hymn does not include the word ਸਰੁ.

62. The sequence of *chhants* and *ashṭpadis* is identical in both the pothi at Jalandhar and the Adi Granth.

63. This hymn of Kabir is found in the Adi Granth, p. 692. The opening stanza in the pothi at Jalandhar appears there as verse number 2, in a variant form:

ਸੋਭਾ ਰਾਜ ਬਿਭੈ ਵਡਿਆਈ॥   ਅੰਤਿ ਨਾ ਕਾਹੂ ਸੰਗਿ ਸਹਾਈ॥

64. From this point onwards through the section on this *rag*, the writing is in the hand of the second scribe. This particular hymn of Ravidas is present in the Adi Granth, p. 694, and begins with what is the second verse in the pothi: ਨਾਮੁ ਤੇਰੋ ਆਰਤੀ ਮਜਨੁ ਮੁਰਾਰੇ॥. For other examples of this change see below, notes 66, and 67; *rag* Basant, notes 90, and 92; *rag* Bhairo, note 106; *rag* Maru, note 122; *rag* Sorathi, note 161; *rag* Malar, note 175. This practice of transferring the second verse of various hymns recorded in the Goindval Pothis to the opening position in the Adi Granth (the original opening verse then becomes the second verse and verses three and following follow in sequence) deserves to be examined closely, to understand the possible reasons for the change.

65. This composition attributed to Trilochaṇ is not found in the Adi Granth.

66. This hymn of Dhanna appears in the Adi Granth, p. 488, and is recorded in the *rag* Asa section. It opens with what is the second verse of the hymn as it appears in the pothi: ਰੇ ਚਿਤ ਚੇਤਸਿ ਕੀ ਨਾ ਦਯਾਲ ਦਮੋਦਰ ਬਿਬਹਿ ਨਾ ਜਾਨਸਿ ਕੋਇ॥

67. This hymn of Trilochaṇ appears in the Adi Granth, p. 695, and opens with what is the second verse in the pothi: ਨਾਰਾਇਣ ਨਿੰਦਸਿ ਕਾਇ ਭੂਲੀ ਗਵਾਰੀ॥

68. The following hymn by Namdev in *rag* Malar is inserted later on folio 165 originally left blank:

ਆਲਾਵਤੀ ਇਹ ਭਰਮ ਜੋ ਹੈ ਮੋ ਉਪਰ ਸਭ ਕੋਪਲਾ॥. . .
ਫੇਰ ਦੇਹੁਰਾ ਨਾਮੇ ਕਉ ਦੇਨਾ ਇਮ ਪੰਡਤ ਕਉ ਪਿਛਵਾੜਲਾ॥੩॥੧॥

Rag Basant

69. The text of the *mulmantar* ends with a *ḍanḍi* (full stop) and ਗੁਰਪਰਸਾਦ is later added to it.

177

70. This *rag* section contains thirty-eight hymns of the Gurus, which all appear in the Adi Granth. The pothi does not use the combination of *rag* Basant-Hindol (nor in all probability did *rag* Hindol even appear in the Goindval Pothis), but in the Adi Granth, six hymns, all from *rag* Basant section of the pothi, appear under this designation. These six hymns are: *chaupadas* number 4-6, and 16; *ashṭpadi* number 1; hymn number 3 in the subsection of the non-Sikh saints.

71. The *rag* Basant section in the Adi Granth opens with the first three hymns found in this *rag* section in the pothi, but then there are changes.

72-73. Both these hymns appear in the Adi Granth, pp. 1169-1170, under the name of Guru Amardas. As far as the text of the pothi at Jalandhar goes, these hymns are attributed to Guru Nanak and are part of the sequence of his eight hymns in *rag* Basant. It is possible that a later scribe mistook the notation on folio 174* (see above, note 9) to indicate the end of the hymns by Guru Nanak, while it was simply there to mark the end of the previous work shift of the scribe. In the Kartarpur Pothi, folio 843, they were first recorded as belonging to Guru Nanak, but later transferred to Guru Amardas; the changed attribution appears in the table of contents (folio 17). It seems that Bhai Jodh Singh somehow overlooked this fact, with the result that the information provided in his *Sri Kartarpuri Biṛ de Darshan*, p. 36, is not entirely accurate; I have checked on this matter myself. It is interesting that in later manuscripts the attribution of these hymns to Guru Nanak recurred from time to time.

74. In the pothi the opening stanza has three verses, but in the Adi Granth, p. 1172, we find the additional verse: ਕਿਆ ਹਉ ਆਖਾ ਕਿਰਮ ਜੰਤੁ॥

75. In the Adi Granth, p. 1172, the last verse has ੳਰਿ instead of ਕੳੁ.

76. In the titles of the hymns numbered 13-15, "Mahala 4" is inserted later. When and why was this done is not clear.

77. When the folios in the Goindval Pothis were framed and the pothis rebound, the folio containing this hymn in the pothi at Jalandhar was dislocated from its original position and bound as folio 300. As a result, this hymn begins on folio 300 and continues on folio 187. The following hymn by Guru Nanak in *rag* Bilaval is inscribed later on folio 186 originally left blank:

ਮਨੁ ਮੰਦਰੁ ਤਨੁ ਵੇਸ ਕਲੰਦਰੁ ਘਟ ਹੀ ਤੀਰਥਿ ਨਾਵਾ॥. . .
ਜੋ ਤੁਧੁ ਭਾਵੈ ਸੋਈ ਚੰਗਾ ਇਕ ਬਾਬਾ ਨਾਨਕ ਕੀ ਅਰਦਾਸੇ॥੪॥

78. In the Adi Granth, p. 1170, the opening verse contains ਸਚੁ instead of ਰਚੁ in the pothi.

79. In the Adi Granth, p. 1176, the opening verse contains ਭਾਗਿ instead of ਸਬਦਿ. The last verse in the Adi Granth does not contain the word ਗੁਰ.

80. In the Adi Granth, p. 1177, the opening verse does not contain the word ਸਚੁ.

81. In the Adi Granth, p. 1177, the opening verse does not contain ਹਉ but has ਗੁਰਸਬਦ instead of ਸਬਦ.

82. The sequence of hymns numbers 21-30 is identical in the pothi and the Adi Granth, pp. 1172-1176.

83. In the Adi Granth, p. 1173, the opening verse contains ਮਨੁ ਤਨੁ, instead of ਤਨੁ ਮਨੁ.

84. In the Adi Granth, p. 1174, the opening verse does not contain the word ਮਹਿ.

85. In the Adi Granth, p. 1175, the final verse contains ਨਾਹਿ ਕੋ instead of ਕੋ ਨਾਹਿ.

86. ਗੁਰਪਰਸਾਦ is later added to the text of the *mulmantar*.

87. In the Adi Granth, p. 1187, the final verse does not include the word ਤੂ.

88. The middle verses of the fourth stanza differ between the pothi and the Adi Granth. The verse in the pothi, ਬਿਨੁ ਰਸ ਰਾਤੇ ਪਤਿ ਨਾ ਸੁਖੁ॥ ਤੂ ਆਪੇ ਕਰਤਾ ਆਪਿ ਆਖੁ॥, reads as follows in the Adi Granth, p. 1188: ਬਿਨੁ ਹਰਿ ਰਸ ਰਾਤੇ ਪਤਿ ਨ ਸਾਖੁ॥ ਤੂ ਆਪੇ ਸੁਰਤਾ ਆਪਿ ਰਾਖੁ॥

89. The opening verse of the fourth stanza differs between the pothi and the Adi Granth. The verse in the pothi, ਇਤ ਉਤ ਸਹਜਿ ਰਵਉ ਗੁਣ ਗਾਵਉ॥, appears as follows in the Adi Granth, p. 1189: ਇਤ ਉਤ ਦੇਖਉ ਸਹਜੇ ਰਵਉ॥

90. This hymn of Ramanand appears in the Adi Granth, p. 1195, and opens with what is the second verse in the pothi: ਕਤ ਜਾਈਐ ਰੇ ਘਰਿ ਲਾਗੋ ਰੰਗੁ॥ This hymn is in the hand of the second scribe.

91. The scribe began to record this hymn of Kabir on folio 227, but crossed it out after writing four verses, and instead recorded it on folio 221*, originally left blank between the hymns of the Gurus and those of the saints. The hymns of the saints begin on folio 222, with the *mulmantar*. Note that at the beginning of this set of blank folios, folio 214*, the second scribe later recorded the hymn of Ramanand referred to in the preceding note. These two hymns are not part of the total count of this subsection.

92. This hymn of Kabir appears in the Adi Granth, p. 1194, and opens with what is the second stanza in the pothi: ਜੋਇ ਖਸਮ ਹੈ ਜਾਇਆ॥

93. This composition by Namdev is not present in the Adi Granth, nor to my knowledge is it available in any other collection of his hymns.

94. See above, note 91.

Rag Bhairo

95. The pothi at Jalandhar contains thirty-two hymns of the Gurus in this *rag*, and all of these are available in the Adi Granth. In the pothi the name of this *rag* is normally spelled as ਭੈਰੋ, while in the Adi Granth it appears as ਭੈਰਉ. At the head of the opening hymn of this section the phrase "Mahala 2" is added. This addition appeared once before; see above, note 10.

96. In the Adi Granth, p. 1128, the final verse has ਸੋਇ and ਨੇੜੀ instead of ਕੋਇ and ਨੇੜੀ in the pothi.

97. In the Adi Granth, p. 1128, the verse contains ਨ instead of ਮਤ.

98. The pothi contains the word ਕੁਲਮਾਨੀ, which appears as ਕੁਮਲਾਨੀ in the Adi Granth, p. 1126. For another instance of this change, see below, *rag Malar*, note 171.

99. There are variations between the text of this verse as recorded in the pothi and that available in later manuscripts.

Goindval Pothis	ਨਰੁ ਤਿਨੀ ਕਰਮੀ ਬਾਇ ਨ ਪਾਹਿ॥
Ms. 1245, f. 1047	ਬਿਨਾ ਗੁਤਿ ਕਰਮ ਬਾਇ ਨ ਪਾਹਿ॥
Adi Granth, p. 1130	ਨਾ ਗੁਤਿ ਨ ਕਰਮ ਬਾਇ ਪਾਹਿ॥

100. In the Adi Granth, p. 1131, the word ਤੁਖ does not appear in the opening verse.

101. The sequence of hymns 7-13 and 14-27 in the pothi appears exactly the same way in the Adi Granth, pp. 1125-1127 and 1129-1133.

102. This hymn of five stanzas appears among the *chaupadas* in the Adi Granth, p. 1133.

103. This hymn of five stanzas is also recorded among the *chaupadas* in the Adi Granth, p. 1133.

104. There is a mistake in the computation of hymns here, due to the preceding hymn not being entered in the total.

105. Giani Gurdit Singh, in his *Itihas Sri Guru Granth Sahib*, p. 565, has assigned this title great importance. Building on this entry in the pothi at

Jalandhar, he has argued that all the saints whose hymns were recorded in the Adi Granth were actual followers of Guru Nanak. More broadly, however, it is evident that the Goindval Pothis pay very little attention to the titles of the hymns of the saints. Consequently, Giani Gurdit Singh's whole argument is not on a firm foundation.

106. This hymn of Kabir that appears in the Adi Granth, p. 1157, and opens with what is the second verse in the pothi: ਇਹੁ ਧਨੁ ਮੇਰੇ ਹਰਿ ਕੋ ਨਾਉ॥

107. This hymn of Namdev appears in the Adi Granth, pp. 1166-1167, with an extra stanza not available in the pothi:

ਜਉ ਗੁਰਦੇਉ ਤ ਸੰਸਾ ਟੂਟੈ॥   ਜਉ ਗੁਰਦੇਉ ਤ ਜਮ ਤੇ ਛੂਟੈ॥

ਜਉ ਗੁਰਦੇਉ ਤ ਭਉਜਲ ਤਰੈ॥   ਜਉ ਗੁਰਦੇਉ ਤ ਜਨਮਿ ਨ ਮਰੈ॥

108. This hymn of Ravidas is present in the Adi Granth, in the *rag* Gauṛi section, p. 345. From this point onward, the remaining hymns in *rag* Bhairo are recorded in the hand of the second scribe. They were written on folios originally left blank.

109. This composition by Namdev is not present in the Adi Granth, nor to my knowledge is it available in any other collection of his compositions.

110. This hymn of Namdev appears in the Adi Granth, pp. 1165-1166, in a radically changed and expanded (twenty-eight stanza) form.

111. This composition does not appear in the Adi Granth, but its theme has close affinity with the hymn referred to in the preceding note. See also Winand M. Callewaert and Mukund Lath, eds., *Namdev ki Hindi Padavali*, pp. 369-370.

112. This hymn appears in the Adi Granth, p. 1164, but does not include the following verses, which appear in the pothi:

ਉਠ ਰੇ ਛੀਪੜੇ ਤੂ ਬਾਹਰਿ ਜਾਹਿ॥   ਉਤਮ ਲੋਕੁ ਬੈਸੈ ਆਗੈ ਆਇ॥

113. The following couplet by Guru Nanak in *rag* Asa is inscribed later on folio 273 originally left blank:

ਬਲਿਹਾਰੀ ਗੁਰ ਆਪਣੇ ਦਿਉਹਾੜੀ ਸਦ ਵਾਰ॥. . .

ਫਲੀਹਿ ਫੁਲਹਿ ਬਪੁੜੇ ਕਰ ਤਨ ਪਰਹ ਸੁਆਹ॥੩॥

Rag Maru

114. In the pothi at Jalandhar *rag* Maru was originally recorded as *rag* Maru-Kedara; later, however, "Kedara" was crossed out from all headings in

181

the text. This is the only *rag* section in the Goindval Pothis that does not contain all the hymns of the Gurus that are found in the Adi Granth. It is possible that the extra hymns in the *rag* Maru section of the Adi Granth may have been recorded originally in the *rag* Kedara section of the Goindval Pothis. Since the pothi that would have contained that section is not extant, it is hard to make a claim about the exact situation with any degree of confidence.

115. In the Adi Granth, p. 989, a couplet by Guru Arjan is prefixed to this hymn. For more examples of this type see below, note 116, and *rag* Ramkali, notes 141, and 143. The reason for such additions is not clear. Pashaura Singh argues that through the technique of addition, Guru Arjan established unity and doctrinal consistency in Guruship; see his, "The Text and Meaning of the Adi Granth," pp. 144-148. Constructed around three or four examples, the argument is not very convincing. Scholars need to look into this issue in some detail.

116. A couplet of Guru Arjan is also prefixed to this hymn in the Adi Granth, p. 990.

117. The sequences of hymns numbers 1-7 and 9-10 in the pothi are identical in the Adi Granth, pp. 989-992.

118. In the pothi, this hymn of Guru Amardas appears among the hymns of Guru Nanak. In the Adi Granth, pp. 993-995, however, it has been taken to its right place with the other hymns of Guru Amardas; there are four additional hymns of Guru Amardas in this *rag* section that are not present in the extant Goindval Pothis.

119. In the Adi Granth, pp. 989-993, there are three additional hymns of Guru Nanak that are not present in the extant Goindval Pothis.

120. The gathering that begins with folio 283 has serious structural problems: the folio containing the writing of Gulam Sadasevak appears after the hymns of Jaidev and Kabir, and the rest of the folios are not in the proper sequence either.

121. Six hymns of the non-Sikh saints present here (3, 9, 10, 12, 15, 17), appear in the *rag* Kedara section of the Adi Granth, pp. 1123-1124.

122. This hymn of Kabir appears in the Adi Granth, p. 1102, but opens with what is the second verse in the pothi: ਪੜੀਆ ਕਵਨ ਕੁਮਤਿ ਤੁਮ ਲਾਗੇ॥

123. In the Adi Granth, p. 1123, the opening verse does not include the word ਕੈਸਾ.

124. This composition by Kabir is not present in the Adi Granth, nor to my knowledge is it available in any other collection of his hymns.

125. The following hymn by Trilochaṇ in *rag* Gujri is inscribed later on folio 299, and part of it also appears on folio 185:

ਅੰਤ ਕਾਲ ਜੋ ਲਖਮੀ ਸਿਵਰੈ ਐਸੀ ਚਿੰਤਾ ਜੇ ਮਰੇ॥

Rag Tilang

126. In the original writing of the pothi at Jalandhar, the hymns in *rag* Tilang were placed toward the end. At the time of the framing of the folios and the rebinding of the pothi, three of the folios containing the hymns in *rag* Tilang got attached to *rag* Basant. In this tangle a folio containing the opening section of a hymn in *rag* Basant got shifted to the end of the pothi; see Chapter 1, pp. 37-38.

Two of Guru Nanak's hymns (ਇਹੁ ਤਨੁ ਮਾਇਆ ਪਾਹਿਆ ਪਿਆਰੇ ਲੀਤੜਾ ਲਭਿ ਰੰਗਾਏ॥ ਮੇਰੈ ਕੰਤ ਨ ਭਾਵੈ ਚੋਲੜਾ ਪਿਆਰੇ ਕਿਉ ਧਨ ਸੇਜੈ ਜਾਏ॥; ਇਆਨੜੀਏ ਮਾਨੜਾ ਕਾਇ ਕਰੇਹਿ॥ ਆਪਨੜੇ ਘਰਿ ਹਰਿ ਰੰਗੋ ਕੀ ਨ ਮਾਣਹਿ॥), and two hymns of Namdev (ਮੈ ਅੰਧੁਲੇ ਕੀ ਟੇਕ ਤੇਰਾ ਨਾਮੁ ਖੁੰਦਕਾਰਾ॥; ਹਲੇ ਯਾਰਾਂ ਹਲੇ ਯਾਰਾਂ ਖੁਸਿਖਬਰੀ॥) recorded in the Adi Granth, pp. 721-722, and 727, are not found in the pothi at Jalandhar. One could argue that these hymns must have been present originally, but they were lost in the transference of folios. We know that at present, instead of having a complete gathering of eight folios at the end of the pothi, we have only two folios appended there; and with three shifted to the *rag* Basant section, we are still left with three folios that must originally have been part of this gathering.

127. This hymn appears in the Adi Granth, p. 721, with minor changes. These changes seem to have resulted from an effort to give proper Persian forms of the words. For example, ਇਕ and ਤੂ of the opening verse of the pothi are changed to ਯਕ and ਤੂਨ in the Adi Granth.

128. In the Adi Granth, p. 721, appears ਮੈ instead of the ਤਉ.

129. In the Adi Granth, p. 725, the last verse does not include ਤਉ.

130. In the Adi Granth, p. 722, the opening verse contains ਤੈਸੜਾ instead of ਤੈਸਾ in the pothi.

131. This composition does not appear in the Adi Granth, see above, note 126, and Chapter 1, pp. 37-38. For its complete text, see Chapter 3, p. 101.

132. This single hymn of Kabir appears on folio 300*, and confirms that the hymns in *rag* Tilang originally appeared toward the end of the pothi.

2. 2. The Pothi at Pinjore

Rag Ramkali

133. The text of the *mulmantar* in the pothi at Pinjore slightly differs from that in the pothi at Jalandhar. For example, the words ਨਿਰਭਉ and ਨਿਰੀਕਾਰ found in the pothi at Jalandhar sometimes do not appear in the pothi at Pinjore, and instead of the phrase ਗੁਰਪਰਸਾਦੁ/ਗੁਰਪਰਸਾਦਿ of the pothi at Jalandhar, ਗੁਰ ਪੂਰੇ ਕਾ ਪਰਸਾਦੁ is recorded in the pothi at Pinjore.

134. The pothis contain twenty-six hymns and three long compositions by the Gurus, all of which appear in the Adi Granth. With the exception of one change (see below, note 142), the sequence of hymns is identical in the pothi at Pinjore and the Adi Granth. The *var* of Guru Amardas in *rag* Ramkali in the Adi Granth is not present in the pothi; for a discussion of this issue, see above, note 2. In the pothi at Pinjore the *rag* variant Ramkali-Dakhṇi appears very frequently, but in the Adi Granth its use is minimal.

135. This hymn includes two refrain verses: the second verse, which regularly appears as the refrain verse of every hymn, and the last verse. The same usage is found in the Adi Granth, p. 877. Instead of ਜੋ ਦਰਿ, the opening verse in the Adi Granth contains ਜਿਤੁ ਦਰ.

136. The hymn in the pothi contains two stanzas, but the Adi Granth, p. 878, has a complete *chaupada*, with the addition of the following verses:

ਦੇਹਿ ਭਗਤਿ ਪੂਰਨ ਅਵਿਨਾਸੀ ਹਉ ਤੁਝ ਕਉ ਬਲਿਹਾਰਿਆ॥੧॥;

ਜਪ ਤਪ ਸੰਜਮ ਕਰਮ ਨਾ ਜਾਨਾ ਨਾਮੁ ਜਪੀ ਪ੍ਰਭ ਤੇਰਾ॥

ਗੁਰ ਪਰਮੇਸਰੁ ਨਾਨਕ ਭੇਟਿਓ ਸਾਚੈ ਸਬਦਿ ਨਿਬੇੜਾ॥੩॥

137. This sequence of hymns 1-12 appears the same way in the Adi Granth, pp. 876-880.

138. This hymn of Guru Amardas is recorded along with his other hymns in the Adi Granth, pp. 908-909.

139. In the pothi, this hymn has twenty verses, but in the Adi Granth, pp. 911-912, there are twenty-one verses. I have been unable to determine whether this variation is the result of the Adi Granth having an extra verse or of different computation.

140. The presence of the complete text of the *mulmantar* indicates that the following three compositions are given privileged status. These compositions are counted separately. As stated previously the variant of

"Ramkali-Dakhṇi" appears frequently in this *rag* section, but interestingly enough it is not found in the title of this composition. For some unknown reason, however, this composition, is entitled *Dakhṇi Aunkar* in the Adi Granth, p. 929.

141. This composition contains seventy-two stanzas in the pothi at Pinjore, but in the Adi Granth, pp. 938-946, the text has seventy-three stanzas. The seventy-third stanza, present in the Adi Granth, is not found in the pothi:

ਤੇਰੀ ਗਤਿ ਮਿਤਿ ਤੂਹੈ ਜਾਣਹਿ ਕਿਆ ਕੋ ਆਖਿ ਵਖਾਣੈ ॥. . .

ਨਾਨਕ ਸਭਿ ਜੁਗ ਆਪੇ ਵਰਤੈ ਦੂਜਾ ਅਵਰੁ ਨ ਕੋਈ ॥੭੩॥

142. The *Anand* appears in the pothi as part of the longer compositions, but in the Adi Granth, pp. 917-922, it is placed after the section of *ashṭpadis*. In Ms. 1245, folio 881, the placement of the *Anand* is similar to that in the pothi at Pinjore.

143. The text of the *Anand* in the pothi contains thirty-eight stanzas, while in the Adi Granth, there are forty stanzas. Referring to "some old tradition," Bawa Prem Singh attributes Adi Granth stanza 39 to Guru Ramdas and stanza 40 to Guru Arjan. See Gursharan Kaur Jaggi, *Babe Mohan valian Pothian*, pp. 47-48; Piar Singh, *Gatha Sri Adi Granth*, p. 94. This issue is really more complicated, however, as the later additions to the text available in the pothi at Pinjore are actually stanzas 40 and 34:

ਅਨਦ ਸੁਣਹੁ ਵਡਭਾਗੀਹੋ ਸਗਲ ਮਨੋਰਥ ਪੂਰੇ ॥. . .

ਬਿਨਵੰਤਿ ਨਾਨਕ ਗੁਰ ਚਰਣ ਲਾਗੇ ਵਾਜੇ ਅਨਹਦ ਤੂਰੇ ॥੪੦॥

ਮਨਿ ਚਾਉ ਭਇਆ ਪ੍ਰਭ ਆਗਮੁ ਸੁਣਿਆ ॥. . .

ਕਹੈ ਨਾਨਕ ਪ੍ਰਿਅ ਆਪ ਮਿਲਿਆ ਕਰਣ ਕਾਰਣ ਜੋਗੋ ॥੩੪॥

The text of Adi Granth stanza 40 is also present in the collections that belong to the followers of Prithi Chand and in all likelihood can be attributed to Guru Ramdas; see Raijasbir Singh, ed., *Guru Amardas Srot Pustak* (Amritsar: Guru Nanak Dev University, 1986), pp. 198-201. Addition to the *Anand* of this concluding stanzas, may have been aimed at bringing its structure closer to that of the *Japji* by Guru Nanak--thirty-eight stanzas and a concluding couplet--the most well known text in Sikh tradition. The reasons for the addition of Adi Granth stanza 34 are not as clear. In my view this stanza, which appears for the first time in Ms. 1245, folio 886, belongs to Guru Arjan. In Ms. 1245, the *Anand's* structure has not yet attained its final shape. Here the last stanza of the *Anand* in the pothi at Pinjore is still at the end of the text, preceded by two new stanzas: Adi Granth stanza 40, here in position 39; and Adi Granth stanza 34, here in position 38. How the stanza appearing in position 39 in Ms. 1245 became Adi Granth stanza 40, and how that appearing in position 38 became Adi Granth stanza 34 needs to be looked into. The latter change is compelling, as there are obvious problems in the relationship of Adi Granth stanza 34 to its present context. It appears in a sequence of stanzas that address various bodily senses: the series opens with ਏ ਰਸਨਾ (stanza 32) and goes on to include ਏ ਸਰੀਰਾ (stanza 33), ਏ ਸਰੀਰਾ (stanza 35), ਏ ਨੇਤ੍ਰਹੁ (stanza 36), ਏ ਸ੍ਵਣਹੁ (stanza 37).

144. A set of folios following 92 are left blank in the original writing of the pothi. On the left-hand lower part of folio 94 is inscribed: ਗੁਲਾਮੁ ਮਸਤ ਤੇਡਾ ਜੇਠ ਚੰਦ. According to Bhalla family tradition this writing is in the hand of Guru Ramdas, and during the pothi's ceremonial opening on the *puranmashi* this folio is normally displayed (see photograph, p. 208).

145. Hymns of the saints actually begin on folio 111, with the *mulmantar*. The few hymns that appear on folios 101-106 are in the hand of the second scribe and were inserted after the original writing of the pothi. We also have two hymns in this hand at the end of the subsection, folios 120-121.

146. This composition by Kabir is not present in the Adi Granth, nor to my knowledge is it available in any other collection of his hymns.

147. This composition of Beni is not present in the Adi Granth.

148. This composition of Namdev is not present in the Adi Granth, but appears in other sources of his hymns; see Winand M. Callewaert and Mukund Lath, eds., *Namdev ki Hindu Padavali*, p. 312; Bhagirath Mishra and Rajnarayan Maurya, eds., *Sant Namdev ki Hindi Padavali* (Pune: Pune University, 1964), p. 43.

149. This hymn of Kabir appears in the *rag* Asa section of the Adi Granth, p. 484.

150. This composition of Trilochan does not appear in the Adi Granth.

151. Teja Singh thought that this composition was the same as one appearing, with some minor changes, in the *rag* Suhi section of the Adi Granth, p. 793; see his "Sri Guru Granth Sahib da Sampadan," p. 140. This observation is incorrect, however. This hymn is not present in the Adi Granth, but does appear in other sources of Kabir's writings; see Bhagavatsvarup Mishra, ed., *Kabir Granthavali*, p. 387; Mataprasad Gupta, ed., *Kabir Granthavali*, p. 291.

152. This composition of Kabir is not available in the Adi Granth, but does appear in other collections; see Winand M. Callewaert and Bart Op de Beeck, eds., *Devotional Hindi Literature*, p. 1: 326; L. B. Ram 'Anant,' ed., *Kabir Granthavali*, p. 321.

153. Hymns of the saints actually begin from this point in the original writing of the pothi and continue until folio 120.

154. This hymn appears in the Adi Granth, pp. 969-970, and contains the following stanza which is not present in the pothi:

ਕਬੀਰ ਦੀਈ ਸੰਸਾਰ ਕਉ ਲੀਨੀ ਜਿਸੁ ਮਸਤਕਿ ਭਾਗਿ॥

ਅੰਮ੍ਰਿਤ ਰਸ ਜਿਨਿ ਪਾਇਆ ਥਿਰੁ ਤਾ ਕਾ ਸੋਹਾਗਾ॥੫॥

Rag Soraṭhi

155. There are thirty-one hymns of the Gurus in *rag* Soraṭhi in the pothi at Pinjore, and all of them are present in the Adi Granth, pp. 595-604, and 634-639. In the Adi Granth the organization of this *rag* section is constructed around number of verses per stanzas. This additional organizational principle results in many sequential variations between the pothi and in the Adi Granth, in this *rag* section, see Chapter 1, pp. 41-42.

156. This hymn of Guru Amardas is repeated on folio 159. It is the only case of duplication in the hymns of the Gurus in the two extant pothis.

157. The pothi does not contain the word ਉਪਜੈ, which appears in the Adi Granth, p. 604.

158. In the Adi Granth, the *ashṭpadis* section is also reorganized on the basis of the number of verses per stanza. This results in significant sequential changes.

159. The Adi Granth, p. 636, contains ਨਿਰਮਲੋ instead of ਉਜਲੋ.

160. See above, note 156.

161. This hymn is entitled ਗਉੜੀ ਭੀ ਸੋਰਠਿ ਭੀ, and appears in the *rag* Gauṛi section, Adi Granth, p. 330, and begins with what is the second verse in the pothi: ਰੇ ਜੀਅ ਨਿਲਜ ਲਾਜ ਤੋਹਿ ਨਾਹੀ॥. There are textual variations between the version in the pothi and the one recorded in the Adi Granth.

162. This hymn of Kabir is identical in both the pothi and the Adi Granth, p. 656. The variation in the number of its stanzas--two in the pothi, three in the Adi Granth--is merely the result of using a different counting system.

163. This hymn of Ravidas appears twice in the pothi; see below, note 167. Interestingly, this hymn also appears in two different *rag* sections in the Adi Granth, in *rag* Sorathi, p. 658, and *rag* Maru, p. 1106.

164. According to a later tradition, the last verse of this hymn originally contained the word ਖ਼ਲਾਸਾ, but this was changed by Guru Gobind Singh to ਖ਼ਾਲਸਾ; see Teja Singh, *Shabadarth Sri Guru Granth Sahib Ji*, p. 654. Contrary to this belief, the word ਖ਼ਾਲਸਾ already appears in the pothi. The five hymns following this one are in the hand of the second scribe.

165. This composition of three stanzas by Kabir is not present in the Adi Granth, but is available in other collections of his writings; see Mataprasad Gupta, ed., *Kabir Granthavali*, p. 311; Bhagavatsvarup Mishra, ed., *Kabir Granthavali*, p. 408.

166. This short composition of two stanzas by Kabir is not to be found in the Adi Granth, nor to my knowledge is present in other collections of his hymns.

167. See above, note 163. This hymn is in the hand of the second scribe. In all likelihood he did not realize that it had already been recorded.

168. This composition of Kabir is not present in the Adi Granth, but is found in other sources; see Mataprasad Gupta, ed., *Kabir Granthavali*, p. 200; Bhagavatsvarup Mishra, ed., *Kabir Granthavali*, pp. 272-273.

169. There are many variations between the text of the hymn in the pothi at Pinjore and the canonical version recorded in the Adi Granth, p. 659. The text that appears in the Adi Granth is the same as that found in other sources; see Winand M. Callewaert and Bart Op de Beeck, eds., *Devotional Hindi Literature* p. 1: 450. The text in the pothi at Pinjore, is as follows:

ਆਰ ਨਾਹੀ ਜਿਤ ਤੁਘਾ ਰਬੀ ਹੋਵੈ ਤਾ ਬਾਉ ਅਰੁਘਾ॥
ਤਾ ਰੈਦਾ ਮੁਰੁ ਖੁਘਾ ਹਉ ਕਿਤੁ ਵਿਧਿ ਪਾਟੀ ਗਢਾ॥੧॥
ਭਾਈ ਰਾਮਅਈ ਗਢਾਵਟਿ ਪਾਟੀ॥
ਅਗੈ ਮੁਰੀ ਏਟਣਾ ਗਢੁ ਨ ਜਾਟੀ॥੧॥ ਰਹਾਉ॥
ਰਵਿਦਾਸ ਭਵੈ ਸਿਰੀ ਰਾਮਾ ਮਇ ਨਾਹੀ ਜਮ ਸਿਉ ਕਾਮਾ॥
ਹਉ ਗਢਿ ਗਢਿ ਬਹੁਤ ਵਿਗੁਤਾ ਵਿਣੁ ਗਢੇ ਗੁਰ ਪਹੁਤਾ॥੨॥੨੩॥

Rag Malar

170. There are twenty-nine hymns of the Gurus all of which appear in the Adi Granth. A hymn of Guru Amardas (ਗੁਰਮੁਖਿ ਕੋਈ ਵਿਰਲਾ ਬੂਝੈ ਜਿਸੁ ਨੂੰ ਨਦਰਿ

ਕਰੇਇ॥), and *Malar ki var* of Guru Nanak, Adi Granth, pp. 1258, and 1278-1291, are not present in the pothi at Pinjore.

171. Instead of ਭੁਲਮਾਨੀ in the pothi, the word appears as ਭੁਮਲਾਨੀ in the Adi Granth, p. 1255. See also above, *rag* Bhairo, note 98.

172. On folio 186 the scribe drew a few lines and recorded the number 16 underneath. For some reason he resumed writing. Having recorded the next four hymns he drew the same notation and again recorded the number 16. This repetition seems to affirm my earlier observation that such notation is a serial marker for the end of one sitting of the scribe. The same pattern is repeated with his next sitting.

173. The information about this section given by Piar Singh in his *Gatha Sri Adi Granth*, p. 96, is flawed. According to him, this hymn is not included in the text of the pothi at Pinjore.

174. According to Piar Singh, three *ashtpadis* in *rag* Malar of Guru Amardas, which appear in the Adi Granth, are not found in the pothi at Pinjore; see his *Gatha Sri Adi Granth*, p. 96. This information is again not correct. One of Guru Amardas' *ashtpadis* is recorded at the end of the *ashtpadis* of Guru Nanak, and the other two are present as numbers 13 and 18 in the sequence of Guru Amardas' *chaupadas*.

175. This hymn appears in the Adi Granth, p. 1292, and opens with what is the second in the pothi: ਸੇਵੀਲੇ ਗੋਪਾਲਰਾਇ ਅਕੁਲ ਨਿਰੰਜਨ॥

176. This composition of two stanzas by Namdev is not present in the Adi Granth, nor to my knowledge is found in other collections of his hymns. This and the following hymn are in the hand of the second scribe.

177. This hymn is present in the *rag* Gond section of the Adi Granth, p. 874, and includes two verses that are not recorded in the pothi:

ਜੈਸੇ ਬਿਖੈ ਹੇਤ ਪਰ ਨਾਰੀ॥   ਐਸੇ ਨਾਮਾ ਪ੍ਰੀਤਿ ਮੁਰਾਰੀ॥੪॥

ਜੈਸੇ ਤਾਪਤੇ ਨਿਰਮਲ ਘਾਮਾ॥   ਤੈਸੇ ਰਾਮਨਾਮਾ ਬਿਨੁ ਬਪੁਰੋ ਨਾਮਾ॥੫॥

Rag Sarang

178. This title beautifully shows the unique status of Guru Nanak in the sixteenth-century Sikh community.

179. In the pothi at Pinjore, the name of this *rag* is written without the nasal, whereas in the Adi Granth the nasal is used. With the exception of one *ashtpadi* of Guru Amardas (ਮਨਿ ਮੇਰੇ ਹਰਿ ਕੈ ਨਾਮਿ ਕੀ ਵਡਾਈ॥), which appears in the

Adi Granth, p. 1233, all the hymns of the Gurus in this *rag* section are found in the pothi. On the upper left-hand corner of the folio on which the text of this *rag* begins is recorded: ਗੁਰੂ ਅੰਗਦ ਗੁਰਮੁਖੀ ਅਖਰ ਬਾਨਾਏ [ਤੇ] ਬਾਬੇ ਦੇ ਅਗੇ ਸਬਦੁ ਭੇਟ ਕੀਤਾ ("Guru Angad created the Gurmukhi alphabet [and] offered a hymn [in it] to Baba [Guru Nanak]"), see photograph, p. 207. Not being in the hand of the primary scribe, this statement cannot be used to support the tradition that Guru Angad was actually responsible for creating the Gurmukhi alphabet.

180. There is a key difference between the text of this *rag* section as recorded in the pothi at Pinjore and the canonical version in the Adi Granth. The *rahau* (refrain) appears in its regular place, as verse number 2, in all the hymns in the pothi included in this *rag*, but for some reason in the text of the Adi Granth, the *rahau* verse is always brought to the opening position. The reason for this change is not at all clear, but there is no doubt that it was made very early. We can see it beginning with Ms. 1245, folios 1098-1099, and 1127-1128.

Photographs from the Extant Goindval Pothis

1. *The Pothi at Jalandhar*
   1. 1. The author studying the pothi during its ceremonial opening on the morning of *sangrand* at Jalandhar

1. 2. The *var* ("blessing"), folio 1*

1. 3. The *var* continues, folio 9*

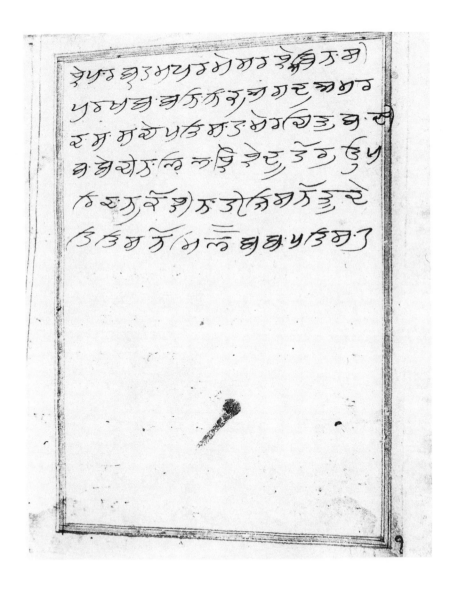

1. 4. The opening hymn in *rag* Suhi, folio 2*

1. 5. The opening hymn in *rag* Suhi continues, folio 2

1. 6. A sample of handwriting of the second scribe, folio 62*

1. 7. A sample of handwriting of the third scribe, folio 186

1. 8. A sign in the *rag* Suhi section denoting completion of the scribe's first shift, folio 9

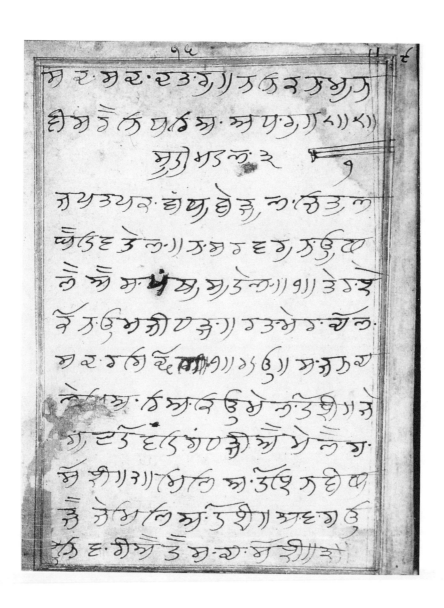

1. 9. A sign in the *rag* Bhairo section denoting completion of the scribe's twenty-third shift, folio 241*

1. 10. The hymn attributed to Guru Ramdas in later manuscripts,
recorded as Guru Nanak's composition in the pothi, folio 137*

1. 11. The hymn attributed to Guru Arjan in the Adi Granth that was
   later inserted in the pothi, folio 137

1. 12. The hymn attributed to Guru Arjan continues, folio 138*

1. 13. A hymn attributed to Gulam Sadasevak, folio 284

2. *The Pothi at Pinjore*

2. 1. The opening hymn in *rag* Ramkali, folio 2

2. 2. The opening hymn in *rag* Sorathi, folio 122

2. 3. The closing verses in *rag* Sorathi, folio 176*

2. 4. The opening hymn in *rag* Sarang, folio 216

2. 5. Mrs. Kanwarjit Singh Bhalla paying obeisance to the pothi during
its ceremonial display on the morning of *puranmashi* at Pinjore

Glossary of Punjabi Terms

This is a revised version of the glossary, which appeared in *Studying the Sikhs: Issues for North America* (Albany: State University of New York Press, 1993) edited by John Stratton Hawley and myself. I am grateful to Dr. Hawley for permitting me to utilize it in the present book.

Adi Granth (*ādi granth*) "original book": the Sikh scripture includes the compositions of the six Sikh Gurus, and selected writings of fifteen non-Sikh saints of medieval India, in addition to some bards from within the Sikh community. The honorific title used for the sacred book is Guru Granth Sahib.

Akal Takhat (*akāl takhat/akāl takht*) "Throne of the Timeless": historically came into being as seat of the temporal authority of the Guru located on the premises of the Darbar Sahib, Amritsar, and developed into the central place where communal decisions are taken.

arti (*ārtī*) "praise": a song of praise.

Baba (*bābā*) "father/grandfather": a term of affection and respect often used for religious figures, including the Adi Granth.

bani (*bāṇī*) "utterances," "compositions": the compositions recorded in the Adi Granth. The hymns of the Gurus are called *gurbani*; those of the saints are *bhagatbani*.

bauli (*baulī*) "well": a large well with steps going down to the water.

Bhai (*bhāī*) "brother": a title applied to Sikhs of acknowledged learning and piety, or any Sikh congregational leader.

bir (*bīṛ*) "volume," "recension": term used for scriptural manuscripts as well as the printed text of the Adi Granth.

chhant (*chhant*) "song."

Darbar Sahib (*darbār sāhib*): "the honorable court": honorific title of the Golden Temple in Amritsar, the holy place of the Sikhs.

Giani (*giānī*) "a learned man": a scholar well versed in Sikh scriptures.

granth (*granth*) "book": scripture.

gurdwara (*gurdvārā/gurduārā*) "Guru's place": the Sikh place of worship.

This term is often translated as literally meaning "door of the Guru" or "door to the Guru," and the word door (*dvar/duar*) is indeed the basis for the term (*dvara/duara*) that describes the interior space to which a door leads. The key area of a Sikh gurdwara is a spacious room housing the Adi Granth, where people sit and listen to scriptural recitation. This room is also used as center for social activity and has a community kitchen attached to it, in which meals are served.

gurmata (*gurmatā*) "the resolution of the Guru": the will of the eternal Guru, as expressed in a formal decision made by a representative assembly of Sikhs.

Gurmukhi (*gurmukhī*) "from the mouth of the Guru," "the script of the Gurmukhs/Sikhs": the script in which the compositions of the Gurus were first written. It has become the script in which Punjabi is written by all Sikhs.

Guru (*gurū*) "preceptor": the mode of God as teacher and guide which in the past was revealed to Sikhs in ten human Gurus, and persists in the form of the Adi Granth.

Guru Granth Sahib (*gurū granth sāhib*) "the honorable Guru in book form": honorific title of the Adi Granth.

hukamnama (*hukamnāmā*) "decree": issued from the Akal Takhat, considered to be binding on the entire Sikh community.

Janam-sakhi (*janam-sākhī*) "birth story": traditional hagiographic narratives of Guru Nanak.

Khalsa (*khālsā*) "God's own": Sikhs who have undergone the initiation ceremony of taking nectar prepared with the double-edged sword and have thus responded to the call of dedicating themselves to God and working for his victory on earth.

Japji (*japjī*): a composition of Guru Nanak that is recited by Sikhs every morning. This is the most commonly known Sikh liturgical prayer.

kirtan (*kīrtan*) "devotional singing": a significant part of Sikh piety.

langar (*langar*) "community kitchen": attached to every gurdwara, from which food is served to all, regardless of caste or creed.

Mahala (*mahalā*): "palace," "section": designates the attribution of the compositions of the Gurus in the Adi Granth: Mahala 1 (Guru Nanak), Mahala 2 (Guru Angad), Mahala 3 (Guru Amardas), and so forth.

mahant (*mahant*) "abbot": title traditionally used for Udasi custodians of the

Sikh gurdwaras. The position tended to be hereditary before the Gurdwaras Act of 1925.

masand (*masand*) "Guru's deputy": authorized leader of a local congregation in the early Sikh community.

mulmantar (*mūlmantar*) "the root formula": the invocation placed at the head of the text of the Adi Granth. It reads: "There is one Supreme Being, the Eternal Reality. He is the Creator, without fear, and devoid of enmity. He is the immortal, never incarnated, self-existent, reached through the grace of the Guru.

Nanak-panth (*nānak panth*) "the way of Nanak": term often used for the early Sikh community.

Nirankari (*nirankārī*) "a follower of Nirankar": a revivalist Sikh movement started by Baba Dayal in the middle of the nineteenth century. At present the movement has bases in Chandigarh and Delhi.

Nirmala (*nirmalā*) "a pure one": a line of Sikh scholars said to have originated during the time of Guru Gobind Singh. Because of their emphasis on Sanskrit learning, their interpretation of Sikh scriptures has a strong Vedantic coloring.

Nath Yogi (*nāth yogī*): a member of a Shaivite sect of ascetics which was very influential in medieval Punjab. The writings of the Sikh Gurus indicate their engagement with these ascetics, whose seats were known as *tillas* ("mounds").

pada (*padā*) "stanza": hymns in the Adi Granth are organized according to number of *padas*. For example we have *dopadas* (two stanzas), *tipadas* (three stanzas), *chaupadas* (four stanzas),. . . *ashtpadis* (eight stanzas).

pothi (*pothī*) "volume": term used for scriptural manuscripts in the early Sikh community.

puranmashi (*pūranmāshī*) "full month": night of the full moon.

rag (*rāg*) "melody": the main body of the text of the Adi Granth is classified under thirty-one *rag* sections.

Ragmala (*rāgmālā*) "rosary of *rags*": a composition that refers to eighty-four *rags* and *raginis* and appears at the closing of the Adi Granth.

rahau (*rahāo*) "refrain": the verse assigned this status is repeated while singing the hymns recorded in the Adi Granth.

rahit (*raihat/raiht*): the Khalsa code of conduct.

rahit maryada (*raihit maryādā/raihat maryādā*): the code of discipline of the

Khalsa; also a specific text on this subject.

sangat (*sangat*) "congregation": With its considerable emphasis on community, Sikhism gives great importance to congregational worship.

sangrand (*sangrānd*): the first day of the month in the local calendar in India.

shabad (*shabad*) "word," "hymn": The term is used to refer both to the divine Word received from God and to a hymn contained within the Adi Granth.

shalok (*shalok*) "couplet," "type of stanza."

Sikh (*sikh*) "disciple," "learner": any person who believes in God, in the ten Gurus, in the Adi Granth and other teachings of the Gurus, in the Khalsa initiation ceremony, and in the doctrinal system of no other religion. This definition, systematized in the middle of the twentieth century, is considered authoritative in the mainstream Sikh community.

Sufi (*sūfi*) "a Muslim mystic": As a group, Sufis had a major religious impact in medieval Punjab. From centers known as *khanqahs*, these saints taught their disciples, fed travelers, and gave medicine to the sick.

taksal (*taksāl*) "mint": Sikh seminaries where religious education is offered.

Udasi (*udāsī*) "melancholic": an order of ascetics begun by Baba Sri Chand, the eldest son of Guru Nanak. During the eighteenth century the Udasis became the custodians of Sikh gurdwaras and the key interpreters of Sikh religious thought. With the beginning of the twentieth century, however, the close Sikh-Udasi link was largely severed, and Udasis increasingly regarded themselves as Hindus rather than Sikhs.

var (*vār*) "ballad": a long composition comprising both *shaloks* and a type of stanza called *pauri*.

Bibliography of Works Cited

In Punjabi

Akali Kaur Singh. *Guru Shabad Ratan Prakash.* 1963. Reprint. Patiala: Punjab Language Department, 1986.

Ashok, Shamsher Singh. *Punjabi Hathlikhatan di Suchi.* 2 vols. Patiala: Punjab Language Department, 1961-1963.

————. *Shiromani Gurdwara Prabandhak Committee da Punjah Sala Itihas 1926 ton 1976.* Amritsar: Sikh Itihas Research Board, Shiromani Gurdwara Prabandhak Committee, 1982.

Badan Singh, Giani, ed. *Adi Sri Guru Granth Sahib Ji Saṭik (Faridkot vala Ṭika).* 4 vols. 1905. Reprint. Patiala: Punjab Language Department, 1970.

Balbir Singh. *Ragmala da Saval te Jodh Kavi ate Alam.* 1945. Reprint. Amritsar: Khalsa Samachar, 1969.

Bhalla, Sarupdas. *Mahima Prakash, Bhag Duja.* Edited by Gobind Singh Lamba and Khazan Singh. Patiala: Punjab Language Department, 1971.

Bhandari, Sujan Rai. *Khulastut Tvarikh.* Patiala: Punjabi University, 1972.

Chakarvarti, Sant Inder Singh. "Sri Guru Granth Sahib dian Biṛan de Bhed." In *Gurmat Sahitt,* edited by Jeet Singh Sital. Third edition. Patiala: Punjab Language Department, 1989.

Charan Singh. *Sri Guru Granth Baṇi Biaura.* 1902. Reprint. Amritsar: Khalsa Tract Society, 1945.

Chaupa Singh. *The Chaupa Singh Rahit-nama.* Edited by W. H. McLeod. Otago: University of Otago Press, 1987.

Chhibbar, Kesar Singh. *Kesar Singh Chhibbar da Bansavlinama Dasan Patishahian ka.* Edited by Ratan Singh Jaggi. Chandigarh: Panjab University, 1972.

Dil, Balbir Singh. *Amar Kavi Guru Amardas.* Patiala: Punjab Language Department, 1975.

Dip, Dalip Singh. *Guru Amardas.* Patiala: Punjabi University, 1980.

Ganda Singh, ed. *Punjab, 1849-1960 (Bhai Jodh Singh Abhinandan Granth).* Ludhiana: Punjabi Sahitt Academy, 1962.

G. B. Singh. *Sri Guru Granth Sahib dian Prachin Biṟan*. Lahore: Modern Publications, 1944.

————. *Gurmukhi Lippi da Janam te Vikas*. 1950. Reprint. Chandigarh: Panjab University, 1981.

Gian Singh, Giani. *Tvarikh Guru Khalsa*. 1891. Reprint. Patiala: Punjab Language Department, 1970.

Gill, Mohinder Kaur. *Guru Granth Sahib di Sampadan-kala*. Delhi: Rabbi Prakashan, 1974.

Gopal Singh, "Adi Granth te usda Prabhav Punjabi Boli ute." In *Punjabi Sahitt da Itihas, Bhag Paila*, edited by Surinder Singh Kohli. Chandigarh: Panjab University, 1973.

Grewal, Amarjit Singh, ed. *Vismad Nad*. Ludhiana: International Institute of Gurmat Studies, 1994.

Gurdas, Bhai. *Varan*. Edited by Gursharan Kaur Jaggi. Patiala: Punjabi University, 1987.

Gurdit Singh, Giani. *Itihas Sri Guru Granth Sahib, Bhagat Baṇi Bhag*. Chandigarh: Sikh Sahitt Sansathan, 1990.

Giani Gurdit Singh Ji. Amritsar: Dharam Prachar Committee, Shiromani Gurdwara Prabandhak Committee, 1991.

Harbhajan Singh. *Gurbaṇi Sampadan Nirṇai*. Revised edition. Chandigarh: Satnam Prakashan, 1989.

Jaggi, Gursharan Kaur. *Babe Mohan valian Pothian*. Delhi: Arsi, 1987.

Jaggi, Ratan Singh. *Varan Bhai Gurdas: Shabad-Anukramaṇika ate Kosh*. Patiala: Punjabi University, 1966.

Janam Sakhi Sri Guru Nanak Dev Ji. Vol. 2. Amritsar: Sikh History Research Department, Khalsa College, 1969.

Jodh Singh, Bhai. *Sri Kartarpuri Biṟ de Darshan*. Patiala: Punjabi University, 1968.

————. *Bhai Jodh Singh Gadd Saurabh*. Edited by Piar Singh. Patiala: Punjabi University, 1986.

Khalsa, Giani Gurbachan Singh Ji. *Gurbaṇi Paṭh Darshan, Bhag Duja*. Ninth edition. Bhindar Kalan: Gurdwara Akhanḍ Prakash, 1990.

Kirpal Singh, ed. *Janam-Sakhi Prampra: Itihasak Drishtikoṇ ton*. Patiala: Punjabi University, 1969.

Mahan Singh, Giani. *Param Pavitar Adi Biṟ da Sankalna Kal*. Amritsar: Khalsa Samachar, 1952.

_____ . "Bahoval vali Pothi Sahib." *Khera* (March 1980).

Nabha, Bhai Kahn Singh. *Gurushabad Ratanakar Mahan Kosh*. 1930. Reprint. Patiala: Punjab Language Department, 1981.

_____ . *Gurmat Sudhakar*. Patiala: Punjab Language Department, 1970.

Padam, Piara Singh. *Guru Nanak Sagar*. Patiala: Kalam Mandir, 1993.

_____ . *Sri Guru Granth Prakash*. Patiala: Kalam Mandir, 1990.

_____ . *Gurmukhi Lippi da Itihas*. Patiala: Kalam Mandir, 1988.

_____ . *Sri Guru Amardas Ji di Bani*. Patiala: Punjabi University, 1979.

_____ . *Punjabi Sahitt di Rup Rekha*. Patiala: Kalam Mandir, 1971.

Piar Singh, "Solvin Sadi de Hor Kavi." In *Punjabi Sahitt da Itihas, Bhag Paila*, edited by Surinder Singh Kohli. Chandigarh: Panjab University, 1973.

_____ , *Gatha Sri Adi Granth*. Amritsar: Guru Nanak Dev University, 1992.

Pritam Singh, "Punjabi Boli." In *Punjab*, edited by Mohinder Singh Randhawa. Patiala: Punjab Language Department, 1960.

Ragmala bare Vichar. Amritsar: Sura Masak Patar, 1986.

Raijasbir Singh, ed. *Guru Amardas: Srot Pustak*. Amritsar: Guru Nanak Dev University, 1986.

Randhir Singh, "Adi Granth da Kal." *Punjabi Dunia* (May 1952).

_____ , ed. *Guru-Pranalian*. Amritsar: Sikh Itihas Research Board, Shiromani Gurdwara Prabandhak Committee, 1977.

_____ , Giani Kundan Singh, and Bhai Gian Singh Nihang, eds. *Sri Guru Granth Sahib dian Santha-sainchian ate Puratan Hathlikhatan de praspar Path-bhedan di Suchi*. Amritsar: Shiromani Gurdwara Prabandhak Committee, 1977.

Sadhu Singh, "Utri Amrika vich Sikh Adhiain da Sarvekhan." *Watan* (Vancouver) 5: 3 (1994).

Sahib Singh. *Gurbani Viakaran*. Amritsar: Rabbi Pustakavali, 1939.

_____ . *Gurbani te Itihas bare*. 1946. Reprint. Amritsar: Singh Brothers, 1986.

_____ . *Sri Guru Granth Sahib Darpan*. 10 vols. Jalandhar: Raj Publishers, 1962-1964.

_____ . *Adi Bir bare*. 1970. Reprint. Amritsar: Singh Brothers, 1987.

Sainapati. *Sri Gur Sobha*. 1967. Reprint. Edited by Ganda Singh. Patiala: Punjabi University, 1988.

Santokh Singh, Bhai. *Sri Gur Pratap Suraj Granth*. Vol. 6. 1929. Reprint. Edited by Bhai Vir Singh. Amritsar: Khalsa Samachar, 1963.

Sekhon, Sant Singh, ed. *Shabad Shalok*. Patiala: Punjab Language Department, 1969.

Sharma, Krishan Lal, ed. *Guru Amar Das: Jivan ate Chintan*. Amritsar: Guru Nanak Dev University, 1986.

Sikh Rahit Maryada. 1950. Reprint. Amritsar: Shiromani Gurdwara Prabandhak Committee, 1978.

Sikhan di Bhagatmala. Second edition. Edited by Tarlochan Singh Bedi. Patiala: Punjabi University, 1994.

Sri Gur Bilas Patishahi 6. Edited by Giani Inder Singh Gill. Amritsar: Vazir Hind Press, 1977.

Taran Singh. *Sri Guru Granth Sahib ji da Sahitak Itihas*. Amritsar: Faqir Singh and Sons, not dated, 1963?

————. *Gurbani dian Viakhia Pranalian*. Patiala: Punjabi University, 1980.

Teja Singh, ed. *Shabadarth Sri Guru Granth Sahib Ji*. 4 vols. 1936. Reprint. Amritsar: Shiromani Gurdwara Prabandhak Committee, 1969.

————. "Sri Guru Granth Sahib da Sampadan." In *Guru Arjan Dev: Jivan te Rachna*, edited by Giani Lal Singh. Third edition. Patiala: Punjab Language Department, 1988.

Udasi, Swami Harnamdas. *Adi Shri Guru Granth Sahib dian Puratani Biran te Vichar*. 2 vols. Kapurthala: Kantesh Pharmacy, not dated, 1969?

Vir Singh, Bhai. *Sri Asht Guru Chamatkar, Bhag I te II*. 1952. Reprint. Amritsar: Khalsa Samachar, 1990.

————. *Santhaya Sri Guru Granth Sahib*. 7 vols. 1958. Reprint. Amritsar: Khalsa Samachar, 1972.

In Hindi

'Anant', L. B. Ram. *Kabir Granthavali*. Delhi: Regal Book Depot. 1968.

Bahura, Gopal Narayan, ed. *The Padas of Surdas*. Jaipur: Maharaja Savai Man Singh II Museum, 1982.

Callewaert, Winand M., and Mukund Lath, eds. *The Hindi Padavali of Namdev*. Delhi: Motilal Banarsidass, 1989.

————, and Bart Op de Beeck, eds. *Devotional Hindi Literature*. Vol. 1.

New Delhi: Manohar, 1991.

Gupta, Mataprasad, ed. *Kabir Granthavali*. Alahabad: Lokbharati Prakashan, 1969.

Hariji. *Goshṭi Guru Mihirvanu*. Edited by Govindnath Rajguru. Chandigarh: Panjab University, 1974.

Mishra, Bhagavatsvarup, ed. *Kabir Granthavali*. Agra: Vinod Pustak, 1969.

Mishra, Bhagirath, and Rajnarayan Maurya, eds. *Sant Namdev ki Hindi Padavali*. Pune: Pune University, 1964.

In English

Bachittar Singh, Giani, ed. *Planned Attack on Aad Sri Guru Granth Sahib*. Chandigarh: International Centre of Sikh Studies, 1994.

Bhagat Singh, *Maharaja Ranjit Singh and His Times*. New Delhi: Sehgal Publishers Service, 1990.

Bosch, Gulnar K., John Carswell, and Guy Petherbridge, *Islamic Bindings and Book Making*. Chicago: Oriental Institute, University of Chicago, 1981.

Cole, W. Owen, and Piara Singh Sambhi. *The Sikhs: Their Religious Beliefs and Practices*. Revised edition. Brighton: Sussex Academic Press, 1995.

Daljeet Singh. *Essay on the Authenticity of Kartarpuri Biṛ and the Integrated logic and Unity of Sikhism*. Patiala: Punjabi University, 1987.

Dewana, Mohan Singh. *A History of Punjabi Literature*. Jalandhar: Bharat Prakashan, 1971.

Fauja Singh. *Guru Amardas: Life and Teachings*. Delhi: Sterling, 1979.

Gandhi, Surjit Singh. *Perspectives on Sikh Gurdwara Legislation*. New Delhi: Atlantic Publishers, 1993.

Gangoly, O. C. *Rags and Raginis*. Bombay: Nalanda Publications, 1935.

Grewal, J. S. *Guru Nanak in History*. 1969. Reprint. Chandigarh: Panjab University, 1979.

_____. *From Guru Nanak to Maharaja Ranjit Singh*. Revised edition. Amritsar: Guru Nanak Dev University, 1982.

Griffin, Lepel H., and Charles Francis Massy. *Chiefs and Families of Note in the Punjab*. Lahore: Government Press, 1909.

Hans, Surjit. *A Reconstruction of Sikh History from Sikh Literature*. Jalandhar: ABS Publications, 1988.

Harbans Singh. *The Heritage of the Sikhs*. Delhi: Manohar, 1983.

217

Hawley, John Stratton. "Author and Authority in the *Bhakti* Poetry of North India." *Journal of Asian Studies* 47: 2 (1988).

_____ . "The *Nirguṇ/Saguṇ* Distinction in Early Manuscript Anthologies of Hindu Devotion." In *Bhakti Religion in North India*, edited by David N. Lorenzen. Albany: State University of New York Press, 1995.

Juergensmeyer, Mark, and N. G. Barrier, eds. *Sikh Studies: Comparative Perspectives on a Changing Tradition*. Berkeley: Berkeley Religious Studies Series, 1979.

Kohli, Surinder Singh. *A Critical Study of Adi Granth*. 1961. Reprint. Delhi: Motilal Banarsidass, 1976.

Lawrence, Bruce B. *Notes from a Distant Flute: The Extant Literature of pre-Mughal Indian Sufism*. Tehran: Imperial Iranian Academy of Philosophy, 1978.

Leitner, G. W. *Indigenous Education in the Punjab Since Annexation*. 1882. Reprint. Patiala: Punjab Language Department, 1970.

Levering, Miriam, ed. *Rethinking Scripture: Essays from a Comparative Perspective*. Albany: State University of New York Press, 1989.

Macauliffe, Max Arthur. *The Sikh Religion: Its Gurus, Sacred Writings and Authors*. 1909. Reprint. New Delhi: S. Chand and Company, 1985.

Mann, Gurinder Singh. "The Making of Sikh Scripture." Ph. D. diss., Columbia University, 1993.

_____ . "The Goindval Pothis." In *Five Punjabi Centuries*, edited by Indu Banga. Delhi: Manohar, forthcoming.

McLeod, W. H. *The Evolution of the Sikh Community: Five Essays*. Oxford: Clarendon Press, 1976.

_____ . "The Study of Sikh Literature." In *Studying the Sikhs: Issues for North America*, edited by John Stratton Hawley, and Gurinder Singh Mann. Albany: State University of New York Press, 1993.

Nirbhai Singh. *Bhagata Namadeva in the Guru Grantha*. Patiala: Punjabi University, 1981.

_____ . "The Collection of the Hymns of the *Guru Granth*." *Journal of Sikh Studies* 8: 1 (1981).

Nizami, Khaliq Ahmad. *Some Aspects of Religion and Politics in India during the Thirteenth Century*. Delhi: Idarah-i Adabiyat-i Delli, 1974.

Pashaura Singh. "The Text and Meaning of the Adi Granth." Ph. D. diss., University of Toronto, 1991.

_____. "An Early Sikh Scriptural Tradition: The Guru Nanak Dev University Manuscript 1245." *International Journal of Punjab Studies* 1: 2 (1994).

Pritam Singh. "Bhai Banno Copy of the Sikh Scripture." *Journal of Sikh Studies* 11: 2 (1976).

_____, ed. *Sikh Concept of the Divine*. Amritsar: Guru Nanak Dev University, 1985.

Randhawa, Harveen Kaur. "Early Printing History of *Guru Granth Sahib*." M. Phil. term paper, Guru Nanak Dev University, 1985.

Shackle, Christopher. *A Guru Nanak Glossary*. London: School of Oriental and African Studies, 1981.

Smith, Wilfred Cantwell. *What is Scripture: A Comparative Approach*. Minneapolis: Fortress Press, 1993.

Talib, Gurbachan Singh. *Bani of Sri Guru Amar Das*. New Delhi: Sterling Publishers, 1979.

Trilochan Singh. *Ernest Trumpp and W. H. McLeod: As Scholars of Sikh History Religion and Culture*. Chandigarh: International Centre of Sikh Studies, 1994.

Trumpp, Ernest. *The Adi Granth or the Holy Scripture of the Sikhs*. 1877. Reprint. Delhi: Munshiram Manoharlal, 1978.

Vaudeville, Charlotte. *A Weaver Named Kabir: Selected Verses, With a Detailed Biographical and Historical Introduction*. Delhi: Oxford University Press, 1993.

World Sikh Meet-1995. Amritsar: Shiromani Gurdwara Prabandhak Committee, September 1995.